THREE PAGODAS

Christian Goodden was born in 1949 in Suffolk, where he grew up. After completing a modern languages degree at the University of East Anglia (Norwich), he went on to do research at Gonville & Caius College, Cambridge, where he was awarded a Ph.D. in 1977 for a thesis on Austrian literature and thought at the turn-of-the-century. In the following eleven years Dr Goodden lectured in English and translation at the Universities of Cologne and Basle, publishing at the same time a variety of articles on German and English culture in journals and newspapers. In 1988 he returned to Britain to work as a freelance translator and EFL teacher. At the same time he started travelling in the Far East, where he met his wife. A keen photographer and creative writer, he currently divides his time between England and northern Thailand, where with his wife he is researching the material for a second book about the Thai-Lao border. He has one daughter.

THAILAND & BORDERING COUNTRIES

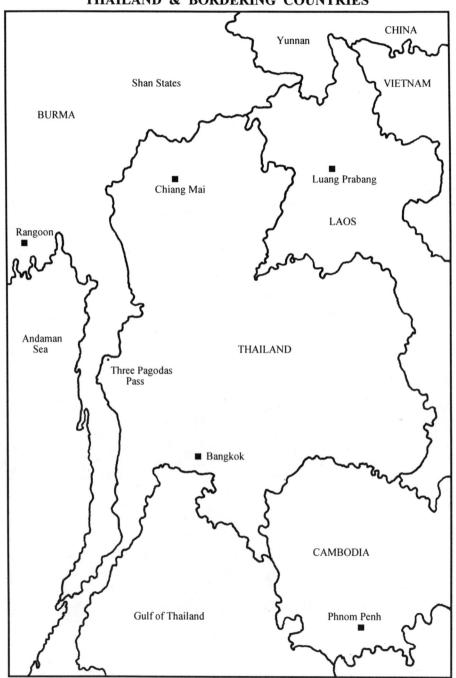

△
△△

THREE PAGODAS

CHRISTIAN GOODDEN

A JOURNEY DOWN THE THAI-BURMESE BORDER

JUNGLE BOOKS
(HALESWORTH)

"BY TRAVELLERS FOR TRAVELLERS"

DEDICATION

For the long-suffering Karen people
as well as for
"Darkie"
and all her brothers and sisters
in the mountains of the Thai-Burmese border

Front cover photo: Karen *loe-si* jungle hunter near Lae Tong Ku

Back cover photo: The Three Pagodas Pass

First published in 1996 by
JUNGLE BOOKS (HALESWORTH)
P.O. Box 15
Halesworth, Suffolk IP19 0DY
England

ISBN 0-9527383-0-9

Text and maps © Christian Goodden
Photos © Christian and Nittaya Goodden

If difficulty is experienced obtaining this book through conventional outlets, copies may be ordered directly from the publisher.

CONTENTS

THE MAPS

ACKNOWLEDGEMENTS

This book would never have been possible without the help of my wife, Nittaya ("Daeng"), who asked countless questions and facilitated the journey at every turn. I must also mark the forebearance of our infant daughter, Tanya, who we took with us on some sections of the trip. She will understand later the not insignificant role she played. A four-year old can slow one down when travelling, but in Thailand can also unlock many doors, and quite especially so in remote areas.

Too many people (notably headmen and villagers) have helped us in the detailed execution of our travelling over several years for me to be able to acknowledge them all individually. Our sincere gratitude is expressed to them collectively. However, for showing us particular kindness I would like to single out for especial thanks the following: Somsak Suriyamongkol and his staff at Wiang Haeng district office; Pastor Somkiet of Wiang Haeng; Witit Terkae of Chong, Wiang Haeng; WNO Major Ta Kong Mong and his kindly wife Chang Soe; WNO Chairman Maha San and his wife Janoo; Karenni Army commander Jo Lae of Pang Yon; headman Boonyeuan Promsermsook of Mae La Oop; Gen. Bo Mya and Minister Sor Shwi Ya Hae of KNLA GHQ Manerplaw, Burma; Sombat Singharaj of Um Pang; KNLA commander Sor Tae Tu of Sa Kaang Thi, Burma; Than Oo of Sa Kaang Thi; "Mr Fixit" Sampan and Sooksi of Boeng Kloeng; KNLA commander Sor Kyi Shwi of Mae Ta Ro Ta, Burma; O-Sae-Tae, Toom Yai and the teachers of Lae Tong Ku; KNLA commander Mor Thaing Chor of Kui Le Toeng, Burma; and the incomparable Joi-ae of Ti Po Mo.

The following travellers met with on the trail also deserve a warm *khop khun kap* and *chok dii*: Soeren and Wanida ("Aeao") Skibstedt of Denmark and Nan Province; Mike Batley of Thailand (no fixed abode!); Peter and Lidya Scheurenberg of Düsseldorf; Thorben (No Name) of Denmark; Béatrice and Didier Dumaine-Chereau of France; Joe Cummings of Lonely Planet; as well as Yai and everybody else at Doi Phukha GH, Nan.

I would like to thank Stephen and Liz Brough for their generous help, encouragement and advice during the long realization of this book, and Sylvia Samms for her patient work printing up black and white photographs.

Finally, I must record my indebtedness to historians Martin Smith and Col. Kanchana Pragadwootisan. From Smith's masterly and compendious *Burma. Insurgency and the Politics of Ethnicity* I have learned a great deal, particularly about the history and politics of the Shan State and of the Karen rebellion, while from Col. Kanchana's *The History of Doi Mae Salong* and his *The 93rd Regiment and Nationalist Army in Doi Pa Taang* (both unfortunately still in Thai) I have gleaned much valuable information about the history and movements of the KMT.

INTRODUCTION

In his books *A Dragon Apparent* (1951) and *Golden Earth* (1952) Norman Lewis wrote that he was visiting Cambodia, Laos, Vietnam and Burma because he wanted to see traditional life there before it changed forever. Also he foresaw that the incoming repressive xenophobic régimes in the region, embracing Chinese-inspired policies of self-isolation, would soon put these countries beyond the reach of the ordinary traveller. The reasons for visiting Thailand in the 1990s are on the first count not dissimilar, while on the second they could hardly be more different. Traditional life in the Kingdom, as elsewhere in South-East Asia, is changing fast and irrevocably, but not because the bamboo curtain is coming down, rather because it is all too rapidly going up. Ancient eastern traditions and lifestyles are being overwhelmed by western influences, and access, expanding in line with a flourishing tourist industry and comprehensive road-building programme, grows daily easier. (Ironically, it has already reached a stage in some environmentally sensitive parts of the country such that, even as these areas are being opened up, they are being closed down again - putting them, indeed, beyond the reach of the ordinary traveller.) Nowhere is this more the case than in Thailand's rural and isolated border areas. One of the aims of *Three Pagodas. A Journey down the Thai-Burmese Border* is to record something of the impact of these far-reaching changes on the peoples and cultures along the margins, to provide a snapshot of an existence in convulsive transition.

Based on the extensive travels of the author and his wife (a Thai national) in northern Thailand over a period of six years, the book is an account of their explorations and adventures in the mountains and jungle of the country's western border with Burma in a 700-km section running from Chiang Dao in the north to the Three Pagodas Pass in the south. *Three Pagodas* is the story of a journey made by motorbike, truck, bus, boat, elephant, and on foot through a swathe of remote volatile border territory, which is home to migrant hilltribes, diverse rare and obscure minority peoples, jungle sects, insurgent guerrilla groups, warlords and heroin traffickers. The book also sets out to show what it is like to make one's way through this remarkable terrain and what life is like for the people living there.

The book grew out of the encouragement of the many friendly travellers the author and his wife met 'on the road' who remarked: "if only we had all your information - you should write it up in book form so that others would then be better informed about where to go, what to see, and what it all means". But *Three Pagodas* is not a thoroughgoing guidebook. It is an anecdotal account of people, places and incidents off the beaten track, supplemented where appropriate with background cultural and historical information. Outline route detail and personally researched maps have been included, but they are diagrammatic only and not to scale, intended to

7

illuminate the text. Intrepid independent travellers who choose to use the book and maps as a resource in an attempt to retrace part or all of the journey described do so entirely at their own risk. The author cannot be held liable for anything that may happen to them and hereby explicitly disclaims all responsibility. At the same time he enters the following warning.

WARNING

Parts of the Thai-Burmese border area are dangerous or potentially dangerous. At the time of writing the Kae Noi - Piang Luang - Pai route, stretches of the Salween and Moei rivers north and south of Mae Saam Laep, sections of "Death Highway", and the wilderness south of Um Pang were dangerous or hazardous. Both flitting out of Thailand and flitting into Burma are illegal. Travellers who cross into the Shan State could be playing with their lives. By contrast, places such as Pai, Mae Hong Son, Mae Or, Mae Sot and Um Pang were relatively safe, already figuring to a greater or lesser extent on the well-trodden tourist trail. But the western border is a troubled area which changes from year to year. What was safe last year might not be so this, and vice versa. Anyone intending to poke about in these corners should either speak Thai, and/or take along a Thai companion, or first ascertain from locals if it is safe to proceed.

In the matter of the transliteration of Thai, Karen and other names and placenames in the book, a spelling has generally been adopted which for an English-speaker or reader most closely resembles the sound of the original word (i.e. a lot of redundant "h's" have been dropped, hence 'pratat' instead of 'phrathat'). The exception to this is with well-established words (e.g. 'Mekhong' whisky, or the Karen HQ of 'Manerplaw'), where it would be churlish to transliterate otherwise.

C. G.
Suffolk, England
1996

MAP 1

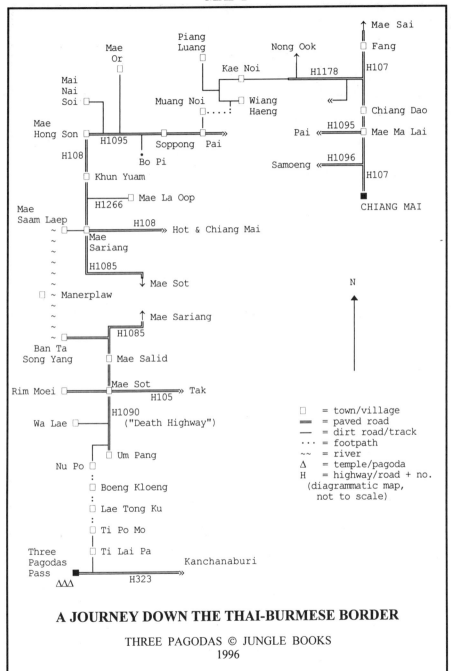

A JOURNEY DOWN THE THAI-BURMESE BORDER

THREE PAGODAS © JUNGLE BOOKS
1996

MAP 2

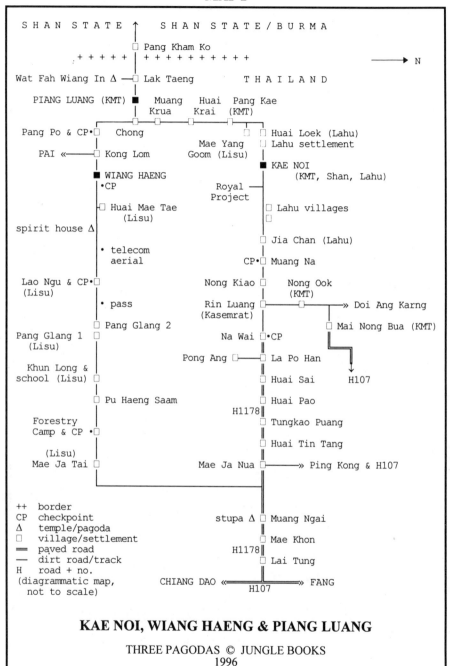

KAE NOI, WIANG HAENG & PIANG LUANG

THREE PAGODAS © JUNGLE BOOKS
1996

CHAPTER 1

MR DONUT COMING SOON

Chiang Mai - Chiang Dao - Kae Noi - Wiang Haeng

Chiang Mai, Thailand's northerly second city, is where adventures are mooted and plans laid. It is the base from which travellers explore the mountainous north of the country, both the western flank towards Burma, and the eastern reaches towards Laos. Later, after rough dusty tours, this onetime capital of the ancient Lan Na kingdom is a welcome place in which to clean up and become reacquainted with western food. But for us, for the moment, it was a convenient spot in which to acclimatize and overcome jet-lag following the 13-hour long-haul flight from Europe. After the gloom of an English winter the intense Lan Na light pricked our eyes.

"The Rose of the North", as Chiang Mai is sometimes known, used to detain us longer, but on recent stopovers we have been increasingly dismayed by developments there. During the late 80s and early 90s the town had its share of changes - the northern capital is no more proof to the transformation sweeping the Kingdom than any other part. But whereas previously the alterations had always seemed modest, piecemeal, assimilable, cumulative, now suddenly the city was convulsed. In the space of twelve months a watershed had been reached, and unfortunately Chiang Mai's legendary balance of traditional charm and modernity, of easy living and commerce, had tipped decisively in favour of the latter.

The northerly rose had lost her bloom. Condomania had struck along the banks of the city's leisurely River Ping. Highrise hotels in the vicinity of the modest "Suriwong Hotel" (now renamed "Novotel") were falling all over each other. Estates of fancy, gleaming white houses, built in "wedding-cake" architecture, were mushrooming everywhere. The Nawarat Bridge, Tapae Road, Chang Klan Road and Charoen Pratet Road were choked with traffic. In a short time our throats were rasping from the exhaust fumes of innumerable *tuk tuks*, motorbikes, *songtaews*, pick-ups and tourist coaches. The air was loud with the noise of engines revving, vehicles tooting and security men blowing whistles. Chiang Mai was becoming more like Bangkok by the hour.

Our guesthouse, which had once been a haven of tranquillity in a leafy lane on the banks of the Ping, was suddenly a dilapidated block on a busy connecting road, overshadowed by a giant condominium and passed nearby by a brand-new river bridge, which roared day and night with traffic. The old Vieng Ping bazaar on the Chang Klan Road, which had once been such an intriguing place to browse among hill-tribe artifacts, had been relegated to a dismal corner of the Anusarn market. Some brash shopping mall was all set to take its former place. The Anusarn market, where we had so often supped inexpensively on *pat thai* or noodle soup, where, Mekhong whisky in hand, we had enjoyed watching the nightly proceedings of the market, was in the throes of an unfathomable transformation. It looked as if a pizza parlour was taking shape in the middle of a car park.

Only fifteen years earlier *farangs* were such an unusual sight in Chiang Mai that schoolchildren used to tail them down the quiet dusty streets out of curiosity, keeping a safe distance for fear of the unknown. Now luxury coaches blocked up the Night Bazaar, disgorging groups of elderly French package tourists, who tried to haggle in French over the price of a pair of fake Lacoste socks. Where once ladies in conical straw hats had sold fruit and other foods from panniers at the side of the Chang Klan Road, now a spanking new shopping plaza was waiting to be opened. In the plate glass windows huge signs proclaimed: KENTUCKY FRIED CHICKEN OPENING SOON, BURGER KING OPENING HERE SOON and MISTER DONUT COMING SOON.

Sooner than expected we were riding out of town. It was a relief to be on our way, heading for the hills. The Chang Puak Road led into the Chotana Road, which crossed the Super Highway and proceeded north in the direction of Chiang Dao. The literature speaks of Chiang Mai as a town of 200,000 inhabitants. But a trip through the Chang Puak and Chotana suburbs tells a different story. If these teeming bustling quarters are taken into account, the true total population of the city must easily exceed one million. From a rental shop in town we had hired a Honda Wing motorcycle. Although getting rather long in the tooth, these 125cc air-cooled 4-stroke workhorses had one great advantage over the other bikes available (the finicky MTX trails machine or the strong but lightweight Dream town bike): a large petrol tank. The roadsters could manage more than 300 kms on one tankful - an important consideration when making a long flit through the mountains or jungle. We drew into a petrol station to fill up and make ready for the ride. On the station forecourt, in the shade of a giant ESSO sign, we strapped one of our two rucksacks onto the Wing's tank with expanders, and pulled on a pair of those maroon acrylic bobble-hats seen everywhere in Thailand, useful for keeping the dust, bugs and diesel flecks of the highway out of one's hair. Preparations were completed with a liberal smearing on our faces of factor-15 sun cream - essential protection in the hills against the fierce oriental sun.

Our plan was to ride north about 50 miles to Chiang Dao and turn west up a side road towards the mountainous Burmese border. We had heard intriguing things about a remote place up there called Wiang Haeng. Our enquiries had revealed that there were apparently two ways to reach this outpost. One was a new dirt road which skirted round the back of Thailand's third highest mountain, Doi Chiang Dao, before it climbed 66 kms up to Wiang Haeng. Evidently this was the new dirt track which had only recently connected the village to the outside world. The other way was a closed road which went up to the forbidden multi-ethnic village of Kae

12

Noi. To the best of our knowledge, no travellers had reached this volatile settlement. The writers of one German guidebook spoke of being unceremoniously repulsed by the Thai military at the first checkpoint along the route. Evidently the track continued after Kae Noi over the border to Namaklwe and Mong Hang, two places in an area of the Shan State (Burma) controlled by opium warlord Khun Sa. But we figured that there might be a track which looped back after Kae Noi, but before the border, southwest to Wiang Haeng. Certainly it would have been odd if two villages which on the map seemed so close together were not linked by some way. Thus, for the first leg of our journey down the Thai-Burmese border, we thought we would try to negotiate this alternative route to Wiang Haeng, before cutting through the mountains from there to Pai.

With the promise of adventure programmed into our journey from the start, our adrenalin was up. But we were elated for other reasons. The open road and the narrowing trail beckoned again - always the occasion for an upwelling of anticipation. What lay ahead? What experiences, surprises and mishaps might befall us? Who would we meet? What would we learn? Where would we end up? Where would we stay, and what would we eat? The answers to these questions could not be imagined in advance. But one thing was certain, that when we did reach our journey's end, memorable things would have happened and we would have met some remarkable people. And this, surely, is the mainspring of travelling. In what at the time often seems hard, dispiriting, bewildering, even senseless, there is the promise of a cache of rewarding experiences and enriching memories.

A succession of sights unfolded beside Highway 107 out of Chiang Mai: the Lanna Golf Course, Chiang Mai City Hall, barracks, the Nong Haw horse-racing course, and some fields with hundreds of horses and donkeys grazing on dessicated grass. At first sight these meagre animals seemed part of a sanctuary or awaiting shipment to the knacker's yard. But in fact they were "cavalry" horses, belonging to the barracks. The better ones, apparently, were even raced at Nong Haw. Thais like a flutter on the horses, and racing took place, so the hoardings announced, every Sunday morning. Other facets of Thai life revealed themselves. Clapped-out mopeds puttered north with bamboo cages, one suspended each side, containing piglets. A troop of hundreds of boy scouts and girl guides snaked its way single file along the side of the road to a camp somewhere. A raucous merit-making band of villagers proceeded to their local temple, bearing money and gifts. A sombre funeral cortège moved slowly out of a village to a cremation site, where the body would be burnt on a pyre. A pick-up among the black-clad mourners bore the gaudy coffin.

About 15 kms from Chiang Mai the chaotic little town of Mae Rim greeted us. Fortunately, we lost here the numerous coaches and minibuses which had thundered dangerously past us on the highway. They turned left into the 1096 side road towards the Mae Sa Valley. Their goal was the plethora of "attractions" developed in this picturesque valley to entertain the package tourists making their 3-day stopover in Chiang Mai. The forest of signs at the mouth of the road indicated the diversions that awaited them: elephant "training" camps, "scenic" resorts, restaurants offering "traditional" food served by waitresses in "authentic" costume, mini waterfalls, and orchid, butterfly and snake farms.

Our route continued north, passing after 27 kms the hilltop temple of Wat Pratat Doi Chom Chaeng. The *wat* stood out because of a long flight of steps leading up to it, which was flanked by two enormous wavy-backed snakelike *nagas*. A further 8 kms brought us to Mae Ma Lai. The market and shops of this busy little trading place seemed interesting enough to warrant a quick look round. Shopkeepers told us that Thais and especially hill-tribe people came down here from the westerly mountains to buy and sell. Of significance for us was the key turn-off left (west) plumb in the middle of the market onto Highway 1095. This was the beginning of the exciting northerly route to Mae Hong Son, some 200 kms distant. Pai, a station on our way, lay up this mountain road, almost exactly half way to Mae Hong Son. The road invited and Pai called, but we were able to resist the temptation. Our rendezvous with Pai would come later, after a more circuitous journey. First there was the little matter of our assignation with Kae Noi and Wiang Haeng.

For the moment, therefore, we carried on in a northerly direction past Mae Taeng and towards Chiang Dao. With the sphere of influence of greater Chiang Mai receding, and with Mae Ma Lai and its strategic 1095 turn-off behind us, the traffic thinned noticeably now. The route began to shadow the River Ping, passing through luxuriant wooded mountain country. A sinuous road cut through steep hillsides of lovely green, golden and brown trees with outsize leaves. Lychee orchards appeared, and we saw piles of orange maize at the side of the road. On the descent to Chiang Dao we were presented on the western side with a view of the massive grey block of Doi Chiang Dao (2180 m.). Indistinct in the haze and against the sun, its summit was shrouded, as always, in cloud.

The district town of Chiang Dao, strung out along the main road some 70 kms north of Chiang Mai, seemed a good place to stop for a *kao soi* lunch and soft drinks. We figured that it might be the last opportunity to eat regular food for a few days, perhaps until Pai. *Ampoe* Chiang Dao sometimes hits the headlines because of fighting to the northwest between the private army of Shan opium warlord Khun Sa and the Wa. For years Sa's Mong Tai Army and various Wa factions have been battling it out along this stretch of Thai-Burmese border for control of territory, certain strategic hills and narcotics-trafficking routes. It might be thought that during such fighting traffic on the Chiang Dao road would be stopped. However, down on the 107 there is little hint of the deadly skirmishing up there - perhaps only some additional troop movements of the Thai Army. The exception to this is when the warring factions bring their wounded down to be treated at their own expense in the local Thai hospitals. A bizarre consequence is that the Thai authorities then have the task of keeping the wounded from the two sides apart, directing, for example, the

Shan wounded to Chiang Dao hospital and the Wa casualties to nearby Fang. Sometimes, ironically, this cannot be managed, and casualties who are mortal enemies in the field have to recuperate in the same hospital in beds side by side.

Five kms beyond Chiang Dao town we found our turn-off. With Highway 107 continuing north to Fang and Taton, our side road, the 1178, headed left (west) off the beaten track up to Kae Noi and Wiang Haeng. Neither of our destinations was signposted. For a short distance we rode on a speedy metalled surface. The villages of Lai Tung, Mae Kon and Muang Ngai came and went. Muang Ngai was distinguished by a special stupa and reconstructed fort commemorating the exploits of King Naresuan. Apparently, around the year 1584 this Thai national hero set up a large military encampment in the village in preparation for one of his five crusades between 1584 and 1592 against the traditional Siamese enemy, the Burmese. Evidently, the valley was a suitable invasion route into Burma, like our ultimate destination the Three Pagodas Pass, much further south. For us, passing through this pleasant rural backwater on a sunny December afternoon, it was difficult to believe that armies of thousands of foot soldiers, war elephants and cavalrymen had passed this way almost exactly 400 years earlier.

Not far from the main road came a second junction. Left (south) was the new dirt road through the mountains to Wiang Haeng (a further 57 kms), while straight on (west) led to Muang Na and the closed track to Kae Noi. It was the parting of the ways. Steeling ourselves, we continued towards Muang Na. We calculated that if we were turned back somewhere, we could always return to this junction and get up to Wiang Haeng the direct way. At worst we would sacrifice Kae Noi and the backdoor approach to Wiang Haeng. Almost immediately came Mae Ja (with its turning northeast back down to Ping Kong and the H107 Prao junction), followed by a string of other small places: Huai Tin Tang (= chair leg stream), Tungkao Puang, Huai Pao, Huai Sai and La Po Han.

We had already passed a first checkpoint. It was hardly a serious one - there was no barrier across the road, and the guard, who was watching TV, did not even glance up as we passed. However, riding through Na Wai, we spotted trouble ahead. A more menacing-looking checkpoint lay at the wayside with a barrier across the road, slightly raised. This was it, we thought. Here our jolly jaunt would be terminated even as it started. We slowed down, wondering whether to stop or whether to duck our heads and scoot through. As we approached, something remarkable happened. The soldier on guard stepped out of his hut and, without looking, went round to the back to relieve himself. As he stood there, back turned, we cruised under the red-and-white barrier and accelerated away. Our burst of speed was short-lived, for immediately the paved road gave out, and we plunged onto a bumpy dirt surface.

THREE PAGODAS

The village of Rin Luang (or "Kasemrat") was distinguished by a school and, unusually, a small Christian church. In the village we noticed a significant dirt road heading north 7 kms to Nong Ook, a large Kuomintang Chinese village (renamed by the Thai authorities "Aroonothai"). The way links up after Nong Ook with another KMT place, Mai Nong Bua (in Chinese Xing Shoon), and also with the new border dirt road proceeding all the way up to Doi Ang Karng. Rin Luang was followed by the villages of Nong Kiao (Lahu) and Muang Na. The latter, 42 kms from Highway 107 (117 kms from Chiang Mai), turned out to be the last place of any consequence before Kae Noi. A relatively large, mixed Shan/Chinese/Thai village, it had shops and other facilities, as well as a military camp. If we had known then what we were to find at Kae Noi, we would certainly have stopped at Muang Na for food and refreshments, and might even have spent the night there. But, of course, one could never be wise before the event. Also, the day was advancing, and we wanted to press on.

At Muang Na we ran into a third checkpoint. Our fear here was that not only would we be intercepted in the ordinary way, but that the guard at the earlier Na Wai checkpoint would have radioed through, so that now all eyes would be peeled for us. With trepidation we glided towards the barrier. There was no point in trying to sneak past this thoroughgoing wayside military post, so with a show of innocence we rode straight up to it and searched the open window. We saw inside two or three soldiers - but also, on the table, empty Mekhong bottles... The guards were either dozing or drunk or both. Again, we ducked our heads, passed under the barrier, and free-wheeled on far enough for nobody to be able to hear us, when we once again wound up the engine. After Muang Na and before Kae Noi there were no more checkpoints. By good fortune and almost without trying, we had entered the closed zone. Our elation at slipping through the net turned out to be very misplaced. What we did not know was that the stretch ahead was one of the most dangerous in all Thailand. Ironically, that first leg of our journey could easily have been the last.

Hard on the heels of Muang Na came the hill-tribe village of Jia Chan. As we put increasing distance between us and the end of the hard road (already 20 kms back), we became more anxious for information about the route ahead. But clearly we could not ask at Muang Na, let alone at the checkpoint. At Jia Chan we found a roadbuilders' camp. Although it was only a modest one, this was good news because, as we had often found, roadbuilders were naturally in possession of reliable route information. Also, they did not tend to put a superfluous obfuscatory gloss on everything, as the military liked to do. We found two men fiddling with a vehicle. There was a way through to Kae Noi, one confirmed, although it was not easy. The main problem, the other man said, was that nobody went up there. He did not elaborate, and the two merely looked at us and our backpacks as if we were not in possession of all our marbles. We asked how far it was now to Kae Noi?. About another 25 kms, they thought. Were there any villages on the way? There were a couple of Lahu villages, but

16

they were off the track. Was Jia Chan a Lahu village? Yes, it was. And then the men went on to tell us an interesting but disquieting story about the village we were in. The place had been relocated to here from higher up because a number of villagers had been killed by Khun Sa in a conflict over heroin.

Heartened by the fact that Kae Noi now seemed to be within our grasp, but discouraged by the thought of another 25 kms of bad road, we set off again. The lingering look the men gave us as we rode away hardly inspired confidence either. In fact, the rest of the trip was one of the roughest, loneliest and most frightening stretches we encountered anywhere on our journey - a baptism of fire. The mountain track threw everything at the poor Honda, and we passed not a single vehicle or person the rest of the way. First, some dramatic limestone outcroppings shouldered up to the road. Covered with a hair of bushes and trailing creepers, these ominous monoliths reared up above the surrounding jungle canopy like weed-bedecked monsters out of some primaeval seabed. Then the dirt road narrowed into a 4WD track, passing through defiles which had us scanning the features ahead and glancing nervously over our shoulders. The vegetation closed in oppressively on all sides. Suddenly we realized we were in deep jungle. Far too slowly the track made its way up a damp thin valley, crossing a series of broken-down wooden bridges. Little footpaths went off to the sides, presumably to the Lahu villages.

At the end of the valley we came to the first of two ridges that had to be crossed. Aggressively, the track zigzagged up the steep mountainside. The tyres of the Wing shuddered and slipped on the rubble surface. And then we laboured down the far side. On the second climb we had a crisis. Grinding up a corkscrew, the motorbike gave up the uneven contest. It came to a halt on the steepest, most boulder-strewn incline. With two up, it was overwhelmed - even in first gear. Of course, the machine would not hold on the steep loose surface, slipped back and toppled over. We, too, came to rest on the dirty stones. Picking ourselves up and dusting ourselves down, we checked that nothing was broken, either on the bike or ourselves. After the screaming of the engine and the noise of our curses, the dark green foliage all around fell uncannily silent. So here we were, stuck with a stalled, underpowered, overheated bike on a dangerous jungle mountainside - already seriously compromised on our first day out.

What to do? If the rest of the route continued in the same way, the bike would not be up to it. The nightmare of a series of crashes ahead flickered through our minds. But the thought of going back was equally appalling - not least in terms of hurt pride. We looked at the tripmeter. Apparently, if the roadbuilders were right, we were almost exactly half way between Muang Na and Kae Noi. So the way back was as far as the way forward. In fact, counting from Chiang Dao or even from the end of the paved road at Na Wai, we had the lion's share of the journey behind us. There should be only another 12 or 13 kms to go. So we decided to go on.

THREE PAGODAS

It would have been very awkward to try to start the Honda on the scree-like hill, so we eased it back to the last twist in the corkscrew and kicked it to life on the flatter outer edge. Then, while one of us scrambled the bike up the rubble to higher, more level ground, the other toiled up behind on foot with a backpack. Fortunately, not too far above, the crest of the second ridge appeared. Thereafter, the track levelled off, skirting round hilltops through conifer woods. Finally, the elevated way began to drop down into a broad valley - a Shan *moeng* - where we came to a fork. A welcome sign pointed left to some Royal Project and right to Kae Noi school. Where the school was, so also, presumably, was the village. And indeed, a couple of kms further (68 kms from the start of the 1178 and 143 kms from Chiang Mai), we coasted into Kae Noi.

Kae Noi was a mixed Chinese, Lahu and Shan village. With a predominantly Chinese nucleus of about 200 families, it was surrounded by a number of Red and Black Lahu satellite settlements, comprising a further 100 families. Mixed into the ethnic hotchpotch were an additional 20 or so Shan families. The Chinese in Kae Noi, like the many other Chinese refugees along this stretch of the Thai-Burmese border, were so-called "KMT" people. With KMT villages figuring so large especially in the early parts of our journey, it is appropriate to sketch in who these Chinese refugee people are and how they came to be here. Readers anxious to press on with the story may like to pass over the following brief excursion into recent Chinese and Thai history, as well as into the rise of the "Golden Triangle" drugs trade.

The KMT

KMT people take their name from a Chinese political party, the Kuo-Min Tang or National People's Party (Nationalist Party). Dating back to the early 20th century, the KMT movement was bound up for most of its history with its leading figure, Chiang Kai-shek. The success of the Nationalists was to curb the power and autonomy of China's many regional warlords as well as to play a major role in repelling the Japanese during their 1931-45 invasion of the mainland. But they were ultimately no match for Mao Tse-tung's Communists. Civil war between Chiang Kai-shek's virulently anti-communist KMT and Chairman Mao's revolutionaries ended in 1949 with the defeat of the Nationalists.

The bulk of the KMT, some 2 million people, including dictatorial Generalissimo Chiang Kai-shek himself, escaped to Formosa (now Taiwan), an island off the coast of mainland China. Here they formed the Republic of China (Nationalist China), nursing plans, unrelinquished to this day, to retake the communist mainland. However, many Kuomintang were cut off during the escape in the southern Chinese province of Yunnan, unable to reach Taiwan. These elements were then forced to flee in their thousands across the China/Burma border into the Shan State, the Wa substate and Kokang. Establishing strongholds along the frontier, the heavily armed KMT remnants schemed, like their Taiwanese brothers, to recapture China. In the early 1950s they made three major attempts to reinvade Yunnan, but all failed.

Holed up in the remote inhospitable fringes of northeastern Burma, the exiled KMT sought to consolidate their position. Winning over some local warlords, and subduing others, they recruited or pressganged local Shan, Wa and Lahu men until soon their army grew to well over 10,000 soldiers. As the "Burmese" KMT grew in strength, they expanded their sphere of operations. From being a force temporarily poised to retake their homeland, they turned into an army of occupation, controlling much of the eastern and southern Shan State as far down as Karenni territory (west of Mae Hong Son). Because of their indiscipline, the Chinese intruders were loathed wherever they went. During the 1950s marauding KMT bands caused considerable death and destruction in much of the trans-Salween region.

The local Shans and Wa were too fragmented to do much about the interlopers, and the central Burmese authorities in distant Rangoon could make little impression either. In the absence of any real resistance, the Nationalist remnants went from strength to strength. Two factors greatly helped them in this. One was covert American (CIA) and Taiwanese backing, largely coordinated through Thailand. In those days Chiang Mai almost amounted to a rear base for the Kuomintang, with General Li Wen-huan, the overall commander of the remnant KMT forces, maintaining an extensive house and compound in the Charoen Rat Road, by the Ping River. The other factor was the swift immersion of the KMT into the narcotics trade. Cut off from the outside world and with no local economic base of their own, they quickly realized that the lucrative gathering, refining and trafficking of opium was an excellent way of sustaining an army and its followers. The other main KMT commander, General Duan Shi-wen, put it thus: "We have to continue to fight the evil of communism; to fight, you must have an army, and an army must have guns; and to buy guns, you must have money. In these mountains the only money is opium." It was basically the KMT in Burma who launched the "Golden Triangle" as the massive source of opium and heroin for worldwide consumption that it has now become. So deeply involved were the Nationalists in the drugs business that it was not long before they tangled with the region's number one opium warlord, Khun Sa. Rivalry between the Shan kingpin and the Chinese exploded in 1967 in the famous Opium War along the Shan-Thai border, a war which grumbled on for years afterwards. In the end, the KMT almost forgot their anti-communist raison d'être and largely degenerated into trading militias, with Generals Li and Duan little more than opium warlords themselves.

A UN-supervised evacuation in 1953 removed many KMT from the Shan State area to Taiwan. But a significant number remained. Along the Sino-Burmese frontier they continued with their infiltration of red China, with their intelligence-gathering and their cross-border sabotage missions.

Finally, the communist Chinese moved jointly with Rangoon to definitively crush the diehard nationalist irritant. In a massive offensive in early 1961 some 20,000 troops of the Chinese People's Liberation Army and 5000 Burma Army soldiers swept the China/Burma border, effectively eliminating the Kuomintang threat - at least as far as China was concerned.

A second evacuation in the wake of the offensive "repatriated" more KMT warriors. Those left, dislodged from northeast Burma, moved south, coming to settle along the Shan-Thai border in villages built just inside Thai territory. The principal KMT redoubts in Thailand, places like Mae Salong, Tam Ngop and Nong Ook, date from this time at the beginning of the 60s. Curiously, the Thais, far from repulsing the Chinese encroachers, welcomed them. To understand why, one has to remember the politics of the period. Almost all of Thailand's neighbours had either gone or threatened to go communist or revolutionary "socialist" - China, Korea, Laos, Cambodia.... In Burma the Communist Party of Burma (CPB) was enjoying considerable success, while, more alarmingly, in the Kingdom itself the Communist Party of Thailand (CPT) was making serious advances in the mountainous jungle areas of the northwest and northeast. There was a very real danger that the CPB and the CPT would soon link up, with Thailand falling as the next domino in South-East Asia to the communists. In these circumstances, and with American approval, the Thai authorities embraced the KMT. The staunchly anti-communist Chinese Nationalists would form a crucial link in the security cordon of friendly rebel armies and ethnic insurgent buffer states the Thais were trying to encourage around their borders to counter the red menace. Thus it was that Gen. Li's 1400-strong KMT Third Army came to establish its GHQ at Tam Ngop (a stone's throw northeast from Kae Noi), and Gen. Duan's 1800-strong KMT Fifth Army came to set up camp at Doi Mae Salong further north.

The Thai government's involvement of the KMT in its security strategy was surprisingly successful. For years, and especially in the 70s, the two Nationalist armies, often referred to collectively as the 93rd Division, did much dirty work for the Thai Army, frequently clashing with the CPT (for example in the Kae Noi/Tam Ngop area), providing military protection during road construction in areas where the CPT was active (one thinks of "Death Highway" south from Mae Sot to Um Pang or of the road from Chiang Kham to Nan), and generally acting as a deterrent to the communists. A proof of the success of the strategy was that in the areas where the KMT operated the CPT had minimal impact. But the cooperation did not come without a price. Unknowingly, in embracing the Chinese, the Thais clutched a viper to their bosom. In the first flush of their enthusiasm they had overlooked the Nationalists' deep implication in narcotics. Suddenly extensive poppy fields sprang up around places like Mae Salong and Kae Noi, and refineries for producing heroin began operating in Mae Salong and Piang Luang (next to Kae Noi). Chiang Kai-shek's remnants had arrived on the Siamese doorstep depleted and dispirited, but now, secure in the knowledge that they enjoyed both Bangkok and CIA backing, they enjoyed a new lease of life. Re-entering the turbulent world of Shan narco-politics from their safe havens just inside Thailand, they began with renewed vigour to finance themselves and their activities through the trafficking of opium, jade, arms and other black-market goods.

It was only in the 1980s that the fortunes of the KMT declined. By then the CPT insurgency in Thailand had largely petered out, while the CPB threat across the border in Burma had also receded. There was little need anymore for the Nationalist veterans to act as a proxy security corps. Rewarded in some cases with Thai identity and with fresh border villages to settle, the KMT had served their purpose as far as the Thais were concerned. But beyond this they had become an anachronism. Mao's victory of 1949 was history, and any idea of the Nationalists reinvading mainland China 35 years on was just wishful thinking. Most troubling from the Thai point of view was the fact that the once highly-valued anti-communist bulwark had virtually degenerated into armed merchant militias. Generals Li and Duan, effectively opium warlords, were mounting military and entrepreneurial forays into neighbouring Burma from Thai soil. World opinion was beginning to tut-tut. All in all, the Thai hosts realized that there was hardly further justification for harbouring a corrupt and embarrassing alien army in their land, and in 1984 they moved against the Kuomintang, ordering them to disband, subjecting KMT villages to a "pacification" programme, and encouraging the 15,000 Chinese dependants to integrate into regular Thai society.

However, the ageing KMT warriors were not entirely played out. In the 1970s, following the Burmese Communist takeover of the Wa substate, Wa refugees started appearing along the Shan-Thai border. The Wa were also involved in narcotics trafficking, and before long they too tangled with opium king Khun Sa, replacing the KMT as his arch-rival. In the late 80s and early 90s the grumbling Opium War along Thailand's northwestern border flared up anew, this time between the Wa and Sa. With a common enemy in Khun Sa, it was logical that the KMT should side with the Wa newcomers. During the 80s the KMT commenced fresh machinations along the border, using their experience and financial clout to build up various Wa factions with a view to challenging Sa and securing cross-border trafficking routes. The new KMT strategy was not without its success.

The Nationalists' informal alliance with the Wa brings the story of the Kuomintang Chinese in the northwest of Thailand up to date. Today the KMT can be found continuing to live along the frontier in a dozen principal outposts, still engaged to a greater or lesser extent in trafficking activities. Their villages are either purely Chinese (Mae Salong) or shared with Shans and others (in our immediate vicinity Kae Noi, Piang Luang and Wiang Haeng). A few are near Wa strongholds or jointly inhabited with Wa people - as we were later to find out.

Kae Noi

Our first impression of Kae Noi was of a desultory and in some way sinister aggregation of mean houses, spread out in a wide featureless basin. An incongruous paved road ran for two or three kms through the Chinese core, after which it terminated in some fields. We scooted up and down this drawn-out main street a couple of times, trying to interpret what we saw. The Chinese influence was palpable. Around the doorframes of the low mudbrick dwellings were various banners, gold Chinese characters on red paper. In the wooden panels of the doors were diamond-shaped pictures of Samurai-like warriors or dragons. One or two richer families had built cement-rendered houses, washed over in characteristic Chinese style with pale green or pink. Mules were tethered in yards, and ox-carts lay around. We tried to find some kind of centre. But there was none, just a snake of dispersed dwellings. Finally, we spotted a couple of low wooden shops side by side. Finding no eating place anywhere, we dismounted at these rudimentary stores and surveyed their minimal provisions. There was the usual assortment of goods one finds in all such village shops - tinned sardines, washing powder, loose tobacco and noodles - but also a selection of tinned produce which had made its way down through the Shan State from China. The Jiin owners eyed us coolly, suspiciously. One woman seemed to have been selling noodle soup, but although it was not late, she refused to serve us. From another lady we bought a rusty tin of chicken curry, years beyond its sell-by date. To this meagre acquisition we added a bar of peanut crunch and some other titbits to see us through the long evening ahead.

Word of our arrival must have spread round Kae Noi like wildfire, for we had hardly been in the village fifteen minutes when a Border Patrol Police truck came scorching along the main street, clearly aiming for us. Four paramilitary *dorchodor*, as they are called in Thai, got out and bore down on us ominously. They demanded our passports, scrutinized the pages (even though none of them could read English), and asked us what we were doing in Kae Noi, making it abundantly clear that we had no business there. We thought trouble was brewing, but actually there was little this officious squad could do. They could not send us deeper into the closed area, but equally they could hardly send us back. If they did send us on - well, that was just what we wanted. Finally, finding no solution to the problem, the *dorchodor* retreated, threatening that they would think about the matter and would return later.

Our next concern was to find somewhere to stay the night. Obviously, there were no guesthouses in such a place, but we had discovered that Kae Noi boasted no fewer than three schools. There is a tradition in Thailand that if you cannot find anywhere to stay in a village, you can fall back on the local temple or, sometimes, the school. We approached the obvious school in the middle of the village. It was a long low wooden affair with an uneven tin roof. Classes were out, but some of the teachers were playing volleyball near their accommodation block. They were very surprised to see us and could not understand how we had got past all the roadblocks. We said we could not find anywhere to stay in Kae Noi and asked if we might possibly spend the night in the school. There was nowhere to stay in the school, they said, and they had no spare space in their block.

Once we had stayed in a school sickroom, and we put it to them that we could perhaps do the same here. After some discussion they supposed that this would be alright. Presently they brought mats and blankets, and even tried unsuccessfully to rig up an electric light. But apart from that, disappointingly, they took little notice of us. Other teachers we have stayed with in other far-flung parts of the Kingdom have proved remarkably friendly and hospitable, offering food, inviting us to sit with them around their evening fire, showing us their village, and so on. But this group, when they had eaten their evening meal, withdrew into their slummy block, shut the doors, switched on the TV, and left us out in the gathering mist and cold. We begged some leftover rice from one of the wives and ate our curry out of the tin. The curry seemed to consist mostly of rabbit or turkey bones. We nibbled at the peanut crunch, which was brittle and sugary. The reception from the teachers was almost as cool as that from the soldiers, and we felt most unwelcome in Kae Noi, even disconsolate. That first night of our journey was one of the least successful ones.

The next morning, finding nowhere to wash, we unplugged a hosepipe which was serving a sprinkler in front of the school, and washed from the tap. The headmaster was at hand, and in an unexpected access of hospitality he brought coffee and tea and biscuits for the three of us to eat at a trestle table in the emerging sun. Over this breakfast the *kru yai* informed us of some interesting details about the village. The bamboo *wat* we had noticed the evening before was inhabited by one solitary Shan monk. The monk had built the *wat* himself just a month or two before. There were at least two Christian churches in the village. One was nine years old and run by an Akha man. The churches were used separately by converted Chinese and Lahu Christians. Of the three schools in Kae Noi, this one in the middle was an ordinary school run by ordinary teachers. It was a Buddhist place, and most of the children were Chinese. Another school, run by BPP teachers, was attended by Christian pupils - mainly converted Lahu. What the third school was we never discovered - perhaps a primary school. The reason why there were so many schools in such a small place was that there was a good deal of antagonism between the religious and ethnic groupings, so that the schoolchildren had to be kept apart. The headteacher was of the opinion that the Shan children were the brightest, while the Chinese were difficult and unmotivated. The authorities, he said, had many problems with the KMT. This had not stopped them, however, from exploiting the Third Army veterans, for the Kae Noi KMT had been used by the Thai government in security work (guarding road construction) and in suppressing the Thai communists. In exchange some had been given Thai identity.

With Chinese youngsters milling around our breakfast table, the conversation turned to us and our project. When the headteacher learned that we had come up from Muang Na, his eyebrows rose in disbelief. He was so scandalized that he called over some of the other teachers. They shook their heads, tut-tutting. Generously, the *kru yai* explained that he thought we had been very brave (read: foolhardy). He would certainly not have made the journey alone. The route was scarcely used at the best of times, but in the winter months, when people had to go down that way, they went in a convoy of several trucks and motorbikes, if possible with armed soldiers. The reason was that the track was preyed upon by cross-border bandits, particularly during the months from December to February. At the treacherous corkscrew where we had stalled the motorbike, a pick-up driver had been shot and killed just two days earlier. After the rice harvest, people were flush with money and were out buying goods. The bandits knew this and so were especially active at this time of year.

The winter months were also the season of the opium poppy harvest. There were heroin refineries, processing at that very moment, only two kilometres behind Kae Noi. The refined drugs found their way down the local footpaths and tracks, bound for Chiang Mai. The traffickers could be jumpy and very dangerous if encountered. Naturally, they did not like being observed going about their business. Especially *farangs* might easily be mistaken for agents of the drug-suppression authorities and took their lives into their own hands. And then there were the battles between Khun Sa's guerrillas and the Wa Daeng or Red Wa. These raged periodically around Kae Noi for control of the poppy fields and trafficking routes. When that happened, the headteacher said, people did not leave the village, but stayed in their houses for weeks on end, eating all their provisions until there was nothing left but salted fish. The *tahaan praan*, Thailand's élite black-uniformed army rangers, were sitting along the border behind Kae Noi, but they were unable to secure the area. Unchallenged, Khun Sa's people infiltrated Kae Noi itself, coming down to buy things from the shops. The authorities and villagers could never recognize them because they were indistinguishable from the local Shans. These were some of the reasons why the Kae Noi area was firmly closed.

Seeing the headteacher's evident concern for our safety, we reassured him that we had no intention of returning to Muang Na, but wanted if possible to go on to Wiang Haeng. He was relieved when he heard this, but worried anew about our fresh proposal. He discussed the matter with the other teachers, but none of them was sure about the possibility of getting on to Wiang Haeng. One thought a way existed, another not. One thought that a border track was under construction, another that it was far too dangerous to venture into those remotest of valleys. Finally, a forestry boy was called, who said that there was a way through, which could be managed by motorbike. Our worry was that we would not have enough petrol for the trip - there was no fuel in Kae Noi. But the *anuraak* lad said that it was only about 35 kms round to the *ampoe*. Just go to the end of the paved street, he said airily, and carry on down the track.

It was time for school to start. The teachers got up and we took our leave of them, thanking in particular the headmaster for his kindness. Before quitting Kae Noi, we wanted briefly to investigate the Royal Project. Accordingly, we went back to the division of the ways at the run-in to the village and followed a track through the fields to the southeast side of the wide valley. Here we found, slightly elevated, the Red Lahu village of Pa Bong Mai and beyond it the Royal Project. There was little sign of traditional costume among the Lahu, and the Project buildings were deserted. But from the reluctant headman of Pa Bong Mai and a large circle of searching onlookers we gleaned that the project, initiated by the Thai royal family, was an old one, some twenty years old, and sought to encourage the local people to grow (instead of opium) temperate fruit trees, kidney beans and certain vegetables. But the best thing about the early morning excursion was the view northwest across the shallow misty *moeng* to Kae Noi proper. The straggling houses, smoke drifting silently through their ka-grass roofs, crouched at the foot of the sinister border hills. Almost more than any other village we visited, Kae Noi was a place with a dark secret.

Back at the school we readied the Honda and set off. We followed exactly the instructions of the *anuraak* youth. The paved street gave over to a dirt road, and the end of Kae Noi was marked by a BPP camp, complete with its sandbag fortifications and machine-gun posts. Outside Kae Noi the sun was completing its job of burning off the overnight mist from the harvested rice fields and luxuriant valleys. The ride was stony and bumpy, making progress slow, but by way of compensation the track was flatter than we had feared. As the teachers had warned us, it passed through some very isolated territory indeed, twisting and turning around the forested hillsides, affording long views into Burma over untouched uninhabited mountain scenery. What we did not know, for better or for worse, was that this stretch along the border after Kae Noi was every bit as dangerous as the stretch up to the village. The truth of this was borne in on us by local Karen friends we were shortly to meet in Wiang Haeng. With typical Karen understatement they said that it was not a road to stop on. A woman in her car had been ambushed and shot at just recently as she drove along the stretch - it was not known by whom, but probably by Lahu bandits.

Fortunately we were oblivious to all this and enjoyed a sunny ride for a long hour round to the village of Chong. Ten kms out from Kae Noi we came across two Black Lahu settlements close together, both apparently with the same name Huai Loek. The second larger one we stopped to look at. Excited people immediately gathered round. A man ushered us up a ladder and into a house. All the others followed, sitting down on the bamboo floor in a circle around us. The man was the village headman and priest, and the room he had brought us into was some kind of church. Handsome pictures of a long-haired hippie-style Christ adorned the walls. The village was ten years old, the pious *pu yai baan* explained. There were nineteen houses, of which seven were Christian. He himself had moved up here from the Mae La Na area, while the people had moved down from Kae Noi. But the real point of interest for us was an impromptu fashion show. Two girls suddenly appeared through the door, having hastily put on festive Red and Black Lahu costumes, beautifully made in Burma. The people wanted nothing more than to show them to us. The Red Lahu (Lahu Nyi) costume consisted of a black tube skirt with a lot of red banding, and of a blue bolero trimmed with red and blue. The Black Lahu (Lahu Na) costume was a mainly black skirt with some red wiggly detailed trimming around the hem, and a short black jacket with long frontal tails, trimmed with intricate small red panels and small silver baubles.

Another 10 kms and a slow descent brought us to several villages bunched at short intervals: the Lisu village of Mae Yang Goom lying a short distance off the track, the new KMT settlement of Pang Kae, Huai Krai and Muang Krua. Finally, the track, now a dirt road, emerged at a T-junction in the village of Chong. Right (west) went to Piang Luang, and left (east) to Wiang Haeng. Chong was a relatively large place, and we stopped to walk around. People were surprised to see us. After all, we were still in the forbidden zone. The word "*chong*" in Shan means *wat*, and near the junction stood a substantial monastery in the Shan style, called Wat Mak Gai Yon. A square wooden structure raised high above the ground on piles, it had a complicated roof consisting of no fewer than seven tiers. In the temple grounds there was a whitewashed stone pagoda with several Buddha figures looking out of niches. They were encircled by a group of praying figures looking in.

The remaining 11 kms of dirt road east to Wiang Haeng was a wider, well-beaten way. We soon discovered why. It was a route taken by log transporters. Laden, they ground past us from behind, and, empty, they came rattling towards us. Each time they left clouds of blinding dust in their wake. Otherwise it was very pleasant along here. The flattish road followed a fertile high-level valley with hills on each side. In the fields people were busy cutting rice and laying it on its side to dry. And there was a string of small self-protection villages. But it was not long before we spotted trouble in the distance. A barrier firmly blocked the road, guarded by two soldiers. It was the Pang Po checkpoint. Wiang Haeng, only a couple of kms beyond, lay just outside the closed area, while Pang Po stood on the threshold. Our problem now, having got in, was how to get out without a lot of unpleasantness. We saw a pick-up coming the other way and slowed down until it reached the post. The barrier went up and the soldiers questioned the people in the cab. They looked like Chinese from Piang Luang. While the guards were thus diverted, we slowly rode through. Of course, they saw us, but they made no attempt to stop us. Their mouths fell open and they stood there speechless. Imagine their puzzlement at seeing a *farang* ride out of a closed area who had not ridden in! They must have thought we had come straight out of warlord Khun Sa's fiefdom in the Shan State.

After the Pang Po checkpoint came the village of Kong Lom. It was followed by the extensive "Godown" logging customs camp. Thousands of logs lay strewn around, lorries were being loaded up and others sat idle in various states of disrepair. At the rear of the compound were some shacks, where the drivers and camp workers lived. Finally, there was one more checkpoint, and then 35 kms after Kae Noi, just as the forestry boy had said (178 kms from Chiang Mai, coming the roundabout way), we entered our first principal objective - Wiang Haeng.

MAP 3

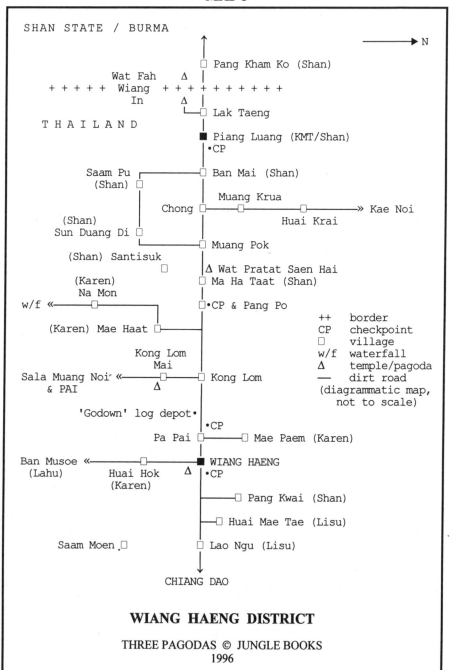

SHAN STATE / BURMA

N

□ Pang Kham Ko (Shan)

Wat Fah Δ

+ + + + + Wiang + + + + + + + + + +
In Δ

THAILAND

└─□ Lak Taeng

■ Piang Luang (KMT/Shan)
•CP

Saam Pu ──────□ Ban Mai (Shan)
(Shan) □

Muang Krua

Chong □────□────□──» Kae Noi

Huai Krai

(Shan)
Sun Duang Di □

□ Muang Pok

(Shan) Santisuk
□

Δ Wat Pratat Saen Hai

□ Ma Ha Taat (Shan)

(Karen)
Na Mon

w/f «──────□───────□•CP & Pang Po

(Karen) Mae Haat □──┘

Kong Lom
Mai

Sala Muang Noi' «──────□────□ Kong Lom
& PAI Δ

'Godown' log depot•

•CP

Pa Pai □────□ Mae Paem (Karen)

Ban Musoe «──────□───── ■ WIANG HAENG
(Lahu) Huai Hok Δ •CP
(Karen)

□ Pang Kwai (Shan)

□ Huai Mae Tae (Lisu)

Saam Moen □ □ Lao Ngu (Lisu)

CHIANG DAO

++   border
CP   checkpoint
□   village
w/f waterfall
Δ   temple/pagoda
—   dirt road
(diagrammatic map,
not to scale)

WIANG HAENG DISTRICT

THREE PAGODAS © JUNGLE BOOKS
1996

CHAPTER 2

THE WIANG HAENG HILTON

Wiang Haeng

At first Wiang Haeng disappointed us. This old Shan village seemed exactly like Kae Noi, only bigger. Here was the same god-forsaken featureless place, spread out on a broad valley floor. What on earth had induced us to spend so much effort reaching it? Perhaps it was just the magic of the name. "Wiang Haeng" had always seemed to conjure up a picture of some wild dusty mountaintop settlement, inhabited by a shifting mixture of dubious peoples, eyeing us suspiciously. But here was the reality, altogether more prosaic. A dismal conglomeration of low buildings was traversed by a dirt road, broad and dusty at this point, which continued on east out of the village with a purposefulness which seemed to suggest that even it had no desire to linger here.

We struck off down a side alley. Paved in cement sections, and lined on each side by single-storey wooden dwellings with tin or leaf roofs, this turned out to be the main street. There were a couple of simple shops and a modest noodle restaurant. Taking a noodle soup lunch, we asked the lady owner whether she served food in the evenings and whether she knew of any accommodation in town. No, she answered simply.

We continued to scout round the village. The centre was a grid of unpaved alleyways and tracks. Wandering among the lowly houses, with their sacks of rice and their chickens scratching around, we caught a glimpse of old-world rural Thailand. In a lane we met three Karen men with their *yaams* or sling-bags. In fact the population of Wiang Haeng District consisted not just of Thais, but also of numerous hill-tribe people. Apart from Shans or *Tai Yai* (= "Big Tai") and modern-day Thais or *Tai Noi* (= "Small Tai"), there were also Karen, Lisu, Lahu and Kachin folk, with an admixture of KMT Chinese.

At the bottom end of town, in a rather decrepit compound surrounded by white walls and overarched by tall leafy trees, we found the Buddhist Wat Wiang Haeng. A ramshackle wooden building in the Shan-style, it was raised on 6-ft stilts and had acres of corrugated iron roofing. Inside we discovered numerous red-painted pillars and a singular collection of some 25 Buddha figures. An emerald green enclosure on the right of the group housed a pair of life-size bronze images, swathed in saffron and gold cloth. Sitting before them were two or three miniature figures, one of them - fifty years old - of solid gold. In the centre of the collection was the main Buddha, resplendent in yellow apparel and made of polished bronze. Facing him from the left were a remarkable group of eighteen merit figures of varying sizes, some quite large, all dressed in saffron robes. They looked like giant wooden Chinese dolls, although the monks told us that they were made of painted cement. Their faces were alabaster with features depicted in fine black lines, with very large elongated ears, and yellow headbands. They were typical Shan Buddha figures. Many sprays of brightly coloured plastic flowers set off the collection, votive *tungs* hung from the ceiling, and instead of the East German grandfather clock that somehow found its way into so many Thai monasteries, there was a surprising cuckoo clock.

A short distance from the temple, in the shade of a large tree, we found a splendid old Shan-style pagoda in an enclosure. The *chedi* was surrounded by half a dozen two-metre high stupas, and outside the enclosure were a number of other, much smaller, urn-like stupas. The pagoda, little gold bells tinkling from the top of its tapering spire, enjoyed a commanding view over the Mae Taeng valley. We thought that the pagoda might be a memorial to the founder of Wiang Haeng. But in fact this lay elsewhere. We later found it north of the main road behind the electricity office. Here, under a young bodi tree, was an old stupa and spirit house. The stupa, whitewashed and in danger of keeling over, contained the ashes of Chao Pu Haeng Sao Wa, an important former Shan ruler of Wiang Haeng.

Also on the south side of the village, between the monastery and the primary school, we stumbled across the remains of some extensive earthworks. At some time great ditches had been dug here, with the earth piled up at the sides. The ditches were full of water, forming a moat. Trees and plants had grown up around the earthworks, and in the misty early mornings or evenings they made a peaceful idyll. Apparently, Wiang Haeng was on King Naresuan's path during his crusades against the Burmese in the 16th century. Perhaps he proceeded up here from his encampment down at Muang Ngai. This would make it possible that the earthworks had been built by his soldiers, perhaps as a defensive system around a forward camp. Or perhaps he made use of ramparts already constructed by Chao Pu Haeng Sao Wa or some other Shan leader to defend the frontier village. Whatever the case, the name "Wiang Haeng" seems to derive from these earthworks. In old northern Thai "wiang" means "moated town".

The explanation sometimes given for the origin of "Haeng" is altogether less plausible. A story from Buddhist literature tells of a wandering monk who came up here to teach the people Buddhism. Resting at nearby Doi Huai Pak Gu mountain, he was approached by a Karen, who offered him some melon to eat. While the holy man was eating this, he cracked or broke a tooth. In old Thai "haeng" means "cracked" or "broken", and the idea of the crack or brokenness was added to the "wiang" to make "Wiang Haeng" - "cracked/broken moated town". But the story does not end there. For the monk threw the melon skin into the river running past Wiang Haeng, thus also giving the local river its name - Mae Taeng means River Melon.

Back at the top end of the "main street", where it joined the "main road", we found a store run by an ample Chinese woman. Her son, fat and with a crew cut, was scooting around at the front in the dirt on a broken child's bicycle. The woman had just finished butchering some animal on a wooden block, and there was a mess of blood and unwanted bits lying around. We asked her if there was anywhere to stay in the village. She motioned with her bloody knife to a building right next to where she was standing. We had not even noticed this wooden shack, which stood absolutely on the corner of the road. Some wag had chalked on the front of it "Vieng Haeng Hilton Hotel". Whether this was an ironic allusion to the chain of luxury hotels or to Lom Jao Prison in Bangkok, known colloquially as the Bangkok Hilton, was not clear. But sure enough one could stay there.

Inside were four walls, full of cracks through which the light filtered, and a crude pallet bed covered with dust. There was nothing else. Seeing the horror on our faces, the woman said that she could bring some things to make up the bed. We asked her how much the room was. One hundred baht, she said with an expressionless face. This was a staggering amount for an unlit, unfurnished shack between the butcher's block and the log transporters. Thirty baht maximum would have been enough. We reminded her that this was Wiang Haeng and that for 100 baht you would normally get a proper room with furnishings, a hot shower and toilet, even in Chiang Mai. Could she not discount a little? No, she could not, came back the answer. It was the only place to stay in town and, moreover, other *farangs* paid this price when they came to the village. Poor deluded other *farangs*! As politely as we could we told her where she could put her room. We would find somewhere else to sleep. With a knowing sickening smile she watched us trudge off aimlessly up the dusty "main" road in the afternoon heat. It seemed to us that even the awful pampered son was grinning.

A few hundred metres up the through road in the direction of Piang Luang we made some useful discoveries. A turn to the right led up to the *ampoe* building and a small post office. On one side of the junction there was a fuel kiosk, where it was possible to buy petrol siphoned out of a drum. On the other was a country hospital. Opposite was a low tin-roofed building with the name "Sayan" (= dusk), which looked like a rudimentary restaurant. And indeed it was. We lost no time in asking if they were open in the evening and what time they closed. They closed, the pleasant lady owner said, when the customers went. We asked her about accommodation, and she suggested the Chinese lady's room, which was the only place in town. We walked back along the dirt road, kicking up the dust and cursing every time a vehicle went past, enveloping us in beige powder. We were still resolved not to go to the rapacious Jiin butcheress and looked the other way as we passed her shack. But our options were running out, and it seemed increasingly likely that in the end we would have to swallow our pride and pay up to stay in her slummy "Hilton". But suddenly we spied a sign pointing to the primary school, and we had the idea to try there, as we had done in Kae Noi.

School for the little ones was just finishing, and the teachers and their charges were all hurrying away. However, we found a janitor locking up the classrooms of the low wooden school building. His name was Rak-kiet. We asked this young foxy-faced man with Mongoloid eyes if there was anywhere to stay at the school. He said that there was no guestroom, but why did we not stay with the Chinese lady? Every visitor to Wiang Haeng stayed there. We explained that the room was dismal and that the woman had tried to overcharge us. Perhaps because he himself was on a modest income, the janitor sympathized with us. He went off to consult with the headteacher. After a while Rak-kiet returned with a bunch of keys, some mats and a couple of blankets, and said it would be alright for us to sleep in the sickroom, although we would have to be up and out before the children arrived the next morning.

The sickroom was little better than the "Hilton". It was a cubicle, nominally partitioned from the most junior classroom, with nothing in it except a narrow child's pallet bed, too short to sleep on. There was no lighting, and the softboard partition had been punched through everywhere with holes about the size of an infant's fist. We laid out our things on the floor and strung up our mosquito net. At intervals along the front of the building there were taps. Later, when it was getting dark and the mist was forming, we washed off the caked sweat and dust of the day, looking out over the playing field.

Remote mountain villages have a habit of shutting down very early, and we were concerned about not getting to *Sayan* in time for supper. But we need not have worried. Three of the half dozen tables were occupied by eaters and drinkers. The restaurant was well placed to catch state employees coming out of work from the district office or hospital. There was no menu - food depended on what was available in the kitchen. The idea was to tell the cook what you wanted, and she told you whether you could have it.

While we were eating stir-fried pork and vegetables, a group of moustachiod bobble-hatted Chinese men came in, evidently from Piang Luang. They brought in with them three one-kilo plastic bags containing some white substance. It looked like pure N°. 4 heroin. Strangely, two of the bags went into the cold drinks fridge, and the other went out to the kitchen. The men ordered Mekhong whisky, soda and ice and sat waiting, rubbing their hands and licking their lips. Not believing that the men should want to chill their heroin, I went over to the fridge to inspect the bags. They contained a mass of white two-inch long worms, each with a tiny black head. The worms had been gathered from rotten wood and were considered a delicacy by Thai and Chinese alike. Sometimes they were cooked in an omelette, but on this occasion they were being deep fried as a snack to accompany the whisky.

Outside, the beginning of the night's convoy of log-transporters started to go past. Old battered vehicles, festooned with lights of every colour, ground past at walking speed, engines screaming. All told, some 45 lorries plied the route between the Shan State and Highway 107, passing down from Wiang Haeng the "direct" way. A typical convoy consisted of 6-10 transporters. Each lorry carried a dozen tree trunks. The number of tons of teak and other precious woods coming this way alone day after day was frightening. But multiply it by the innumerable cross-border logging points all down the 2000-km frontier with Burma (not to mention the crossings along the Cambodian border), and one could get some idea of the environmental rape that was going on in Burma's virgin forests now that there was little left to plunder in Thailand. Much of the wood, apparently, went to Japan, while some ended up as furniture in the houses of Thailand's new rich. The logging at Wiang Haeng, which came from Khun Sa territory through Piang Luang, was one of the most substantial operations in Thailand. When we commented to people at *Sayan* on the size of the convoys, they laughed, saying that the ten or so lorries we would see tonight were as nothing compared to what happened in November after the rainy season. Then, to make up for time lost when the road down to Chiang Dao was impassable and to reduce the vast stockpile that had accumulated, convoys of more than thirty transporters went past nightly. At a dozen trunks per vehicle, that was nearly 400 teak logs a day.

The vehicles travelled at night, partly so as not to inconvenience other road users, partly to remain as inconspicuous as possible to ecologically concerned onlookers, but also because it was cooler at night and the engines did not overheat so easily. It was a wonder how these lorries, negotiating first gear gradients and hairpin bends, groaning under their loads, the trees audibly cracking, ever got down the mountains at all. Often, of course, they did not, or not at once. It was common to see them broken down or crashed, usually in the most problematic places, with chocks under their wheels or the load spilled all over the roadside. Frequently the families of the drivers travelled along too, so that when one did come across a breakdown, it was not uncommon to light upon a little domestic scene - food being cooked over a roadside fire, people eating or sleeping in the shade of the lorry, and even a lineful of washing strung up between a cab mirror and a jungle branch.

At about 9.30 p.m. most people had gone from *Sayan*, and the owner began shuttering the front. Once again we walked up the dusty main road, more groping our way this time. There was electricity in Wiang Haeng but no street lighting. The moon helped, otherwise it was pitch black. In few places have the stars seemed so bright and tangibly near. Outside the teachers' block we found the janitor, his wife and some of the teachers sitting round a crackling wood fire, well wrapped up in anoraks, scarves and hats. As in many other mountain villages down the Thai-Burmese border, it was downright cold at night during the winter months of December, January and February - not something one would normally associate with tropical Thailand. In many places too, as we had already seen in Kae Noi, there was a thick mist, which the sun often did not burn off until mid-morning. Wiang Haeng was no exception, and as we sat with the teachers, wedges of fog visibly shifted around the corners of the buildings in the light from the windows.

A TV was on in the porch of Rak-kiet's billet and everybody was watching an interminable Thai soap opera. A villager and a BPP man came and joined in the gentle fun. Seeing us arrive, they became interested in our story, and so against a background of sentimental soap we told them about Kae Noi. Most of the group had never even heard of the place, let alone been there. We took the opportunity to quiz them about local routes. But the result was not satisfactory. It was the same vagueness and confusion, even from people who should have known better, that one found all over Thailand and which could so infuriate the western mind, with its rage for order and clarity. Thus no one knew if there was a way down to Pai, although someone thought there was a way up through the Huai Nam Dang National Park to Wiang Haeng from somewhere along the Mae Ma Lai - Pai road. We asked about visiting Piang Luang, but the fogbound gathering around the wood fire were clear about one thing. The road to Piang Luang was closed to all outsiders after Pang Po, putting the border village firmly out of bounds.

With a torch the janitor lent us, we picked our way over to the school building and cleaned our teeth over the railing of the veranda. It could not have been often that the flowers in the bed below got a dowsing of "Darkie" toothpaste and bottled water. Then we retired into the sickroom, only fractionally more salubrious than the "Vieng Haeng Hilton". We got into our sleeping bags on the hard wooden floor, pulled down the mosquito net and settled down to a cold sleep, surrounded by bottles of Stomachic Mixture, Thimerosal Mixture, Rubbing Alcohol and Scabicide Emulsion. The beam of the torch picked out a wall diagram showing how to insert a coil into a woman's vagina - rather out of place in a primary school. The night was punctuated by terrifying crashes, as large fruits from some overhanging tree fell onto the tin roof of the building.

After what seemed like only a couple of hours - actually it was 7.30 a.m. - the janitor threw open all the classroom doors of the school. Children began arriving, even though school did not start until 9 a.m. Several eager curious faces peered at us in our sleeping bags through the holes in the partition. We got up, dressed and washed, watched by a group of pie-faced bobble-hatted infants. Outside, the mist was so thick that it was impossible to see even halfway across the playing field. Later, at 9.30, when the whole school was lined up for assembly by age, size, sex and class, the smallest at the front and the tallest at the rear, the mist was still so thick that the children at the back of the files tailed off into obscurity. The janitor's wife had set up a stall at the side of the field and was selling sweeties, biscuits and grilled meatballs. She was doing a brisk trade, the children eating their titbits in a ring around a blazing wood fire.

Sayan was already open, and we took coffee for breakfast there. This was one of those accommodating places where, in addition to the coffee, they automatically served unlimited China tea. Foregoing a Thai breakfast of rice soup or pork with garlic and pepper, we filled up on coconut cake.

While we were contemplating how to spend the day, a gang of youths in nondescript clothing rode up on MTXs and other motorbikes, parked and hung around. They were bristling with guns, and one, wearing a white headscarf and dark glasses, had a walkie-talkie, which he used all the while. They eyed us as they spoke, and for a moment we wondered if they were not Khun Sa or Red Wa bandits. But on one of the motorbikes was painted in small letters *Grom Pa Mai*, meaning that they were forestry-protection boys. Their guns were US-made Mossburg 3-shot large bore warning rifles. They had an unenviable and dangerous job, patrolling the forest trails and seeking to apprehend anyone involved in illegal logging.

It seemed a good idea to call in at the *ampoe* office to see if we could glean any interesting information about Wiang Haeng district. In true bureaucratic fashion we were handed with a succession of *wais* from one official to another until finally we were sitting in the office of the district chief himself. He was a laid-back young man with a Chinese-looking face and the name of Somsak Suriyamongkol. He came from Korat and confessed that he had only been in Wiang Haeng a month. Thai civil servants in the fast track are moved around fairly speedily, but what this raw remote district must have seemed like after worldly Korat could only be imagined - probably like Siberian exile. Nevertheless Somsak was committed and knowledgeable and proved to be one of the most helpful district officials we ever came across.

Wiang Haeng, he thought, could be as old as 700 or 800 years - at all events it was quite old. The Shans were probably the first to settle the area, and they were followed by Thais, Karens, Lahu, Lisu and KMT. Out of a total district population of some 9000 people (2250 families), a good third of these were hill-tribe and minority people, the Chinese of Piang Luang accounting for the lion's share of the latter. There were some twenty villages in the *ampoe* (excluding Wiang Haeng itself), with approximately half of these based on Wiang Haeng and half on Piang Luang.

Wiang Haeng lay at about 2500 ft above sea level, and more than 90% of its total surface area of 700 sq. kms consisted of mountains and national park. That left only 50 sq. kms for villages and fields. There was a severe shortage of agricultural land - something typical of these border settlements - which meant that many people kept livestock as a way of earning a living. Some hill-tribe people cultivated opium poppies, and others were still involved in logging, which was unfortunate because the area was the watershed of the River Ping. One of the priorities of the *ampoe* was to try to provide more crop land and more water for irrigation.

Until recently Wiang Haeng had been no more than a self-protection village. Administratively, the area had consisted of two far-flung precincts or *tambons* within the ambit of *ampoe* Chiang Dao: *tambon* Wiang Haeng itself and *tambon* Piang Luang. It still consisted of these two precincts, but in May 1981 Wiang Haeng was given branch or sub-district status of its own, and in October 1993 accorded full district status. The reason for the promotions was that the area was too remote from Chiang Dao. Prior to the construction of the access dirt road in 1982, Wiang Haeng and the surrounding villages had been completely cut off from the outside world. It had taken officials three days to walk the 80 kms from Chiang Dao to Wiang Haeng and four days to walk the 98 kms from Chiang Dao to Piang Luang, making communication, administration and development understandably difficult. But there were other reasons too for the upgrading of administrative status. Wiang Haeng was a mountainous area, sharing a 35-km border with the Shan State. This meant that there were (and still are) numerous problems connected with illegal logging, opium-growing and heroin-trafficking, subterfuge immigration, contraband, and communist insurgency. The border area was also a haven for fugitive criminals. It was thought that all these things could be better dealt with by an independent authority on the spot.

However, the situation remained problematic because during the long rainy season (May - October) the road became virtually impassable, leaving the district isolated for weeks on end. To illustrate the point, the chief produced some photographs, which showed a mixed convoy of vehicles hopelessly bogged down in a 2-ft deep quagmire of rutted slimy mud. It was common for people to use snow chains in these conditions - a practice frowned upon by the Highways Department because the chains churned up the mud even more, completely destroying the road. When people tried to make the journey in the rainy season, they took meals with them to eat on the way because no one ever knew how long the trip would take.

In the photo album we noticed some other pictures showing an intriguing-looking temple, and we asked what it was. It was the famous Shan *wat pratat* at Piang Luang, Somsak said. The pictures had been taken during the *poi sang long* festival, which they held there every year, just as they did in Mae Hong Son. This was a wild colourful festival, held when local Shan boys went to become novice monks. Unfortunately it was not possible to visit the *wat* because the area was closed off for security reasons. Just a few days before, two French travellers had tried to go there, but had been rejected at the Pang Po checkpoint.

It seemed as if the interview was at an end. We thanked Somsak for his time, and he escorted us down to the entrance. Shaking hands with him there, we asked if it was really impossible for us to go to Piang Luang and view the forbidden monastery and pagoda. Now that we had seen the photos of them, our appetite had been whetted. And, of course, the fact that the *wat pratat* was out of bounds merely made it all the more alluring. But Somsak held out little hope. The matter did not rest with him, he regretted, but was in the hands of the military. However, he volunteered to see what the could do.

This set in train a process quite out of proportion to a visit to a border village and monastery. Back in the chief's office again, we waited a long time while half the officials of the *ampoe* fussed around trying to make radio contact with the military. A small radio could not get through, so they brought into play the district's principal communications system. The long and the short of it was that we got permission for the trip. But that was not the end of the story. Permission was not permissible without a permit. And now the district office had to make out a permit. This absorbed the other half of the officials for more than an hour, and necessitated visits to various rooms, kowtowing to numerous intermediate bureaucrats, and explaining our story for the umpteenth time. We were surprised that there was not some pre-printed form for making out such a permit. But either such permission-giving was rare or else things were never quite so simple. A special paper had to be invented and typed up on the spot. Finally, the document was ready, and we emerged triumphantly with it into the mid-morning light. The little letter came to have a value far in excess of what it was intended to have. We subsequently used it many times to sway checkpoints or obstructive *dorchodor* to gain access to restricted or closed zones.

CHAPTER 3

POPPY MEN

Piang Luang

We started immediately for Piang Luang. As far as Chong the way retraced the route we had come in on from Kae Noi. We passed the checkpoint just outside Wiang Haeng, the "Godown" logging camp and Kong Lom village. Then we drew up at the implacable Pang Po checkpoint. Here the Frenchmen had been turned back. It seemed to us that the two soldiers remembered us from our trick the day before. But there was nothing they could do. They scrutinized our permit and waved us through. How sweet were the licit illicit kilometres after the barrier. Between the villages of Ma Ha Taat and Muang Pok we noticed something we had not seen when coming from Kae Noi. A steep flight of steps with serpentine dragon-headed *nagas* on each side led abruptly up from the roadside to an ornate hilltop pagoda with a commanding view over the paddy fields and the distant border mountains. It was Pratat Saen Hai. A *pratat* is a particularly important pagoda, said to house an authentic relic of the Lord Buddha. As such, this pagoda would attract pilgrims all the year round. After Muang Pok came Chong, and there again was the dun 7-tiered monastery and the turn-off north to Kae Noi. From now on up to the frontier the front tyre of the Honda carved a new furrow on the flat stony road. Passing through Ban Mai, we entered an amphitheatre of cultivated hillsides, dotted with Chinese tombs. The mountains closing around us were the border. After a couple more kms we suddenly drew up at the gates to Piang Luang.

The entrance to the village was an obstacle course of barriers and other obstructions. Bridging the road was one of those wooden portals which mark the approach to many rural Thai and hill-tribe villages. The soldiers at the box checked our permit and made us surrender our passports. The reason for this, they explained, was that policemen in or beyond the village might confiscate them, compelling us to carry heroin in order to get them back. This was a sign of the contempt with which the Thai police were viewed not just by the military. After the military checkpoint at the outskirts of Piang Luang, there were no further controls right up to the border.

Piang Luang was a thriving, relatively large, mixed KMT and Shan place. In spite of the Shan *wat* in the village, the visitor might have been forgiven for thinking he had stumbled into a small market town in Yunnan, southern China. Things were more developed than we had expected. Numerous stores lined the main street, there was moderate traffic, and everyone enjoyed electricity. But while the village was more advanced than the KMT outposts of , say, Pa Taang on the Laos border or Mae Or north of

Mae Hong Son, it was nowhere near as developed as Doi Mae Salong. Many of the dwellings were still single-storey and made of mud or wood with leaf or tin roofs. The doorframes were decorated with the same paper mottos we had seen in Kae Noi - red strips bearing goldleaf ideograms. In the main street there were tea houses with KMT veterans in faded military fatigues and peaked caps, drinking glass tumblers of amber China tea, smoking waterpipes, reading Chinese newspapers from Taiwan, or simply passing the time of day. We found several noodle soup shops and stopped for lunch in one of them. A tasty bowlful of Chinese egg-noodles was accompanied by a side dish of pickled cabbage and toasted sesame seeds.

Outside one store a very old Chinese lady with a bent back and miniscule bound feet was sitting in the sun. When we asked if we could photograph her, she spent a long time arranging her cap, collar, cuffs, rings and bracelets until everything was just right. Pleased as punch at the unfamiliar attention, she gave us two coconut patties from her granddaughter's shop. On a more disquieting note, we noticed too many fairly new MTXs, emblazoned with signs like "P6", which suggested that they might have originated from the hire places of Pai and have been stolen from motorcycle trekkers. It would be very difficult for a foreigner or even the Pai owner to locate a bike in Piang Luang, let alone recover one from the nearby Shan State.

Most of the villages along the border of the Shan State and Thailand are associated in some way with the warlords and private armies operating on the Burmese side. Piang Luang is no exception. Its history is intertwined with the fortunes not only of the KMT, but also of the two veteran Shan opium barons Mo Heng and Khun Sa. The village is identified especially with Mo Heng. For the purposes of further illuminating both Piang Luang and this "Golden Triangle" stretch of the border I include next a thumbnail sketch of him and his activities. Again, hurried readers will be forgiven if they skip over the following section as well as the pages after it devoted to Khun Sa.

Warlord Mo Heng

The wobbly Shan leader Mo Heng, also widely known as Gon Jerng or Korn Jerng, was born in Burma in 1926. During his early years he belonged to or founded a succession of small political parties and rebel armies - a switching which came to characterize his whole career. An early move of his, surprising considering his subsequent fervent anti-communism, was to become a member and then a commander of the Communist Party of Burma. But at the age of thirty he transferred into Shan nationalist politics, joining in 1958 the Noom Soek Haan or Young Warrior movement. This small underground resistance group, in the vanguard of the wider Shan nationalist uprising, was based on Piang Luang, and Mo Heng's long association with the border outpost dates from this time. It was while with the Young Warriors, fighting against the Burma Army, that he lost his left arm. A period in mainstream Shan nationalist politics followed, with Mo Heng rising through the ranks of the Shan State Army (SSA), the principal army of Shan nationalism at that time, and ranging far and wide in the Shan State. But in 1968 he broke with the SSA and returned with a following of 1000 men to Piang Luang.

Here in the same year Mo Heng reunited with the original "Young Warrior", one Chao Noi, and together they formed in 1969 the Shan United Revolutionary Army, which had as its HQ the Pang Mai Soong camp just behind Piang Luang. Soon, however, SURA vice-president Chao Noi, dismayed by the course his partner was steering, dropped out of the organisation, leaving the army almost exclusively in Mo Heng's charge. For the next fifteen years the SURA, Mo Heng's single greatest achievement, became virtually synonymous with him and also with Piang Luang.

In the late 1960s and early 1970s Piang Luang was a different place from what it had been in the late 50s. Meanwhile the Kuomintang refugees had arrived, and now the frontier village housed a sizeable detachment of soldiers of Gen. Li's KMT Third Army, whose GHQ was stationed at nearby Tam Ngop (northeast of Wiang Haeng and Kae Noi). Already disaffected with the brand of Shan nationalism mainstream bodies like the SSA were purveying, and seeing which side his political bread was buttered on, Mo Heng underwent in 1969 a radical change of heart, falling in with the KMT. After all, were they not, as he had also become, virulently anti-communist? Mo Heng's expedient but unholy alliance with the alien Chinese army, which lasted as long as his SURA, led him to be sharply criticised by other insurgent leaders. He had sold out, betrayed the Shan cause. The former plucky underground rebel commander had turned into a mere adventurer, no longer the revolutionary idealist of yore, but just another warlord.

The criticism was not wide of the mark. For while it was true that the SURA frequently clashed during the 70s with the Communist Party of Thailand along the northwestern Shan-Thai border, Mo Heng and his pocket army operated out of Piang Luang in easy concert with the KMT, the two forces financing themselves through trafficking opium and jade or through taxing contraband crossing the border at Piang Luang and Mae Or (another village under their joint control further west), and doing eachother's dirty work across in the Shan State. Actually, the cosy coexistence of the SURA and the KMT in Piang Luang was something of a three-way affair, for quietly colluding with the two militias was the Thai Army. Just as the Siamese authorities had welcomed the KMT as a buffer against Burmese communism and also as a check on their own CPT, so they sanctioned the presence of Mo Heng's anti-red SURA, turning a blind eye to its more or less open drug-trafficking activities. Historian and Burma-watcher Martin Smith reports in his Burma: Insurgency and the Politics of Ethnicity *that, when he visited Piang Luang in 1984, he found a booming town with a thriving black market, frequented by hundreds of traders and colourful hill-tribe people. Opium and heroin were both freely available, and he saw a Thai Army colonel giving training to SURA troops.*

The long SURA-KMT marriage of convenience lasted until 1984, when Mo Heng embarked on a new piece of adventurism. Opium king Khun Sa and his powerful private Shan United Army, which like the KMT and SURA had been tolerated by the Thais in their border territory as part of their counter-communist strategy, had recently been expelled by the Thai Army from the Kindom. In 1982 they pushed the overweening warlord out of his stronghold in Ban Hin Taek (near Mae Salong) back into Burma. The repercussions were dramatic, felt the length of the Shan-Thai border by all the many peoples living there. As the SUA swept southwest in a deadly scramble for new land and to control new cross-border trafficking routes, minority groups as far down as Mae Or were battled and displaced, including the KMT, the Wa, the Lahu and various Shan factions. Mo Heng and his SURA at Piang Luang were no exception. By 1984 Khun Sa was knocking insistently on their backdoor. He had overrun the territory behind Piang Luang, interdicted the (for the SURA) vital caravan and trafficking route leading back from the village into the Shan State, and begun a blockade of Mo Heng's HQ. The stranglehold was such that SURA income slumped by 80%. 1984 was also the year the Thais moved against the KMT, not shunting them over into Burma, but simply emasculating them - although in one sinister incident thirty KMT inhabitants of Piang Luang were mysteriously massacred by Thai Army rangers. Seeing the star of the KMT on the wane, and with Khun Sa menacing triumphantly at his rear, Mo Heng could not help but read the signs. In an opportunistic about-turn characteristic of him (and typical of the tortuousness of Shan rebel politics), he made a series of abrupt changes. As easily as he had once sided with the KMT, now he suddenly terminated his 15-year alliance with the Chinese Nationalist remnants, dissolved his SURA, made a call for Shan unity, and formed a new faction, called the Tailand Revolutionary Council. Based like its predecessor at Piang Luang, the new body would, the Shan leader declared, have no part in narcotics-trafficking. But that was not all. Only a short time later, in early 1985, Mo Heng merged his fledgling TRC with Khun Sa's SUA. The new organization, now some 4000 soldiers strong, retained the name (temporarily) of Tailand Revolutionary Council, and Mo Heng even became its president. But the real power lay with Sa, who took charge of finance and the military. Within two years the new outfit of the two Shan warlords was renamed the Mong Tai Army or Army of the Tai (Shan) Land - a name which it still bears today.

With the amalgamation of Mo Heng's and Khun Sa's armies, Piang Luang effectively fell under the dominion of South-East Asia's pre-eminent warlord, Khun Sa. From 1985 on the new force engaged in unchecked drugs-trafficking, acquiring through the resulting wealth an awesome arsenal of modern weaponry bought on the Thai markets. Soon, virtually the entire Shan-Thai border from Takilek/Mae Sai in the east to Mae Or/Mae Hong Son in the west was under the control of the two warlords.

Numerous photographs in MTA propaganda show the short, pug-faced, one-armed, chain-smoking Mo Heng in the shadow of the taller, open-faced, affable, imperious, chain-smoking Khun Sa, the two of them taking a salute, reviewing an MTA passing-out parade, or sitting around the conference table. Finally, in 1991, at the age of 65, the inveterate turncoat (although lifelong devout Buddhist) Mo Heng died, leaving Khun Sa in sole control of the MTA, the Piang Luang border-crossing, and the Shan hinterland behind the village - a situation unchanged until today.

The forbidden temple of Fah Wiang In

Piang Luang was not only a village with a history, but a place of architectural interest. Just beyond it lay the remarkable *wat pratat* Fah Wiang In. This Shan monastery was singular in that it exactly straddled the border. No one tried to stop us going beyond the village, so we ventured on to see what happened. It was certainly exciting travelling down a dirt track not knowing whether we had crossed over into Khun Sa territory. The road dropped down from Piang Luang, proceeded for a couple of kms to a settlement, and then forked. We asked where we were. It was Lak Taeng. Straight on went immediately to the border, and left went up a steep track to the monastery.

Wat Fah Wiang In consisted of many buildings, but its large celebrated pagoda was on a hill in Thailand while the *viharn*, the building containing the Buddha images, lay on a hill in Burma or the Shan State. The boundary ran precisely through the middle. While we were looking around, we were taken in hand by a small serious man in his late twenties, who wanted to show us the complex. We asked him if he was a guide. He said that it was his duty to show visitors round, and he declined any payment. His name was Toeng-Leng, he was Shan, and it transpired that he was a guerrilla from Khun Sa's Mong Tai Army.

We looked first at the pagoda. This impressive and ornate affair was surrounded by a curious circular building. Inside, the building was divided up into twelve segments, each forming a little "chapel" containing a mural. The twelve chapels referred to the lives of the Buddha, and each painting depicted a scene from one of his reincarnations. The murals were garishly painted in a naive, surreal style. In one a man was disappearing into the earth, the ground cracking dramatically around him. It was difficult to know exactly what was happening in each picture because the captions were only in Shan. The pagoda was not old. It was built in 1969 to commemorate some eminent Shan monk. A glass case in the circular building housed his bones together with a wax figure of him wearing his old glasses. More recently Mo Heng used to come here and to the *viharn* to pray, ever accompanied by an armed bodyguard, and since 1991 the pagoda had contained his remains too.

Most of the other buildings also looked fairly new, although at the back of the compound there were some old wooden buildings, which might have been part of an original *wat*. The *viharn* contained three golden Buddha

42

figures. One of them was a splendid piece in the Shan style, with an extravagant bronze winged crown. Toeng-Leng said that there were 101 monks in the monastery, most of them boy novices. We saw some of them in their saffron robes running around behind the *viharn*, trying to fly kites. We also saw a number of white-clad shorn-headed nuns. Our companion expressed the hope that when the whole monastery was completed, his state might have achieved independence. Unfortunately, real independence would probably remain a pious hope, as Rangoon liked to remind the Shans when the Burma Army passed this way. They had shelled the *wat* a year or two previously. One shell which had not detonated hung near the *viharn*. Its casing served as a gong. With a grim irony the junta forces liked to return to Wat Fah Wiang In to make their presence felt exactly at the time of the *poi sang long* festival.

There were some other, secular buildings on the side of the monastery compound in the Shan State. One was a printing press. All flew the Shan nationalist (MTA) flag - a green, red and yellow tricolour with a central white moon. Immediately below the monastery hill was a school, which we were invited to visit, and the buildings of Pang Kham Ko village. Behind this village the logging road wound off down a narrow secluded valley towards the Salween river. Immediately to our left and right, Toeng-Leng pointed out, at the head of the valley, were two Shan military posts, guarding the pass. Khun Sa's Pang Mai Soong camp lay nearby.

Our soldier friend told us something of his history. When he was young, he had been sent to a Christian school in Chiang Mai along with twenty other Shan boys. He had been sponsored by missionaries, who wanted to encourage him to become Christian. After school, he had wanted to study further in college, but he had been recalled by Khun Sa along with the other boys to defend Hin Taek, Sa's GHQ at that time, which was being attacked by the Thai Army. Subsequently Toeng-Leng had been sent by his leader to fight alongside the Karen National Liberation Army opposite Mae Sot district against the Burma Army. So his education had been broken off. He said that of all the people he had fought against, the Wa Daeng (Red Wa), now Khun Sa's arch-enemy, frightened him most - literally almost to death. This was because they were tenacious fearless fighters. Once Toeng-Leng had been caught by the Thai police in Mae Hong Son. He had been imprisoned there until Khun Sa's men had bought his release. We noticed that whenever this quiet MTA soldier mentioned Khun Sa, he always used the reverential Shan title "Chao" - "His Grace/His Excellency". Thus Toeng-Leng was of the opinion that His Grace was now in the process of stepping down from being leader. His Excellency was getting tired of being vilified by the world's press as "the opium king", "King of the Jungle", and so on. Now Toeng-Leng was based at Pang Kham Ko, where as a reserve he was on permanent call. His duty meanwhile was, along with other soldiers, to show visitors around Wat Fah Wiang In. It seemed to us that this burgeoning temple complex, together with the school at its foot, was something of a propaganda showpiece for Khun Sa and his cause.

We did not want to leave Piang Luang without having a brief look at the actual border crossing to Sa's territory. So we left the *wat* and went back down to Lak Taeng. Beyond the houses was an area where the log lorries were serviced and repaired, and beyond this, in a gloomy sinister defile, the frontier checkpoint. This was nothing more than a squalid cement blockhouse, a couple of leaf and tin-roofed shacks selling noodle soup and other goods, and crude wood and barbed wire gates, blocking the road. From time to time the gates were opened to let through a pick-up, which was thoroughly searched. Bicycles and small motorbikes also plied back and forth, as well as pedestrians. An odd assortment of people hung around the checkpoint. One bent old Chinese man with grey hair offered us jade, amber, anything.... What did we want?

The checkpoint used to be manned by rebel SURA/TRC/MTA personnel, but now half a dozen *tahaan praan* rangers were in charge. It was the duty of these crack black-uniformed troops, trained in jungle survival and much feared by minority hill groups, to guard Thailand's most sensitive border areas. To us, however, they were friendly enough. Three of them sat on a bench at the side of the road, peeling a mound of garlic. With their loose neckerchiefs and floppy hairstyles, they looked far from intimidating, reminding us rather of effeminate boy scouts. Like Somsak of the Wiang Haeng district office, the boys were from Korat. We asked them about the possibility of crossing to the other side. More interested in their garlic-peeling, the rangers had no objection. The temptation to flit across the border was great. But Somsak's admonition not on any account to cross into Khun Sa territory rang in our ears. Also we remembered the warning words of the guards at the entrance to Piang Luang. For once discretion really did seem to be the better part of valour.

Warlord Khun Sa and the "Golden Triangle"
No account of the Thai-Burmese border would be complete without a sketch of Khun Sa. It is this colourful warlord's fiefdom which abuts Thailand for almost the whole of the northwesterly Shan stretch of the border, from the Laotian frontier in the east to Mae Hong Son in the west, and it is his intimidating presence which is most mightily felt in the "Golden Triangle" region. No account of Piang Luang either would be complete without an outline of Khun Sa. The village marks one of the very few vehicle crossing-points into and out of his territory, meaning that now the Shan narcotics kingpin has come to be just as closely associated with Piang Luang as once his right-hand man Mo Heng was.

Khun Sa, alias Chang Chi-fu, was born in 1933 or 1934 in the Loi Mo district of Mong Yai State - one of the 30-odd former Shan mini-states of Burma. Sa is a self-appointed leader of the Shan people, and yet actually he is only half Shan. His mother, certainly, was a Palaung Shan, but his father was Chinese, the paternal ancestors hailing originally from the old Chinese-Shan principality of Norng Sae (Talifu) in China. Both Sa's parents died while he was still young, although his mother survived her husband long enough to remarry a local noble. It was on the strength of the stepfather's nobility, as well as because there was a tradition of district chieftainship in his real father's family, that Sa assumed the honorific "Khun", meaning Lord (princeling). Playing down his Chinese background with a view to improving his Shan credentials, he then dropped the name Chang Chi-fu to become known as Khun Sa.

The orphaned boy was brought up amid the tea plantations of Loi Mo by his paternal grandparents. A powerful early influence on him was the oppression of the KMT as they expanded rampaging through the Shan State after 1949. The sight of Nationalist intruders one day expropriating mules from his grandfather apparently led the young Sa to vow that at some time he would drive the KMT from his homeland. It has been said that the future warlord learnt his trade from the KMT, either working under or for them, but Sa himself denies this, maintaining that, always a freedom-fighting Shan nationalist, he had mixed it with the KMT from the start. Whatever the case, the KMT came to be his arch-enemy for a full thirty years.

Khun Sa started out in the early 1960s with a small clandestine rebel outfit. Two factors transformed it. One was his entry into the opium trade, and the other was the legitimization of his force as a ka kwae yae *or government-backed local defence militia. Sa began buying opium up in the Wa substate and transporting it, escorted by his embryonic army, down to the Thai border, where the refineries and export possibilities were. The mule trains grew ever bigger, with the result that more and more profit flowed to his force, allowing him continually to expand it.*

The ka kwae yae *scheme was invented by Gen. Ne Win and the Burmese authorities to help bring under control the worrying situation of the early 60s in the Shan State. The Shan* sawbwas *(traditional feudal princelings) were becoming increasingly restless, liberation groups were mushrooming, a general Shan uprising seemed imminent, the Communist Party of Burma was flexing its muscles, and the KMT were marauding. The strategy was a double one. It was thought that, in persuading some (quasi-)nationalist factions such as Khun Sa's over to the government side, Rangoon would have fewer hostile groups to worry about and at the same time gain militias able to assist with security. The deal was that if the militias would police their local areas and counter the threat of both the Shan insurgents and the CPB, as well as the KMT, the Burmese authorities would sanction the militias and, turning a blind eye to their trafficking activities, allow them to continue financing and arming themselves through the opium trade. Sa, never slow to spot an opportunity, and astute at seeming to side with an authority while actually using and undermining it, agreed to the Burmese deal. Thus it was, improbably and ironically, that the young warlord's private force, soon to emerge as the Shan United Army, came to masquerade for a decade as a kind of volunteer home guard!*

The ka kwae yae *idea backfired on Rangoon. Neither the Shan insurgents nor the CPB were halted. There was no lessening of lawlessness either. Rather, the scheme, which eventually produced about twenty "local defence militias", many originally little more than bandit bands, launched some of the most notorious warlords and their armies in the "Golden Triangle". A massive proliferation of weapons and drugs in the Shan State followed. Far from policing their patches, the militias simply abused their positions to line their pockets and strengthen themselves. With no one was this more the case than with Khun Sa and his SUA. Blessed by the authorities, the warlord prospered inordinately. He already had in his pocket his own Loi Mo district and corners of the Wa substate. Soon he added control of Kentung and the Laos border area. In the early years Khun Sa had had to pay taxes to the KMT when his opium mule trains passed through their territory or arrived at their outposts along the Thai border. But now his caravans became so large and his SUA so powerful that he was no longer minded to pay the Chinese. The challenge for supremacy was not lost on the trafficking Kuomintang, who, seeing their main means of survival threatened and in a bid to snuff out the upstart Sa, attacked one particularly large (16-ton) shipment of opium, sparking the infamous Opium War of 1967. The attack, which resulted in a bitter four-day battle with heavy losses all round, was won by neither side. The larger Opium War was similarly inconclusive. It rumbled on for years afterwards, with the SUA and the KMT vying for control of the trafficking and the smuggling routes over the Shan-Thai border.*

A great survivor in the "Golden Triangle", Khun Sa soon bounced back from this upset, as he did also from the next setback. In 1969 he was arrested by the Burmese in the Shan State capital of Taunggyi, apparently on corruption and trafficking charges. For four years he was held in Mandalay prison until one of his lieutenants, abducting two Russian doctors working at Taunggyi hospital and holding them hostage, extorted his leader's release. Sa did not return home immediately, but stayed a year or two longer in Rangoon. Finally, around 1975 or 1976, he managed to escape back to the Shan State. He resurfaced next at Hin Taek ("Toed Thai"), the village inside Thailand (near Mae Salong) which for a number of years afterwards was to be his principal HQ. The Thai authorities welcomed Khun Sa onto their soil, just as they had done the KMT and Mo Heng's SURA, as a plank in their anti-communist border-security strategy. Meanwhile the ka kwae yae *scheme had been wound up by the Burmese in 1973, and for six years or so the SUA, while the master was incarcerated, had been out of his control. Now, at Hin Taek, Khun Sa set about rebuilding his army. He re-immersed himself in the narcotics business as never before. Basking in the patronage of various high-ranking Thai Army and police officers, he operated for six years with impunity out of his new stronghold. But the best news for the SUA leader was that his arch-rival, the KMT, was being broken. Around 1973 the People's Army of the CPB together with the Burma Army definitively dislodged the Chinese Nationalist remnants from the Shan State, pushing them over the border into Thailand and ending their 20-year long control of opium trafficking in Burma. Khun Sa, reinvigorated and poised in Hin Taek, stepped in to fill* the vacuum. Where once the KMT had controlled 90% of the heroin issuing from the "Golden Triangle", now he was in control of 70% of it. In the mid-70s Khun Sa emerged as South-East Asia's premier drugs warlord, a position he has not relinquished since.

The warlord's notoriety began to embarrass his Thai hosts. Not only was the Hin Taek area a funnel for vast amounts of drugs passing into Thailand and on out to the wider world, but Khun Sa's SUA was assassinating the odd CIA and US Drugs Enforcement Administration official, angering the Thais' main ally, the Americans. There were other considerations, too. The threat from the communist parties of Burma and Thailand was receding by the early 80s, making the SUA less necessary. But what really stung the Thai authorities into action was the discovery that Sa was buying large quantities of opium from the Burmese communists - the very people he was supposed to be undermining (it had always been his practice to buy from anyone and everyone). Worse still, he moved freely through CPB-controlled territory and was even reportedly harbouring Chinese arms for the Thai communists. In January 1982 crack Thai Army rangers and BPP troops launched a massive attack on Hin Taek, backed up by tanks, artillery and warplanes. In the ensuing fierce battle scores were killed and wounded, but the strike was successful, and a thousand SUA men retreated over the border into the Shan State (Sa, it is said, was tipped off by powerful Thai friends and escaped). The Hin Taek heroin-producing hub was smashed, and the opium king dispatched from Siamese soil.

Never a man to be worsted, Khun Sa retaliated against his former hosts by sacking Mae Sai and stopping and burning dozens of vehicles on the Mae Sai-Chiang Rai highway. On the Burmese side of the border he initiated 1983-84 a reign of terror, fanning the smouldering border war with the KMT, attacking and displacing numerous small ethnic groups and rebel armies, and creating the biggest shake-up along the Shan-Thai border since the arrival of the KMT. In one memorable action an SUA hit-squad blew up the Fah Ham residence in Chiang Mai of Gen. Li, the commander of the KMT Third Army. When the dust had settled along the border, Khun Sa had established camps notably at Doi Larng (opposite Mai Ai), at Mong Mai (near Mae Or/Mae Hong Son), and at Piang Luang. At the latter place, as we know, his SUA units straddled the corridor leading from the village to the interior of the Shan State, all but cutting the lifeline of Mo Heng's SURA. The upshot was the swallowing in 1985 of Mo Heng's force by Khun Sa's, the new combined army later being renamed the Mong Tai Army. Both at Doi Larng and Mae Or Sa's strongholds were compromised by adjacent Wa positions, but at Piang Luang the warlord was in sole control. Mo Heng's old base, the starting point for three main trafficking routes into Thailand - one down through Kae Noi, one down through Wiang Haeng, and one down to Pai - must have been the jewel in Khun Sa's crown.

By 1985 Sa dominated virtually the whole 200-km Shan-Thai frontier. His trafficking flourished accordingly. He claimed to control two thirds of the cross-border narcotics trade with Thailand, approximately 1000 tons of *opium a year. As the money rolled in, his MTA swelled. Soon it comprised some 6000-8000 properly trained and heavily armed men. Khun Sa was the uncontested opium king of the "Golden Triangle". The only force which could perhaps have moved against him was the Burma Army. But, as in earlier decades, Rangoon's stance was curiously hands-off. In thirty years Khun Sa has had, compared to all the other rebel groups in Burma, a remarkably easy ride with the authorities. Possibly they remembered his early "work" for them as a ka kwae yae commander. Perhaps they throught the game of pursuing the powerful warlord into his remote jungle kingdom not worth the candle. But probably they had reached some kind of understanding with him. It was reported in the 80s that at secret meetings with him senior Burmese military figures had agreed that he could pursue his trafficking activities unmolested if in exchange he would allow free passage through his territory for the teak which Rangoon had begun selling to the Thais for desperately needed foreign currency. The hemorrhage of logs today through Piang Luang would seem to substantiate such a deal. With the Thais themselves, Sa's relationship was also surprisingly sweet. Now that he was no longer on their territory, they had no special quarrel with him. Rather the reverse was the case. The hardwood was coming through, as were the regular shipments of white "N°. 4", which yielded hefty kickbacks for army and police officers at the border crossings and on the mountain roads leading down from the frontier. At the instigation of the Americans, the Thais put a price on Sa's head, but the bounty was so laughable that no one bothered to try to collect it. It would have been an easy matter to do so, as Sa had a safe house in Mae Hong Son and even, apparently, property off the Sukhumvit Road in Bangkok. Of the Thais Khun Sa scoffed: "If you feed them, they are friendly" and "Why should they fight or capture their moneytree?!"*

Around 1987 the "Prince of Death" or the "Poppy Man", as the world's press liked to dub Khun Sa, sought to clean up his image. He tried to attenuate the significance of opium-growing, the drugs trade, the MTA, and his cause. He invited journalists to his Ho Mong GHQ, who were surprised to find not a warlord of legendary ruthlessness, but an affable, astute and articulate host, a man who took pleasure in promoting Buddhist and Shan culture. The reason so much opium was grown in the "Triangle", the Shan champion explained, was simply economic dependency. "If you ask the peasants to stop growing poppies, they will have nothing left to barter for rice." He himself was not an opium warlord, but a Shan nationalist and freedom fighter. With the MTA he was fighting a war of liberation against Rangoon for an autonomous Shan State. Sa did not deny his involvement in trafficking opium and heroin, but claimed it was a necessary evil. He had only entered the narcotics trade to fund his army and finance the struggle. Actually, he was anti-drugs and wanted nothing more than to eliminate the curse of opium from the Shan State. He reminded the journalists - and through them the world at large - that on several occasions he had proposed to the US that they buy from him the

48

entire opium crop of the "Golden Triangle" in exchange for economic aid. For US $100m a year for five years the Americans could stop the flow of heroin from the "Triangle", and the Shan State would benefit from an aid programme which would eradicate the poppy, substitute other crops, and develop the Shan economy. "If I can win the Shan State, 8 million Shans will be happy, but if I solve the drug problem, the whole world will rejoice." Sa reiterated his offer, but as on previous occasions it was turned down by Washington, which did not deal with "criminals". Cynics pointed out that Sa was only changing his tune because his share of the world narcotics market was declining in the face of a flood of drugs from places like Columbia. But perhaps also an ageing Khun Sa, with his eye on the history books, wanted to acquire respectability before he quitted the stage. The warlord's problem was that his change of heart came rather late. Perhaps he really was now a freedom fighter, but meanwhile he had become so much tainted by the corruption of the narcotics world that few believed his offer. This was a pity, as the offer, which still stands, could well be genuine.

Khun Sa's virtual monopoly of drugs trafficking along the Shan-Thai border ended around 1990, when a new opium war flared up, this time between Sa and the Wa. The two factions had already skirmished sporadically throughout the 80s, but the confrontations, for example at Mae Or (Mae Hong Son), had been of little consequence. Now the jostling for power and for control of the frontier was deadly serious. The difference was that the Wa, already backed by the KMT, were substantially reinforced by a body of Wa Daeng or Red Wa, Wa who up in the Wa substate had for years sided with the Burmese communists, but who now in the wake of the 1989 CPB mutinies and the demise of Burmese communism came south to the Thai border. Here they joined up with pockets of Wa already in place, forming the new United Wa State Army, and began muscling in on Khun Sa's scene, notably on the Doi Larng range. Sa's MTA attacked the UWSA, but in a battle which intensified right through to 1991 - the bitterest fighting, the MTA conceded, it had ever been involved in - things did not go entirely Sa's way. He was obliged largely to pull his troops out of his base near Mae Or so as to relieve his beleaguered Doi Larng stronghold, and in the end the Wa secured a piece of the ridge.

Khun Sa's latest move, a provocative one, was to declare in mid-December 1993 the independence of the Shan State. A large number of Shan leaders and observers gathered in his Ho Mong GHQ to promulgate under his direction a constitution, at the same time instituting a 70-seat two-house parliament, with Sa, his relatives and lieutenants holding key offices. All laws issuing from Rangoon were annulled, and all SLORC junta troops on Shan land were required to leave. Sa invited recognition for his newly independent country from the UN and the nations of the world, and he crowed that in the years ahead the MTA would be strengthened to as many as 100,000 guerrillas.

THREE PAGODAS

The Burmese reply to all this bravado was a massive offensive against Khun Sa. In the dying days of 1993, 6000-10,000 government troops gathered on the west bank of the Salween, closing off a 120-km section of the river. Fighting started opposite Wiang Haeng, precipitating the flight of hundreds of refugees (especially Lisu) over the border at Piang Luang, where they were housed in camps at Chong. Rangoon claimed that it had seized two refineries belonging to Sa. Sa, holding many of his troops in reserve to protect his other refineries, rushed a sizeable number of MTA guerrillas to block the Burma Army. They ambushed a column of 1000 SLORC soldiers crossing the Salween in longtail boats, killing many. At the height of the crisis Sa warned the Burmese that if they advanced, he would destroy Takilek/Mae Sai - by no means an empty threat considering his earlier sacking of the town. At the same time he claimed that the offensive against him was merely cosmetic. The two refineries seized were not his, but had been set up by the Burmese so that for effect they could then be captured. This may well have been true. The MTA spotted farangs *(probably US DEA officials) among the Burmese on the west bank of the Salween, suggesting that the offensive and the seizures had been stage-managed to impress the DEA (and congressmen back home) with a view to justifying American aid to Rangoon. And, indeed, in early 1994 the offensive seemed to peter out. The Burmese may not have liked the Shan State declaration of independence, but either they did not have the stomach to pursue the opium king into his border lair or else they had never intended to do so anyway.*

Before our trip to this section of the border, we had wondered why Piang Luang (but also Kae Noi - and in early 1994 Wiang Haeng too) was so firmly closed to outsiders. In retrospect, as we made our way back to Wiang Haeng, the reason, or rather cocktail of reasons, was obvious. There was the danger of cross-border bandits and robbers, of the kind who lurked around Kae Noi. There was the intermittent danger of attacks and shelling by the Burma Army. There was the risk for outsiders of being mistaken by the KMT or the MTA (if *farangs* crossed the border) for hated DEA officers. There was the matter of the massacre of KMT people at Piang Luang, which the authorities no doubt preferred to remain a secret. But the real murky secret was the trafficking in the area. Kae Noi was a drugs smuggling village like other KMT border settlements, and Piang Luang was a veritable funnel for heroin passing from Khun Sa's territory into Thailand. The drugs came over the border in pick-ups and in secret compartments cut into the Burmese teak on the log-transporters. And it was in this respect that the Thai authorities quite especially did not want outsiders snooping around Piang Luang. They did not want the lid lifted here on an easy relationship with the notorious Khun Sa, nor on the collusion with him of corrupt Thai police and army officers (on one police truck we saw drums of acetic anhydride, a chemical vital in the heroin-refining process), and not either on the questionable tripartite cooperation of the Thais, the illegal Rangoon junta and Khun Sa in the shameful matter of the logging - something internationally condemned.

CHAPTER 4

SPIRIT WELL

Wiang Haeng - Sala Muang Noi - Pai - Bo Pi - Mae Hong Son

Back in Wiang Haeng, we were refreshing ourselves at *Sayan* when we had a piece of luck. It was Friday, and employees from the district office, the post and telecommunications offices, and the hospital opposite were leaving work for the weekend. Everyone was in a grand mood, all the more so because next day was a Buddha day, a reason for special celebration. No one was more buoyant than a fellow in his early thirties who was roaming around on a large white trails bike looking for diversion. This was the excellent Witit Terkae, a Karen from the nearby hamlet of Mae Haat. He spotted us immediately, parked his machine, and introduced himself. He was a hospital employee, although his actual place of work was the health clinic in Mae Haat. He was involved in family planning and had in the past worked in UN-sponsored hill-tribe development schemes. A broad-faced, short-haired fellow, who had enjoyed education in Chiang Mai, he now lived in Chong, where his wife ran a shop selling domestic appliances, and did some tailoring on the side.

Witit was instantly likeable. He seemed overjoyed to meet a *farang* and began showing us numerous kindnesses. He paid for our tea and snacks, pointed out to us (three-up on his motorbike) hidden aspects of Wiang Haeng, and invited us for nips of pre-prandial *lao kao* at the store next to *Sayan*. As the evening wore on, he became more and more eager, his altruism, embarrassingly, seeming to know no bounds. To our eternal shame, we began to grow suspicious of this rather flash, Thaiized character. What could he want of us? Why should he take such an interest in us? He liked to meet foreigners, he explained, was teaching himself English and wanted to practise what he had learnt. But more than that, he wanted *farang* visitors to get a good impression of Wiang Haeng and Thailand. When he had met westerners in the past, they had all too often left complaining of this or that, and that had hurt him. We also got the impression that this keen-minded Karen-Thai was simply bored of everyday life up at remote Wiang Haeng district. He was looking for contact, interest. But if on that Friday evening we were made for him, much more so he was made for us. On all our travels down the border we hardly met a more helpful generous man.

We were worried that, with the school closed for the weekend, it might be awkward to continue staying in the primary school sickroom. "Don't worry about that", Witit said, "the janitor Rak-kiet is a friend of mine. We'll go down and sort it out." ("Don't worry" and "so-and-so is a friend of mine" were favourite expressions of his.) And just as we had feared, when we got back down to the school, Rak-kiet had disappeared and all the

51

MAP 4

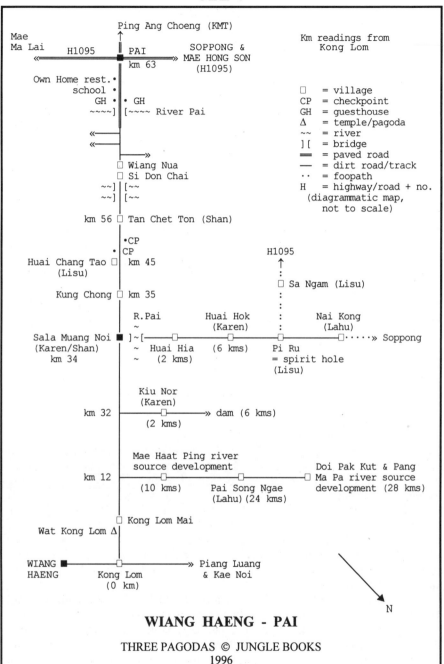

```
                    Ping Ang Choeng (KMT)
Mae                      ↑
Ma Lai                   |   SOPPONG &          Km readings from
         H1095       ■  PAI  MAE HONG SON           Kong Lom
    «===============═══»  (H1095)
                    km 63
Own Home rest.•                             □  = village
      school •                              CP = checkpoint
        GH •  • GH                          GH = guesthouse
      ~~~~]  [~~~~ River Pai                Δ  = temple/pagoda
                                            ~~ = river
    «━━━━━━━━━                              ][ = bridge
    «━━━━━━━━━                              == = paved road
            └━━━»                           —  = dirt road/track
         □ Wiang Nua                        •• = foopath
         □ Si Don Chai                      H  = highway/road + no.
       ~~]  |[~~                              (diagrammatic map,
       ~~]  |[~~                               not to scale)
  km 56 □ Tan Chet Ton (Shan)

         •CP
      •  CP                         H1095
Huai Chang Tao □  km 45              ↑
     (Lisu)                          :
                                     □ Sa Ngam (Lisu)
  Kung Chong □ km 35                 :
                                     :
         R.Pai    Huai Hok           :    Nai Kong
          ~       (Karen)            :    (Lahu)
Sala Muang Noi ■ ]~[——□———□————□———□·····» Soppong
(Karen/Shan)      ~  Huai Hia   (6 kms)  Pi Ru
   km 34          ~  (2 kms)             = spirit hole
                                           (Lisu)

         Kiu Nor
         (Karen)
  km 32 ——□————» dam (6 kms)
         (2 kms)

         Mae Haat Ping river
         source development            Doi Pak Kut & Pang
  km 12 ——□————————□————————□ Ma Pa river source
         (10 kms)  Pai Song Ngae      development (28 kms)
                   (Lahu)(24 kms)

         □ Kong Lom Mai
Wat Kong Lom Δ|

WIANG ■━━━━━□━━━━» Piang Luang
HAENG    Kong Lom    & Kae Noi
         (0 km)
```

N

WIANG HAENG - PAI

THREE PAGODAS © JUNGLE BOOKS
1996

teachers had gone down to Chiang Dao or Chiang Mai for the weekend. However, Witit knew where the janitor's private house was - in the middle of a pineapple field halfway between Wiang Haeng and Kong Lom. On the way out to the pineapple plantation we suddenly turned off the main road, still three-up on the trails bike, into a long side track running down to an isolated building in the middle of some fields. It was Wiang Haeng Christian Church. Behind the simple box church building was a long motel-like block, where the priest lived. "What are we doing here?" we asked our new friend. "Don't worry", Witit said, "the priest is a friend of mine. You can stay here." And indeed the priest and the Karen seemed to be on good terms. Within a short time it was all fixed up that we should stay in the guestroom of the pastor's block.

While Witit went off to regulate things with the janitor and at the same time recover our backpacks from the school, we made acquaintance with the priest. Most obligingly, this chubby-faced, quiet-spoken man, called Somkiet, unlocked a simple spartan room with a large double bed and electric fan. There was nothing else in the room except nails in the walls for securing a mosquito net. But the priest, although he was really cooking his supper in the kitchen, set about rustling up blankets, sheets, pillows and even pillow cases. At the back of the block he showed us a *hongnaam* cubicle (wash and toilet facilities combined), and soon we were showering with rainwater from a tank warmed by the sun. On a table on the veranda at the front of the building jars of tea, coffee and Ovaltine appeared, together with a clump of bananas and a pyramid of oranges. There, waiting for Witit, we chatted to our new host.

After two nights in the sickbays of primary schools, all this was luxury indeed. Here was the real "Wiang Haeng Hilton", and we told Somkiet so. It was nothing, he demurred, just simple Christian hospitality. From time to time westerners, mostly Americans, came up from Chiang Mai to express solidarity with his mission or help him plant church rice, and he had meanwhile learned what "farangs" liked. We voiced our fear that we were putting him to a lot of trouble. Not at all, he smiled, there was not a lot to do up here, he did not get many visitors, and he was glad of the company. He elaborated about the church and his work. The church had been built by missionaries between 1985 and 1991. They had left two years previously, leaving him in charge as the first Thai priest. The church had 49 members, mostly Lisu people. He held a service for them once a week. There was another church in the village, a Baptist mission for the Karens. While Somkiet was speaking, we noticed that he had outsized Buddha-like earlobes - hardly appropriate for a Christian minister. Another odd thing was that the priest had put into a cassette player a tape of Christmas carols (it was in the weeks running up to Christmas), which played over a loudspeaker system he had rigged up. So, as we chatted on the veranda and watched the oriental sun go down over the mountains behind Chong and distant Kae Noi, we were regaled with "Jingle Bells" and "God Rest Ye Merry Gentlemen" - in Thai, of course.

Witit knew of a second better restaurant in Wiang Haeng and insisted on taking us for supper there. It was a new place, set back from the main road and positioned by a small artificial lake. It belonged to a teacher ("a friend of mine") and as yet had no name. From Somkiet's veranda we could see its fairy lights winking in the distance. There was a direct way over to the restaurant from the church, and so, guided by Witit, we picked our way under a full moon through the dry stubbly rice paddies towards the lights.

The little lake was being used to breed freshwater fish, and it was not long before a trout couched in coriander leaves and a fiery fish *tom yam* soup in a steamboat were on the table. Best-quality Sangthip whisky appeared, a bucket of ice, soda, more dishes of pork and fresh ginger, of stir-fried mixed vegetables and so on, and soon we were well into a feast that must have cost the health worker a week's wages. But Witit was in his element, kept saying how much he liked *farangs*, and what a pleasure it was for him to see us happy. As the Sangthip began to course through his veins, his English improved remarkably. All sorts of stories came out. One concerned his father. Years ago his father had been walking down to Pai when he had been bitten in the bottom by a tiger. The wound had hurt so much that doctors had given the poor man opium to alleviate the pain. Unfortunately, the father had then grown addicted to opium. With the breadwinning father incapacitated, and the family having to buy ever more opium, they had all become impoverished. Witit told of how he and his mother had had to make long treks alone in search of opium, sometimes as far as Pai (65 kms away). It was only when the father had finally died that the family's fortunes had improved. This background may have explained Witit's motivation in life and relative affluence.

We were the guests of honour at the restaurant, and the teacher-owner brought to our table a plateful of *yaku*. This was a Shan confection made specially to offer to monks on Buddha days, such as was the morrow. It was a brownish sticky cake, like flapjack but softer, and made of glutinous rice, sugar cane, coconut and peanut. The wedge-shaped slices were dusted with sesame seeds. Trying the *yaku*, we learned that some of Witit's relatives had dug up in their gardens both at Mae Haat and Chong pipes, pots and other relics from the ancient Lawa people. Our ears pricked up. The few surviving Lawa now lived in a mountainous area much further south, near Mae Sariang. If what the Karen said was true, the finds would seem to indicate that at one time, pre-dating the arrival of the local Shans (Tai Yai) and the Siamese Tai (modern Thais), the Lawa had lived right up here in Wiang Haeng district, perhaps constituting the original inhabitants of the area.

Witit recounted details his mother had told him about the Japanese in Wiang Haeng during WW2. They had pressganged local people to act as porters in their invasion of Burma from Thailand. But they could not have had things all their own way in this isolated area. Recently a mass grave of Japanese soldiers had been unearthed at nearby Sala Muang Noi. We asked Witit where that was. It was a Karen village halfway between Wiang

Haeng and Pai. Witit had relatives there. This casual titbit of information made us sit up. The village seemed to lie on our onward route. The detail was all the more interesting because we had once tried to get up by motorcycle to Wiang Haeng from the Pai end, but had failed miserably. The track had been so difficult that we had given up after about 20 kms. Our abiding fear was that we might be frustrated again on this crucial link down to Pai. Was there a way down to Pai from here, we asked, and what was it like? For the first time that evening Witit's face clouded over. There was a way, but it was very bad, and dangerous. We could not possibly get our Wing down there. Even in a 4WD truck it was virtually impassable. No one went down there. The only sensible way to get through was on foot. But to halfway Muang Noi it was more than 30 kms - an awful long way to trek in one day. The outlook seemed bleak. "But don't worry about it", our Karen friend said, "let me see what I can do."

We wanted to leave Wiang Haeng for Pai the next day. But the next day Witit had arranged with a friend to go down to Chiang Mai in a pick-up he owned. He was torn between honouring his arrangement and trying to help us. The more we discussed the problem of getting through the mountains to Pai, the more the spice of an adventure with us attracted him. Finally the matter was settled - fantastically in our favour. He would take us on the Saturday, if it was possible, in his truck as far as Sala Muang Noi. There he would leave us with his Karen relatives and return the same day to Wiang Haeng. We would have to find our own way down the second half of the route to Pai. His trip to Chiang Mai he would delay until the Sunday, and on that Sunday he would also be able to take our redundant motorbike with him in the back of his pick-up to Chiang Mai, returning it to the hire shop. The plan could not have worked out more perfectly for us. But Witit declared himself very satisfied too. He would still get to Chiang Mai, but would also have the pleasure of a day out with us. In the euphoria of the moment another bottle of Sangthip appeared, and we all drank too much late into the night.

When Witit finally arrived the next morning, he was in high spirits. We could tell from his breath that he had already been drinking. We took our leave of Somkiet the priest, left the Honda with him, and made a small contribution to his church effort. Then, in Witit's ageing blue pick-up we blasted down the dusty stony road past Rak-kiet's pineapple patch in the direction of Piang Luang. Almost immediately the truck drew up at a shophouse in Kong Lom village. "A friend of mine", Witit said, "don't worry." We did worry, because in front of the house there was a table with a litter of glasses and half-empty Mekhong bottles on it. Around the table sat half a dozen men, clearly determined to waste no time in celebrating Buddha day. We feared either that we would have to join the party or that the noisy crew might want to come with us. But only one man was to come with us, a Thai in his twenties called Ekerin Poon Nu.

Witit and the lean wiry-haired Ekerin disappeared into the house. Presently they emerged wearing military combat gear and bearing provisions for the trip. Witit had asked me what I liked eating, and I had said, not giving the matter much thought, but trying hastily to settle on something as innocuous as possible, "Chiang Mai sausage". So they put into the truck sticky rice, chilli dip, a bottle of Mekhong whisky and, taking me literally, a long coiled Chiang Mai sausage. Behind the seats in the cab they also stowed "just in case" an assault rifle, two pistols and three hand grenades. Into the open back of the truck they tossed, for good measure, a hunting gun, wrapped in a sack. We questioned the two about this mini-arsenal, and Witit confessed that he was terrified about the trip - not so much about the outward journey to Muang Noi, but about the way back, which they would have to do in the night. He would never have gone with us on his own, which was why he had asked his friend to come along. Ekerin was a regular Thai Army soldier, in fact a paratrooper who had been trained by the Americans.

Soon we were on our way. At a junction in the centre of Kong Lom, a side road went off southwest, out past Wat Kong Lom, through the new satellite settlement of Kong Lom Mai, and towards the hills. The road, already a narrow dirt track, bumped through some outlying fields, before starting to climb. Then, twisting and turning around the hillsides, it climbed over three ridges in succession. The way, a major heroin-smuggling route from Piang Luang down to Pai, passed through completely uninhabited mountainous forest. During the 34 kms from Kong Lom to Sala Muang Noi we passed not a single hut or vehicle or person on foot. The absence of vehicles, even 4WD machines, was hardly surprising - the route proved, as Witit had predicted, virtually impassable. The main problem was that on the central ridge section the track degenerated into a series of precipitous rutted gulleys. The two boys in the cab picked out a way for the truck as best they could. We stood in the back, clinging onto the rollbar, being tossed this way and that. The wheels inched from boulder to boulder, grinding up, teetering, and lurching forward. The vehicle underside scraped repeatedly on the rocks. On the steepest downgrades, where the surface was gravelly, the pick-up slithered, its rear end threatening on the curves, where the outer edge fell away, to tip off the mountainside. Alarmed, we made ready to jump from the vehicle should this happen. Initially, Witit and Ekerin were worried too. Witit said later that they had wanted to go back, but had not been able to find anywhere to turn round, and so had had to continue. But as they got into the expedition, they warmed to it. The two friends were like boys out on an adventure. We saw them through the rear window of the cab chattering, joking and, maniacally it seemed to us, passing the Mekhong from one to the other, which they drank straight from the bottle.

Presently they drew up on an elevated flat piece of track. Ekerin had seen something he wanted to take a potshot at. He came round to the back and aimed the hunting gun up into the tree tops. None of us could see what it was that he wanted to shoot. There was a loud report, and a bird flapped away. Then the sizzling countryside fell eerily silent again. We kept looking over our shoulders into the endless lonesome *mai teng* and *mai rang* trees, wanting to press on. But the boys decided it was an excellent spot for a picnic. They began fiddling around, as Karens do, slashing at the vegetation with their survival knives and unpacking the food on the pick-up's tailboard. While the soldier recharged his gun, Witit hacked off two sections from a fat bamboo and fashioned two drinking cups. I had brought a plastic bottle of purified water with me and was not amused when he poured half of the precious liquid into the green cups and threw the rest away. Taking my plastic bottle, he then sliced it in two, making two more crude containers. Decanting half the water from the bamboo sections into the two new plastic "cups", he then liberally topped up all four with whisky, and we each had a drink. The boys thought the makeshift bar a hoot. Then the Chiang Mai sausage came out. And so, with slices of sausage and balls of sticky rice in one hand, and our warm whisky in the other, we had an impromptu lunch standing around the truck on a heroin trail in the middle of nowhere.

Waving a machete with a piece of sausage spitted on the end, Witit pointed out wild orchids growing from the tree tops. They hung down like dark clumps of weeds from the uppermost boughs. Through gaps in the woods he indicated pink sakura trees and yellow *buatong* growing on the mountainsides. Ekerin narrated mad stories about his commando training with the Americans. For some reason he and the other soldiers had had to stand for days on end in water. And when during their jungle survival training he had subsisted on centipedes and rats, the softie GIs had munched throughout on secret chocolate bars. Two kms short of our halfway goal, we passed a turning northwest (right) to the Karen village of Kiu Nor and a small dam. After that, a long descent brought us to Sala Muang Noi, almost exactly midpoint between Wiang Haeng and Pai.

Sala Muang Noi

A relatively large village with a mixed Shan and Karen population, Muang Noi straddled the River Pai. A new bridge was being built over the water, and it was impossible to drive across to the western side. So Witit parked his pick-up in the grounds of the new health centre. His idea was to get us billetted there, where the medic in charge was "a friend of his". But alas, the day being a Saturday (moreover a Buddha day), the friend had gone away for the weekend, and the building was locked up. Picking our way on foot through the scaffolding of the new bridge, we searched around the houses on the other side. Finally the boys lighted on one poor unsuspecting household, and we all crowded in. The owners were Karen, evidently distantly related to Witit. What was happening and what was being arranged was quite inscrutable to us, and so we kept our own counsel. But it seemed that some corner of the large wooden dwelling would be our bedplace for the night.

We wanted to go out and explore the village, but Witit and Ekerin had other ideas. Soon the four of us were sitting cross-legged on a platform at the rear, while the lady of the house brought plate after plate of snacks. The boys intended to continue the day as they had started it, and once more laid into the whisky. Most of the snacks were either too fiery to eat or made of things one would not want to eat anyway. But a plate of roast buffalo morsels was tempting, if only to soak up some of the afternoon alcohol. Unfortunately, a scruffy young chicken also had designs on this. Numerous domestic animals besieged the platform, but none was more persistent that the chicken - or "chor" in Karen. With a constant cheeping and fluttering it kept returning to the platform, strutting among the plates and pecking at them. We shooed it away a few times, and when that became tiresome, Witit picked it up and threw it across the backyard. Undeterred, the brazen chicklet returned. Ekerin moved to teach it a lesson, and in its panic it placed a scaly foot exactly in the middle of the roasted buffalo morsels. We thought the paratrooper was going to wring the bird's neck, but he simply cloched it with a heavy pot, from under which it cheeped inconsolably, denied access to the snacks. The *chor* was in prison, we suggested, which set the boys chuckling again...

Finally, when it was already dark, our two friends broke off the party, saying that they had to return to Wiang Haeng. They grew steadily more serious as we neared the truck. We tried to persuade them to stay the night and start back early next morning. But they would not hear of it. They checked their cache of weapons, took leave of us, and disappeared into the nighttime jungle. The thought of the two of them trying to drive up that atrocious way in the dark made us apprehensive too - and with justification. When, months later, we saw Witit again, he said that they had not reached Wiang Haeng until two in the morning. In fact, they had almost not got back at all. He did not elaborate, and we felt sure that they had had an accident. At all events, we never saw the blue pick-up again (Witit had "sold it - it was getting rather old"), and in our minds there was no doubt that the Karen and his soldier friend had written it off on that return journey.

Our lodging in Muang Noi was not a typical Karen house raised on stilts, but a regular two-storey building made throughout with wooden planking. The disorder was great, and every room looked like a lumber room. Normally when passers-by stay at a Karen dwelling, they sleep on a communal platform at the front. But we were allocated pride of place upstairs in a lobby, where the family shrine was. There, under a shelf decked with Buddha figurines, flowers, a miniature bespectacled monk and a mysterious old tea tin, we unpacked out rucksacks and rolled out our sleeping bags. In the backyard there was a barnlike shack - probably the original house. In this, a very old man and woman lived, the parents of either our host or hostess. They never moved from the shack and tended three blackened kettles, which were permanently on the go on a fire that burned night and day. Washing was either in the River Pai or with a pot and dipper on the platform at the rear, where we had had our little party. The dipper was half a tin can nailed to the end of a stick, and with this we tried to have a wash. Seeing that no more food would be forthcoming that evening, we went to the aged grandparents and made Ma-ma instant noodles with their boiling water. The granny smoked a pipe throughout, and the grandpa constantly rolled his own green cheroots. The impudent chicken was on the loose again, and darting around on the bare earth floor, it ran the gauntlet of gobs of spit from the ancient pair. Neither of them could speak a word of Thai, and we could speak no Karen, so communication was reduced to an amiable exchange of signs. Electricity had reached Muang Noi three years previously, and our house had one of the few TVs in the village. Back in the living room of the main house, we found 25 people of all ages sitting in a crescent around the box, but also crowding the doorway and hanging in through the windows. A Thai thriller was showing, and we noticed that many of the viewers took the film literally. Gasping and flinching when something dramatic happened, they had difficulty telling TV make-believe from reality.

The next morning, inspecting Muang Noi, we realised what an attractive place it was. With the tight valley of the River Pai running through the middle, the settlement was surrounded by lush vegetation and dominated by nearby Doi Pa Poeng (or Toe Nae Lae in Karen), a wooded hump with a sheer northern cliff face. It was also a traditional village, many of the Karen inhabitants wearing their costumes. The women had on red hand-woven tube-skirts and terrycloth turbans, while the men were dressed in baggy black pants and jerkins, their attire topped off by a ubiquitous bobble hat. At the high end of the village we found a fine small monastery, surrounded by flowering *sh'bar* bushes and *lantom* trees. In the midst of their heady perfume, a monk explained to us that Muang Noi was about 40 years old and originally Shan. A few Karens had then arrived, followed by more, until they predominated. They had intermarried with the local *tai yai*, creating a truly mixed Karen-Shan village. We learned from the bonze something of advantage to us. Most days a lorry came up to the dam from Pai. Usually it went back down the same day - he could not say when - and we might be able to get a lift with it.

We were doubtful whether the lorry would come on a Sunday, but nevertheless thought it worth trying to intercept the vehicle. So we went back down to collect our backpacks. On our way through the simple leaf-roofed houses we came upon a disturbing sight in somebody's front yard. Although the late-morning sun was very hot, a wood fire was blazing. A man was lying next to the fire, so close that his clothes were singeing. He was wrapped in innumerable blankets, had on three woollen balaclava helmets one over the other, and his feet were bound up in hemp sacking. The bundled figure looked like the Michelin man or a mummy, and the only part of him which was visible was a panel of face, which was waxy white and had a black moustache. The man was shaking uncontrollably and over and again asked for the fire to be made hotter. He was bitterly cold, he complained, and had a terrible headache. Of course, the man had malarial fever. The circle of onlookers explained to us that the fever came on always at the same time of day. Why don't you go down and get the doctor, we suggested, fearing that the man might die. That was the problem, they replied, the doctor had gone away for the weekend.

We took up position by the road in a corner of the health clinic compound. Opposite was Muang Noi's tiny "Private Licensed Post Office", no more than a shed. It was just as firmly shuttered as the clinic. Behind the post office was the timeless veering cliff of Toe Nae Lae. It seemed to mock us in our wait in the blazing midday sun. We searched incessantly up the dusty track, but no vehicle came. It was incredibly boring and frustrating waiting there. The seconds and minutes and hours ticked slowly by. The only thing to contemplate was the grisly detail that Witit had told us - that our waiting station was the place where, when the health centre had been built a year or two earlier, workers had unearthed the mass grave of Japanese soldiers who had been massacred in WW2. They were probably killed by Karens as the Japanese withdrew from Burma back into Thailand at the end of the war. In 1945 Karen and Karenni underground forces, organized and armed by the British, killed an estimated 12,500 troops of the Japanese 15th Army, as it retreated in disarray through Burma's eastern hills and back across the Thai-Burmese border.

In the end our waiting was rewarded. At teatime an orange lorry came bumping towards us from the direction of the dam. We waved it down and asked if we could ride to Pai. The driver was happy to take us, and as the back was full of oxyacetylene cutting and welding equipment, he bade us climb up into the cab. And so we began the second half of the trip down to Pai. It was every bit as bad as the first half, if not worse. Immediately after Muang Noi we splashed through two fords and passed an outlying hamlet, Kung Chong. Then the lorry broke its way over a couple more ridges of the type we had crossed earlier. The flora was part jungle, part highland woods, the trees being a mixture of pine and teak, *mai teng* and *mai rang*. The most severe section of the entire 65 kms from Wiang Haeng to Pai was probably around the Lisu village of Huai Chang Tao. Here a dozen wickedly steep climbs and descents were aggravated by a succession of hairpin bends. This had been our waterloo on that previous attempt at the route. The driver carefully edged the lorry around the bends. After the Lisu village (45 kms from Kong Lom), we passed the first of two checkpoints. Both were manned intermittently, our driver explained, their sole purpose being to catch drug smugglers. On the day we passed them, both posts were deserted. After one more ridge, we finally left the mountains, coming down into valley country at the Shan village of Tan Chet Ton (= seven palm trees) (km 56). From there it was a straight run on through the villages of Si Don Chai and Wiang Nua, across the River Pai, and into Pai town itself.

Pai

Pai was a dreamy squat little place, set in a hot wide basin. Lying almost exactly halfway along the 200-km H1095 route from Mae Ma Lai to Mae Hong Son, this Shan town was enjoying a mini-boom. For the increasing number of people proceeding anti-clockwise round the Chiang Mai - Mae Hong Son - Mae Sariang - Chiang Mai loop, the town made an obvious first stopping point. There was not a lot to do in Pai, either in the town itself, or in the immediate vicinity. The central grid of streets, lined with single and two-storey houses, could be walked all round in half an hour or so. Some people used the town as a base for trekking in the mountains further afield. Pai lay on the edge of a well-trekked area to the northwest. Others used it as somewhere to linger for a week or two. In choosing tranquil low-key riverine Pai in preference to Chiang Mai or other overtly touristy resorts, they were not making a mistake. One diverting feature close at hand was the KMT village of Ping Ang Choeng, renamed by the Thai authorities Santichon (= peaceful river). Situated west of Pai, four or five kms up a dirt road, the village was unusual for a KMT settlement in that it was in the lowlands and not up on the mountainous border. We were told that the 20-30 Chinese families had recently been resettled there from notorious Hin Taek, where they may have been "friends" of Khun Sa. This would have explained the frosty welcome and veiled looks we received when we stopped by at Ping Ang Choeng.

We stayed a couple of days in Pai, and at first the little town captivated us. The laid-back atmosphere was relaxing, and there was minimal traffic and pollution. After Kae Noi, Wiang Haeng and Muang Noi it was also undeniably pleasant to re-enjoy the creature comforts of relative civilization. *Own Home Restaurant* provided a remarkably varied menu with good friendly service. One could spend an inexpensive week here eating one's way through molee Indian curry, barbeque chicken, Thai stir-fries, moussaka, Burmese food and Japanese tempura. And *Charlie's Guest House*, centrally located in the main street, proved an adequate lodging, with hot showers, an attractive inner courtyard with garden, and somewhere to hang out one's washing.

But gradually Pai palled on us. Above all, it was an unreal place - indeed, all "Pai in the Sky", as the name of one guesthouse had it. For such a small rural community, it had a disproportionate number of guesthouses, trekking agencies and restaurants. They had mushroomed to service all the *farangs* who now saturated the town. However, these were not the seasoned travellers and trail-blazing bikers of yore, but (at the risk of sounding patronizing) couples pushing infants in buggies, maladroit elderly tourists, and groups of pink-skinned youngsters, fresh in from their home countries, hobbling around with blisters after a first trek and bitten all over by mosquitos and bedbugs. Our room at *Charlie's* was really no more than a box, utterly devoid of furniture, and for this they charged prices rivalling those in Chiang Mai. In the self-regarding *Tai Yai* restaurant, we met arrogance and contempt from the Thai-Shan owner. Woe betide anyone

MAP 5

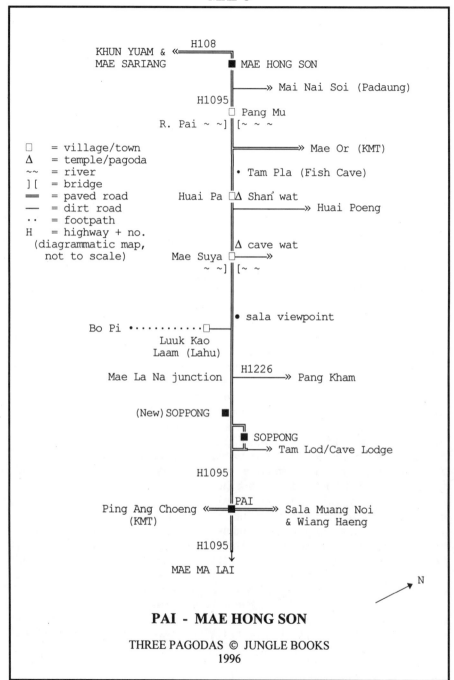

KHUN YUAM & «══════ H108
MAE SARIANG

■ MAE HONG SON

─────────» Mai Nai Soi (Padaung)

H1095

□ Pang Mu

R. Pai ~ ~] |[~ ~ ~

□ = village/town
Δ = temple/pagoda
~~ = river
][= bridge
══ = paved road
── = dirt road
·· = footpath
H = highway + no.
  (diagrammatic map,
  not to scale)

────────────» Mae Or (KMT)

• Tam Pla (Fish Cave)

Huai Pa □Δ Shan' wat

────────────» Huai Poeng

Δ cave wat

Mae Suya □──»

~ ~] |[~ ~

• sala viewpoint

Bo Pi •··········□

Luuk Kao
Laam (Lahu)

Mae La Na junction   H1226 ──» Pang Kham

(New) SOPPONG ■

■ SOPPONG

──» Tam Lod/Cave Lodge

H1095

□ PAI

Ping Ang Choeng «════ ■ ══» Sala Muang Noi
  (KMT)   & Wiang Haeng

H1095

MAE MA LAI

N

PAI - MAE HONG SON

THREE PAGODAS © JUNGLE BOOKS
1996

who went there as a *farang* with a Thai wife or girlfriend. He would be served last or not at all and made to understand that he was *persona non grata* in the company of a prostitute, which was odd, as the owner seemed to be married to a *farang* woman, and the insinuation could equally have been made the other way round. Pai also had a discreet drugs scene. Some of the trekking guides could be seen in dim corners pushing the dope that had found its way down from the Shan State. Correspondingly, not all the people hanging out in Pai were there only to enjoy the river view or the local atmosphere. Finally, after 8 p.m. the townlet was dead - unless one joined the throng in an establishment with the authentic Shan name of *Chez Swan*. Here a pretentious French menu and inflated prices were matched by the clientele inside. The sight of them through the glitzy windows, posing and regarding each other, made us want to scurry on the next morning.

Pai - Soppong - Luuk Kao Laam

The next leg of our journey was to take us west from Pai along the 1095 to Soppong, Bo Pi and Mae Hong Son. From Chiang Mai there were two ways to Mae Hong Son. A circuitous southerly route took in Hot, Mae Sariang and Khun Yuam, an all-day journey of nearly 400 kms. And a shorter, more difficult route went north via Mae Ma Lai, Pai and Soppong, some 250 kms. Until recently virtually all traffic for Mae Hong Son had taken the southerly road, painfully negotiating the famous 1800 bends on the way. But with the completion of the 1095 road in the early 1990s, more traffic had started to use the northerly route. The 1095 was originally laid out by the Japanese in WW2 as a way of supporting their war effort in Burma. It was to take another fifty years before this tortuous dirt track through the mountains and jungle was to become properly serviceable. At the time of our journey, the road was alphalted throughout except for a small section between Pai and Soppong.

With our Honda Wing back in Chiang Mai, we decided to travel on by bus. Of course, when the stumpy orange mountain vehicle pulled into Pai bus station mid-morning, it was already full. But, tossing our backpacks onto the pile of luggage and other bundles near the rear door, we managed to squeeze in next to an elderly monk. The holy man, supposed to be a model of abstinence, was using the opportunity of the stop to surreptitiously smoke a worldly Khrong Thip cigarette out of the window. We soon discovered the disadvantages of bus riding in Thailand. It was dreadfully hot and cramped. For a long-thighed *farang*, the tightly packed seats meant having to sit either legs wide apart, suggestively, or legs parallel and to one side, female fashion. Whatever way, as the bus jolted and shuddered along, it was physical torture.

Progress was very slow. In fact it took a good two hours to complete the 40-odd kms to Soppong. This was partly on account of the twisting and climbing, but also because every mile or so the bus stopped to pick passengers up or let them down. They were mostly hill-tribe people. Soon the central aisle and the standing area near the backdoor were chock-a-block with Lahu, Lisu and Karen in their colourful costumes. In the crush we lost sight of our luggage. These mountain people never travelled except with a great deal of encumbrance. The women had snoozing infants in slingcloths on their backs. The men had their shoulderbags, cardboard boxes with animals in them, and small boys to look after. All had bundles of vegetables, which they stowed under the seats, or sacks of maize or rice, which they sat on. They had their pipes or their betel-chewing paraphernalia with them and juggled all this with packed lunches of sticky rice and boiled eggs or dried meat. Somewhere behind us a cock crowed.

Interesting as it was to literally rub shoulders with these tribespeople, the encounter had its less appealing side. Teeth blackened from years of betel-chewing and maws reddened from the latest mouthful leered at us from close quarters. If the mountain people were near a window or door, they would lean out to eject a stream of carmine juice. Sometimes the children could not wait until the bus stopped, but peed straight onto the floor. At the end of long journeys, the mountain buses were often awash not just with plastic bags and soft drink cans. Nor were the hill people very good travellers. Perhaps because they were unused to the motion of the bus, they easily got sick. Unfortunately, when we later came to retrieve our backpacks, we found that someone, probably a hill-tribe child, had deposited the contents of their breakfast on them.

The tribespeople got on and off the bus in the most unlikely places. We would round a corner, and there would be a little band of Lahu or Lisu flagging us down in the middle of nowhere. Then they rode a mile or two, perhaps to go to a field or to visit friends, and would alight by a tiny path leading off into a wall of jungle. The bus was driven by a young man in sunglasses and minded by a couple of busboys, who hung the whole time right out of the doors. Every time the vehicle stopped, they leapt down and placed wooden chocks behind the wheels. Then, with a shout of "bai" to the driver, they would snatch out the chocks, scamper alongside the bus as it moved off, and jump aboard. Occasionally, the chocks were used for a novel purpose. On particularly steep upgrades the vehicle, engine labouring, edged forward so slowly that the boys were easily able to walk beside it. Then, just as it was about to shudder to a halt, they popped the chocks behind the wheels, the driver stirred the gears, selected first, the bus moved forward again, and they pulled the chocks away, clambering in.

On the run out from Pai, the hot air of the valley floor blew through the bus as if from a giant hair-dryer. But as the road rapidly ascended, and the baking flat fields gave way to the stepped paddies of narrow secluded valleys, the warmer air was interspersed with wedges of cool. Soon we were in the damp chill of the high jungle and mountain forest. Incredibly slowly the bus climbed to almost 5000 ft, finally emerging on top at Pang Ma Pa police box. The pass was marked with stunning bluish vistas of wooded cordilleras receding miles north to the Burmese frontier. And then it was 2000 ft down the far side of the ridge, past Lisu people on hillsides harvesting ginger, towards Soppong.

People around us began acting strangely at this point. Rummaging in their bags, many produced handkerchiefs or scarves, which they tied around their heads in such a way that only a slit was left for the eyes. The effect was sinister, and to anyone passing we must have looked like a busload of bandits. The reason soon became apparent. Suddenly the bus plunged into the last unmade section of the 1095. Where there was no oncoming traffic, this did not matter much. We simply left a terrible dusty wake. But when a vehicle did come by, the bus was filled with a 30-second blinding choking cloud of orange laterite particles. It was just our luck that on one of the hairpin bends, 12 inches deep in the treacherous bulldust, we came across a convoy of log-transporters. The bus juddered to a halt to let the groaning beasts past. They ground up round the hairpin slower than walking pace. Indeed, the swarthy Shan or Burmese crew accompanying them were easily able to run back and forth past the vehicles, managing the convoy and warning oncoming traffic with red flags. As each transporter passed the bus, its engine blasted us with hot air and another whirl of orange powder. By the time we got to Soppong, nobody cared much anymore about trying to keep clean. In particular the monk beside us seemed quite untroubled. But then the dirt was exactly the same colour as his saffron robes.

In Soppong a busload of orange zombies disembarked to dust themselves down and seek food and refreshments. While others took a hasty fried rice or noodle soup, we settled for hawker food at the side of the main street and found a girl selling *salapao* - steamed white rice dumplings with a minced meat or black bean filling. Soppong was a small one-street Shan place. Muslims also lived there, and they may have been the descendants of migrant *jiin haw* traders, as we saw Chinese lettering on some notices. Apart from the shops and a couple of primitive fuel stations, there was not a lot else. As usual, the police station was the biggest building in town, and in front of a mini-hospital stood a large sign in Thai warning of Aids in Mae Hong Son. The bus was an important line of communication in a place like this, bringing not only mail and the latest gossip from the district towns, but also entertainment in the form of visitors. So for fifteen minutes, as long as the bus stopped, the local people studied us while we studied them. The ambience of Soppong struck us as peaceful, colourful, relaxed, idyllic.

While we were snacking beside the bus, a long mule train sauntered past. Out on the main road again, we soon overtook the laden beasts, led and cajoled by their Shan minders. On the far side of Soppong, at the side of the 1095, a new piece of town was beginning to spring up. Probably it would soon usurp the main town itself, with the original section declining into a quiet backwater. After that, the jungle swallowed up the road again. Seeing that we were nearing our next destination and did not know exactly where to get off, we asked one of the busboys to warn us. When he heard that we wanted to visit the mysterious Bo Pi ("baw pee" = "Spirit Well"), he grew concerned. "Aren't you afraid of the spirits?" he asked. The bus climbed up again several kms, before emerging into a marvellous terrain of blue-black lumpy mountains with extensive vistas. It was the finest scenery between Pai and Mae Hong Son. On the south side lay a deep valley with a tiny picturesque village in the bottom, nestling at the foot of a towering mountain. Here, a dozen kms out from Soppong, the bus drew up. It was time for us to get off. Bo Pi was somewhere down there by the village. We extricated our luggage from the pile and clambered down, watched by all the passengers, who wondered why we should alight in the middle of nowhere. And then the bus departed, leaving us alone in the midst of this fairytale landscape. We watched it disappear, its emergency drum of diesel lashed to the roof.

Luuk Kao Laam

A short distance back down the road we found a track leading to the valley floor. We followed it down for a couple of kms. The afternoon heat was blistering, and we were hungry from having eaten only *salapao* dumplings. As we approached the small village, we had the impression that we were walking into an unsuspecting nest to disturb it. The houses and their surroundings were utterly silent and peaceful. We passed a primary school and entered a deserted dusty village square. There was one tiny shop, but it was locked up. Finally a boy came, bringing a key. Then his mother arrived. The shop was disorderly, with almost nothing for us to eat or drink. The village was called Luuk Kao Laam and was a Lahu settlement. Most of the people were out in the fields. We felt slightly dissatisfied, sitting in front of the shop, but the next piece of news disappointed us even more. Somehow we had imagined that Bo Pi was this village or perhaps part of the mountain behind it, but it transpired that Spirit Well was some way off in the mountains, too far to go there and back before dark. Nor was there anywhere to stay at the Well. Thus, if we wanted to visit it, we would have to stay the night at the village and walk there next morning.

It was too late to climb back up to the road and go on to Mae Hong Son, so we decided to embrace the fate of Luuk Kao Laam. A clinic near the square was closed, but we found a second school functioning. Inside one solitary teacher was surrounded by a score of Lahu elementary pupils. As soon as we poked our heads in through the door, lessons were hopelessly disrupted. The teacher, a young Thai, felt he had to attend to us, and the children grew excited. In his living quarters to one side of the classrooms, the man made a wood fire so that we could boil water to make instant noodles. Then, while we ate around the smoky hearth in his kitchen, he tried to rescue his class. The children kept coming to look at us, and soon he called an end to school for the day, preferring anyway to chat with us. Learning of our plan, he offered us the school storeroom for the night. The room, wedged between his bedroom and a classroom, had a pallet bed and a wall of teaching materials, all covered with dust, but otherwise it was not bad accommodation.

There was not a lot to see in Luuk Kao Laam, and when we had finished our inspection, we went for a wash. The washing place was outside the village. It consisted of a deep well with an old plastic oil container on the end of a length of rope. A group of adolescent Lahu girls were taking their evening shower there. In clinging wet sarongs and with streaming long black hair, they soaped and scrubbed and tipped icy water over themselves. We tried to do likewise, much to their amusement. With the day drawing to a close, we took up position in a little pavilion overlooking the central patch. People were returning from the fields, young men were playing football, kicking up the dust, and children came to toy with us. The youngsters, with slightly hooded eyes, were forward and unafraid, and we realized that they were used to seeing *farangs*. Altogether, during our overnight stay we found the Lahu of this village a boisterous, loud, confident, self-reliant people. In an incomparable setting, Luuk Kao Laam was near the main road and accessible to the one or two Suzuki hire jeeps which turned up most days with tourist visitors. But if the children were cheeky and the adults inured, there was no begging and none of the souvenir stalls and ethnic tat found in some hill-tribe villages.

Our supper was a repeat of our mid-afternoon lunch, only augmented. A woman sold us some greens from her field, and the teacher picked herbs from the school garden. Once again around his kitchen hearth, we enjoyed a much tastier Ma-ma noodle soup, supplemented with mountain rice and tins of tuna and sardines we had bought in Pai. A final touch of luxury was Lahu *lao kao* mixed with the electrolytic soft drink Sponsor - a vernacular gin and tonic. While we were eating, people began arranging folding chairs in the largest classroom at the other end of the school building. And soon half the village crowded in. It was a meeting called by the headman. Two things were on the agenda. A cow had been stolen outside the village and slaughtered on the spot, and the assembly was to decide what should be done. And the next day was to see a visit by the governor of Mae Hong Son province, who was coming to distribute aid to the village. The meeting had to draw up plans to receive him.

A party of Hilltribe Development Authority men had already arrived in advance of the governor, and tiring of the deliberations at the other end of the corridor, they came to join us. They brought with them bottles of local hooch, and soon a party was in full swing. Many Lahu, hearing the conviviality and seeking respite from village politics, also came by, cramming the little wooden kitchen. Finally, the *pu yai baan* himself absented himself from his own meeting to investigate the rival moot. Squatting on the bare earth floor in pride of place, he sucked on a silver-banded pipe. The Hilltribe Development men in their high-spirits had invented a game, whereby lots had to be drawn to see who could ask us a question. By chance the headman pulled out a winning lot. He said: many Lahu girls and also some boys wanted to marry *farangs*, and what did I think of the idea. I pointed out to him that, tantalizing as the idea was from the point of view of both the Lahu and the *farangs*, there would be some big problems. How would the couple communicate, and where would they live? A westerner would hardly be content with life in Luuk Kao Laam, and the Lahu lass or lad would hardly want to go and live in a strange faraway country. The headman pondered the matter, poking the fire. Then he asked about English football. Hearing that we lived near Norwich, his face lit up. Apparently very satisfied with the exchange, he then got up and returned to his session. "If there is anything you need, just come and ask me", he said. His meeting went on very late, as did numerous follow-up gatherings around wood fires all over the village. People stood, wrapped in blankets, under the brilliant moon and stars, warming themselves on the embers, smoking and turning over the issues discussed earlier. Some may well have stood there all night, but we retired to our platform bed. As we slept, condensation dripped off the tin roof onto our heads. In the dead of the night we stirred in our sleep to hear someone enter the school and creep around....

Preparations for the governor's visit continued from an early hour. The folding chairs were removed from the school to the dusty central arena nearby, where they were set out in rows. The Thai flag was run up a white pole. Everyone fussed around. These visits by the authorities can sometimes spell bad luck for anyone else passing by. Life is disrupted, nobody has any time for you, and the village takes on a prettified artificial gloss. It has often been our fate to arrive somewhere just before a member of the Thai royal family was due to descend. But on this occasion the visitation had its upside. The entire village, from the tiniest toddlers to the hoariest elders, had turned out in their best festive Lahu costume, something they might otherwise have done only during their New Year or at a marriage. Some two hundred people had hunkered down to wait, in lines of fifteen or twenty, alternating male/female, and with the youngest on the right and the oldest on the left. These were Sheh Leh Lahu, a distinctive subtype of Black Lahu. The females wore black baggy pants, leggings, and a three-quarter-length jacket, open at the front and with long vents at the sides, which gave the impression of having three tails. The black tunic was strikingly edged with white, and often the arms were trimmed with red and blue banding. The front opening was fastened with large ornamental silver discs. Most of the older women had their hair drawn up in topknots and wore white towel turbans. We noticed characteristic silver earrings in the shape of a pendent "S", the lower part whorled like a coiled snake. The men were in black baggy trousers, the legs joined Hmong-like down to the knee, leggings, open loose black jackets, and red sashes. A few of the oldest men also had turbans, while babes-in-arm were fussed with the most exquisite little caps. The Lahu are handsome, angular-faced people, and these colourful Sheh Leh were as impressive a hill-tribe gathering as any we saw.

Finally, a small convoy of vehicles swept in, half a dozen heavily armed bodyguards leapt down, sealing off the entrances to the square, and the provincial governor with a posse of minions went to the front of the crowd.

He made a short speech and then personally distributed the presents - blankets and other useful things for the adults and packages of biscuits and sweeties for the children. Afterwards the gathering broke up and everyone intermingled. It must be said in favour of the governor that this busy man, no doubt fulfilling a tedious duty, was kind enough to come over to us and exchange pleasantries. And then suddenly the suave dignitary, quilted in an anorak against the early morning chill, was back in his minibus. The convoy swept out of the village in a cloud of dust, probably heading for another three or four such distributions, and the official visit was over.

Bo Pi - "Spirit Well"

Seeking out the headman, we asked him if he could find someone to guide us to Bo Pi. That was not so easy because the local people were frightened of going there. But he collared a couple of boys who were among the children who had twitted us the previous evening. They were both eleven years old. One, called A-pichai, had Mongoloid eyes and no hair on his head except a little on top, the back and sides having been shorn. Taking our revenge on him for the evening before, we said that he looked like a pineapple. The other lad, Jak-gaek, a beautiful chubby-faced boy with a sense of humour, found this endlessly amusing. He began chaffing his friend, just as we chaffed them and then they us, setting the tone for an anarchic expedition.

A footpath ran out of the back of Luuk Kao Laam and began climbing steeply. We thought the scramble could not last for long, but it was relentless, quite knocking the stuffing out of us. The heat from the mid-morning sun was sweltering. Our mouths were soon dry and our bodies bathed in sweat. The path threaded its way up a headlong jungle-lined gorge. Every so often it passed the out-of-village pigpens of the Lahu, and at each one we stopped to get our breath back and cool off. The boys would already have arrived long since. They would be idly fiddling with a twig, their faces still with a fresh cool bloom. "What kept you so long?" they chirped mischievously. After thirty or forty minutes the stiff climb ended, and we reached a col. There was a secluded poppy field in it, and we stood among the poppies enjoying the faint breeze wafting up from the other side.

Beyond the poppies was a resting area with bamboo benches among some trees. After that the path descended into a remote hinterland. Through the trees we could see mountains, isolated valleys, the odd patch of hillside under cultivation, cliffs and forest. We asked the boys where the path ultimately led. It went to a waterfall, they said, otherwise they did not know. They thought that a long way off was a Lisu village. We were certain that there were extensive poppy fields in that hinterland. Descending from the col, we came to a fork. The fork was marked by fresh banana palms on the ground and the smoking remains of a fire. Lahu had caught a wild boar there yesterday, the boys explained, and they had cooked it on the spot.

There was more than one "spirit well" in the area, and A-pichai and Jak-gaek showed us first a small one. Hidden in the trees, it was a deep dark shaft in the mountainside. Into it the boys dropped rocks, which hit the water in the bottom with a splash. But nothing prepared us for the real Bo Pi. Climbing up to a rocky rim in the forest, we suddenly peered over, not so much into a well, but into a mighty chasm. Here, one hour out from Luuk Kao Laam, was a massive unnatural hole in the mountainside, the bottom appearing to have sunk 150 metres into the earth. There was no way down into Bo Pi, as the sides all around the chasm were sheer or overhanging cliffs. At the foot of the tallest cliff, the one shouldering uppermost into the mountain, was a great gloomy cave. It looked like the bowl of some giant theatre or stadium. The mouth of the cave was full of boulders, while hanging down across the mouth, like curtains before the bowl, were stalactites and creepers. Some of the air roots falling from the cliff face high above were hundreds of feet long. Trees and bushes grew far below on the floor of the "well". It was as if, when the mountainside had collapsed in on itself, they had simply continued to grow in their new subterranean location. The boys dropped rocks into Bo Pi, and after a free fall of several seconds the boulders splashed resoundingly, as if into a lake. But apparently there was no water down there, and the noise must have come from the rocks smashing through the tree tops.

Peering over the rim gave us vertigo, and when we realized that the rocks we were clinging to were overhanging, we retreated a bit. Stumbling upon Bo Pi was altogether bizarre, like looking into a prehistoric volcano or into some monstrous aberration from science fiction. Few Lahu came here, and none had climbed down into the bottom of Bo Pi or would ever do so. They believed spirits lived in the well and were frightened of them. Local people frequently heard cries and roars issuing from the well, echoing off its walls. They thought these were the howlings of restless spirits down there, but also of numerous wild animals supposed to lurk in the depths. We told A-pichai and Jak-gaek they should stop throwing stones into the chasm, or they would upset the spirits, which would come and get them in the night. With boyish bravado they declared all that stuff and nonsense, and yet at the same time they grew thoughtful. While they were contemplating the possibility of being snatched in their sleep, we crept round behind them and suddenly made a ghostly bellowing sound. They leapt up in alarm, nearly over the cliff, and it took them a long time to see the humour of the joke.

If no Lahu had been into Bo Pi, it seemed that almost no one else had been down there either. Evidently, there was no way in except to climb down the cliffs. But at Luuk Kao Laam villagers said that recently two *farangs* with ropes had passed through, intending to explore the well. Apparently, they had successfully descended, but one of them had then fallen ill, suffering either a mild heart attack or from heat fatigue. Of course, these events simply reinforced the Lahu in their beliefs about Bo Pi. In fact, Spirit Well is what is known geologically as a collapsed doline.

Over aeons underground streams created a cavern inside the limestone mountain, the roof of which then collapsed. There are numerous such dolines in the karstic landscape of this and other areas of Thailand (e.g. Nan province), and Bo Pi is one particularly dramatic example.

On the way back to the village, we met two Lahu women resting on the benches in the col. One of them was the mother of Jak-gaek. When she heard that the two boys had been dropping rocks into Spirit Well, she grew very angry. She cuffed the pair repeatedly, saying that the spirits would get angry and misfortune would befall their families. For all their trouble, our high-spirited duo had got a bad fright from us and a maternal scolding. By the time we got back to Luuk Kao Laam, they looked thoroughly disgruntled. So to cheer them up, we gave them 20 baht each, and they scampered off triumphantly.

Luuk Kao Laam - Mae Hong Son

Back up on the main road, we figured that it would be some time before a bus came from Pai, so we decided to try our hand at hitch-hiking. Within minutes a wealthy Thai couple pulled up in a flashy speeding pick-up. They were going all the way to Mae Hong Son and bade us hop into the back. The remaining 53 kms of this leg of our journey, therefore, we enjoyed from the vantage point of a Toyota Mighty X, or whatever it was called. With our backs to the cab and the wind howling past our ears (bobble hat time again), we watched the mountains and jungle slip by. The remainder of the 1095 was every bit as spectacular as the earlier stretches. On the ridge crest soon after Luuk Kao Laam there was a roadside *sala* with a view over that same inky green mountainscape rolling north we had admired from the bus the day before. An exhilirating elevated road brought us slowly down to the Nam Kong river and the village of Mae Suya. Just beyond the village, in a claustrophobic landscape of towering monoliths, our hosts pointed out to us a cave hermitage set at the foot of a cliff face. A solitary monk lived in this grotto temple, long twisted lianas hanging across its entrance. And then the steep twisting road set about climbing over two more ridges.

Ascending one of these, we came upon a disaster. Just before a blind bend there were pieces of bush on the road - the Thai warning of some mishap ahead. Cautiously rounding the corner, we found a log-transporter upside down in the drainage channel at the side of the road. Evidently it had come too fast down the hill and lost control on the corner. Twenty or so wheels stuck up in the air, and the load of teak logs was spilled everywhere, including on top of the lorry. The cab was crushed beyond recognition. It was clear that the driver and probably a couple of mates were dead inside, and we did not dare to look too closely. Our friends stopped their pick-up to find out if anything could be done. They were told that the police had been alerted, but had not arrived yet. It would be some time before they or an ambulance could come from faraway Mae Hong Son. The atmosphere among the people standing around the lorry was noticeably gloomy, but as there was little anyone could do, our hosts motored on. For a while, mindful of this *memento mori*, they proceeded carefully, but soon it was business as usual again, rushing headlong downhill and screeching round corners, often on the wrong side of the road. Later in Mae Hong Son we chanced upon some people who knew that an Austrian motorcyclist had been the first to come upon the accident. According to the Austrian, the driver and his mate had managed to scramble out of the cab with only minor injuries. They had been remarkably lucky.

On the far side of the second ridge, a dream road swung down through jungle and woods, skirting the touristy and uninteresting Tam Pla or Fish Cave, to emerge on the River Pai valley floor at Pang Mu. There remained a final ridge to climb, after which, 100 kms of jungle and mountain from Pai, we approached Mae Hong Son. Forking left in the outskirts, we suddenly found ourselves riding up the long main street into the town centre.

CHAPTER 5

TUK-TUKS IN SHANGRI-LA

Mae Hong Son

In spite of a recent boom, Mae Hong Son (the last syllable is pronounced "sorn") remains essentially a backwater idyll. Cut off in the far northwestern corner of Thailand and almost 1000 kms from Bangkok, this small town lies on a broad valley floor, surrounded by hills and mountains. Immediately to the north is the Burmese border and the Shan State, and to the west, also across the "Myanmar" frontier, is the Kayah State, controlled by the Karenni Army. To the east and south stretch vast tracts of mountainous jungle and forest.

The town sometimes goes by the name of "Muang Saam Mok", meaning "town of the three mists". This arises from the fact that in each of the three seasons of the year it can be affected by a different kind of mist. In the winter, ground fog grips the valley, which only burns off when the sun gains its mid-morning strength. In the hot season, the air is heavy with the spicy-smelling smoke of slash-and-burn agriculture. And in the wet season, fine misty rain blankets the town. It is a continental climate up here with extremes of weather. At night in the cool season, temperatures can approach zero. In the hot season, especially in March and April, they can soar to a baking 40°+ Celsius. In the monsoon season the heavens open, and it can rain heavily for days on end.

The origins of "Muang Saam Mok" are said to lie in elephant corralling. Records show that in 1831 the then ruler of Chiang Mai sent an expedition to this region to survey the western border. The expedition set up camp on the banks of the River Pai at Pang Mu, a few kms north of present-day Mae Hong Son town. The explorers found the locality populated with Shans or Tai Yai (= big Tai). Mixing with them, the new arrivals came to appoint the Shan Pa Ga Mong as leader at Pang Mu (mu = wild boar, pig). But then they discovered that an area not far south was rich in elephants, and set up a second camp there. Here, too, the camp intermixed with the indigenous Shans to grow into a regular settlement, and Pa Ga Mong's son-in-law, San Khon, was appointed leader. The two Shan headmen became involved in logging, floating teak wood down the Rivers Pai and Salween to sell in Burma. Father and son-in-law grew rich, and their respective villages developed, especially San Khon's. Known as Muai Tor (after the celebrated temple with six pagodas on its northerly hill - the ruins can still be seen today), the elephant village expanded so rapidly that in 1874 the Chiang Mai authorities declared it a town. In 1893 the region achieved provincial status, being incorporated in 1900 into the northern Siamese Payab "Circle". Muai Tor, renamed Mae Hong Son after a local river, became the provincial capital. Then, as now, both town and province were predominantly Shan. In the course of this century migrant hill-tribe and other minority people have moved into the province, resulting in a mix of an estimated 50% Shan and 50% Karen, Hmong, Lahu and KMT. Thais of modern-day Thailand hardly show up in these statistics at all, and where they do exist, they are confined largely to the towns (Mae Hong Son, Mae Sariang and Pai). Today in Mae Hong Son town, with its population of about 7000, the Siamese account for only some 2% of the townsfolk, whereas 98% are Shan. This is another factor which gives the town its "exotic" feel.

If sheer remoteness and exotic ethnic feel are one appeal of Mae Hong Son, Jong Kham lake just south of the centre is another. Held by some to be the prettiest lake in Thailand, its banks have been landscaped and planted with colourful tropical flowers and bushes. At the rear of the lake tall palm trees overhang the water, and behind them, in the background, loom the first of the scrubbily wooded mountains which recede hundreds of kms south and east from this oasis.

On the southwestern bank of the lake two magical monasteries lie side by side. Viewed from across the water, Wat Jong Kham sits on the left, while its twin, Wat Jong Klang, sits on the right. The original building of Jong Kham was apparently constructed in 1827 by a local Shan chieftain and his wife, Praya Singhanat Racha and Chao Mae Nang Mia. Said to be the first temple to be built in the province, it takes its name from the fact its pillars used to be decorated with gold (*jong* = pillar, *kham* = gold). Jong Klang, on the right, started out as a pavilion where people could rest, before being turned into a *wat* in the 1860s. A room in this temple houses a celebrated collection of 30-40 antique wooden figures. Between three and four feet high, the dolls represent people from the Buddha story. They have come from Burma and the Shan State - the Shan ones are tattooed. Together the two temples form a chaotic complex of wooden tin-roofed buildings and golden pagodas. They are built in that ramshackle Shan-Burmese style which tops off the *viharns* with tiers (more than eight high in this case) of rusty corrugated sheeting, adorned with intricate iron filigree. If one sits beside Lake Jong Kham in the early evening, looking out over the crimson sprays of flowers to the deepening green of the palms and the gathering purple of the mountains, watching the fish come up to nibble at an insect supper, contemplating the dark gold reflections of the pagodas rippling lazily in the surface of the water, one might be forgiven for thinking that one had stumbled upon Shangri-la.

Mae Hong Son used to be an inside tip passed on by the few who were prepared to rough it round the northerly Pai route on trails bikes or endure the gruelling 12-hour bus ride south via Hot. But word of the town's mystique got out, and now a small but steady stream of visitors passes through. The handful of guesthouses and small hotels of just four or five years ago has mushroomed into more than thirty places to stay of all types. Similarly, where in the past so few people arrived that in the evening over a beer on the main street it was possible to spot the newcomers individually, now Airbuses disgorge parties of well-heeled package tourists, who are ferried down to the brand-new Tara Imperial Hotel or Holiday Inn at the bottom end of town, and buses plying both the northerly and southerly approach routes let down clutches of young backpackers with squeaky clean clothing and equipment. What have they all come for, and what will be their effect on the town? Mae Hong Son is only a small rural place - quite boring if one cannot savour atmosphere - and there is not a lot to see outside town.

In many ways Mae Hong Son typifies developments in Thai tourism in the 1990s. A relatively small destination is being allowed to boom, but with little regard for planning or the longer term consequences. Get-rich-quick seems to be the order of the day. Whether sleepy backward places like this can cope with the boom, and even whether the boom will last, is open to doubt. In some places the tourism might perpetuate itself, not grounded in anything much the locality has to offer - mini Las Vegases in the middle of nowhere (like the "Golden Triangle" at Sob Ruak) - but in others the bubble will probably burst. How on earth can a town of 7000 Shans justify some thirty resorts, hotels and guesthouses? And even if the tourists do come for a while, might they not suddenly switch to somewhere else - not Mae Hong Son but Luang Prabang or Hanoi?

Interestingly, Thai Air has recently suspended its Airbus flights to Mae Hong Son on the grounds that they were not cost-effective. The suspension met a storm of protest from the local hoteliers and restauranteurs who had just invested so much money. But the volume of visitors was not quite as expected, and many of these pretentious places will no doubt go to the wall. Indeed, as we walked round some of the new guesthouses, it was noticeable how empty many were and how the owners came running out onto the street to try to entice us in. On the other hand, there is a long-term development strategy for Mae Hong Son which might have these investors laughing all the way to the Thai Farmers bank. As with Mae Sai in the northernmost part of Thailand, there are plans to connect the provincial capital with selected locations in Burma. Airlinks could be forged with Loi Kaw in the Kayah State, with Taunggyi in the Shan State, and with famous Mandalay.

The friendly Thais who had given us a lift to Mae Hong Son dropped us outside the bus station in the main street. Our first task was to fix up somewhere to stay. Eschewing the numerous new overpriced guesthouses, and not wanting to make the rounds of the popular traditional haunts, we decided to try the *Sanguan Sin Hotel* (*sanguan sin* = preserve art). Old rooming houses like this usually have plenty of beds available at modest prices. Sidestepping the touts who were hanging around the bus station to intercept new arrivals and bring them to the guesthouses, we set off down the main street towards the central intersection. A turn south into the Singhanat Road brought us quickly to our goal. In a dusty, rather squalid yard we found a large wooden building, but no reception. A knock on the door brought out a woman, but she appeared to speak no Thai, let alone English. However, she knew well enough what we wanted and led us across the yard to another wooden building opposite. We passed through a scruffy storage room and went upstairs. In a dark corridor with rooms leading off on both sides, the woman opened a door. This was to be our lodging. It was 60 baht for the room, and any number could stay in it. The bed alone would have comfortably slept three.

Just as there was no reception, so also there was no communal room, and no food either. We closed the door and sat down on the bed. The room was a large gloomy box with dark teak beams and slatted wooden walls. A small neon tube clung to the ceiling, but its garish light hardly penetrated the dusty corners. A small mirror hung on a nail on the wall. The windows and gaps between wall and ceiling were covered over with ancient fine wire mesh, but this was full of holes. On wires over the bed somebody had strung up a mosquito net, but it too was full of holes and, judging by the dust accumulated on it, had not been used for many moons. We had the impression we were sitting in a lumber-room. The walls of our box were so thin that it was possible to hear straight into all the other lodgings along the corridor. Over the passage someone coughed, and in the room next to ours a fan whirred. Periodically people shifted on the bed.

The teak building had heated up all day in the sun, and our lumber-room was like an oven. There was a fan, a ridiculous little thing placed on a chair, but it made no difference. Perspiration formed on our foreheads. It seemed a good idea to cool off with a shower. But that meant grappling with the mysteries of the traditional Thai ablution. A corner of the room had been partitioned off, and inside this dank cubicle were the famous earthenware pot and dipper and next to them a French-style toilet with a hole and two footpads. Beside the toilet was a slime-encrusted cement tank with more water in it and a second plastic dipper. As a concession, perhaps to *farangs*, there was a crude shower nailed to the wall with a spray head like that of a watering can. The cold-water-only shower nevertheless dribbled warm water that had heated up all day in the pipes. As a luxury, there was even a small wash basin. It might be supposed that there was not much scope for sabotaging a wash basin. But, no, the cockeyed tap, when it was turned on, rotated freely in its socket. Getting it to work was a matter of holding the barrel with one hand and turning the tap with the other. Then it was possible to wash hands and face - except that the waste water shot straight down through the plughole and onto one's feet. From there it drifted lazily across the floor and disappeared who knows where.

Sleeping was hardly easier than washing. Towards midnight the heat in the room was still oppressive. Getting our own mosquito net up seemed to involve stringing it first in every conceivable wrong way. Perspiration again bathed our bodies, and it was nearly time to brave the shower again. But finally the net was up, and we lay down stark naked on top of the bed with the fan on. The heat made sleep difficult, although later in the night the temperature dropped agreeably. We tossed and turned, falling in and out of a light sleep. All night long some creature seemed to call from the neon strip light. Mic-mac, it went, mic-mac, mic-mac, five times in all, and always on the fifth call making a slight downward attenuation. It was a gekko, of course, but in our fitful hallucinating sleep it could have been a bird or some local monster emerging out of the three mists... Suddenly I awoke with an intense sharp pain on my thigh, as if someone was sticking pins in my skin. I reached for the torch and in the beam saw a column of small orange ants crossing the sheet and climbing over my body. Finally, the refreshing coolness of dawn was conducive to deep sleep. But almost immediately a dreadful racket started up. Loudspeakers blared out Thai and western pop music, and there was a repeated hammering as if someone was making furniture in the middle of the night. The ballyhoo seemed to be going on right outside our room. Later, when we went to investigate, we found that the hotel backed directly onto Mae Hong Son's main morning market.

It was the racket of the market kicking off between 5 and 6 a.m. that drove us after a couple of days to exchange the *Sanguan Sin* for the *Siam Hotel*. Situated at the eastern end of the main street, this friendly hotel had nice big cool rooms for 120 baht which were ideal for sleeping in. The *Siam* was a typical Chinese place. Inside a characterless cement block, the rooms, on two storeys, surrounded a central hallway, in which guests parked their cars and motorbikes at night. The decor was all cream and brown and pale green, and if the hotel was a little spartan and functional with its institutional tiling, it was at least clean. There were good ceiling fans in the rooms, the bathrooms and showers were adequate, and, amazingly, soap and toilet paper were provided.

The restful nights at *Siam* put us more in the mood for enjoying the market. Mae Hong Son's market was one of the most remarkable we saw anywhere on our border travels - on a par with the bazaar of Mae Saam Laep on the banks of the River Salween or the black market of Sa Kaang Thi, south of Um Pang, in Burma. But it was not so much the variety of fruit and vegetables, meat and fish, sweetmeats and smoking requisites, household goods and clothes, that was interesting - although this was tremendous enough - rather the unparalleled mix of people milling around. The market rapidly became for us the most exciting feature of the town, and soon no morning was complete without an hour or two spent sitting by the entrance, watching the people and the goings-on. This was where dust-laden 4WD trucks came in to park, having come down from outlying villages up in the mountains, on the border, even from across in the Shan and Kayah States (by the same token this was the place to look for lifts to these rough places). There were turbanned Shans, baggy-trousered Hmongs, moustachiod Chinese, Khun Sa agents, "long-neck" Padaung women, suave educated Burmese people of unknown origin (perhaps dissident students or military men), people large and small, young and old, upright and bent, decorous in their costumes or wild-looking with squint eyes and tousled hair. The conversation was a hubbub of Shan, Thai,

THREE PAGODAS

Chinese, Hmong, Lisu, Karen, Kayan, Burmese, Wa... Trucks were being loaded up with wholesale items for resale in hill-tribe villages or with consumer goods to be taken into Burma. Drivers had brought down truckloads of produce to be sold in the market or directly off the tailboard. Rolls of 500-baht banknotes were flashing such as one otherwise only ever saw in gangster films. And here and there in the crowd were individuals conspicuous for their masses of heavy gold jewellery and Rolex watches. These were people who could only have got so rich locally from trafficking heroin or jade or armaments.

In the pre-boom days a walk up Mae Hong Son's long main street was like a walk up the main drag of wild west town. On each side there was a line of two-storey shophouses, many of them still teak, and people looked out inquisitively, cooly, as if to say: What brings you to Shanville? But in 1992 we were horrified to discover that the very first *tuk-tuks* had arrived, a sure sign that a sea change in the fortunes of the town was underway. These are those bizarre motorized tricycles, half-motorbike half-car, that typically ply the streets of Bangkok or Chiang Mai. Now the dusty streets of Mae Hong Son were reverberating to the characteristic sound of their two-stroke engines, and the locals in their shopfronts were breathing in not the mists of the three seasons, but the reeking blue fumes of the three-wheelers. One would have thought that the town was small enough for people to be able to get about on foot. Can it really be that there is no development officer who cannot see that the *tuk-tuks*, far from providing a service and thus encouraging tourism, will actually only drive visitors away?

The arrival of the *tuk-tuks* had been accompanied by a proliferation of tour agencies, motorcycle rental places, bakeries, restaurants and souvenir shops up and down the main street. Mostly they were run-of-the-mill places, of the sort to be found in Pai and elsewhere. But one stood out: *Fern Restaurant* at the bottom (western) end of the main drag. This distinguished eating-house with superb decor was serving up gourmet cooking. We tried mixed seafood in a delicious curry sauce of lemongrass, fresh green peppercorns and spring onions. Amidst all the innovations of Mae Hong Son, however, old favourite details remained. At the entrances to the side *sois*, thickets of crude handpainted signs still sought to lure the newcomer to various guesthouses. And the pavement boards still advertised treks or whatever with a novel syntax: DEAR TRAVELLERS! WHO DON'T HAVE MUCH TIME? WHY YOU DON'T COMMING HERE. WE ARE DON'T DISAPPINTED. FREE MAP OF MAE HONG SON. SIGHT SEEING - KAREN V., PLA CAVE, HOT SPRING. TREKKING - MEO, SHAN, K.M.T. V. NEAR BORDER. CAR, MOTORCYCLE, BICYCLE, GUIDE - FORRENT TO CHEAP ASK HERE. Who could resist such blandishments?!

We were walking up the main street one morning when a *farang* woman approached. She appeared not to be a tourist, and we fell into conversation with her. It turned out that she and her family lived in Mae Hong Son and that she would be very pleased if we came round one evening to eat with them. She seemed a pleasant enough lady, so we took up her offer and that same day, towards evening, went round to her house, armed with a family-sized bottle of Coke. The house was a local affair raised high in the air on stilts up a side alley. It soon became clear to us that she and her husband were American missionaries, that they had just returned from a stint in the bush and had not had any real contact with westerners for the best part of a year. From time to time in remote places we had suffered as a result of these proselytizing zealots - we had been mistaken for missionaries ourselves and been made to feel very unwelcome. So we took a dim view of their cultural imperialism, and an evening with Norma and Marvyn did not bode well. But in the event things turned out pleasant enough.

The American duo had five children - three girls and two boys. The bashful youngsters were exactly stepped in age and height, so that when they were lined up against the living room wall to be introduced to us, they fell away from top left to bottom right in a perfectly sloping line. Norma explained that she and her husband were educating their children themselves, and from a meagre cache Marvyn brought antiquated books for me to inspect which introduced the elements of physics, the countries of the world, and so on. There was an air about this hospitable couple which reminded us of self-sufficient American pioneers heading out west in waggons, taking with them all their worldly possessions, their culture and their education.

The children were very curious about me, as if they had been starved of "white" company. In particular the oldest child, a girl of about 15 or 16, sized up the visiting *farang* the whole evening. So this was what a real young man was like, she seemed to be thinking to herself. The children were also quite embarrassed about their parents' religiosity, even the youngest. During grace they fidgeted uncomfortably, sneaking glances one after the other to see what our reactions were. "Lord bless this good food, which in Your bounty and wisdom You have seen fit to place on our table", Marvyn intoned. "May the sweet Lord protect my good wife Norm, our five fine children and our household. We endeavor to follow You in Your ways. And we think especially today of our new friends, Chris and Daeng, who You have sent to share our table, and we ask You to include them in Your blessings, and hope that You will go with them when they leave on their further travels...."

The children were looking increasingly at the food, which was in danger of getting cold. But finally the prayer was over, and we all tucked into a weird combination of American and Thai dishes. There was jackfruit curry, fried morning glory, brown rice, but also corned beef hash and our 2 litres of Coke. During the meal the oldest girl grew in confidence in her relations with me. The initial stolen glances developed into a sly unmistakable flirtation. I felt sorry for her. In her staid homespun schoolgirl frock she was bursting into nubile womanhood. Brought up to be clean-living, and deprived of contact with boys of her age, she was fairly smouldering with sexual frustration. During supper we made the mistake of asking Marvyn how he and his family came to be in Mae Hong Son. His rambling screwball answer had us looking at our watches, thinking of a beer in the night market, and more than ever pitying the children. "When many years ago I was a college student in the state of Ohio, the good Lord saw fit to send to me a pretty girl who was to become my dear and loving wife, and we resolved to follow together the ways of the Lord, and...." The story went on a full ten or fifteen minutes, until the sharper-minded Norm began noisily clearing away the dishes. We never did find out how he and they came to Mae Hong Son.

How god-fearing Norma and Marvyn would have viewed Mae Hong Son's famous *poi sang long* festival we could only guess at. This Buddhist celebration, held all over Thailand during the school summer holidays, marks the time when a number of 10-16 year old boys are ordained novices. The expression "poi sang long" is actually Shan (in Thai it is called *buat naak* or *buat luuk kaew*), and at some Shan places like Mae Hong Son and Wat Fah Wiang In behind Piang Luang the festivities take a particularly extravagant form. The young postulants are paraded round town, their heads shorn, on the shoulders of relatives, mostly older brothers. However, they do not wear the simple white robes seen elsewhere in Thailand, but are dressed up in fancy costumes. They put on white jackets adorned with sequins, rosettes and medallions, and sport turbans, lavishly decked with flowers. The boys' faces are so prettily made up with red lipstick, green eye-shadow and rouge that the uninitiated onlooker could be forgiven for mistaking them for fanciable girls! They flutter fans before their faces and make their way up the thronging streets under high festive parasols. The swaying procession is accompanied by a band, beating out a throbbing frenzied rhythm on cymbals, drums and gongs. Many people dance as if possessed. Alcohol and sweat are on the air. Slowly the ecstatic parade makes its way through the streets, ending up at Wat Jong Kham by the lake. Later in the day the boys exchange their finery for monks' robes, after which they take their first vows.

In the middle of the main street, on the south side, there was a small all-day food market. Three or four stalls fronted a cavernous gloomy sheet metal building, inside which the food was prepared and relatives of the cooking ladies watched TV. A dozen folding tables and chairs stood between the food stalls and the road, and these proved an excellent place to watch the town proceedings over a drink or a Thai meal. Perhaps because of the food market's position or its modest prices, it tended to attract *farang* travellers. Here Germans and Dutch, Aussies and Poms sat, a Singha beer or a fruit shake in hand, swapping information or trading tales. But it was popular with local people too, who dropped by to pick up a snack of pork satay or charcoal-grilled corn-on-the-cob. Right beside the tables was Mae Hong Son's central police box. A conspicuous sign read: WELCOME TOURISTS, WE'RE PROUD TO SERVE YOU, but an enquiry revealed that none of the three or four policemen could speak a word of English. Dressed smartly in their uniforms, they lounged around, fiddled with their walkie-talkies, disappeared on mysterious errands on their Honda mopeds, or discreetly indulged in a bottle of Mekhong at "their" table behind the kiosk.

Mae Hong Son is dominated on the north side by Doi Kong Mu. The top of this 1500-metre high mountain is shared by Wat Pratat Doi Kong Mu and a soaring telecommunications mast. A landmark of the town are the temple's two pagodas. Both house the relics of eminent monks. The larger one, built in 1860, contains the remains of Pra Maha Mok Kallana Tera, which were brought here from Burma by the builder Chong Tong Su and his wife Lek. The smaller pagoda was built in 1874 by Praya Singhanat Racha, an early local Shan ruler. It is said that the hilltop used to be a hideout from which Karen bandits made raids on the Shan townspeople. A flight of steps makes a direct ascent up the front of the mountain to the *chedis*. It is a stiff climb, but worthwhile for the wonderful views northwest over jungle and forest towards the Shan State. The view south and east reveals the town of the three mists laid out at the foot of Doi Kong Mu, with the mountainous hinterland beyond. Down at street level, from the tables of the food market, the monastery can be seen high above the rooftops. At night, lights on the pagodas and on the mast twinkle magically in the darkness.

One evening we were sitting after supper at one of these tables. An assortment of acquaintances had gathered, of the kind one meets on the road. There was the middle-aged civil servant from Australia, who had suddenly decided that there was more to life than pen-pushing. This likeable fellow was having the time of his life and subsequently ran off with a Chiang Mai waitress. There was the lanky Dutchman who divided his year between the Netherlands, where he had a psychiatric practice, and the Far East, where he indulged his proclivity for young men. There was the Thai airforce man from Korat, who in a way untypical of the gregarious Siamese was travelling round the northwest on his own. And there was the wheeler-dealer from Germany, drifting round the Kingdom in the company of a fractious dark beauty he had met down south on the island of Ko Samui. The German had vague revolutionary ideas, but uppermost in his mind at that moment was a plan to live in a boat moored off Pattaya or Puket. He thought that in this way he could live cheaply both inside and outside Thailand, avoiding all the problems of visas and taxation. We were going through the viability of his scam when a western monk, shorn and in saffron, shuffled past. The *farang* bonze caused a momentary stir in the languid ebb and flow of the conversation. Why did the German not turn to the cloth, we suggested half seriously, perhaps that would answer his needs? It was still quite warm, we were sitting in our shirt sleeves, the ice was melting in the bucket, the policemen were fiddling nearby, sweetcorn and *gai yang* were grilling over the charcoal, and the lights on Doi Kong Mu were winking up above. Suddenly the Australian, his mind roaming over past, present and future, said: "It's fantastic here. We should drink in the beauty and atmosphere of this idyll. In the years ahead it's memories of evenings like this that we'll have to live off."

MAP 6

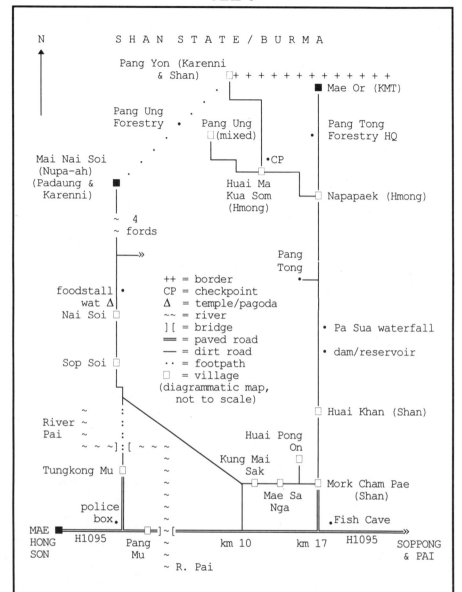

MAE HONG SON - MAE OR & MAI NAI SOI

THREE PAGODAS © JUNGLE BOOKS
1996

CHAPTER 6

DARK SECRETS

Mae Or

When we were supping with the two American missionaries in Mae Hong Son, they suggested we visit the border KMT village of Mae Or, some 50 kms to the north. It was a good day out, they said blithely, although the way up there was no piece of cake. "Backtrack down the 1095 in the direction of Pai," Marvyn explained, "pass Pang Mu and the Pai river bridge, and turn left (north) after about 10 kms. If you miss that turning, there is a second chance at km 17. If you reach the Fish Cave, you have gone too far." We jotted down the instructions on a scrap of paper.

As we knew the route to be demanding and had not yet retrieved our Wing, we decided to hire an MTX trails bike locally. Perched high on the yellow contraption and with a minimum of encumbrance, we set off, exactly following the missionaries' directions. Sure enough, 10 kms out from town there was a turn-off. A country road, filthy with rust-coloured bulldust, then cut through the villages of Kung Mai Sak and Mae Sa Nga, arriving after a further 9 kms at Mork Cham Pae. The streets of this large Shan village confused us, seeming to go round and round the houses. But soon we joined the other (metalled) route in from Highway 1095 and found our way again. Villagers told us to follow the signs for Pa Sua waterfall.

We motored on through a weird moonlike landscape. The trees and bushes on each side of the road had been discoloured orange and beige from the dust of the road and looked frozen and lifeless, as if turned to stone. At the base of a massive ridge lay the Shan village of Huai Khan with its roadside shop. Beyond it the way began to climb. Up and up it went, past some outlying settlements and a dam. We were beginning to wonder what all the fuss was about when, shortly before Pa Sua fall, the water in our MTX boiled. The engine overheated and, with a complete loss of power in the throttle, we ground to a halt. The bike would not restart, so we stood awkwardly by the side of the dirt track, letting the engine cool down. By good fortune we had a litre of drinking water with us, which we poured into the radiator. The disadvantages of the fancy MTX compared to the simple air-cooled Wing were becoming clear.

Arriving at Pa Sua waterfall, we ran into a German couple just leaving. We suggested riding on together as a foursome, but they said that they were going down again. They had only wanted to see the falls. Judging by their exasperated downcast faces and by the dirt all over their machine, it looked as if they had crashed somewhere higher up, had argued together and decided to cut short their trip. And off they went. Before continuing, we stopped to look at Nam Tok Pa Sua. Steep earth steps descended to the fall, where some four cascades poured into basins full of water. After the hot dusty ride, it was luxury to be able to bathe in these and then dry off on the burning grey slabs of rock. The dip was a trifle eerie. Apart from ourselves, there was not a single soul at the secluded falls, and, lingering on the rocks, we had the impression that unseen eyes were watching us from the dense jungle all round or that perhaps someone was quietly cocking a rifle. The fact that our motorbike was out of sight also made us apprehensive, and sent us scurrying on.

On the central stretch of the ride, from the dam to above Pa Sua, we came to two or three extreme gradients. On one of them bits of wrecked indicator light and rear-view mirror lay strewn in the dust, suggesting that this had been the waterloo of the German couple. Our guess was that the climb was so steep that with two aboard they had run out of power, had stalled and crashed. Profiting from their mishap and remembering our own spill on the way up to Kae Noi, we decided that one of us should scramble the bike up the worst sections, while the other toiled up behind on foot. Our prudence still did not save us from a tumble anyway. If we tricked the mountain on the way up, it claimed us on the way down. The problem was that always on the severest inclines and in the tightest corners there was six inches of bulldust covering round fist-sized stones. If going up was rather like riding up a scree, coming down was like motorcycling down a ski run. The brakes, of course, would not hold the bike, and the engine would not slow the machine sufficiently either. So, with the front wheel skittering, there was nothing to do except let go and hope for the best. We were doing just that, when the front wheel hit a stone, turned to one side, slipped, and over we went, adding our quota of plastic and glass to the shards in the dust. But never mind, a new mirror was only 60 baht in Mae Hong Son and the footrest could be straightened out for free. Wise people simply unscrewed the mirrors from hire bikes on trips like these.

Not much higher up, on another protracted upgrade, our MTX overheated for the second time. We had refilled our plastic bottle at the waterfall and once again topped up the radiator. We cursed the showy macho-looking machine and vowed never to take one again. While we were waiting in a shady corner for the MTX and also ourselves to cool down, strange people kept surprising us by issuing from the jungle all around and walking slowly past, staring. They were hill-tribe hunters, probably Karen, and were armed with stovepipe guns and machetes. We thought of the raiders who not so long ago used to infest Doi Kong Mu. Standing in the middle of nowhere with a broken hire bike made us feel vulnerable.

But soon we were on our way again. The road now cut deep through stunning jungle scenery. The sides of the narrow dirt trail were lined with an encroaching wall of green-gold *mai rai* and *mai sang* bamboos, cracking and singing in the heat. Thrusting up through these were young banana palms, their vanes a delicate translucent pale green. Overarching the palms were tall *mai bong* bamboos, their ends hanging down like coachmen's whips. And towering above all of them were the mighty *mai huak* bamboos (the ones used for building) and the lofty trees of the forest. The vibrant colours were a feast for the eye - the brilliant green of the vegetation and the intense orange of the trail contrasted vividly with the delphinium blue of the sky.

We passed a turning left (west) for Pang Tong, where the Thai royal family has a small palace retreat, and then, finally, the road came out on top, emerging into highland plateau country. The mountains and hills all around were largely denuded, and the colours seemed flatter, bleached out by strong UV irradiation. It was a more sober landscape up here and pleasantly cooler. The road continued on at a high level until it reached Napapaek. This Blue Hmong village was memorable for the many black pigs roaming around and also for a *wat*, which, oddly, was a Shan one. A little shop was serving noodle soup, Hmong-style. A way off left through Napapaek went to the Blue Hmong village of Huai Ma Kua Som, to the mixed hill-tribe model village of Pang Ung, and ultimately to the Karenni and Shan refugee village of Pang Yon across the border. Our MTX tripmeter had clocked up 19 kms from Mork Cham Pae to Napapaek, which left another 8 kms to Mae Or.

Pang Tong Forestry HQ passed us to the west, and on the approach to our destination there were indications of some agricultural assistance project. Finally, a small sign welcomed us to Mae Or itself (also often spelt "Mae Aw"). Passing a couple of unmanned barriers, we rode down into the village by a black burnt hillside on the left. Opposite this was a strange lake, with a lot of dead trees sticking up out of it. They had been drowned during the creation of a reservoir right next to the village. People later told us that the lake was essentially natural. Water was already there, and all that had happened was that it had been "improved" by the construction of an embankment through the middle. And in fact, to the east of Mae Or we later found the other half of the original lake. An grandiose sign on the embankment announced that it was called, mysteriously, "Richpool". This was an attempt, which had gone wrong coming through Thai, at "Misty Lake"! In the cold early mornings the reservoir was covered with mist.

Mae Or

Mae Or lay in a basin, ringed around by high deforested hills. Windswept and eerie, the mountains stood there in silence, as if hiding some dark secret. This remote settlement seemed like the end of the world, and it was certainly the end of Thailand in the northwest. The village was a bleak backward collection of long low huts with split bamboo walls. Here and there were mud hovels with grass roofs. All had bare earth floors. Some dwellings had small gardens around them, with roses blooming. Others had tall treelike constructions next to them. We studied these, as we had never seen them before. They were long poles with spars at the top. From the spars, pieces of meat were hanging on string. They were drying in the sun and wind. It seemed as if each pole bore an entire dismembered pig or cow.

Nothing was missing. The hooves and tails were there along with lumps of drying brown flesh. Silhouetted like gallows against the mountains, these "meat trees" reinforced the sinister atmosphere. As at Napapaek, we found numerous animals running around - the same black pigs, black and white ducks, turkeys, chickens and dogs. But there were not many humans to be seen. A few old men were smoking in dark corners, but they ignored us.

All this was a far cry from Piang Luang, even from Kae Noi. And Mae Salong, the leading KMT outpost, was a veritable metropolis in comparison. The reason for the backwardness of Mae Or was no doubt its sheer inaccessibility. The dirt road up had been engineered by the Thai army for security reasons and, while suitable for military vehicles or shanks's pony, was not much good for anything else. But another factor was that Mae Or was still relatively young compared to the major Kuomintang villages of 1961 vintage. Founded twenty years earlier by people breaking away from Nong Ook (Aroonothai), near Kae Noi, it had not had as long to develop. Then there was the fact that Mae Or, piously renamed "Raakthai" (= love Thailand) by the Thai authorities, was a dangerous flashpoint, where warlord Khun Sa's Mong Tai Army, the Wa National Army, the KMT and the Thai Army were all entrenched in a four-way stand-off. Because of sporadic fighting in the border hills immediately behind the Mae Or, the village had been closed off from external influences until recently. If the outside world could not get in, few people could get out. Hardly any of these General Li Third Army veterans or their descendants had Thai ID cards, which meant that they could not travel down to trade or attract business in. The benefit for the visitor, of course, was that Mae Or, still undeveloped, remained an authentic Kuomintang settlement.

We were absolutely filthy with orange dust from the ride up, and so went over to the far side of the reservoir to clean up. Here we found a little jetty, where we could wash and try to freshen our clothes. We shook out the laterite powder, dipped shirts and headscarves in the reservoir, and laid them out to dry in the sun. On the hillside behind us were some official-looking buildings. Presently, we climbed up to have a look. One complex was a new health centre. The other was a paramilitary BPP base. Both were quiet. Behind them a little path led up to the top of the hill. We climbed up and on the summit found some of the *dorchodor* soldiers engaged in building a new temple. That in itself was not interesting (the *wat* contained a Buddha figure in the Shan style), but the view north over Mae Or to the border was.

A BPP officer joined us to explain. Like a commander surveying a model of some theatre of war, his finger pointed out over the basin. The village at our feet consisted of about 120-130 houses or families. The border mountain behind the village to the right, Doi Lan, was Khun Sa territory. The mountain opposite to the left was Wa territory. Here two arch-enemies sat facing each other eyeball to eyeball, just as they did on Doi Larng, near Mae Ai. Mae Or itself, of course, was occupied by Khun

Sa's former arch-enemy, the KMT, who were now allied with the Wa. Periodically fighting flared up for control of both the hinterland, with its trafficking routes, and the border, with its access to Thailand. The last time this happened, the MTA bombarded Mae Or, many shells landing unexploded in the reservoir, where they lay to this day. It was impossible to go up into the hills around Mae Or or to walk along the border because each of the three parties (MTA, WNA and KMT) had laid mines, and none knew where each other's minefields were. Ironically, the situation was actually worse than that. Each rainy season earth got washed over the mines, meaning that the parties no longer knew where their own mines were. It was literally a minefield up there. A day or two before our visit a truck had been blown up by a landmine when driving along one of the mountain tracks. One person had been killed and the other passengers injured. But we did not need reminding of the dangerousness of Mae Or, for in February 1990 two *dorchodor* friends of ours from the Pang Mu BPP camp similarly ran over a landmine up here. When we met them shortly afterwards, one had a leg and an arm in plaster, and the other had had a leg amputated. The reason why the village was so hotly disputed was, of course, that it was strategically important in the heroin-trafficking business. It was a funnel by which drugs, emanating from Kokang and the Wa substate and passing down through the Shan State, entered Thailand, reaching Mae Hong Son and the wider world by the very road we had come up. This, then, was the dark secret of those sinister bald 6000-foot hills just behind Mae Or - they were the scene of landmines, nighttime heroin shipments, and deadly skirmishing.

After the rough and tumble of the ride up, we were very hungry and thirsty. But a strange thing about Mae Or was that there was nowhere to eat or drink. We searched around, but could not find a shop anywhere. A gaggle of children had slowly formed and began following us. We asked them where we could get a Coke, and they took us to the house of an old Chinese lady. This ample Kuomintang matriarch was making chopsticks at a table outside. Wearing a straw hat and wielding a machete, she was not to be hurried and went on to cut another three or four sticks, before finally condescending to fetch two warm Pepsis, for which she overcharged us. But we were in no mood to argue.

Most of the children drifted away, but one or two remained, seemingly fascinated by us. One was a girl with a Tibetan-looking face, and the other was a bewitching lass of fourteen with a remarkably dark complexion and flashing white teeth. She immediately caught our eye. We bought them each a drink, and the four of us talked for a while. Where adults from the migrant minority peoples frequently spoke no Thai, their children often could because they were taught the language of their adopted country at school. The dark-faced girl was so arresting that we asked her if we could take some pictures. Although hopelessly bashful, she did not mind, and so under the watchful eye of the matriarch we composed some portraits of the photogenic nymphet. Probably unbeknown to her or the villagers, she was strikingly beautiful. Her black-yellow skin was framed by jet-black hair, her almond-shaped eyes slanted slightly upwards, the nose was petite like that of a Siamese cat, and her teeth fractionally glinted out of sensuous everted lips.

We commented to our "model" on the duskiness of her skin. She was not at all surprised and confessed that her nickname was "Darkie" (as in English). This was an allusion to a well-known brand of Thai toothpaste. On both the tube and the box there was a picture of a negro with a soot black face and gleaming white teeth, together with the brand name "Darkie". Every time the villagers had seen the girl, they had been reminded of the toothpaste and begun to call her by its name. The nickname "Darkie" had stuck. (Recently there was some legal wrangle over the right to use this brandname, resulting in the toothpaste suddenly being rechristened an enigmatic "Darlie".)

The fuss we were making of Darkie, tilting her head and arranging her hair, made her the centre of attention among the people who had gathered around. For a moment or two she was a filmstar. That was nice because we found out that her family was very poor, almost the poorest in the village. Darkie had to work for another household, doing the washing and the washing up, in order to pay for her clothes and schoolbooks. Her real name was Tiamjit Sae Li. She had two brothers and two sisters. One of the sisters worked for some people down in Pang Mu. In exchange for the work, they sent her to school. The sister only came back up to Mae Or once a year. We asked Darkie if she or her family ever went down to Mae Hong Son. They never did, she replied, because they were too poor to pay the fare.

After the soft drinks and the photographs, Darkie took us to her home to meet her mother. The "house" was a broken-down bamboo hovel with a grass roof, even more abject than those around it. In front were two or three black pigs in a makeshift pen. It was gloomy inside (no electricity, of course), but after a second or two we could make out the main features. A blackened kettle was sitting over a fire in a hearth. On the hard earth floor a pail of water was standing with several white discs of bread in it. These, we were told, would be grilled for supper. The beds were simple platform beds with a mat of split bamboo over a wooden frame. Darkie's was at the front of the hut in a room which was open to the sky. The grass roof had fallen in, leaving gaping holes. It must have been freezing sleeping there at night. The mother was sitting on a stool chopping away the outer layers from the stem of a young banana tree. These would be eaten by the pigs, while the tender core would be eaten by the family. She apologized for the state of the house, adding that she had built it herself. Then we learned the main reason why the family was so impoverished. Her husband had died ten years earlier. With the principal breadwinner gone, she had been left to bring up five children on her own.

Looking at Darkie and seeing how much she differed both from her mother and her brothers and sisters, we wondered if she was not just fatherless, but perhaps the orphan of another family, or a wildcard - maybe the product of a liaison between her mother and a dark stranger up in the Wa hills to the north. Given the chequered history of the migratory minority peoples from Yunnan and northeast Burma, this could well have been the case. Confirmation of our suspicion came when we once showed our Darkie photos to a perceptive KMT man in Mae Salong. "Why, she looks just like a Wa girl!" he exclaimed. Of course, we could not question Darkie, any more than we could quiz the mother, and so for the moment the dusky beauty's dark past remained a secret.

The Mae Or part of our story would not be complete without an account of developments a year or two later, when we revisited the village. Taking a lift from Mae Hong Son market with a young Hmong man called Pan-na, who for 50 baht each drove us all the way to the border in his pick-up, we arrived on the last day of the Chinese New Year. On the way we noticed changes. After Huai Khan a new metalled road was being blasted up into the mountains, scarring the hillsides and destroying quantities of jungle and forest. Napapaek had expanded, with a new first section, and electricity pylons now ran all the way to Mae Or, providing it with power. At the entrance to the KMT village itself, we found a new store, and on the northeast side there was a brand-new wooden school. But the most welcome innovation was that in the centre some simple shops and eating places had sprung up. We took lunch in one of the latter, and a lady fried up for us a delicious plateful of ribbon egg noodles, dried Chinese mushrooms, greens and deep-fried dried beef. An accompaniment of pickled cabbage was served, and the meal was washed down with endless tumblerfuls of golden China tea. The beef seemed familiar somehow, and then we remembered it was the product of those "meat trees" we had once seen.

While we were lunching, a Thai police truck screeched to a halt in the dusty central compound. Two policemen got out and began searching around, making enquiries. A lot of villagers came over to see what the fuss was all about. We gathered that the policemen had stopped two Hmong youths on a motorcycle down on the 1095 road and had discovered that they were carrying heroin. The Hmongs had fled, trying to escape up the Mae Or road. But the police had followed them, chasing them through Napapaek all the way to Mae Or, where their escape route ran out. The punishment in Thailand for heroin-smuggling is death by Heckler & Koch machine gun, so the youths were in fear of their lives. At first the policemen did not find them. But they were clever. They waited around all afternoon in quiet corners, drinking tea and whisky with the locals. Finally, one of the boys crept back into the village and was caught. It was common knowledge by then that the two lawmen intended to extort a large sum of money from the Hmongs in exchange for not turning them in.

When the commotion had died down, a grey-haired Chinese man walked past whom we had once met in Nong Ook. It turned out that he worked in Mae Or in the health clinic as an acupuncturist. When we had last seen him, he had been visiting relatives in that other KMT outpost (it was from Nong Ook that in the 1970s people broke away to form Mae Or). He was pleased to see us, and we fell in with him. He gave us a tour of the village, showing us things we had not previously seen. Near the secondary piece of lake there was a mushroom farm. The fungi did not grow from compost beds, but from notches which had been cut into a ramshackle army of upright wooden logs. Around the village there were orchards, where temperate fruits were cultivated. Tea was also grown, processed in Mae Or.

In every household people had pasted fresh red and gold paper banners around their door and window frames. And in each front yard a pine sapling had been planted in the dirt. Our greying friend explained that these were practices associated with the New Year celebrations. The Chinese believed the saplings brough them "greenness" - health and prosperity. The young pines did not remain in the yards forever, but were removed after a week or so. During our walk we ran into the commander of the BPP base. The afternoon was progressing, and he asked us how we were going to get back down to Mae Hong Son. A Hmong man was coming to collect us in his pick-up, we lied through the teeth. That was good, the *dorchodor* chief replied, because *farangs* were not supposed to stay up at Mae Or overnight. Actually, we intended to try and sleep a night or two at the village, and when the commander was gone, we asked the KMT veteran if there was anywhere to stay. Not really, he said, but just for tonight, while the celebrations were ending, we could stay in the health centre. There were a couple of medics temporarily camping up there while they organized a hygiene course for the village housewives, so the place was opened up.

The acupuncture man showed us our lodging. It was in a spacious lecture hall, where every morning the hygiene course took place. There were no beds, but we could use some of the tables. While he fetched a pile of blankets, we put four tables together in the centre of the hall. The problem would be not to fall off in the night, and so we formed a barricade by placing chairs all round the tables, their backs facing inwards. The medics had made tea and coffee outside on the balcony. While we were chatting out there, we spotted something we had not seen before. It was a very tall bamboo pole on a forward hillock to the west of the village. On top was a white flag. We supposed that it indicated a BPP look-out post or defensive position. Oh no, our Chinese friend corrected us, it was to orientate Wa soldiers and let them know that they were near a safe haven. Questioning him about this, we discovered something which we had not remotely imagined of Mae Or, and which was not mentioned in the guidebooks, was not, indeed, generally known at all, that the village, besides containing KMT people, was a rare Wa place. Now that we knew it, the fact seemed blindingly obvious, and we kicked ourselves for having overlooked such an important feature during our first visit. And so by chance we wrested from Mae Or its deepest secret, one of the best-kept secrets of the whole Thai-Burmese border.

Seeing our interest, the KMT man pointed out to us a wooden building near the entrance to the village. That was the Wa National Army HQ, and we could go and make ourselves known there. He gave us the name of a man to ask for. The building was actually not so much a military headquarters, but a Wa hospitality house and a kind of pension, where Wa guerrillas injured in fighting could recuperate. Inside we found a man sleeping on a mattress who had been traumatized in a battle, and also an intelligent young Wa man who had been working down at the Three Pagodas Pass with a French aid organization. He spoke good English and said that he was staying in the building while he passed through Mae Or. When we had explained ourselves, he called out of a side room two WNA officers. Both were wearing jungle-green camouflage jackets, and both had the black brown faces characteristic of Wa people. One, simply known as Jerng, had a rugged face and the wild, piercing, evil, slightly hooded eyes that we have also come to associate with Wa people. The other was Major Ta Kong Mong (alias Ying Kuang Sae Jao), the area commander of the WNA troops stationed over the border, opposite Mae Or. If Jerng looked fearsome, impressive, diabolical, Kong Mong was altogether softer and more sympathetic. A taciturn round-faced fellow with boyish hair falling forward over his forehead and a hesitant sloping moustache, he had a roguish way which immediately attracted us. It seemed that he also warmed to us because, although we had no business with the WNA, he took us under his wing.

More tea appeared - one could spend all day drinking tea in these villages - and we sat in a circle around the teapot and glasses in a big room, the walls of which were decorated with Kachin Independence Organization posters, Karen National Union calendars, and such like. We asked Kong Mong about the Wa and Mae Or. Wa people first came south to the Thai border around 1973 in the wake of the Communist Party of Burma takeover of their homeland, but they did not move into Mae Or until the early 80s. At one time there had been a joint KMT/WNA force of 300-400 soldiers garrisoned at the village, but now the WNA was back on the Burmese side of the border. We learned that the meagre body of troops was currently stationed opposite three places: Mae Or, Pang Yon and Nai Soi - all local to Mae Hong Son. At present 36 Wa families lived in Mae Or, accounting for a third of its inhabitants.

In some albums of old photos we saw a lot of pictures of the same tall slim man. That was Maha San, Kong Mong explained. Described by some as the last "king" of the Wa, and by others as just another Shan warlord with another private army (the Wa are also involved in opium-growing and trafficking), the legendary Maha San was the most famous and important Wa person alive. The son of the last feudal lord (*sawbwa, chao fah*) of the Wa mini-state or principality of Ming Noen (also referred to as Ving Ngun), the princeling Maha San was leader of the Wa National Army and chairman of the Wa National Organization - the WNA's political wing, which was affiliated to the ethnic rebel NDF grouping. Here were photos of a younger Maha San in combat gear, directing a battle or reviewing troops, or with an open shirt and smoking a cigarette with Shan leaders at the conference table. Kong Mong surprised us by saying that Maha San was his brother. At first we did not take him seriously, thinking that he was using "brother" in the same loose way that Thais used "cousin". But it turned out that the two were indeed real brothers, not even half brothers.

The Wa

The homeland of the Wa is the Wa State or substate, an utterly remote mountainous area in northeast Burma composed of hundreds of former microstates or fiefdoms, ruled by erstwhile sawbwas or feudal lords. If, geographically, it is wedged between the River Salween to the west and the Chinese border to the east, and between Kokang to the north and the Shan plateau to the south, culturally it is overshadowed by the Chinese and the Shan. No reliable statistics exist for the number of Wa living today. Propaganda we acquired from the WNO optimistically put the figure at 2-3 million. A more accurate estimate might be 1-2 million (including Palaung-Wa), which would take into account half a million Wa thought to be living over the Chinese border in Yunnan. Several thousand Wa live along the Thai-Burmese border, several thousand (in the form of Lawa) exist in Thailand itself, near Mae Sariang, and the remainder, perhaps half a million, either live in the Wa State or have intermarried with and been assimilated into various other ethnic groupings. The Wa State is the most backward region in Burma, and that is saying something, as Burma itself is one of the least developed nations in the world (bracketed along with other LDN-status places such as Ethiopia and Chad). Very little is known about the Wa - the only thing at all widely known is that until recently they were headhunters. They are not related to the Shans (Tai Yai), or the Thais (Tai Noi), or the Burmese or Chinese, but they are related to the ancient Lawa of Thailand. Their language, like that of the Lawa, is Austro-Asiatic, related to the Mon-Khmer linguistic family. Through intermarrying, through internal political dissension, through being divided and ruled by other occupying forces, and through serving away in other peoples' armies, the Wa have become widely dispersed and fragmented. They are one of the most obscure, neglected and marginalized of all the minority peoples in South-East Asia.

Kong Mong invited us to take supper with him down in the centre of the village. When we walked down at 7 p.m., it was already quite cold, and we could see our breaths. On the last evening of the Chinese New Year the celebrations were petering out, but there was still some fun and games. A lot of people were roaming around, including WNA soldiers who had crossed over from their camp on the other side. Jumping-jack fire crackers were being let off, men were gambling in smoky dens, there was traditional dancing, special food was being eaten, and the youngsters danced until the small hours in a disco rigged up in the meeting-pavilion of the central compound. The Thai hit popsong of the moment was played over and over again until everybody was thoroughly sick of it.

Outside a Wa house near the noisy central compound several tables had been set out. People kept dropping by to eat, drink tea, and chat. We sat down at one of them and were joined by Kong Mong's wife, Chang Soe, and their two children, a boy and an older girl. Chang Soe, a fearsome-looking lady with a bullish face, was actually much kindlier than she appeared. The best thing about her from our point of view was that she was a mine of information. Kong Mong was very helpful, even spoke some English, but he was not by nature forthcoming and on that particular evening his mind was half on the gambling, to which he sloped off at intervals. So it was from the Thai-speaking Chang Soe that much of our insight into the Wa came. Under our very noses a wild Wa boy with a stubbly moustache and hair gathered up in a topknot prepared a chicken. He killed the bird in the kitchen, the unprotesting animal dying without so much as a cluck. Soon its feathers were off, it was in pieces, and the parts were being washed in water. The boy seemed especially interested in the bird's organs and innards. Nothing was wasted. In particular I remember him carefully holding lengths of intestine up to the light, whether to check that they were clean or to read the omens it was not clear. We were drinking some pleasant Chinese peach *lao*, and after an hour the chicken was served up chopped and fried, and folded into spaghetti-type egg noodles. There was also tofu and mushroom soup, tofu strips stir-fried with mixed vegetables, omelette, and a fiery pickled vegetable accompaniment. It was a feast fit for a king.

Quizzing Kong Mong, we tried to piece together the complicated family background of this noble Wa scion. His grandfather was called Ta Hlang and his father Maha Pong. Maha Pong, the last *sawbwa* of Ming Noen, had married three times. By the first wife he had had his oldest son, Maha Kwang, now deceased. By the second wife, Ye Lu, who was still alive in Taiwan, he had had the three brothers Maha San, Kong Mong and Kong Ko. Maha San, as the most senior surviving son, had inherited the title of Maha (*maha* is an honorific similar to *khun* or *chao*) and for a while had also taken over the father's name of Pong. By the third wife, father Maha Pong had had one son Maha Ja. Maha Ja was widely referred to as "the younger brother", and the interesting thing about him was that in 1986 he joined Mo Heng's and Khun Sa's TRC (later MTA). This was strange as the Wa and Khun Sa were bitter enemies. But even more bizarre was the fact that Maha Ja was commander of Khun Sa's Doi Lan MTA base just a stone's throw from Mae Or. Brothers from the same family commanded mutually hostile forces living next door to each other. There were also two daughters (sisters) somewhere along the line, but one was dead, and the other, Nam Cha, lived in Taiwan with her mother. Chang Soe disappeared to return enthusiastically with three ancient black and white photos. One showed Ye Lu ("Ama"), Kong Mong's mother, an ample round-featured lady. The others were pictures of Ta Hlang, the grandfather, and Maha

Pong, the last *sawbwa* himself. Here were old feudal chiefs with Fu Manchu moustaches and straggly chintuft beards, with white turbans, and with angular faces which seemed slightly European. Looking at these faded photographs was like looking back into some incredibly exotic and mysterious past, like having a direct link with the times of Kublai Khan or Marco Polo.

While we were poring over the photos and trying to disentangle the family relationships, another couple came to join our table. We did not take much notice of them at first - a lot of people were coming and going. The woman, fresh and attractive, looked Chinese, while the man, with his dark pitted face, had to be another Wa. "More Wa people for you", Kong Mong said lightly, mischievously, "and part of the family too." They were all watching me trying to sort out a family tree in my notebook. "And where do you fit in?" I quipped, addressing the man and pointing to the mess of lines, "Who are you?" "I am Maha San", said the dark face in a deep soft resonant voice, "and this is Janoo, my wife." We looked up, stunned. Here we were suddenly, all unprepared, face to face with the leader of the Wa, the illustrious "king" in exile, whose house in Chiang Mai, we subsequently discovered, was sought out by a succession of Shan leaders, NDF chairmen, dignitaries, politicians and journalists.

As we got over our surprise and came to terms with our good fortune, we learned that Maha San and his wife had come up to Mae Or to take part in the Chinese New Year. Many Wa were celebrating there along with the KMT, but in addition, Janoo, it transpired, was of mixed Wa and Chinese extraction. Maha San and his wife were every bit as affable and helpful as Kong Mong and Chang Soe, and from them, on this and other occasions, we learned much else about Maha San himself, his family, his life, the Wa, their history and culture. Maha San was 49 years old (in 1996), was born in Ming Noen, and had three daughters. It surprised us to hear he was so young because he looked older. When we later put this to Kong Mong, the brother confessed that Maha San had once been addicted to opium, which had aged him. We noticed also a vain touch. The princeling dyed his grey hair jet black. Nevertheless, this tall, slim, in some ways boyish man, with hooded crack-like eyes and a wedge-shaped face reminiscent of that of his father and grandfather, was every bit the distinguished personage we had expected. The nobility did not end with him, for his wife Janoo was the sister of the formidable Mrs Li Ching (Li Yi Sing). That Chinese-Wa lady was married to Ai Hsiao-hsu, son of the last Wa *sawbwa* of Yawngbre, and together the couple commanded the other major (larger) Wa faction down on the Thai border, the Wa National Council - recently incorporated into the United Wa State Army. The two Wa princeling leaders, therefore, with their separate pocket armies (the Red Wa UWSA was not affiliated to the NDF), were related through the sister wives.

We commented to Maha San and Kong Mong that they looked so unalike that we could not believe that they were really brothers. They were, they countered, it was just that Kong Mong took after their mother, while

Maha San looked like their father. On the subject of semblances, we produced our photos of Darkie. Both brothers recognized the girl immediately. They confirmed what we had come to suspect, that our poor "princess" was (at least in part) Wa. Her mother was KMT, while her dead father had been Wa. We asked our hosts what they thought of the road construction, which in the end would reach Mae Or, bringing with it tourism, which would change the village. We had learned at the district office in Mae Hong Son that Mae Or was due for development. The cultivation of temperate fruits and tea-growing would be further promoted, and the village was to be officially designated a place of touristic interest. It was possible that ultimately Mae Or might become another Mae Salong. Kong Mong and Maha San were aware of the potential disadvantages, but in general they thought that the village was so backward that things could only go up. There were lighter moments too. Suddenly, the BPP commander came by, stopping at our table. Of course, he remembered that he had forbidden us to stay overnight and that we had promised to skedaddle. But he said nothing, either because he saw who we were with or because he did not care. He helped himself to our peach whisky and talked a lot about how he liked young girls. Then he continued on to the disco. What with all the fruit *lao* and tea, as well as the teeth-chattering coldness of the night, we all had to keep slipping out. Once, when I returned, I said that in English we called this "going to see a man about a dog". "In Wa", Maha San replied, "we say that we are going to shoot a rabbit." "There won't be many rabbits left around here in the morning", Kong Mong finished, and everybody laughed.

One thing that puzzled us was the connection between the Wa and the Lawa. They were the same race of people, Maha San explained, only separated by history. There had been a time centuries earlier when Wa people lived all over northern Thailand. But they had been squeezed first by the Mon and then by the conquering Tai (Thais and Shans). Many Wa had migrated north, inhabiting the mountains which were now the Wa homeland, but some had stayed on as Lawa, being progressively confined to the mountains northeast of Mae Sariang. Latterly a few Wa were moving back down south again. The languages of the Wa and Lawa were closely related, and our friends claimed that old people of the two groups could still communicate. The obliging Chang Soe jumped up again, running to fetch a beginners' book in Wa. What surprised us about it was that written Wa was set down using the Roman alphabet - a practice shared, apparently, by Kachin. Kong Mong gave us the little book, and it led to an interesting discovery later in our journey.

The Wa had been living alongside the Shan so long that Wa culture was now in many respects Shan. They were Buddhists, although there was still a degree of animism (no ancestor worship), and the Wa New Year and other celebrations tended to follow Shan customs. Wa National Day was on 21 January. We asked whether the Wa had a traditional costume. Without our noticing, Kong Mong instructed the lady whose house we were sitting outside to go and change, and presently she emerged in full costume to answer our question tangibly. There was a handwoven maroon wraparound skirt, with wide black and thin gold banding. She wore also a close-fitting black velvet jacket, which had two long central flaps - like ties - hanging to the knees. The jacket was abundantly decorated with silver pearls, buttons, dangles and a butterfly. Down one side hung a cherry red sash. Many Wa we saw carried green shoulder bags.

Maha San and recent Wa history

Maha San's life and the recent history of the Wa, of how they came down to the Thai border and to Mae Or in particular, are very much of a piece. Traditionally, the Wa substate had been an inaccessible mountain region peopled by wild headhunters and ruled by hundreds of feuding clannish sawbwa *princelings. Even the intrepid British administrators of Burmese colonial times had scarcely ventured into Wa territory. Ming Noen (= silver mine), the fiefdom of one of the most important Wa* sawbwas, *was where Maha San was born in 1947. Burmese Independence, a year after his birth, would have been little felt up in the Wa hills, but another contemporary event, the arrival of the KMT from 1949 onwards, certainly was. Thousands of heavily armed Chinese Nationalists, fleeing Mao's communist revolutionaries, poured across the Sino-Burmese border into the Wa homeland. The marauding invaders were so much more powerful and cohesive than the fragmented locals that they quickly established themselves as an army of occupation, ironically providing for a decade the only effective overall "government". The present close relationship between the Wa and the KMT along Thailand's northwestern frontier dates back to the forced cohabitation of the two groups in Wa territory during the 1950s. Around 1960-61 the Chinese People's Liberation Army together with the Burma Army jointly swept the KMT (those who had not been evacuated to Taiwan or who had not already migrated south) from the Wa substate, driving them down to the Thai border.*

The beginning of the Shan nationalist uprising (1959-61) brought the unwanted attention next of the Burmese. The Wa have always identified with the Shan, and their land is normally considered a substate within the Shan State. Where earlier many chieftains had fallen in with the KMT, now they sided with the Shan nationalists. The Burmese intervened, disarming some sawbwa *militias, but encountering resistance in others. The Wa of Ming Noen, led by a youthful Maha San and his older brother Maha Kwang, successfully fought off the Burma Army. The early 1960s also saw the start of infiltration of the Wa hills by communists from China. Many Wa, disillusioned with the outgoing KMT, and not wishing to side with either the Shans or even their own Wa nationalists, were attracted by the promises of the communist newcomers. A people traditionally disunited in themselves were now split in their allegiance to at least four political forces: the Shans, the Burmese, the Wa nationalists, the Chinese communists - even a few KMT stragglers.*

DARK SECRETS

The communists flourished. Mutating in the mid-60s into Communist Party of Burma units, they set up their North Eastern Command in the Wa substate, based on the "capital" Pang Sang. As the period of the KMT invasion ended, the era of CPB occupancy began. The central authorities in Rangoon, seeing the confusion on their northeastern border and alarmed at the growth of the communists, intervened anew. In the ensuing war between the CPB People's Army and the Burma Army, Wa territory was split. One tactic the Burmese used to regain overall control was the ka kwae yae scheme. This was that strategy, employed in the Shan State (netting Khun Sa), whereby hostile ethnic groups in exchange for not supporting active insurgents could gain legitimacy for themselves as government-backed local defence militias. Once on Rangoon's side, they could continue to police and tax their patches, as well as pursue whatever other interests they had (trafficking), confident that they would not be molested by the authorities. One Wa leader to take up the offer was the 22-year old Maha San. In 1969 he marched his Ming Noen force of nearly 1000 rebels over to the government side, pledging loyalty to the Union of Burma. At the time, as he explained, it seemed the most expedient thing to do. He was under threat from all sides - from the Shan State Army, from the Burmese, from Khun Sa's trading militia operating nearby, and now from the CPB. The switch also seemed the best way of halting the advance of the communists in the Wa substate. But as things turned out, the move was unfortunate in more ways than one. The Wa cause was further split, the CPB proceeded to triumph completely, and the ka kwae yae militias were anyway disbanded in 1973. The Ming Noen princeling had backed the wrong horse.

1973 was altogether a watershed in the history of the Wa people. It was the year when the Burmese communist takeover of their homeland became complete. Rangoon was checked, the SSA was marginalized, and the last KMT stragglers were definitively ousted. The seizure also spelled the effective end of traditional Wa sawbwa power and rule. The Wa people themselves were divided vis-à-vis the CPB, hopelessly so. The majority decided to go along with the communists. They believed the party line that, in supporting the People's Army, they would be fighting for a free and independent Wa state and would be in the vanguard of a movement to liberate the whole of Burma. This section of the Wa, under the leadership of the Wa chieftains Kyauk Ni Lai and Pauk Yo Chang, formed the origins of the Wa Daeng or "Red" Wa. But a sizeable portion rejected the CPB. An estimated 10,000 families fled south and west, a veritable Wa diaspora. Maha San led about 2000 refugees down through the Shan State to the Thai border, while Ai Hsiao-hsu, another Wa sawbwa son, brought a further party. Kong Mong, Maha San's younger brother, followed later. The Wa settlements along the Shan-Thai border date back to this flight.

For Maha San the years after 1973 were time in the political wilderness. He settled first in an important Shan rebel base opposite Mae Hong Son and near Mae Or. There in 1976 he formed his Wa National

Army, which he sought to build up with a view to retaking the Wa homeland. Meanwhile Ai Hsiao-hsu had settled along the Thai border further northeast. He founded his own faction, the Wa National Council. Both militias enlisted a steady stream of recruits from the Shan State, notably from among the thousands of refugee Wa families. But it was the WNC, soon to become a rival of Maha San's WNA, which grew faster. Even in exile the Wa remained divided.

In 1978, following a split with his Shan hosts, Maha San moved to Piang Luang, where he found Mo Heng's Shan United Revolutionary Army in cahoots with Gen. Li's KMT Third Army remnants. Assisted by the two armies, the Wa princeling continued in his attempt to build up his WNA, but some of his commanders were unhappy about the collaboration and broke away. The refugee Wa, already divided into WNA and WNC, fragmented even further. Around 1981-82, in a tripartite agreement with Mo Heng and Gen. Li, Maha San decamped with his pocket army to Mae Or. The WNA was given the task, relieving the SURA, of controlling both the Mae Or border crossing and the vital caravan route from the crossing back to the River Salween. In those days whoever held the crossing point could levy a tax of 100 baht per head of cattle passing through Mae Or and 400 baht per horse carrying jade - not inconsiderable sums.

A year later, in 1983, Maha San allied the political wing of his WNA, the Wa National Organization, with the important National Democratic Front. Neither the SURA, nor the KMT, nor even Ai Hsiao-hsu's WNC, were members of this anti-Rangoon alliance of some dozen ethnic insurgent organizations, based at Karen rebel GHQ in Manerplaw, and so Maha San contrived to alienate himself yet further. It was while he was away fighting with the Karens (through the NDF now allies of his) that Khun Sa, dislodged from Hin Taek in Thailand and having swept down the Shan-Thai border, seized the Mae Or border-crossing point and wrested control of the Salween caravan route from the Wa. In 1984 Maha San returned to try to recapture the Mae Or gateway.

War raged around Mae Or in the early months of 1985. The WNA, aided by the Mae Or KMT and by mortar units sent up by the Karens, battled with Khun Sa troops. Hundreds of soldiers on each side were killed or wounded in pitched battles, shelling and hand-to-hand fighting that went on sporadically for some years. The result was a compromise. The Wa did not recover the Salween route, but they did regain the westerly half of the Mae Or border crossing, while Khun Sa held on to the easterly Doi Lan half. The result is reflected in the the disposition of Wa/Sa forces at Mae Or today.

Up in their corner the other main Wa faction on the Thai border, the WNC, was similarly embroiled in the 80s in bitter conflict with Khun Sa. Retreating from Hin Taek, Sa's army pushed the WNC off the Doi Larng ridge. However, during the decade Ai Hsiao-hsu's Wa flourished in a way that Maha San's did not. Besides recruiting widely, they received military help from a variety of sources - the KMT Third Army, Kachin and Shan groups, and the Red Wa of the Wa homeland. The latter in particular were a source of powerful reinforcement. Following the CPB mutinies in 1989 and the demise of Burmese communism in the Wa substate (indeed throughout Burma), the Red Wa sent down some 1500 ex-CPB regulars to bolster the WNC. They were seeking an outlet for their opium and also to compromise Khun Sa. And there, conveniently, was Ai Hsiao-hsu's faction already sitting on the Thai border. Now the Wa army of the homeland and the WNC joined up to form the United Wa State Army, currently the strongest of the Wa forces. It was due to this merger with the ex-communist Wa that Ai Hsiao-hsu's men themselves became "tainted" with "redness" and known in the Thai press as Wa Daeng (unlike Maha San's WNA). They muscled in on Sa, aiming to recapture the strategic Doi Larng heights. In the winter of 1989-90 the long-smouldering Opium War flared up anew, with bitter fighting continuing into the early 90s. But the Red Wa were only partly successful, seizing back the southwesterly Doi Laem half of the heights. Today the Wa Daeng face Khun Sa in a tense standoff on the ridge, a disposition very similar to the WNA/MTA confrontation down at Mae Or.

In 1989, up in the Wa substate, Wa troops, who formed the bulk of the CPB's fighting force, were in the forefront of the Burmese communist mutinies. They stormed the CPB GHQ in Pang Sang, smashed Maoist and Soviet communist icons, and drove the old CPB leaders and cadres into China. The present era of an inscrutable incumbency in the Wa substate by Wa (Daeng) themselves began. Surprisingly, their leader, Kyauk Ni Lai, negotiated a ceasefire with the SLORC junta in Rangoon, the deal being that if the central authorities allowed the Wa to develop their land and conduct "business" as they saw fit, the UWSA would not attack Burma Army troops and would refrain from allying with other ethnic insurgent groups. The situation in the 1990s was almost ka kwae yae *territory revisited.*

Six months after the 1989 mutinies, Maha San and a delegation of WNO and Karen officials travelled up to the homeland with an escort of 100 to test the political waters and see if all the various Wa factions could not be consolidated and perhaps brought into the fold of the National Democratic Front. Their reception was not what they had expected. First, Maha San found that his old manorial family home in Ming Noen had gone - not destroyed, but dismantled to provide materials for other buildings. Then, in Pang Sang he was arrested by Kyauk Ni Lai's men and put in jail. The reasons for this were several. The Red Wa, although no longer communist, were still left-inclined and suspicious of an old feudal lord like Maha San. Further, Kyauk Ni Lai was apparently piqued by the popular support the son of the last Ming Noen sawbwa *still enjoyed. When the local peasants heard of Maha San's presence, they came crowding to touch their forelocks to the former princeling. But in addition a rumour had spread that Maha San and Khun Sa had allied and that the two of them were coming north to take over Wa territory. The fear was not entirely unfounded, for Maha San had indeed made overtures to Sa, going to him in 1987 for talks and to arrange some kind of a truce between their two armies. The rapprochement had been such that Khun Sa had facilitated the passage of Maha San's delegation up through MTA territory to the Wa substate. In the end Maha San escaped from prison. One account says that he bribed his jailors, another that he was released by the Wa Daeng for fear of the prince's popular support. Whatever the case, Maha San fled to China, where he made his way south through Laos, to return to Mae Or in 1990. There he has remained until the present day, periodically visiting NDF HQ at Karen Manerplaw, and with lieutenants like Kong Mong nurturing his few hundred "democratic" WNA troops.*

With his NDF credentials Maha San may well be more politically correct than his main Wa rival on the border, Ai Hsiao-hsu. Yet the tide is running (for the moment at least) with the other leader and the UWSA. Whatever his distinction and draw, Maha San with his WNA remains reduced and isolated, a fragment among fragments. His fate is typical of the fate of the Wa as a whole. As Chang Soe put it pointedly, the Wa are incorrigible side-changers. First they are with the KMT, then the Chinese communists; now it is the NDF, now the Burmese; one moment it is the CPB, the next Khun Sa; for a while it is the Shans, and then the Karens. But the Wa have switched allegiance once too often - even by the standards of local Shan politics. They are their own worst enemy. For in the process they become factionalized, fragmented and marginalized. However, looking at their plight in another way, nothing has changed. The Wa are now what they were in the old days, a disintegrated collection of rival groups, the only difference being that some are now down on the Thai border.

We did not want to leave Mae Or on this second visit without finding out what had become of Darkie. Since our first visit the bashful maiden must have grown up into a marriageable young woman. What had happened to her in the meanwhile? Was she perhaps a humble washerwoman in Pang Mu or Mae Hong Son, or might she now be married with a "darkie" of her own? We went round to the family hovel and asked her mother. Darkie was no longer in Mae Or, but had gone down to Chiang Mai to work. The mother did not know exactly where or at what. Her unconcern about her daughter struck us as odd. Our disappointment at not seeing Darkie again turned to alarm and then despair when the mother narrated vaguely what had happened. Some "people" had come up from Chiang Mai to Mae Or to take the girl down to "work". It was a depressingly familiar story. Then the mother produced a letter from Darkie. We noticed straightaway that the postmark was Bangkok, not Chiang Mai. The mother had not seen this, but only complained that she never heard from her daughter and that Darkie never sent her any money. Inside was a sad little letter with a Bangkok address, which we noted down. It said: "I am alright. I miss you all. Don't worry about me...." and so on. But there was no mention of her work or the people she was working for.

DARK SECRETS

Hill-tribe settlements, rural Thai communities and the villages of the Burmese hinterland are full of examples of poor gullible parents being tricked of their daughters by scouts making an attractive downpayment and promising that the girls would be given a nice job and would be able to send back money at regular intervals. And Bertil Lintner in his *Land of Jade* has reported that impoverished Wa peasants used to settle a debt to (mostly Chinese) moneylenders by forefeiting their daughters as slaves. We had visions of Darkie sold into slavery, a poor mountain girl working in the brothels or sweat shops of Bangkok. Of course, the true explanation could have been more innocent, but somehow the details did not add up. The next time we were in Bangkok we tried to follow up the address. The trail led to teeming impenetrable Tonburi. There we spent an entire afternoon with local *tuk-tuk* drivers, getting ever deeper into a maze of appalling slums and sweat shops. Sometimes, when we scented we were getting close, the quarter was manifestly Chinese, encouraging us to hope that perhaps after all Darkie was "merely" working as a maid or a nanny with a family connected with the KMT of Mae Or. But we could not find her, and in the end we had to give up. The address simply did not figure, leading us to conclude that it was false. So we never found out what happened to our dusky Wa friend, and we were left fearing the worst. Darkie's was a true Wa fate and the darkest secret of all.

CHAPTER 7

THE DRAGON AND THE WIND

Mai Nai Soi

Returning to Mae Hong Son from Mae Or, we stopped off at the Border Patrol Police base in Pang Mu, where two soldier friends of ours were stationed. These were the pair who had been injured in the landmine explosion up near the border. It was in their camp that we first heard about the presence of "Long Neck" or "Giraffe" people in the Mae Hong Son area. The incapacitated *dorchodor* and their chums thought that somewhere in Pang Mu three "Long Neck" women were living clandestinely. But it must have been just a rumour, because an intensive search for them turned up nothing.

The "Long Necks" are Padaung people (pronounced 'padorng') from the Kayah State (also known as the Karenni State) in Burma. They are a minority subgroup of the Karenni, who in turn are sometimes subsumed as Red Karens under the Karen people. The Padaung are celebrated because some of their women wear rings to elongate their necks. Normally these Kayah could not be seen anywhere except deep in Burma, but on account of the Burma Army campaigns against the many ethnic insurgencies in the country during the late 80s and early 90s, a few had fled to the Thai border to live in the outermost reaches of Mae Hong Son province. Because these Padaung were refugees, they would return sooner or later to their homeland in the hills northwest of Loi Kaw.

The obvious intrinsic interest of the "Long Necks", combined with the fact that they might be only temporarily accessible, made us all the more anxious to try to track them down. We continued our enquiries in Mae Hong Son town, and here all roads seemed to lead to a company called "Singha Tour". Evidently this outfit had the Long Neck junket all sewn up, to the extent even of being in cahoots with the Karenni Army guerrillas who controlled the far side of the border and "minded" the Padaung refugees. We learned from *Singha* that Long Necks could actually be seen in two places. One group, the one more regularly visited, was located southwest of *ampoe muang* at a place called Nam Pieng Din. Reaching them involved a river trip and crossing over into the Karenni State. The other group lay northwest of Mae Hong Son at the village of Mai Nai Soi (= new Nai Soi), also known as Nupa-ah. This second village could be reached with difficulty by 4WD vehicle or motorbike, and lay a couple of kms just inside the Thai border.

Singha Tour could take us to "see the Long Necks" at Mai Nai Soi for 600 baht per person. This seemed a whopping amount for a couple of hours with some colourful people, located, by all accounts, not so far from Mae Hong Son. So we politely declined and determined to try to reach the refugees on our own. In fairness to *Singha,* half the fee went to buying off the Karenni Army, a toll that the freelancer could not avoid either. Also, the way to Mai Nai Soi proved so poor that the tour agency really earned their money.

Knowing now the name of the long-neck village, there remained only the problem of finding out how to get to it. In the office of the tour company we noticed a rough map drawn on the wall. Making a mental note of it, we later checked it against a military map at Pang Mu BPP base. The 24-km run began by heading out east from Mae Hong Son on Highway 1095, just as we had started for Mae Or. Three or fours kms out of town, after passing a roadside reclining Buddha, the route then turned left at a police box. Now a gravelly dirt road wound through woods and banana groves, passing the village of Tungkong Mu with its school, until it surprisingly reached a 200-metre long suspension bridge. This slender footbridge over the River Pai was just wide enough for a motorcycle. Beneath the bridge there seemed to be a ford, but in late December it looked to us too deep for conventional vehicles. We saw men standing knee-deep in swirling water sorting boulders and sand, probably for building purposes.

After the suspension bridge, the track narrowed to a woodland path, but soon it rejoined a metalled way. The village of Sop Soi came next, with its new-looking Burmese-style temple. Most of the rest of the route followed a horribly dusty road, with some steep gradients. The trail curved round the mountainside in the company of the Pai river. In the morning sun, the pale yellow powdery road surface ran out blindingly bright before our front wheel. The vegetation on either side had become coated with this lemon dust, giving it the same weird frozen lunar quality we had seen on the way to Mae Or. We soon discovered why - empty logging lorries thundered along here heading for the border to reload. When they came, they raised an indescribable dust cloud, so thick that we were reduced to a fumbling crawl. But never mind, the particles soon settled, and then the morning sun shone with renewed splendour on the lush welcoming countryside. It was fine riding along here. The MTX was behaving itself, and we, without a care in the world, felt glad to be alive.

Nai Soi, the village before Mai Nai Soi, was a fair-sized place. Some of its inhabitants had distinctly Burmese, dark-skinned faces. They wore *longyis* and had cheeks powdered with *tanaka.* The houses were typical of those in a "model village". Their entrances had wooden portals, each bearing a sign, inscribed white on blue, citing the names of the relevant family members together with a line or two of sententious sugary poetry. A Shan-style *wat* in the village passed us on the left, and on the way out of Nai Soi we were surprised to find an inviting-looking eating place. More remarkable still, its menu board, hung out in front, was in English. Our greed got the better of us, and we dismounted for a 20-baht mid-morning lunch of chicken with ginger and green peppers, accompanied by rice and a bowl of bouillon, all freshly cooked. But it was fortunate we stopped because the food situation in the long-neck village turned out to be poor.

After Nai Soi our troubles began. A river had to be forded four times. The water was not so deep, between six and twelve inches, but the stones on the bed were round and slippery. The shallowest places skirted weirs, making it a delicate manoeuvre to thread a way through the shallows, but without wobbling over the weirs. Of course, at the fords there were lots of people, especially children, watching riders get their shoes wet and occasionally tumble with their bikes into the river. The trials of the fords were followed by the tribulations of the forest path. For four kms a narrow steep-sided track cut through cool damp jungle. By turns muddy and gravelly, the path included for good measure some testing upgrades. Along here, just in front of us, two adult elephants suddenly lumbered out of the trees, together with a mahout - a sure sign that we were in Karen territory. At intervals suspicious-looking individuals dotted the trail, seemingly up to no good. And altogether this bumpy ride became increasingly scary. The final test was a treacherous boghole. It could not be avoided, as the sides of the path were too steep. So the choice was either to pick a way along the rim of the slimy hole, pushing the bike as we went, or boldly to ride straight through it. With relief we emerged into a clearing and spotted the entrance to the long-neck village.

Mai Nai Soi (Nupa-ah)
There were in fact two sets of houses at Mai Nai Soi. The first was the Padaung settlement, but behind it, well hidden one km along a jungle trail, lay an extensive new Karenni refugee camp, complete with school and field hospital. While the "exotic" Long Necks were in danger of being overexposed, with photos of the same two or three women appearing ever more frequently in the press and travel brochures, the "ordinary" Karenni of the refugee camp behind were conveniently kept out of sight. The entrance to the village was a short "street", with a row of bamboo huts on each side. Two of these were rudimentary shops, selling water, drinks, Mekhong whisky, instant noodles, biscuits and so on. Another was the home of so-called "Miss Silver", and a fourth was a guard-box/reception point belonging to the Karenni Army (KA).

As we drew up, Miss Silver appeared from her hut to intercept us. This Shan lady acted as an interface between the Padaungs and visitors, and she straightaway escorted us to the KA box. There a couple of Karenni soldiers, vaguely dressed in fatigue uniform, demanded the 300-baht entrance fee Singha Tour had told us about. We argued with the guards about this. The charge was a lot even by western standards, and extortionate for Thai or Karenni circumstances. But apparently there were no exceptions to the toll, although by mentioning *Singha Tour* we did exact a 50-baht discount. The fee was all the more galling when we discovered that Thais were able to enter the village free. It was small consolation for such blatant racial discrimination that part of the money apparently went to supporting the Padaung village, while another part went to the school and hospital behind. No doubt the major portion flowed to the war chest of the anti-SLORC Karenni insurgents.

Miss Silver came from Burma and at the time of our visit had been living in Mai Nai Soi for a year. She was 45, divorced and had four children. A son was at school in Chiang Mai, one daughter was with her, and two other children were in Burma. We never found out what her real profession was, but she may have been a teacher. A sharp businesswoman, Miss Silver was cheerful, obliging, informative and likeable. With her squint-eye she mixed a certain coyness into her forthrightness. In the village she was a lifeline for visitors because she was the only person to speak some English (although very little Thai), whereas the Padaungs spoke neither English nor Thai. The Shan lady took us in hand and showed us round the village.

The Padaung settlement consisted of fifteen families and some twenty houses. It had been in existence for three years. The village was located in a narrow valley, out of which three or four hills rose steeply on all sides. Most of the houses were sited on one favourable hillside, but others stood on the valley floor. Nupa-ah, to use its Kayan name, lay deep in jungle. All around thin silvery trees shot straight-as-a-die to an immense height. Even among the dwellings numerous trees had been left standing, providing shade. The houses were made of bamboo with grass and leaf roofs, and nearly all were raised off the ground on stilts. Some were quite large. At first sight it was an idyllic scene here. It was peaceful and cool, green and shady. A stream trickled through the village, and smoke drifted up from fires both inside the huts and out. Fertile vegetable patches and pig pens were dotted around. Chickens scratched and fluttered, and children played marbles in the dust. Closer inspection, however, revealed that the camp was already quite polluted. Plastic bags and bottles, Coke cans and other rubbish lay everywhere, even in the stream. These did not come from visitors, but from the Padaungs themselves. Accustomed to banana-leaf wrappings, they did not appreciate the non-biodegradability of plastic or aluminium packaging. Of course, there was no mains water supply - water came from the stream - and there was no electricity either. After all, this was a refugee village, a temporary camp. The people did not want to be there, but had been forced by the Burma Army to flee to Mai Nai Soi from their real homes.

One of the long-neck ladies in the village, Ma Nang, could speak a smattering of Thai, and she confirmed this last point to us. It was pleasant enough in Nupa-ah, she said, but she was homesick and like the other Padaung villagers wanted to see her relatives again. Home was a four-day walk away. The main problem was that, as refugees, they were not allowed by the Thai authorities to own land or work. This meant that they had to rely on handouts from relief agencies and earn what they could from tourism. They did not object to visitors coming to the village; nor did they mind being "on display" and being photographed (about 100 visitors a month came on average, and sometimes 50 a day in the high season, but during the monsoon months few or no people). The tourists even provided the bored Padaungs with some welcome distraction. What they objected to was not being able to earn their own money and keep.

Some wild allegations have been made about the plight of the Long Necks in Thailand. Some have said that the Padaung are compelled to stay in Thailand by the Thai tourist authorities to promote tourism in Mae Hong Son province. Others have written that the Padaungs are virtual prisoners of the KA. Certainly there have been some unsavoury incidents in the recent past involving long-neck women, and in general their plight resembles that of another exotic minority, the *"pi tong luang"* or "Spirits of the Yellow Leaves" (Mrabri people near Nan). Tim Forsyth in an article in the *Bangkok Post* (9-11-91) reported that seven long-neck ladies were taken from Burma by a Shan man from Soppong to be sold to a resort near Chiang Mai, where they were to be exhibited in a kind of human zoo. The Shan was arrested and the women taken to Mai Nai Soi. And we witnessed a piece of exploitation of the Padaung on the day of our visit. A handful of the bizarre-looking women - actually mostly children - were going to be taken down to Mae Hong Son to be shown at a fair. When towards evening we saw them in the back of a pick-up waiting to set off, we were reminded of a group of Mrabri we had once seen being taken away from the jungles of Nan to be exhibited like freaks in Chiang Rai. But otherwise the allegations hardly square with what we learned. The Long Necks had fled their homeland because Rangoon had moved against Karenni rebels there. Padaung men had risked being pressganged into portering munitions for the SLORC troops. Their land had been extensively mined, and as if to prove the point, the headman at Nupa-ah, one Alphonso Zawthet, had only one leg, the other having been blown off when he had recently stepped on a landmine. The truth may be that, now that the Padaung refugees are in Mai Nai Soi, it is very convenient for both the Thai tourist authorities and the KA to have them continue to live there. Maybe a deal has been struck over their heads - the Karennis can have their refugee village in exchange for tourists being able to visit the exotic ladies. The Padaungs, while not being prevented from going, have probably not been encouraged to leave either. Whatever the case, one certainly hopes that they can safely return to their homelands soon.

The Padaung "Long Necks"

Miss Silver took us from house to house, introducing us to some of the Padaung women. At the same time she filled in background information. The "Long Necks" were just one of a dozen ethnic minorities in Burma's Kayah State. Only some 7000 Padaung tribespeople existed altogether, of which about 300 lived as refugees on the Thai border. By no means all Padaung women lengthened their necks. During our visit we found only 17 females wearing the rings. (From another source we heard that there were altogether 30,000 Padaung in the Kayah State, of whom 500 women still wore the rings.) Of the fifteen families in Mai Nai Soi, all were animists except one, which was Christian.

The Padaung had their own language, but could speak Karen and some Burmese for communicating with Karens, Karennis and others. They ate rice, vegetables, curry, pork, chicken and jungle game such as snakes. They made a spirit drink out of *kao goi*, but like Karen people as a whole did not cultivate or smoke opium. Some adults chewed betel nuts, leaving their mouths stained red and causing them to expectorate red juice. Men, women and children alike spat incessantly, first loudly clearing their throats. - an unedifying performance from such beautiful people. Miss Silver maintained that the women were unbelievably slow in preparing themselves for the day, putting on their headscarves and other paraphernalia. She said that, even compared to other ethnic minorities, the Padaung were relatively undeveloped and naive, making them easily exploited.

Most of the men were away, either hunting or helping to build in the Karenni refugee village nearby. Others were over in Burma serving in one of the rebel armies. As we walked from house to house we found the long-neck women busy with their domestic tasks. They were cooking or sewing, fetching water or returning from a wash. Some were sitting making baskets or putting together roofing panels. Others were engaged in one of the stages of weaving. These weaving ladies sat before their huts spinning yarn operating simple looms on the entrance platforms to their houses. We found the oldest lady of Nupa-ah putting the finishing touches to a 4-ft long scarf. We tried to speak to her, but all verbal communication was impossible. Next morning we bought the finished, brilliant red scarf from this lovable diminutive grandma for 100 baht. Many of the long-necks had samples of their weaving for sale outside their houses - scarves, shoulderbags and lengths of skirt material. They made attractive mementos and also had the virtue of directly supporting the refugees.

It has to be said that the long-necked Padaung women make one of the most extraordinary sights of all the peoples in the world. In addition to wearing the mass of gleaming bronze rings around their necks, they have golden coils of varying lengths around their lower legs. As if that were not enough, they also like to wear numerous silver and bone armbands, the whole attirement giving them an armoured appearance. Over their upper bodies they wear simple white V-necked shifts, and below most have checked "tablecloth" wrap-around skirts. Many wear leggings, and all sport capacious dark pink headscarves, secured above the fringe with aquamarine headbands. Much of their clothing and most of their weaving is in the green and red or pink colours characteristic of Karen peoples. The chins of the ladies rest on their neck rings on a small tasselled rectangular flap of material.

Looking at these women, we were struck by a haunting melancholy beauty. They had prominent high cheekbones, modelled angular faces, flattish broad noses, and lovely coffee-coloured skins. Their eyes were intelligent and their mouths wide. Because of the rings, their heads were pushed up and away from their bodies, making the heads seem detached.

This gave the Padaung women a remote, serene, unintentionally haughty and supercilious look. The fact that they could not easily turn their heads added a slightly pained expression to their demeanour, as if they were all suffering from a crick in the neck. Further, many of the long-neck women, their bodies seemingly depressed away from their heads, looked unusually thin and elongated.

Miss Silver took us next to look briefly at the Karenni refugee camp. It lay five minutes beyond Nupa-ah along a jungle trail. The beginning of the path was marked by an immense tree. With intergrowing sections, and as if rippling with muscles, the tree was sacred and had a small shrine in front of it. Once a year the Padaung villagers cleaned up the base area, and two old people sacrificed a chicken or other animal to the spirit of the place. Further up the path we came to a fork. Left went to a military checkpoint, beyond which the land was mined, and right went to the refugee camp. Some 1000 Karennis lived in this new village. The neat construction of the houses and the orderliness of the whole camp contrasted immediately with the general scruffiness of the Padaung settlement.

High up on a hill, to the right of the entrance, we spotted a small wooden church. With its cross and prominent Virgin Mary, it testified to the fact that many Karennis were Catholics. There was also a field hospital, a large wood and bamboo hut with a leaf roof, which was staffed by a doctor and three nurses. The camp school, with 172 children divided into six classes, was a serious, well-organized affair. The 96 boys and 76 girls studied Karenni, Burmese, English, maths, geography and science. Their teachers had names like Koo Rae, Tha Wo, Boo Moe, Hser Moo and Ki Mia, but also Victoria and Monica. The headmaster's name was Aung Win, and at thirty years of age he was the oldest member of staff!

Wanting to stay longer than an hour or two in Mai Nai Soi, we asked Miss Silver if it was possible to sleep overnight. Yes, we could - the village had a guest hut, which we could take for 20 baht. We hid and locked our motorbike in the Shan lady's vegetable garden, and in the late afternoon she took us to the hut, right in among the Padaungs. We immediately realized our mistake, but with night falling it was too late to set off back for Mae Hong Son. The hut was primitive indeed, and the facilities worse. That night at the long-neck village was possibly the worst we spent anywhere - worse than Kae Noi and worse even than nights later spent deep in the jungle on the way down to the Three Pagodas Pass.

Leaving us with some *pak gaad* greens, which she thought we could fry for supper, Silver indicated with her boss-eye that the washing place was in the stream. Then she departed. We could have stayed and eaten with her, she volunteered cheerily, but that evening she had to accompany some Long Necks down the fair in Mae Hong Son, and she would not be back till late. When we had got over the shock of the hut, which was a broken-down bamboo shack on stilts with one entire side open to view, we examined the *pak gaad*. This was a green vegetable with yellow flowers, but the leaves were limp and faded, and the flowers had black specks all over them.

Never mind, perhaps they would taste good when fried up with oil and fish sauce. But where was the oil? There was none. Perhaps we could buy some in the shop or borrow a drop from the Padaungs. But this problem was as nothing compared to what we found when we went next to inspect the "kitchen", adjacent to the hut. It clearly had not been used for months, possibly years. Two or three rusty blackened pots, full of dust, lay on the ground. But beyond that, there was nothing - nothing to clean them with, no spoons or plates, no matches, not even firewood. Even to begin to cook a meal, we would have had to go looking for wood, borrow an axe, and begin chopping up firewood. The situation was hopeless. We gave the mouldering greens to some pigs and marched off down to the shop, prepared either to eat biscuits for the evening or to starve until next day. This was an experience which taught us henceforth always to carry with us emergency supplies.

From one of the shops down at the entrance to the village we bought some instant noodles and other things. The shop, it transpired, was run by a Shan pharmacist and doctor. When we explained the situation, he altruistically invited us to spend the evening in Miss Silver's hut. Just push open her door, he said, you will find oil, fish sauce and other things in her kitchen. Who were we to decline? The charcoal embers were still glowing in Silver's earthenware brazier, so we stoked up the fire, boiled water for soup and tea, and ended by getting a passable supper. By 7 p.m. the village was quiet, and an hour later the jungle-bound settlement was dead. Fearing that soon everyone would be asleep, we stumbled back up the paths in the darkness, stopping at a couple of Padaung houses to beg candles, matches and an oil lamp. And then we made ready for a long night.

In the light of the oil lamp, we dimly made out that someone had kindly deposited mats and a heap of blankets in our hut. We laid these out on the creaking uneven bamboo poles of the floor, strung up our mosquito net, and at 8.30 settled down to sleep. Once or twice figures appeared in the darkness at the open side of our hut, peering in at the two strange visitors in their net with the flickering pinpoints of light. But then they disappeared. All night long chickens and other animals scuffled around under the hut. The last thing I remember was the background orchestra of jungle frogs and grasshoppers, against which a little girl in her hut nearby was singing a plaintive Padaung song.

The following morning we tried to discover something about the enigmatic rings. With the aid of Silver, the Shan pharmacist and Ma Nang, we gleaned the following. As we already knew, not all long-neck women wore neck rings. It was a matter of family tradition, they explained. If the mother and grandmother wore them, the daughter might do so too. But there was no inevitability in this, and increasingly mothers asked their daughters if they wanted to continue the tradition. Increasingly, the daughters were refusing. When they wore the cumbersome rings, they stood out at school, and it was not practical for them to take part in activities such as sports. For these reasons, the long-neck tradition would probably die out before too long. One report has it that, with the Burmese discouraging the rings in the Kayah State, the number of women still wearing them there has sharply declined recently.

The rings were first put around a girl's neck when she was either about seven or eleven years of age. Initially four or five were put on, and then, at intervals of roughly five years, more were added. Up to the age of about twenty, the girls could remove the rings permanently. If they did so, they had to wear blankets around their necks for a while to support the neck, but the neck muscles could regenerate themselves. After about twenty, a girl could no longer dispense with the rings. Actually, the rings were not a set of individual rings at all. They were one continuous spiral or coil. The coils were made of Burmese bronze, and a complete spiral, 30 cms or 1-ft high, weighed between four and five kgs. Another misconception attached to these rings. It was not that the rings elongated the neck, but (according to X-ray tests carried out by the National Geographic magazine) that the rings squashed down the woman's collar bones and ribs. New bronze spirals came only from Burma, and there was a shortage of them for upcoming young girls. Old Padaung ladies, it seemed, took their rings with them to the grave.

There remained the simple and obvious question of why the Padaungs wore the rings. Was it cosmetic or what? A lot of apocryphal stories have been circulated in connection with this. A well-known one, now repeated by the Shan medicine man, ran that in the old days, when the Padaung men went hunting for four or five days in the jungle, tigers would come into the village and drag off the women in the hunters' absence. The women took to wearing rings to prevent themselves from being seized by the throat by the tigers. Ma Nang laughed on hearing this. The explanation, she said, was to do with Padaung mythology. According to this, man was the wind, while woman was a beautiful dragon. The original dragon-woman was impregnated by the wind to give rise to the first Padaung people. Ever since that time Padaung women had worn rings around their necks and legs in imitation of the first beautiful dragon-mother figure. We noticed how nowadays the coils had a practical purpose too. They were the preferred place where the Padaung ladies kept their banknotes. When, before leaving Mai Nai Soi, we went to buy our completed handwoven scarf from the village's oldest long-neck woman, she promptly tucked the 100-baht note down behind her rings.

CHAPTER 8

WORSTED IN WIZARDRY

Mae Hong Son - Khun Yuam - Mae La Oop - Mae Sariang

Taking leave in our minds of the poised long-neck ladies, of Darkie and our new Wa friends, we headed off from Mae Hong Son to Mae Sariang on the next leg of our journey. We had meanwhile recovered our Honda Wing from Chiang Mai. Riding south on it down Highway 108, we were also saying goodbye to the Shan section of the Thai-Burmese border. Until midpoint Khun Yuam, Karenni territory (the Kayah State) would shadow us to the west across the border, after which we would move into regular Karen country, on both sides of the border. For the rest of our journey, therefore, from Mae Hong Son all the way down to the Three Pagodas Pass, the Karen world was to be our new milieu.

What the trip down to Mae Sariang lacked in eventfulness (only a handful of villages en route), it made up for in terms of scenery and riding pleasure. Especially the first half of the 165-km journey was a motorcyclist's dream. Not far out of *ampoe muang*, before Pa Bong, a sign pointed down a dirt road to the village of Huai Dua and the River Pai - an area used in the shooting of Vietnam War-style films. Then the 108 began to climb steeply until it reached a viewpoint (km 18). From here one could look out headily over a deep V-shaped valley, dammed at the mouth, which sliced back into the mountainous eastern hinterland. After that, in a protracted descent, the narrow road twisted down to Huai Pong.

This initial section accounted for many of the celebrated 1800 curves between Chiang Mai and Mae Hong Son (coming by the 365-km long south route via Hot). Stopping in some places, we were able to line up four or five bends in a row, making a nice picture with the telephoto lens. The snaking road breasted endless ravishing wooded hillscape, before plunging like a roller coaster through an alternation of mountainous jungle and valley floors. These secluded floors, stepped with bright green paddies, were a sudden tonic for the eye. But the 108 was also a poor road - at least at this end. Its surface was filled with countless potholes, and its edges had frayed away, reducing the metalled part to single track. When an oncoming vehicle appeared, someone had to swerve out into the dust. It could not be long before this first section reverted to dirt road, after which reconstruction work would begin, lasting years.

After Huai Pong a rather better road continued on down through Mae Surin village and over a high plateau, before reaching - some 70 kms out from Mae Hong Son - the district town of Khun Yuam. At the outskirts a sign indicated the 1263 gravel road east up to the much vaunted Mae Surin waterfall and also to fields of *buatong* - golden flowers which every November covered the hillsides near the Hmong village of Mae U-kor.

MAP 7

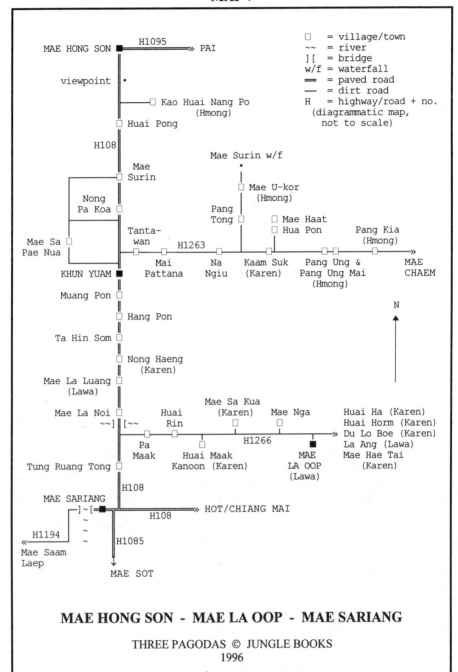

MAE HONG SON - MAE LA OOP - MAE SARIANG

THREE PAGODAS © JUNGLE BOOKS
1996

Khun Yuam

We were seduced into stopping over for a night in midway Khun Yuam not by the town itself, but, unusually, by a guesthouse. This was not the new place at the bottom end of town, nor the shuttered block halfway down the main street, but a tucked-away ranch-style complex at the northerly top end - a veritable oasis in an accommodation desert. It was run by an ageing Frenchman and was called, appropriately enough, *Ban Farang*. Amiable solicitous Monsieur Roger had an eye for detail and a feeling for ambience. His rooms were clean, comfortable and well-appointed, with thoughtful extras. This was the only lodging we ever found which had a UV mosquito electrocutor in every room. The place was a-twitter with an entourage of Shan girls, some from Burma. The pretty, round-faced Burmese-Shan lasses in the kitchen spoke not a word of Thai, let alone English, but they had learned to turn out a respectable *cordon bleu*.

Khun Yuam's busy main street lay tipped down the side of a steep hill. There was not a lot to see here. Although not immediately apparent, the town was a big logging centre, with Union Par Co. one of the key operators. Every third or fourth house down the main drag was involved in some way with the extraction and processing of hardwood from nearby Burma's virgin forests, and many of the shops were little more than fronts for dubious timber middlemen. Parked before their houses were dirty battered logging lorries, the trailing rear axle section of each one jumped up onto the back of the main lorry as if the two parts were copulating. In spite of the fact that Karenni territory lay to the west, Khun Yuam was actually a Shan outpost. The charm of the town was that it had remained traditional. Many of its buildings were still wooden shophouses. In the evenings tall thin *tai yai* housewives in conical hats sold savouries or sweetmeats directly out of their front rooms.

From Khun Yuam a flattish, relatively good road snaked for a long way down a valley. A succession of mountainsides and valley-floor paddies was punctuated by the villages of Muang Pon, Hang Pon, Ta Hin Som, Karen Nong Haeng and Mae La Luang, an assimilated Lawa place. The Honda was in its element, swinging through exquisite sunlit oriental countryside. We breasted groves of red-flowering lacquer trees, but there were also depressing sights - a number of massive log depots. Stopping once for a rest, we found at the roadside a carpet of outsize, dried-out teak leaves, measuring 2-ft long by 18 inches wide. They cracked like popadums under our feet. Further on, a Karen boy waved to us with a 5-ft brown snake he had caught. And then a truck overtook us, with a fully grown bull elephant in the back. At the moment the vehicle hauled past us, the beast decided to do a mighty piss, with the result that on our run in to Mae La Noi we had a free shower.

About thirty kms short of Mae Sariang, Mae La Noi was another assimilated Lawa village. The survivors here of the ancient people were now physically and culturally indistinguishable from local Thais. Seeing that we were about to head off into the hills again, we took a good lunch at one of the roadside eating places and stocked up with a few emergency provisions. We wanted to investigate Mae La Oop, a mountaintop Lawa village said to have remained traditional. *Songtaew* drivers were sitting around, waiting for the morning market to finish, and we quizzed them about the way up. For once they were gratifyingly precise. It was a dirt road (H1266), which started just south of Mae La Noi and went east 27 kms up into the mountains. It was not a bad road.

The drivers were right. Just beyond the bridge at the bottom end of the village a fair dirt road began wriggling its way into that vast highland wilderness that extended right across to Mae Chaem and the Doi Intanon massif (Thailand's highest mountain). Gently but uninterruptedly it climbed out of the River Yuam valley all the way up to Mae La Oop. The outlying villages of Pa Maak and Huai Rin gave way to the halfway Karen villages of Huai Maak Kanoon (south side) and Mae Sa Kua. The latter village in particular enjoyed an incomparable setting. About one km north of the track, it was an island cluster of roofs on a hilltop in a sea of forest. Tiny glints of Karen cerise (from washing hung out in the sun) could just be made out between the brown leaf rooftops in the endless canopy of green. Beyond it, to the north, the isolated settlement was backgrounded by bluish mountain ridges.

Presently, the road emerged from the forest cover into denuded upland country. Bald rounded mountaintops, covered only with scrub, receded mile after mile in every direction. Here and there, in the steep folds between the hillsides, lay out-of-the-way patches of terraced paddy. The headman of Mae La Oop later confessed to us that the Lawa themselves were responsible for this deforestation, having over the centuries cut all the trees down for house-building and firewood. The high-level trail continued for some distance through this bleak open cool terrain until, rounding the shoulder of a mountainside, we suddenly caught sight of our destination. La Oop, a concentration of wooden dwellings, lay on the far side of a valley, perched on the crest of a ridge like some precarious Tibetan outpost. It was but a short ride further until we came to the entrance to the outpost. Signs at the entrance said that the 1266 continued to the Karen villages of Huai Ha, Huai Horm and Du Lo Boe, as well as to the remote Lawa hamlet of La Ang (a further 28 kms). Ultimately the elevated dirt road would be pushed through to Mae Hae Tai, linking the area up with faraway Mae Chaem.

Mae La Oop

With 160 houses and the benefits of electricity, Mae La Oop was a relatively large and developed Lawa settlement. There were a couple of tiny stores, a fair-sized school at the bottom (southwesterly) end, a small temple, a health centre and some kind of government development building. But otherwise it was a traditional place, similar, for example, to Chang Mor - another typical Lawa village. The main street, an uneven surface of stamped earth and humps of polished rock, ran the length of the flat ridgecrest. From time to time dust squalls, caused by strange hot-air turbulances convecting up out of the valleys, scorched along it. Black pot-bellied pigs rooted around everywhere, along with dogs, chickens, buffaloes and cows. We even saw sheep in Mae La Oop. These domestic animals were kept for eating or trading, but also for sacrificing. Essentially the houses lined each side of the main street. Simple primitive affairs, high on stilts and mostly with grass roofs, they were nevertheless solidly built of wood and had spacious front platforms. From their mountaintop eyrie at nearly 4000 ft these Lawa enjoyed spectacular views to the north and south.

Near the village centre we found a group of people busy with ropes, levers and plumb lines, erecting the frame of a new house. We stopped to quiz them about accommodation. Everybody - man, woman and child - gathered round. They had dark coppery careworn faces, and virtually all except the infants were smoking a short pipe. The women and the older men were in some sort of costume, and the children all had hacking coughs. Most of the females were diminutive, and in general these people looked downtrodden, but they were very friendly. There was nowhere to stay in Mae La Oop, they reported, and no eating places either. We suggested the headman. Ah, the *po luang*, they said (a dialect word for *pu yai* or headman), yes, we could try there. It was the tin-roofed house over there with the new extension.

The headman, a pleasant fellow of about forty called Boonyeuan Promsermsook, was happy to let us camp in his new extension if we did not mind the total lack of furnishing. With no alternative, we naturally gratefully accepted his offer. His wife and daughters moved to bring us refreshments from the gloomy smoky kitchen at the back. We expressed a desire to clean up a little first. Immediately we ran into the two major problems of staying in a Lawa village - food and water. Living on a mountaintop might be defensively sound and agreeably cool, but it was hardly practical waterwise. Whereas most other hill-tribe and minority peoples douched themselves regularly towards sundown, the Lawa seemed never to wash at all. Of course, no rivers or streams ran up here, but there were large circular cement tanks around the village which collected rainwater. The Promsermsook family directed us to one of these near the school. But three months out from the end of the rainy season, the tank was already empty. We brought our problem to the village schoolteachers, and they invited us to wash in the "bathroom" under their house. But the modest plastic urn in their *hongnam* held hardly enough water to rinse our hands, let alone take a bodywash. Increasingly peeved, we returned to the *po luang* to report our fruitless errand. He referred us to a cubicle near his house which contained a cement trough, half full of water. But this had clearly not been used for some time. The water was infested with small wormlike organisms jack-knifing hither and thither. Preferring to remain dirty for two or three days than to risk picking up some awful tropical disease, we gave up the idea of trying to wash in Mae La Oop. It was not pleasant later that evening having to slip into our sleeping bags caked in sweat and dirt from the ride. The situation was salvaged to some extent the next day, when we discovered a spring halfway down the mountain. A twenty-minute walk down a zigzag path brought us to a pipe sticking out of the hillside, which dribbled water. Here we were able to clean up a bit, but we saw no Lawa doing likewise.

The headman and his womenfolk were exceptionally hospitable, bringing food three times a day. But it was always cold rice, a kind of marrow soup, a saucerful of tinned sardines, and bananas. We were glad of our emergency provisions from Mae La Noi, although instant noodles and coconut cake for breakfast, lunch and dinner was not a big improvement on the recurring marrow stew. The food problem in Mae La Oop was not helped by the fact that the drinking water (from heaven knows where) came from dirty old oil containers. Also the water, tea and even *lao kao* was drunk from metal goblets and glass tumblers ingrained with grime, while the food was served on enamelled tin plates which looked as if they had never been properly washed up. The situation was little different at Chang Mor, another Lawa village we once stayed in. It struck us as remarkable that a people so ancient as the Lawa and with an early history apparently so illustrious should now be so backward and unfastidious. Theirs seemed to be a civilization in steep decline.

Out on the balcony we had noticed chains and padding which looked like elephant working tackle, and we asked Boonyeuan if the Lawa used elephants and if he himself had any. They did use them, he replied, for dragging logs, and he himself had two elephants. Actually, until recently he had owned four, but had sold two in order to pay for his extension. While we were sitting on the bare wooden floor, eating our Ma-ma noodles and toying with the pee-coloured marrow soup, a succession of people called by to consult with the *po luang*, but mainly to gawp at us. They included the teachers, who were finalizing arrangements for some celebration on the morrow, village elders come to pass the time of day with their leader, women suckling babies, and half the children of Mae La Oop. After a while Boonyeuan brought from the kitchen some home-made rice whisky, which his wife was in the process of distilling at that very moment. We had brought with us a "flattie" (a half bottle) of Mekhong and added it to the supply. The Lawa made their *lao kao* out of rice and yeast only, and were partial to it, the headman being no exception. He liberally helped himself first to our Mekhong and then to his hooch. It was the beginning of an evening of conviviality which went on until the small hours. We took advantage of the opportunity to question the *po luang* and older villagers about the Lawa. Not least the people themselves were all agog to hear details and stories from their culture.

The Lawa people and culture

The Lawa did not call themselves Lawa, nor Lua (the Thai appellation), nor even the L'wa of old Thai chronicles, but La-wua. They were related to the Wa of NE Burma, and there were about 10,000 of them living in Thailand, accounting for 1.5% of the country's hill-tribe population. Most lived in this area, on the Bo Luang plateau, situated northeast of Mae Sariang and northwest of Hot, but there were a few living in other parts of the Kingdom, notably in Kanchanaburi province. In this mountain refuge Lawa lived in 22 villages, Boonyeuan calculated, and that included the five villages of the Chang Mor group, but excluded places like Mae La Noi in the Yuam valley or even Hua Lin, west of San Pa Tong (near Chiang Mai), in the Ping valley, where Lawa lived nearly or totally integrated into Thai society.

The Lawa are the remnants of an original Wa/Lawa race which hundreds of years ago, predating the arrival of the Tai peoples and even of the Mon, inhabited wide areas of present-day northern Thailand. Where they came from before that is not known for sure. One school of thought suggests Khmer territory (Cambodia), while another Malaysia and further south. The anthropologist Gordon Young believes their origins are Austronesian, from the south, and detects in the Lawa race hirsute, slightly negroid, Polynesian/Micronesian features, not the smooth-skinned Mongoloid features of peoples from the north. Some 2000 years ago, therefore, the Ur-(La)Wa may have migrated north, settling in northern Thailand as the first inhabitants there of recent history, i.e. discounting prehistoric inhabitants. Around 500-600 AD the Mons came from Lopburi to found their Haripunchai kingdom in the Ping valley, notably at Lampang and Lamphun (Lampoon). They chased the indigenous (La)Wa out of the fertile lowlands. About 500 years later the conquering Tai peoples began filtering down from the north. They pushed out the Mons and further squeezed the (La)Wa, relegating them to the mountainous areas of the provinces of Chiang Mai, Mae Hong Son, Chiang Rai, Supanburi, Kanchanaburi and Utaitani. In the mid-13th century AD the Tai took Haripunchai from the Mon to form Lan Na. Simultaneously they took Sukhothai from the Khmers. As the mighty dual Mon-Khmer civilization neared its end in Thailand, the first Tai kingdom was established in northern Thailand.

Migrating south, therefore, the Tais found (La)Wa already inhabiting the Shan plateau and parts of northern Thailand. It is said that until recently the rulers of Chiang Mai paid yearly tribute to the Lawa as the original owners of the land. The Lawa for their part claim with some justification to have founded Chiang Mai and, in particular, Wat Chedi Luang, the city's oldest temple and pagoda. The po luang of Mae La Oop told us the same story of the dispersal of the (La)Wa that Wa prince Maha San had narrated at Mae Or, only the other way round - seen from the Lawa point of view. One original folk had inhabited northern Thailand until displaced by the Mon and the Tai. While one group had moved to the Ob Luang plateau, becoming the Lawa, another had struck north to become the Wa of the Wa State in northeast Burma.

The airing of these details led an old man in our circle to rehearse a celebrated mythical account of the origins of the Lawa. They had actually once lived in the Salween valley area, but had been chased out of it into the Yuam valley by an extraordinary huge boulder. The Lawa had run up the narrow bed of the Mae La Noi river, but the rock had still pursued them. Finally the rock had lost sight of the fugitives and paused. A bird told the Lawa that they were safe where they were because the rock could not find them. This was how the Lawa had come to live in the inhospitable mountains above Mae La Noi. But the boulder was still in the stream where it had stopped, which was why, when people used the path down the La Noi streambed, they fell silent near the big boulder, for fear that it might start chasing them again if it heard their language. Another elder spoke of a time before the arrival of Mon and Tai rulers when the Lawa had had their own kings. The last of these was a certain Khun Luang Wilanka, and another legend accounting for the dispersal of the Lawa centred on him. Evidently he was involved in a magic contest with Chaam Taewi, the Mon Queen of Haripunchai (Lampoon). Worsted in the wizardry by this lady, Wilanka and his people beat a hasty retreat into the mountains to the west.

The Lawa language, variously classified as Austroasiatic or Austronesian, is related to Mon and Khmer, as well as to Khmu and Mrabri (the language of the "Pi Tong Luang"). To our non-expert ears it was Lao-sounding, reminiscent of Khmu. And, of course, as Maha San had claimed, it was related to Wa. The po luang *said that the Lawa for their part were able imperfectly to understand Wa people. Many words were the same or similar, for example the words for tree, house and dog (khao, nyie, so). We were able to put this beyond doubt when we fished out the beginners' Wa book Maha San's clan had given us. From the book we read out a list of Wa words and phrases, which some of the older Lawa present were able to identify for us in Thai. But their recognition of the Wa words and the link between Wa and Lawa was more remarkable than this. The literature says that Lawa has no written form. That may be true traditionally, but not in terms of recent history. When we handed the Wa booklet to our hosts, one or two of the oldest men were able to read it. The booklet was written in the Roman alphabet, so these Lawa elders were not just understanding Wa, but understanding it in written (Roman) form. They must have been able to read it on the basis of written Lawa, perhaps similarly systematized in the last hundred years (by missionaries?).*

We wondered if the Lawa had clannish hereditary chiefs, like the Wa mahas *or Shan* sawbwas, *with power and status being passed down through certain "noble" families. The* po luang *confirmed this. The headmanship had been in his family for three generations now, he said, although the Thai authorities were currently trying to stamp out the feudal practice by democratizing the way chiefs were chosen. Peter Kunstadter reports that these special families enjoy a* samang *(= khun, chao) lineage, some, apparently, being able to trace their pedigree back to the last Lawa king,*

Khun Luang Wilanka, or at least to one of his princes. Villagers owed allegiance to their chief, the samang *receiving payments of meat and money. With his ritual knowledge the* samang *was also held to be the local guardian of Lawa culture.*

Besides the samang, *Boonyeuan explained, Lawa villages also frequently had a* lam, *a spiritual leader who was often the oldest man in a group. The* lam *and to a lesser extent the* samang *were able to summon up the spirits. Animism was an important part of Lawa life. Some controversy attaches to the religion of these people. It is usually said that they are basically animists who have acquired a veneer of Buddhism. But there is another school of thought which believes that the Lawa were originally Buddhists who lapsed into animism after their displacement into the hills by the Mons. Whatever the case, the signs of Buddhism, at least in the Lawa villages we visited (Mae La Oop, Chang Mor and Om Pai), were few, while the signs of animism were many. La Oop had a small, apparently new wat, almost an afterthought, and the odd house had a tiny spirit shrine on its balcony, containing a Buddha image or amulet. But we saw plenty of cotton wrist strings, mirrors positioned beside doors into houses, and star-shaped bamboo Solomon's seals above the lintels - all animist devices for warding off evil spirits. In La Oop Christianity may have had a better hold than Buddhism. We were told that there were 46 converts in the village, won by a missionary who had now gone, leaving a Lawa priest in charge.*

The Lawa believed in a great pantheon of spirits. Spirits, divided into benevolent and malevolent, dwelt in all things, including humans, and people believed in them because their existence had repeatedly been demonstrated. It is worth detailing some of these spirits because they reflect the animism of so many hill-tribe and minority peoples in the border areas of Thailand. There were the spirits of the heavens, the sky, the mountain, forest, village, village entrance, house, people, the human body, and ancestors. Some of these could be further subdivided. The heaven-dwelling spirits included the important spirit lords of whole areas and of towns, while the forest spirits comprised the spirits of the virgin jungle, certain kinds of tree, fallen trees, landslides, streams, white ants and so on. Humans, like other creatures, were inhabited by 32 special spirits or souls. Illness was when the body was invaded by a bad soul or when one of its own souls departed. When that happened, either cotton yarn was tied around the invalid's wrist and neck or the departed soul was invited to re-enter the person's body via a boiled egg! It was not just the wrist cords, mirrors and Solomon's seals which could ward off evil spirits. Members of a household could be protected against bad spirits, illness, theft and misfortune by the house spirits, which might reside, for example, in a large spider. An interesting belief of the Lawa was that certain people were inhabited by the spirits of tigers. This enabled them to carry out amazing feats of strength or endurance. They could, for example, cover great distances very fast, and were held actually to be tigers.

This colourful world of spirits could be engaged through propitiation, divination, shamanistic communication, exorcism and the mechanisms of deflection and protection already mentioned. Especially the lam, *but also the* samang *or old people, could be agents in these processes. They could summon up spirits and cast out bad ones from ill villagers' bodies. Omens could be read in an animal's entrails, for example in a chicken's gall bladder. If the bladder was shiny and full of liquid, the auspices were good, and ploughing, say, might be commenced. If that was not the case, and the omens were bad, there might perhaps be some swapping around of fields among families to create a new disposition of circumstances. The spirits could be approached and propitiated either by giving them food or by making sacrificial offerings to them, which often amounted to the same thing. The headman singled out for us two important propitiatory ceremonies held annually in Mae La Oop. One was to honour the ancestors. The Lawa were ancestor worshippers, and every July the villagers offered one buffalo to the spirits of their forebears. The other was an offering to the spirit of the village. Made every 10 November by the two oldest inhabitants of Mae La Oop, it involved the sacrifice of eight pigs or cows or whatever - the type of animal was rotated, while in other Lawa villages the number of animals offered differed. Small pieces of meat were placed on an altar for the relevant spirit to eat. The spirits did not have big appetites, the* po luang *observed drily, nor did they like chilli peppers. This meant that the sacrifice of a buffalo or of eight pigs left the villagers with a jolly good feast. Altogether, with so many different spirits, there was no shortage of work - and eating - to be done.*

When, therefore, a Lawa villager died, he or she became a spirit. The Lawa did not burn the corpses of their dead folk, like the Buddhists, but buried them. The death was followed by a wake, with the sacrifice of animals, and eating and drinking. In general, the mourning seemed to resemble Karen funerals. The corpse was kept in the house, and the local youngsters processed around it, singing.

Courtship and marriage was a business for the Lawa hardly less involved than their animism. To the amusement of our little gathering, Boonyeuan explained how a would-be bridegroom went and "captured" his sweetheart, holding her secretly for one week. Then he went to the girl's parents to "confess". All being well, a date was fixed for the wedding, and the suitor paid to the bride's family a bride-price - a certain amount of silver. Animal offerings were made, and in La Oop a buffalo was slaughtered, to be eaten during seven days of marriage celebrations. Regulated by tradition, the bride-price consisted of a fixed amount of old silver coinage, to which was added eight pairs of candles as well as betel nuts and leaves. Boonyeuan's wife fetched a bag containing such money. In it were silver Indian rupees bearing the heads of "Queen and Empress" Victoria, and Kings Edward VII and George V. But more interesting for us were some examples of old Thai currency. These were the celebrated "dog's penis" pieces, so called because of their shape. One was stamped

2411, making it 125 years old. The giving of the bride-money was to some extent ritualistic. The eighteen or so pieces were not so much actually given away, as just symbolically handed over. They tended to remain in the owner's family, passed down from generation to generation. Poor people could borrow the special money for the duration of a marriage ceremony, returning it afterwards.

The Lawa were mostly monogamous, and divorce was unusual. Residence was traditionally patrilocal. After marriage, a woman moved to her husband's house, although sometimes a couple set up a new house of their own. She did not move in with him if he was remarrying, when understandably she would not want to live in the house of his ex-wife. In that situation he might move into her house. People mostly married in the winter. In the winter of 1993/94 ten couples got married in Mae La Oop. An interesting detail was that some of the older villagers in La Oop were married to Khmu people. Khmu sometimes came across from northeast Thailand or from Laos to marry Lawa. The relation of the Lawa language to Wa, but also to other tongues in the Mon-Khmer family, such as Khmu, H'tin and Mrabri, has already been mentioned. But the affinities do not end there. Obscure but undeniable connections exist between these ancient indigenous peoples. Although widely dispersed, they continue to have truck with each other. The po luang *of Chang Mor told us that his father was a Khmer trader who had come over this way from Cambodia, married a Lawa and stayed.*

The showing of the dog's penis pieces encouraged several people to slip away and return with family heirlooms. The Lawa are traditionally skilled silversmiths, and soon the floor was awash with silver. One elder in particular emptied out of a *yaam* a cascade of items. As he was old, single and childless, he offered to sell some of them to us. Here were chunky Lawa bracelets; pairs of large cup-shaped earrings; sets of antique Shan betel boxes, repousséd with animals and mythical figures and engraved on the base with Shan or Burmese lettering; characteristic Lawa pipes in silver and wood, in the shape of a U-tube and embellished with silver wire; and a strange Lawa coronet in the form of an expandable band, decorated on one side with a kind of upstanding diamond or star. The hoard put the headman in mind of a favourite Lawa legend which related to other treasure. There used once to be a book, complete with maps, which showed where all the treasure of the Lawa, mainly silver, was buried. Unfortunately, one of the Siamese kings had got hold of this and hidden it. He had then died, and the inventory had been lost for generations. But there was a rumour that the treasure book had recently been found in Chiang Dao cave....

It was already after midnight, late by hill-tribe standards. Many people had drifted away, but some remained, unwilling to pass up any titbit relating to their culture or history. Eventually, even these lingerers disappeared, leaving just the headman and ourselves. We were weary and would gladly have retired too, but *po luang* Promsermsook insisted on just one more nip of *lao kao* - to round off a pleasant evening. Finally, he got up too, and, our heads reeling from too much tipple with insufficient substance in our stomachs, we crawled into our sleeping bags. Our dreams were a welter of rolling boulders, treasures troves, King Wilanka, Wa words and Khmu people.

Only an hour or two later, at 5.30 a.m., we were awakened by clumping across the wooden floor. We tried to hide our heads inside our sleeping bags, but to little avail. Wailing Lawa music regaled us from a cassette recorder, and outside millions of cicadas made a piercing racket in the trees. Poking our heads out after a while, we found the headman sitting exactly where he had been the evening before. He was cleaning and playing with some kind of rifle, making a loud snick every time he pressed the trigger. A bottle of *lao* already stood in front of him together with a small glass. It was as if he had not moved the whole night long. There was a silver workshop in Mae La Oop, the headman mused. He himself would be busy with the teachers that morning, but we might like to visit it on our own. We breakfasted on more stewed marrow and cold rice, and then, eager for a wash, searched out the dribbling pipe halfway down the mountainside. Refreshed, we set off up the main street to investigate the silversmithery.

The workshop was located in a house near the entrance to the village. It was only a small affair. With a set of primitive tools two young men were transforming small stamped bullets of silver into bracelets, fine chains and exquisite round repoussé boxes. The finished products were sold in Chiang Mai's Night Bazaar. It was not so much these objects that interested us as a strange stone artifact which the boys showed us. This was antique and fitted pleasingly into the palm of the hand when one wrapped one's fingers around it. It was smooth to the touch and seemed to us to be vaguely shaped like a duck. Smirking, the young men explained that the stone imitated a woman's genitalia. It was only when we examined it more closely that we saw their point. The stone was articulated. A male half fitted snugly into a female half. The two could be wiggled slightly, but not parted. The stone was an erotic object which a boy fondled in his hand when he went to flirt with a girl. It was supposed to bring him good luck on his errand.

·In many houses in La Oop women were weaving on their balconies. The Lawa were not just fine silversmiths (and workers of iron), but also skilled weavers. Their looms were of that simple type where one end was attached to the house wall, while the other formed a backrest. When a woman, sitting on the floor, leaned back against the rest, she tautened the warp strings and could then weave across her lap. The women were mostly weaving material for skirts and shoulderbags. With La Oop being a traditional Lawa village, one of the joys of a visit there was the spectacle of the women and older men in costume. The clothes were not like Wa costume, except in the matter of the skirt. Rather they seemed to us to show some Karen influence (the Lawa and the Karen have become closely associated over the last century or two), something which *po luang* Promsermsook flatly denied.

The women wore a tube skirt, basically black or indigo or blue with horizontal banding of dark red or pink, but also sometimes of azure or white. They had a white or beige smock top, reminiscent of the Karen shift. On their lower legs were indigo leggings, held in place by black bands, and above these, just below the knee, were bangles made from the lac tree, which were thought to contain a protective spirit. Sometimes "leggings" were worn on the arm, held in place by a silver band. The most distinctive thing about Lawa women were their numerous strings of small beads. The preferred colour for these was coral, but red, yellow and azure were also common, strings of each layered in swathes one over the other. In the ears big cup-shaped "drum" earrings of silver were worn, making large holes in the women's ear lobes. In Chang Mor we saw some ladies wearing beads suspended from their ears and looped under the chin. And then, of course, there was the white or pink *yaam*, and the inevitable little pipe. The men's costume, by contrast, was very simple. Baggy, off-white, heavy cotton trousers were complemented by an open jacket in the same colour and material, the whole reminiscent of a judo outfit. Many men were tattooed. The tradition was to bear two tigers on the back for fending off evil spirits, and to have densely tattooed emblems (such as cat figures) down the thighs, making it look as if the men were wearing culottes.

We searched the faces of the Lawa in Mae La Oop. Sometimes it seemed to us that the wide-eyed children looked like "Yellow Leaf" Mrabri infants we had seen, while some of the girls had Darkie's beauty. Other times we thought we saw in their mothers the placid round faces of Khmu and Lao women, while the men, with their dark angular faces and (for orientals) unusual hairiness of face and limb, resembled the wild sharp-featured hirsute Wa. But these people remained enigmatic. Here was a race, like their cousins the Wa, waiting to be understood. And if their history was obscure, the investigation and archaeology of Lawa prehistory had not even started. Almost the most enigmatic question was how a people apparently once so prominent could now be so reduced. Their ancient faces were unmistakably careworn, and behind the openness, friendliness and hospitality there was an undeniable squalor. The villages were impoverished and disorderly. Their agro-economy was near subsistence level, with many Lawa men working as itinerant labourers. Sanitation was poor, and clothing was mostly dirty. Kitchens were gloomy and soot-encrusted, and cups and plates were unbearably grimy. The food was unappealing, and water was lacking. The Lawa, like the Wa or Mrabri, seemed to be a tribe hopelessly compromised in history by the appearance of other peoples, in this case by the Mons, Khmers, Tais, Burmese, and latterly even the Karens.

Mae Sariang

27 kms back down off the mountain and a further 30 kms south of Mae La Noi we reached Mae Sariang. Had we not spotted signs suddenly reading "Hot: so-and-so-many kms", we would have sped clean past the town on a bypass. A last-minute turn west just after a petrol station slewed us into the beginning of Mae Sariang's long main street, the Wiang Mai Road. Until the 1960s, when Highway 108 was first built, the town, like Mae Hong Son, was another utterly inaccessible place on the remote northwestern fringes of the Kingdom. Even afterwards few penetrated here unless they were cattle dealers or Karen National Union and Thai Army officers come to liaise about border security. Things remained that way until the late 80s, when the town began to figure in the itineraries of people making the Chiang Mai - Mae Hong Son loop. In the early 90s a handful of intrepid travellers realized that Mae Sariang lay not only on the road north to Mae Hong Son, but at the gateway to the marvellous new 1085 border route south to Mae Sot. But these visitors and the ever-so-slight boom they brought with them has scarcely more than stirred the spot's age-old calm.

What at first seemed to us an unremarkable backwater quickly grew on us as an intriguing little nest. Like Nan or even Pai, Mae Sariang was an authentic, laid-back, minding-its-own-business kind of place which could easily in its own right claim the visitor for a pleasant relaxing stay. It was also in our experience a town almost like no other made for running into like-minded travellers. Anyone looking for a travelling companion would be much better advised to linger here (or in similar places like Mae Sot or Nan) than in a confusing metropolis such as Chiang Mai. Mae Sariang's variety of religious buildings told that its 7500 inhabitants were a good mix. As we scooted around the streets, we found Burmese/Shan-style temples for the Shans and Thais, a mosque in the market area for the Muslim Indo-Burmese and Chinese, and a Christian church in the main street in part for Karens. A 10-ft high phallic *lak muang* or town pillar, standing in front of the old police station and covered in squares of gold leaf, was a focal point for animist tendencies. This old police headquarters, situated in the Mae Sariang Road next to the new station, was a fine teak building. It was one of the many old wooden houses and shophouses still standing which made the town so pleasing to the eye.

Our hunt for accommodation in Mae Sariang was characteristic of the search that had to be embarked upon every time one arrived in a new provincial town. Proceeding down the Wiang Mai Road away from Highway 108, we spied first a promising-looking place called *New Mitaree* or *Mitaree Guest House N°. 2*. The reception was spic and span, and a Chinese lady led us down a lot of clean corridors past pristine rooms. The odd thing was that they were all unoccupied. Finally, we came to the room she had singled out for us, and inside we found very agreeable accommodation with a hot shower. It seemed a bargain at 120 baht per night. But back at the reception, we discovered the scam. Fortunately verifying the rate before we moved in, we learned that the room was suddenly 240 baht - 120 per person. Of course, we showed the lady a clean pair of heels. But who would have wanted to stay in this complex anyway? In the maze of concrete corridors and rooms a guest would have felt about as comfortable as Rudolf Hesse in Spandau Prison.

We called in next at the *Mitaree Hotel* in the town centre. A large typical Chinese establishment, it must have been the original which spawned the *New Mitaree*. For an acceptable sum the management wanted to put us in the shabby hotel annexe. Everything inside and out was painted pale green, and our room neighbour would have been a bent old Indian man, renting by the month. Checking out the beds in every room, we soon discovered the reason for his bowed posture. They all rose at the foot and head ends. Sleep would have been impossible except by lying on our backs. While we continued to scout round town, a youth on a moped drew level with us. He was touting for custom for a guesthouse with the singular name of *See View* and invited us to come and have a look. But when we got there, there was no sea or lake or indeed any view to see, except a sand quarry with a row of parked tipper trucks.

Mae Sariang GH had acceptable rooms but no hot water, and *Hunter GH* had appeared, only to disappear again. It was all typical of the guest-house scene in Thailand. Places mushroomed overnight, to go under just as suddenly, and standards went up and down like a yo-yo. Our quest ended at the *Riverside GH*, a typical traveller hang-out. The four-storey building was built on the steep southern bank of the River Yuam. A bamboo bridge from the main house crossed the sluggish flow to a spur of scrubby parkland on the far side. Here, in a bend of the river, a clutch of primitive bamboo bungalows supplemented the bedrooms in the house. Overlooking the Yuam and the parkland was a pleasant balcony restaurant with a travellerish menu, listing dishes half *farang*, half Thai. Around the walls were maps and details of local tours, together with a mini-library of well-thumbed paperbacks and magazines from countries around the world. In this relaxed place there always seemed to be someone to chat to.

After a first night in one of the cool gloomy spartan rooms underneath the restaurant, we moved across the river into a bungalow. The bungalows were much favoured by "smokers", and in the one next to us a serious withdrawn Japanese boy had settled in for the season. To get a hot (= lukewarm) shower, we had to stagger over the swaying bridge to the bathrooms in the main building - no piece of cake at the best of times, but in the dark or after Mekhong (or a good smoke) a hazardous adventure. One of these bathrooms had a feature to titillate the exhibitionist. The window, glassless but barred, looked directly into a cage of monkeys. Precisely at the moment one was stark naked and trying to adjust the shower, they came to the window and stared in. Another titbit amused us at the *Riverside*. One morning we were having breakfast on the balcony when two girls, aged about fourteen, both very ordinarily dressed in jeans and T-shirts, tried to come in. They were Karen prostitutes. The lady at reception threw them out, but they remonstrated, saying that they had been in before and they only wanted to meet some men. She shooed them away again, but just as they were going, she relented, saying that they could come in if they paid 5 baht each.

With accommodation sorted out, the next priority was food. *Renu* restaurant in the main street had inviting décor, but always seemed empty. *Ruan Prae*, an eating place in a side street not far from *Renu*, boasted a celebrated cook, but was never open. Which left *Intira*, the restaurant almost opposite *Renu*. It was *Renu's* misfortune to be situated facing *Intira*, for without doubt *Intira* was the most satisfactory eating place in Mae Sariang. It had good food, prompt service and fair prices, which meant that no evening was complete without a meal and a drink in it. The teenage fetchers and servers were assiduous and rewarded faithful customers in discreet ways - large portions or discounted bills. The décor was unprepossessing, and yet the place hummed equally with local people and *farang* visitors. The food was not connoisseur's fare, but their fried beef in tomato sauce or renowned chicken with basil and chillies was most acceptable.

Opening onto the busy main street, *Intira* could be a noisy place. But sitting there of an evening just before New Year watching the local people and events outside, we could begin to get our finger on the pulse of Mae Sariang, appreciating its real *raison d'être*. A constant stream of cattle trucks rumbled loudly up the main street, beginning a long night journey to Chiang Mai or Bangkok. BMWs, fabulously expensive by Thai standards, were parked at the roadside. Groups of traders and dealers made their way into the girlie "singing place" adjoining *Intira* to drink Chivas Regal. It was a mini Mae Sot. The town, booming on the back of a flourishing cross-border trade, was a major transit point for goods - notably cattle and teak, but no doubt other valuable commodities as well - coming across from nearby "Kawthoolei", the Karen State, in Burma.

CHAPTER 9

REBEL HQ

Mae Sariang - Mae Saam Laep - Manerplaw

Prince Maha San had recommended to us in Mae Or that we should visit Manerplaw. Said to mean "Victory Field" or "Land of Victory" and pronounced "Ma Noe Plo", Manerplaw (I shall adopt the established spelling) was the GHQ inside Burma of the insurgent Karen National Union and its military wing, the Karen National Liberation Army. It was also the HQ of the National Democratic Front, the principal anti-government alliance in Burma of a dozen ethnic rebel organizations, of which the Wa National Organization was one. Maha San, leader of the Wa and chairman of the WNO, thought that on the strength of our connection with him we stood a fair chance of reaching this supreme rebel HQ. He had given us the names of contacts en route who might help us and the name of somebody to ask for when we arrived. All this set in train a little side trip from Mae Sariang west to the border which we would certainly have abandoned, so terrible was the way, had not the ultimate goal been so alluring.

We had first to get down to Mae Saam Laep, a village on the River Salween, which at that point formed the frontier. The 46-km ride down "Highway" 1194 began innocuously enough. The road left Mae Sariang on the western side by Wat Kitti Wong, crossed the Yuam river bridge, and swung south and then west. Almost immediately the logging route to the Salween hamlets of Mae Kong Ka and Mae Sa Koep branched off right. Our road wound out through the fringes of town, past outlying villages and through lurid green paddy fields. A modest paved affair, it afforded a glimpse of rural Thailand in a wide fertile valley. The lakeside *Baitong* restaurant yielded to an isolated petrol station, and after the village of Huai Sing (km 15) the paved section of road gave over to orange dirt.

Huai Po (km 20) was immediately followed by Tatafang Police Station, where for some inexplicable reason an amiable policeman politely saluted us. The 1194 now plunged into forested hill country, climbing up and up to a pass, before descending at length into marvellous jungle scenery. In a ravine tall trees, covered in moss-like epiphytic plants, dripped with lianas. Several herds of emaciated cows and buffaloes, 20-50 strong, came against us. Driven by solitary Karen boys with knapsacks, they had wandered from deep inside Burma, crossed the Dawna Range, ferried or swum the Salween, and were now nearing the end of their epic journey. Sadly, beyond Mae Sariang only a truckride separated them from the slaughter-houses of Chiang Mai and Bangkok.

To better cater for the trade in Burmese livestock (and also timber), the 1194 was slowly being improved. In this middle section we came across a

MAP 8

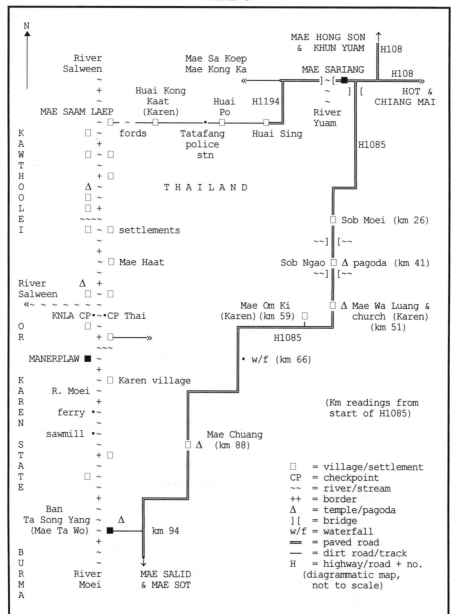

```
N
↑
                                        MAE HONG SON ↑
                                       &  KHUN YUAM    H108
         River                 Mae Sa Koep
         Salween               Mae Kong Ka      MAE SARIANG    H108
                       +                          ]~[■            HOT &
                       ~      Huai Kong                  ~   ] [  CHIANG MAI
                            Kaat        Huai    H1194      ~
         MAE SAAM LAEP     (Karen)      Po          River
                      ~ □ ~  fords  □    □     □    Yuam
K         □ ~          Tatafang                     H1085
A         +            police
W         □ ~ □        stn
T         ~
H         + □
O         Δ ~              T H A I L A N D
O         □ ~
L         □ +
E       ~~~~                                    □ Sob Moei (km 26)
I         □ ~ □ settlements
          ~                              ~~] [~~
          +
          ~ □ Mae Haat              Sob Ngao □ Δ pagoda (km 41)
          ~                              ~~] [~~
River   Δ +
Salween   □ ~ □                                □ Δ Mae Wa Luang &
«~ ~ ~ ~ ~ ~ ~           Mae Om Ki               church (Karen)
     KNLA CP•~•CP Thai    (Karen)(km 59) □          (km 51)
O       □ ~
R       + □————»              H1085
      ~~~
  MANERPLAW ■ ~          • w/f (km 66)
       +
K      ~ □ Karen village
A    R. Moei ~                        (Km readings from
R        +                            start of H1085)
E   ferry •~
N        ~
  sawmill •~
S        + □          Mae Chuang
T        ~          □ Δ  (km 88)
A        ~
T      □ ~                              □  = village/settlement
E        ~                             CP = checkpoint
         ~                             ~~ = river/stream
  Ban    ~                             ++ = border
Ta Song Yang ~   Δ                     Δ  = temple/pagoda
 (Mae Ta Wo) ~  ■   km 94              ][ = bridge
         +                             w/f = waterfall
B        ~                             ══ = paved road
U        ~                             —  = dirt road/track
R     River     MAE SALID              H  = highway/road + no.
M     Moei      & MAE SOT                (diagrammatic map,
A                                         not to scale)
```

MAE SARIANG - MANERPLAW - BAN TA SONG YANG

THREE PAGODAS © JUNGLE BOOKS
1996

number of bridges under construction. The roadbuilders' encampments lay at intervals beside the route. It was not long before we reached the cutting edge of the improvements. Bulldozers and levellers were hacking a way along the side of the valley through virgin jungle. Now we were routed onto an old track along the ravine floor. Ominously it was strewn with large boulders which had rolled down from the workings above. This was the first hint of the trouble ahead. Weaving our way through the rocks, we suddenly drew up at a river. On the other side lay a ramshackle Karen settlement, named Huai Kong Kaat. We could see that the track picked up on the far bank, passing through the dozen huts. Clearly the river had to be forded. Some children at play gleefully spotted a *farang* coming, and in an instant the whole village had turned out. Luckily we rode without mishap through the water and on up through the hovels. As we passed, not one person moved or said anything, which was strange. Later we learned that *farangs* hiking to Mae Saam Laep had several times been robbed in this ravine, some near the village.

After Huai Kong Kaat the real nightmare began. The track ran for seven or eight kms down the bed of the river, dishing up a mess of mud, water, sand, gravel, stones and small boulders. Where the bed widened, the river broke up into a network of rivulets and islands. Here the track kept losing itself, and we cast around trying to find a way through. In a short space the water had to be forded between fifty and sixty times. It was filthy exhausting work, and these last few kms alone took us on our Wing the best part of two hours. What was particularly galling was the knowledge that before long people would be swanning down here in minibuses on a fine new road. Towards the end we even nearly missed the way into Saam Laep, which veered off to the right up the river bank. Continuing on down the riverbed, we all but ran into the Salween. But that would not have mattered - it was the way the cattle and the trading trucks came.

Mae Saam Laep

Ascending the right-hand bank, we passed through one of those wooden arch-like portals which typically mark the entrance to obscure villages and hit the first houses of Mae Saam Laep. A sign by a police box required visitors to report with their passports and enter their names in the register. However, the policeman on duty seemed unconcerned, and we rode on into the narrow main street. This was a long winding rutted mud road, clinging, like the outpost itself, to the precipitous eastern bank of the Salween. It was immediately noticeable that both the number of stores and the profusion of their merchandise was quite out of proportion to the size of the village, which was strange, until we remembered that Mae Saam Laep was one of the principal gateways by which goods entered and left Kawthoolei, the Karen State, in Burma. Indeed, with Rangoon itself seeking increasingly to cash in on these gateways - Kawmoorah (Ko Mu Ra), Wa Lae and the Three Pagodas Pass, for example, all fell to the Burma Army at the start of the 90s - Mae Saam Laep was rapidly becoming the most important of all.

THREE PAGODAS

A steep flight of steps led down from the main street into the Salween riverbed. Outside the rainy season the famous river, which coursed down to Burma from China and Tibet, withdrew here into a narrow central channel, lined on each side by black craggy rocks. With the waters receded, extensive banks of white sand lay exposed. They were so dazzling in the intense light that we had to screw up our eyes. The strong dosage of UV radiation had blackened the skins of the local people and burnt out the colours all around. Down on these scorching sandbanks we found to our surprise numerous small blue lorries. They were no ordinary vehicles, but were covered in searchlights and had their exhaust pipes and air filters sticking up above the cabs. For a moment we wondered it they actually crossed the Salween, but, considering the depth of the river and the power of its current, that was clearly impossible. Also the trucks were all waiting for something, although far and wide there seemed to be nothing that they could possibly be waiting for. It was enigmatic and suspicious. In the shade of some of the lorries the owners and their families were sitting having lunch. We quizzed them about the mystery, but got only evasive answers. Finally, one man volunteered that he was expecting some cattle "and other things". The lights and exhaust systems were designed for the way back down to Mae Sariang. Often the trucks ploughed back up the riverbed in the night. When I photographed one of them, a man came over and harangued me, saying that I should confine myself to taking pictures of nature, not of his truck. We began to feel uneasy in this out-of-the-way place.

It was a motley collection of people hanging around at Mae Saam Laep. The fact that there was no sign of any authority, other than the solitary policeman at the entrance to the village, hardly lessened our feeling of disquiet either. Nowhere was this more the case than in the market area, laid out on the sand at the foot of the village. Two lines of makeshift stalls with leaf roofs curved down towards the river. Of course, there were many Karens in the village, but they were mostly not the traditional type one met all down the western Thai border with their pink and green clothing and shoulderbags. They were wearing no costume at all. There were Thai wheeler-dealers taking advantage of the cross-border trade and of the smuggling. There were unaccountable black-faced Burmese in *longyis*. There were Burmese Indians with little beards, their black faces and white eyes peering out of the gloom of their shops, scrutinizing us. Some of the women and girls in the market were heavily made up and in fancy clothes quite incongruous for such a rough place. They were prostitutes, waiting to accompany a flush trader or grimy backwoodsman to some shabby hut. At the bottom of the market alley, by the water's edge, we found a shack with a snooker table in it. It was flanked by two gambling dens. Groups of men squatted on the sand floor around mats which were divided up into sections with symbols of chickens and other things on them. The dice, with corresponding symbols on their sides, were watched intensely, and, depending on how they fell, substantial banknotes changed hands.

Gambling was illegal in Thailand, but we got the impression that in this respect, as in many others, the authorities here turned a blind eye. Anything went in Mae Saam Laep. It was extraterritorial, controlled by neither the Thais, nor the KNU, but a law unto itself. The village was altogether one of the rawest, most riveting and exhilirating corners we found anywhere on our journey.

The market was a cornucopia of merchandise which even Mae Sariang could hardly match. For such an isolated spot the colourful assortment of fresh produce, groceries and other household items was all the more remarkable. But on the other hand the village was where Karen potatoes met Thai condensed milk, and dried Burmese prawns from the Andaman Sea intersected with yellow noodles brought down from China. Overestimating the facilities of Manerplaw, we made a mistake in not stocking up with provisions here. A vegetable and fruit stall was piled high with immaculate cauliflowers, the choicest *mange tout* peas, tomatoes, potatoes, cabbages, shallots, garlic, green aubergines, ginger, green and red chilli peppers, pineapples, coconuts, oranges, water melons and jujubes. Next to it was an Aladdin's cave of cooking oil, bottles of pork fat, shrimp and fish paste, fresh fish, dried fish, eggs, peanuts, Singha beer, *lao kao*, bottled water, black tea, rice, noodles, bread rolls, blocks of cane sugar, tubes of ground pork meat, dried bananas and mushrooms, prawn crackers, and sachets of sunflower seeds for snacking on. Packs of dark brown discs caught our eye, and we enquired what they were. *Tua now kap* or "rotten bean squash", a lady laughed, using northern Thai dialect. They were compressed roundels of dried-out yellow bean mash, used for making curry sauces and chilli dips. And then there was a smoking counter. Bundles of Burmese Best Thukita cheroots, 50 for 10 baht (a terrific bargain), were stacked up alongside mounds of loose tobacco and cartons of Thai Khrong Thip cigarettes, contraband Marlboro and various Burmese and Chinese brands (for example, Fortune, Hunter, Horse and Xinxing). A round-faced Burmese-looking girl minding the stall was also doing a brisk business in betel chews. From a variety of pots she took different kinds of betel paste and spread them on green leaves, which were then folded up, bought by the customer and chewed. The litter of messy tins and caked spatulas on the spattered counter was a bit like an art class in an infants' school. And all this was not to take into account the ironmongery stalls, clothes shops and refreshment stands.

At the end of the market alley, by the Salween, there was a small bay, where some 25 longtail boats of all sizes were moored. Some were very large, and it was these which were used for bringing the livestock across the river, either transporting the animals on board or swimming them over with their heads roped to the sides. Teak logs were manhandled across in a similar fashion, and of course the *hang yao* provided a regular service for people, ferrying them and their goods back and forth, as well as up and down the river. On the far side of the swirling fast-flowing Salween, directly opposite Mae Saam Laep, there was little except mountains and jungle. A clearing on the other bank was littered with hardwood trunks waiting to be floated across. Behind them, on a knoll, stood two buildings - perhaps a Karen "customs" point, where taxes would be levied on everything passing through. A track went off past the knoll into the interior. Looking back towards Thailand, we could take in the whole of bustling sinister Mae Saam Laep in one sweep. The longtails with their Thai or Karen flags and massive engines lay tied to the "beach". The empty trucks waited sizzling in the sun. The gambling sheds and market straggled across the sand to the steep hillside. The tiers of wooden houses of the village proper perched precariously on the hillside on long stilts. And above the village a small Burmese-style *wat* crouched in the background.

At the upper end of the market, in a small eating place, we ordered gravy noodles with pork and greens. While we were waiting for the food to arrive, we noticed a pair of booted feet sticking out through a curtain across a doorway. Behind it a walkie-talkie could also be seen hanging from a chair back. Presently, a KNLA officer emerged, rubbed his eyes, and continued with whatever he had been doing before his nap - perhaps travelling upriver. As we ate, a continuous stream of men went past, humping sacks of rice and other necessities down to the longtail boats. We asked our cooking lady about accommodation in Mae Saam Laep. It was this lady who told us about the robberies on the road up from Mae Sariang. She said that there had once been a guesthouse in the village, but that it had burnt down in mysterious circumstances. The headman sometimes let out rooms, but if we wanted, we could stay in her house.... We thanked her, saying that we were hoping to travel on. This led us to ask her if she knew how we could find our contacts. Maha San had told us of some dissident Burmese students operating clandestinely in Mae Saam Laep who should be able to help us on our way. The village was a large place, we explained, and it would be difficult for us to hunt out the contacts on our own. The cooking lady knew exactly who we wanted and, lowering her voice, indicated where we could find them - at the back of a certain shop.

Sure enough, when we asked at this shop, two Burmese men in sarongs appeared. Communication was difficult because they spoke no Thai, although one of them had a smattering of English. But they soon understood what we wanted. They themselves had no direct link with Manerplaw, they explained, but were agents for the ABSDF HQ of Daungguin, thirty minutes by boat upstream (north). Why did we not go there instead? Lying, we said that we wanted first to go to Manerplaw for New Year, but would come on to them afterwards. It was a stroke of luck that we never visited their camp, for a few days later it was attacked by the Burma Army, a number of student revolutionaries perishing. The two men bade us sit down while they went to make enquiries. The contacts seemed to us to be not quite all they had been cracked up to be, and we began to fear that we would never get to Manerplaw. But we were wrong. Soon they returned and reported that everything was arranged. Suddenly, we were overtaken by events. A *hang yao*, which we could travel on, was now waiting for us. It would leave for Manerplaw in five minutes, and we should get down to the water immediately. There was a big problem with our motorbike, we remonstrated. Should we leave it here or take it with us or have it transported back to Mae Sariang? Give us the keys, one of the duo pressed, we will sort it out. We surrendered our £1000 hire bike to unfathomable people we had never seen before, hurried to get our backpacks from the noodle restaurant, and strode down to the longtails. We arrived to see the Honda being lifted aboard one of them, where it was lashed down. We climbed in too, along with a dozen other passengers, and within minutes the boat set off with a great roar of its outsize engine. We had not even had time to ponder the wisdom of our move, let alone make a few hasty purchases for the trip. As we headed off to an unknown fate in a murky region very far from anywhere and embroiled in a civil war, we reflected that, well, at least there was no turning back now. On the backrest of one of the boats' seats was painted in English: BE HAPPY AND SMILE. In the circumstances it was the best and only thing to do.

Fifty baht each bought us a thrilling two-hour boat trip south down the Salween. It was a ride precisely along the border - the west bank was Burma, while the east Thailand. The river itself, which touched Thailand only for a short distance on its passage through "Myanmar", was claimed by the Burmese. These *hang yao* plied the Salween at a fair lick. When an oncoming boat zipped past, there was scarcely time to see who was aboard. Our longtail bore mostly Karens who had been shopping or trading, but there were also two Burmese monks, as well as a girl who was returning home from college for the New Year break. The boat was manned aft by an expressionless driver and fore by a youth with a paddle, who was drunk. Between the passengers and the driver was a mountain of prawn crackers in cellophane bags. Someone in rebel Kawthoolei obviously had a soft spot for the crunchy titbit. The bows of our craft sliced through the water, sending up each side an arced curtain of glistening droplets, while in our wake a long plume of spray was churned up by the single thrashing propeller. The riverbanks to left and right alternated clumps of black jagged rocks and sandy coves. Tiny settlements flashed by, *chedis* punctuated the hillsides, people were fishing with nets in the shallows, and here and there a sawmill stood at the waterfront. Passing the sawmills, all on the Burmese side, we could see how the cut timber was floated across to Thailand on bamboo rafts. Tributaries came down to meet the river on both banks, and sometimes a track ran up from the water's edge. Ahead the monolithic peaks of the Dawna Range loomed. Not far after the Thai village of Mae Haat, set in an area of reafforestation, we came to a major confluence. It was where the Moei river flowed into the Salween. The princely Salween, which had been running north to south, now turned northwest into the Burmese heartland, while the knavish fast-flowing Moei, which unusually ran north, headed off upstream (south) along the border towards distant Mae Sot. We struck off into the mouth of the Moei.

Amost immediately we came upon a serious KNLA checkpoint mounted on the Burmese bank. Armed rebel soldiers in sunglasses ordered the longtail to pull over. They checked the papers and business of everybody aboard, and of course we fell into their hands. A tense five minutes followed. Diagonally opposite on the other bank stood a Thai military post. We could see its soldiers watching us and the proceedings through binoculars. The situation was difficult not least because the Karen guards could speak no Thai, while we could speak no Karen. Altogether Thai was of little use down here - English, if anything, was the fallback language. But these boys could speak no English either. Judging by the way they were shaking their heads, things did not look promising, and we were convinced that they would send us back. After all, what business had we up here, especially at GHQ Manerplaw? The guards seemed particularly unhappy about the motorcycle and our backpacks. It was clear to them that we were no ordinary trippers from Mae Sariang taking a spin out on the river. Shouting across the water that separated the boat from them, we tried to explain in Thai and English that Maha San had sent us and that we were going to visit the Wa representative at Manerplaw. But nobody had heard of Maha San or knew of any Wa representative. There were a lot of ordinary Karen civilians hanging around the checkpoint, waiting with their bags for a boat north. Now the words "Maha San" and "Wa" were on everyone's lips. The people, like the guards, chewed over the concepts, tentatively, unsure whether the taste would prove bitter or sweet. Suddenly, it bore in on us just how obscure Maha San and the Wa actually were, at least down here in Karen territory.

Finally, the KNLA soldier in charge delivered his verdict in Karen. One of the two monks leant over and relayed the message to us in broken English: "Cannot go further, must to go back now". We grew very dispirited. It seemed such a shame to have got all the way to Mae Saam Laep and then with the aid of the student contacts so far downstream, just to be repulsed by a handful of youths on the riverbank. At this point the college girl intervened. She elicited from us what our purpose really was. As she could speak Thai and Karen, she was able to clearly convey to the guards what we wanted. They appeared to relent. Did we have any documentation with us? We handed over our passports, which they scrutinized. As they appeared now to be in two minds, we further passed over for good measure Maha San's personal card and a wallet of photos we always carried with us. The card spelled out Maha San's membership of the NDF, while among the photos was a shot of a KNLA commander we had met on another occasion. Somebody recognized the commander, and that did the trick. To everybody's relief the boat moved forward again.

We breasted some rapids, rounded a large island midstream, and passed some kind of staging post, situated by a confluence on the Thai side. It was not long before the longtail slowed down to stop apparently in the middle of nowhere. There was a beach, an escarpment behind it and, growing on top, a lot of trees. The driver motioned us to get out. We queried if this was

Manerplaw. It was, confirmed the other passengers. Nobody else got out, although one or two people who had been waiting on some rocks got in. All the men present helped us lift the Honda onto the beach. Then the boat sped off, leaving us stranded with a motorbike in Burma. It was all quite different from what we had imagined. Where was the famous GHQ, where were all the houses and soldiers, and where was the checkpoint processing new arrivals? In the shade of a large boulder we spotted two youths with rifles. We also noticed a rickety sign on two poles in Karen lettering. We asked the boys what it read. "Manerplaw", they said. "Where is the village?" we enquired. "Up the escarpment", they replied, uninterested. Our surprise, upon arriving at Manerplaw, at not finding what we had expected was just the first of a series of re-evaluations we were obliged to make at rebel HQ.

Manerplaw
Pushing the bike across the sand and stones to the foot of the escarpment, where we left it for the moment, we climbed up a steep flight of earth steps to emerge at a control post, hidden in the trees. Opposite it was a 6-ft satellite dish aimed heavenwards, but full of fallen leaves. The checkpoint, a wooden hut with a tin roof, was manned by a youngster. Like his predecessors on the river, he spoke only Karen. Unlike them, he was not at all concerned about us, or, rather, he did not really know what to do with us. Finding that he put no obstacle in our way, we wandered on through some large wooden houses and stumbled all at once on the heart of Manerplaw. Around a parade-ground cum playing field were a number of substantial office buildings, while on the far side was the Karen National Liberation Army General Headquarters itself. We were amazed at how easy it was to breeze into Manerplaw, the resistance nerve-centre that the Burma Army had spent years trying to capture.

Looking for some reception or information bureau, we strolled around. No one challenged us, which was remarkable as we could have come with a bomb for GHQ. But then there were not many people around anyway. The overriding impression we got of Manerplaw was not of a bustling fortified garrison, but of a cool relaxed spot, shady under trees - the pervasive tranquillity broken only by the distant growl of longtails on the Moei. We had timed our visit to coincide with New Year. This was not because of any special celebrations here (nothing special did happen - the Karen New Year was two weeks later), but because we wanted to avoid the New Year (the western one) in Thailand. The celebrations for this had degenerated in recent years into a national bunfight, with mayhem on the roads and widespread drunkenness. In Manerplaw we had picked the right place to come. Battered old trucks with no number plates languished in sleepy sunlit corners, the clack of a typewriter drifted lazily out of an office window, giant butterflies wafted by, and on the hour a muffled bugle sounded somewhere.

Poking our heads into a few windows, we asked where reception was. Over in the corner of the parade-ground, people said. Everyone was friendly, orderly, civil. Sure enough, there was a reception point across the ground, but it was unattended. It was while we were looking there that we began to notice sentries discreetly dotted around, at intersections or on corners, especially in the vicinity of the GHQ building. In a house marked Karen Women's Organization we asked if there was an information office anywhere. We were pointed back in the direction we had come from, towards the Moei. Behind an empty barrack house we found the office. It too was deserted, although after a while a man appeared. After we had introduced ourselves, he sat us down to fill up a long form, one each. It was not easy to do this. The questions asked: "Purpose of visit?", "Intended length of stay?", "Representing which organization?", "Rank?", and so on. We could hardly write: "Just popping by to have a look." The forms were borne away by the man to another building. After a quarter of an hour another man appeared, apparently some secretary. He asked us all the same questions, but ended by flabbergasting us with the enquiry: "And which minister is it that you have come to see? You understand that the ministers are busy people, but I will try to secure an appointment for you." Actually, we had no desire to interview any minister. We wanted only to form a writer's impression of Manerplaw. But to say so would have undermined our credibility, and so, not quite daring to go for C-in-C and KNU president Bo Mya himself, we blurted out almost at random: the Minister for Education and Culture. A meeting with this gentleman was duly arranged for the afternoon of the following day. The encounter with the information office and the secretary revealed another unexpected aspect of Manerplaw - it was a grave, bureaucratic place. It was as if with all the paperwork the Karen authorities were trying to conjure into existence a world which did not properly exist.

The secretary escorted us next to Manerplaw's hospitality house. A simple wooden affair with a nice veranda, this was soon to be replaced by regular accommodation being noisily hammered together next door. Washing was done outside from a cement water tank with the aid of a dipper, while sleeping was attempted in a series of cubicles, separated by 6-ft wooden partitions. These cubicles - a kind of dormitory for officers - had no roofs (except for the overall roof of the building high above), and were screened off from the corridor by flimsy curtains across the doorway. Journalists and TV crews from all over the world came to Manerplaw to get the latest news from source of the long-running insurgency. During our stay in the hospitality house we overlapped with two radio reporters from Germany. They were a pair of humourless spinsterly ladies, one older and one younger, and when they were not going from one appointment to another, thet sat fiddling on the veranda with their notebooks, cassette recorders, water filters and other paraphernalia. They were snobbishly contemptuous of us, not deigning once in three days to recognize our presence, let alone mouth a friendly hello. It was as if they thought that we were somehow poaching on a patch they wanted all to themselves, as if our presence somehow detracted from their feeling of exclusivity. A seasoned aid worker we met elsewhere in Kawthoolei said that the behaviour of the two Germans was typical. Probably Manerplaw was the only part of the border they had seen. The more trivial the journalist, she said, the more self-important and snooty they were. She had met at HQ some of the world's most famous reporters, and they were invariably the friendliest.

To stay at the hospitality house we were charged a hefty (by local standards) 200 baht per person per day, although that did include three daily meals. Clearly the sum was a nominal one, with the fat constituting an involuntary contribution to the war effort. We rather got the impression that the new "guesthouse" being built next door was to put up not just delegates to the occasional NDF or DAB conference, but possible future tourists. The Karen authorities had perhaps spotted some potential here.

The secretary indicated to us a way round the escarpment by which we might bring our motorbike up to our lodging. After we had settled in and washed, we went to retrieve the Honda. We also took a first scout round Manerplaw. Again we were struck by the calm of this well-established place. Lofty mature trees surrounded the central parade-ground, shading the various organizational and command buildings. Perhaps the trees were planted in 1975, the date KNU/KNLA GHQ was first established in Manerplaw. It was difficult to imagine that the area had repeatedly been the scene of bitter fighting. Yet the air-raid shelters everywhere (mostly bunkers dug sideways into earth banks), as well as the series of checkpoints on the tracks out north and south, bore witness to the fact. The last such attack had been in 1991. Unlike many other gateways to Kawthoolei (pronounced "ko thu lae"), which had fallen in the late 80s and early 90s to the Burma Army (mostly quickly being retaken by the Karens), Manerplaw had never been captured. But this was hardly surprising. Owing to its position, the place looked virtually impregnable. Situated furthest to the rear (east) of the Karen State, it lay sandwiched between the protective waters of the Moei border river and the shield of the Dawna mountains. The jungle-clad slopes of this towering range rose straight up immediately behind the KNLA GHQ building itself.

Manerplaw's quietness was also in part due to the fact that not many ordinary people lived there. We had expected an extensive village, bustling with children and animals. But we found a community of about 100 houses with only two or three tiny shops - a far cry from Mae Saam Laep. In fact Manerplaw was not a regular village at all and much less the capital of the Karen State, as is sometimes assumed. It was primarily a military camp, with all the earnestness and spartan regimen that that implied. Certainly there were people in Manerplaw, about another 1000, but they were all troops stationed in barracks mostly north of the centre. However, things did liven up a bit towards evening, when people returned from working in the fields and some soldiers came back from day exercises.

There were two primary schools in Manerplaw and a secondary school not far away. On the north side was a Baptist church, and power came from a hydroelectric plant, generating locally. Besides the KNLA GHQ building itself, as well as the hospitality house and the information bureau, our tour of inspection turned up a communications centre, an administrative office, a clinic and a couple of central barracks. Away from the village centre were a series of buildings, all of wood and bamboo, housing the representations or headquarters of numerous organizations, including the Karen Youth Organization, the Karen National Defence Organizaion, the Palaung State Liberation Front, the important Democratic Alliance of Burma (DAB), the National Democratic Front (NDF), and many more. The NDF HQ was itself home to an alliance comprising the Arakan Liberation Party, the Chin National Front, the Kachin Independence Organization, the Karenni National Progressive Party, the Karen National Union (KNU), the Lahu National Organization, the New Mon State Party, the Pa-O National Organization, the Palaung State Liberation Party, the Shan State Progress Party, and Maha San's Wa National Organization, together with all their corresponding armies. Inside the NDF HQ was a colourful array of the flags and emblems of all these political parties and military wings. The DAB HQ was home to an even bigger alliance, which included the NDF and a number of other movements. Manerplaw was the meeting place of a veritable potpourri of ethnic groups and military factions, and, walking around, one could on any one day bump into a sample of representatives from them. The danger at rebel HQ, a danger that not a few visitors succumbed to, was of getting sucked into an endless investigation of these fascinating minority groups and their insurgent efforts. Many were the people in the village who spent days on end consulting, asking questions and taking notes.

On returning to our lodging, we found our supper already laid out on a table in a gloomy back room. The pattern was always the same. The food, prepared by some cooking boys, was put out irrespective of whether the guests were there to eat it or not, so that if the guests were late or the meal was early (which happened most of the time), the food was left to go cold. We sat down to the cold supper with an unaccountable American, who was "just passing through". The joyless German women preferred to eat on their own out front on the balcony. The offering was threefold. There was a meat and potato curry, cabbage fried with tomato, and omelette. Rice, of course, was also served, and coffee afterwards. Unfortunately, the meat was almost exclusively fat and gristle, and the curry was swimming in oil.

Later on our journey we were to enjoy some fine Karen cooking, and *Yang* hospitality in general was to prove unsurpassed among that of the minority peoples, but this first meal at Manerplaw was an introduction to typical run-of-the-mill Karen fare. Unlike Thai or Chinese cooking, it was more in the style of Burmese food - heavy, bland and greasy. In three days of breakfasts, lunches and suppers there were some variations. Chicken replaced beef in the curry, cauliflower was fried with tomato instead of cabbage, noodle was served as a change from rice, and once for breakfast we had an intriguing deep-fried rice pillow, filled with chick peas. But always the dishes were cold and greasy, the chicken (for example) consisted of pieces of chopped up neck, and no meal was complete without egg in some form, mostly fried or boiled. We took to putting the boiled eggs in "doggie bags" for redistribution during our walks. The fare proved no problem for the punk-style American. He ate it like a horse, and we began to wonder if he was not a soldier of fortune who had just returned from the front and months of jungle diet. In the matter of food and drink, we made another discovery about Manerplaw - it was a dry village. The reason for this was that the leaders of the KNU and KNLA were predominantly Baptist and Seventh-Day Adventist and had imposed a prohibition on alcohol in GHQ. Nowhere was beer or whisky to be had, not even *lao kao*. So our New Year's Eve in Kawthoolei passed off completely teetotal.

The next morning we explored on foot the tracks running south and north of Manerplaw. To the south the impressive new HQ of the Karen Youth Organization was fronted by a series of signs bearing the slogans: TO HAVE MORE UNITY AMONG THE ETHNIC GROUPS, TO BUILD UNDERSTANDING AMONG THE FUTURE LEADERS OF THE ETHNIC GROUPS, TO EXCHANGE CULTURE OF DIFFERENT ETHNIC GROUPS and TO DEFINE PLAN FOR FUTURE ACTIVITIES AMONG THE GROUPS. Some serious youths inside tried to embroil us in a heavy political discussion in broken English right after breakfast. We found a little shop and also a couple of "cafés". Outside the "KNU Finance Department - Supreme Headquarters", a wooden building with plaited bamboo walls and a leaf roof, a battered Toyota pick-up was parked in the shade of a banana palm. The vehicle's front bumper, headlight mounting and front offside carrosserie was lashed on with a rope running up to the rollbar, while on a side panel some wag had sprayed "OK".

The dusty jungle track south was punctuated by a series of checkpoints and barriers. So near to GHQ, they were not trivial affairs, but on the other hand no one tried to stop us in our exploration. After the NDF and DAB offices we found Manerplaw's church, called the Redeemer Church. A side track, signposted "Daw Aung San Suu Kyi Road" in honour of the Nobel Peace Prize-winning heroine of Burma's 1988 democracy uprising, led down to the Moei. Also on this road a tranquil side ravine housed the representation of the All Burma Young Monks' Union. A flamboyant sign on the portal overarching the entrance to the *pongyis'* compound read: LONG LIVE HOLINESS - REVOLUTIONARY AREA. Burma had a tradition of militant monks, and the ochre robes we could see hanging in the ravine would have been no strangers to bloody front-line action. A tiny sawmill also lay to one side of the route. Here two men, their bodies glistening with sweat in the morning sun, were laboriously sawing a tree trunk lengthways with a 6-ft long, double-handled saw. The resulting beams were remarkably true, and from time to time they paused in their slow rhythmic efforts to oil the blade.

THREE PAGODAS

An hour's walk out from Manerplaw we came to a third checkpoint. Situated high up on a Dawna mountainside, it had a commanding view over the Moei. The guardhouse and barrier were manned by a lady soldier and a boy, both of the KNLA. The Karen military had servicewomen, and some of them could be seen at HQ. She was holding an automatic weapon, while he in true *Yang* fashion was puffing at a cheroot. Both could not have been more than teenagers. She looked about 17 or 18, while he, with his boyish round face and quavery deep voice which sounded as if it had just broken, must have been only 14 or so. The girl was also singular in that she was barely 4-ft tall and had a squint eye, which could not have helped her shooting - or perhaps it did. He, a spindly playful creature with hair down to his shoulders, was hardly taller. The lady sentry was dressed in camouflage jacket and trousers, a wide-brimmed hat and flip-flops, while the boy had regular army trousers and boots, a military cap with KNLA badge, but also an ordinary civilian shirt and a kind of tea towel tied around his waist. We could not help wondering how effective they would really be if the enemy suddenly appeared round the corner. Conversation with the two was impossible. But they were happy enough to sit with us for a while on a table next to the sentry box. We passed on to them our boiled eggs from breakfast. These they peeled and ate on the spot, dropping eggshell into the dust. The soldier girl's flip-flops fell from her feet. Incised into the top of each was the enigmatic message I KISS. Whether "I" was "I" (me) or "1" (one) we never discovered.

Investigating the track north was a different kettle of fish. If the southern end of Manerplaw was the political quarter, the northern was the military. Over the road up here was a series of arches which all bore the message in stark white letters on black: GIVE ME LIBERTY OR DEATH - KNLA. We walked under them humbly. They were a grim reminder of the seriousness with which the Karens took their struggle for self-determination, of the whole *raison d'être* of Manerplaw, and of the deadliness of the forty-year old insurgency against Rangoon. But passing under one arch, we could not resist a smile. A large pot-bellied pig trotted beside us. Did the looming slogan apply equally to the *Yang* porker?

Beyond the arches we came across Kawthoolei Military Training School with its adjacent barracks. The KNLA emblem (two horns and a drum superimposed on a sunburst) blazed from a coat of arms above the entrance to the school. The barracks were simple affairs. Each was a wooden longhouse, raised on stilts, with a roof, but open at the sides except for a low wall. Inside, the length of the two long walls, each soldier had a metre or two of space for his bed and belongings. Opposite the school was another parade-ground cum football pitch. A match was in progress between Karen soldiers and some guesting Shan troops. The clothes of the spectators were an interesting mix of green camouflage fatigues and checked *longyis*. Between the pitch and the river stood an open-air lecture hall. The Four Principles of the Karen struggle, almost exactly as first formulated in 1950 by Saw Ba U Gyi (the first Prime Minister of the

provisional Kawthoolei government of the day) were pinned up in here: 1.
FOR US SURRENDER IS OUT OF QUESTION, 2. THE RECOGNITION OF THE
KAREN STATE MUST BE COMPLETED, 3. WE SHALL RETAIN OUR ARMS, and 4.
WE SHALL DECIDE OUR OWN POLITICAL DESTINY. A military cemetery
adjoining the hall was a poignant reminder of those who had embraced
death in the pursuit of liberty. About 200 overgrown graves were marked
by simple wooden Christian crosses, almost every one with RIP etched on
it. The details on the crosses showed that most of the deceased were Karens
and Mons, as well as ABSDF student guerrillas. Their dates of their deaths
were variously 1990, 1992 and 1993.

At sundown we returned to the guesting Shan soldiers, now off-duty.
There were hundreds of them. On the breast pockets of their jungle-green
uniforms, bright yellow flashes announced: SNPLA (Shan National
Peoples Liberation Army), while their shirt sleeves bore red sunburst
badges, and their caps had red stars. Evidently part of a new or renamed
army, it was, we were later told, a Pa-O outfit which had joined the Shans.
To us many of the troops looked like Wa. They were wild-looking men of
all ages and sizes. Their skins were black-brown, and many had wispy
chintuft beards or moustaches. Some were already quite old and greying,
while others were mere boys of twelve or less, their voices not yet broken.
There were men with bits of ear missing and decayed brown teeth, others
with scarred lips and squint eyes. These pitiful people almost made a more
profound impression on us than anything else in Manerplaw. Scattered in
the scrub around their barracks, they had divided up into groups of three or
five or ten. Many had improvised windbreaks to shield themselves and
their camp fires from the chill evening breeze. Those who had not already
gone to rest in the long huts were cooking, or brewing tea, or strumming
guitars, or cleaning their weapons, or smoking, or lying in hammocks made
of old rice sacks. Hanging from the trees or lying on the ground was every
kind of gun and grenade launcher. It was as if troops had decided to set up
camp for the night in the middle of a battlefield. Passing from fire to fire,
we tried to see what the groups were cooking. It was always the same.
Youths squatting in broken-down shoes or in cracked rubber ankle boots
were stirring two pots, one containing a stew of green leaves and salt, the
other rice. It was a meagre diet to sustain a hard boring life.

Earlier that afternoon, we had made our visit to the Minister of Education
and Culture. By mistake we arrived for our appointment half an hour early.
This was because we had not noticed a 30-minute discrepancy between
Thai time and Burmese standard time. The minister turned out to be Saw
Shwi Ya Hae, the Karen Central Committee member who in 1989 led the
first NDF delegation up to the Wa State in the wake of the CPB mutinies to
see if the Wa defectors could be brought into the democratic fold. Shwi Ya
Hae welcomed us into his wooden house near the Moei escarpment. An
assistant accompanied him, and at a table in an anteroom a male secretary
picked out keys on an ancient typewriter. There was evidence of

duplicating equipment, and dusty piles of roneod pamphlets lay stacked up on the floor. The minister, in regular civilian trousers and a fashion camouflage jacket, bade us sit round a large table. He had short hair and a military moustache, and spoke good English. An urbane, educated, soft-spoken man, Saw Shwi patiently answered our many questions about the Karens, their history and culture, and the insurgency. I shall try to represent what he said not in the form of an interview, but as a digest. Readers impatient to continue the travellogue may care to omit the following.

Karen people and culture

The Karens (the emphasis is on the second syllable) are usually classified as belonging to the Sino-Tibetan group of peoples (Karennic branch). Like many other peoples in South-East Asia, they derive from China, possibly from Mongolia. At all events the Karens are thought to have originated from further west than other Sino-Tibetan peoples, such as the Lahu, Lisu and Akha. Karen legends speak of their tribe coming from "Tibi Kobi", which may be Tibet and the Gobi Desert. The Karens date their present era back to 739 BC, making it longer even that the Buddhist era, let alone the Christian one (in 1995 the Karen year was 2734, the Thai year 2538), but whether this date refers to the origins of the Karen people or to their most recent migration into Burma is not clear. Certainly they have been living in Burma for a very long time, predating the arrival of both the Mons and the Burmans. The migration of the Burmans into Upper Burma in the 9th and 10th centuries AD displaced the Karens first into central Burma and then into southeast Burma. In the 18th century the Karens began crossing the River Salween, some migrating into western Thailand. Today the area of Karen settlement is southeast Burma and western Thailand.

The majority of Karens, the plains Karen, live in the Burmese Delta and Lower Burma. A minority, the hill Karens, live in the remote hills to the east and across the Thai frontier. On the Burmese side of the border Karen territory extends from Victoria Point in the far south 500 miles up to approximately the level of Mae Hong Son. On the Thai side Karens are spread across some fifteen provinces, from Prachuab Kiri Khan in the south to Chiang Mai province in the north. As we saw, Karens can be found as far up as Wiang Haeng district. Like their brothers across the border in the eastern reaches of Burma, the Karens of Thailand are all traditional hill or "tribal" Karens, with their distinctive red costumes. It is these Karens who concern us on our border journey. To the central Thais they are known as "Kariang" ("Kaliang") while in northern Thailand they are called "Yang". The hill Karens of western Thailand and Kawthoolei are often referred to as "hill-tribe" people, yet they are neither mountain dwellers, nor migratory people, but settled farmers who cultivate paddy in the low hills and lowlands. Some Karen villages in Thailand, such as Mae Ramoeng behind Mae Salid, are over 200 years old. Nor should it be forgotten that in terms of settlement in the region the Karens of Burma are an older people than the Burmans and, for that matter, the Thais of modern Thailand.

142

With a population estimated at 4 million (possibly 6-7 million if their Karenni, Pa-O and Kayan cousins are taken into account), the Karens hardly constitute a minority tribe either. Of this total, some 275,000 live in Thailand, making up fully 50% of the total "hill-tribe" population there. No fewer than a score of subgroups exist among the Karen, some rare and "exotic". In Thailand by far the largest group are the S'gaw or "White" Karens, accounting for 80% of the total, while the colourful Pwo Karens, who live only south of the latitude of Mae Sariang, make up most of the remaining 20%. Less than 1% of Thai Karens consist of Karennis, Kayans, Pa-Os and others. The different subgroups speak a variety of Karen languages and dialects. S'gaw and Pwo are considered basically mutually unintelligible. But the groups can communicate with each other through a common standard Karen language (or through Burmese). Based on S'gaw, it has both a spoken and a written form. Written Karen is very similar to written Burmese. This is because the American Baptist who put S'gaw Karen into writing in the early 19th century used the Burmese alphabet. The Karen languages do not fit easily into the usual linguistic classifications. Given a Karennic grouping of their own, they are sometimes described as Tibeto-Burman and sometimes as Sino-Tibetan. The Karens like to borrow words from Burmese, Thai, Mon and Shan, and many have a smattering of Northern Thai (Lao), which they speak with a thick accent.

The tribal Karens mostly build their settlements in the lowlands or low foothills, often at an altitude of around 500 m. and sometimes higher. A village can comprise as few as three or four houses, or as many as 100. Sala Muang Noi was large by Karen standards - an average village might have 20-30 families. The houses, as we saw at Muang Noi, are raised on stilts and are made of wood and bamboo, with their characteristic platform out front. Villages typically have no central shrine or meeting place or ceremony ground. As their villages are sedentary, the Karens have rice paddies, maize fields, vegetable gardens, and chilli and sesame plots. On the hillsides they also grow mountain rice, but no poppies - the Karens are not involved in opium, either in producing, refining, trafficking or selling it. But their (mostly subsistence) economy is not only agricultural. They keep domestic animals and, famously, elephants. The Karens are the only people in Thailand still to keep elephants in the ordinary way - authentically, for working, and not for show or tourist purposes. Wherever one goes in Karen country, it is not long before one encounters the lumbering beasts. Only relatively rich Karens have elephants, as the animals are expensive to keep. They are used for transporting goods through the jungle and over the mountains, as well as for pulling logs. Sometimes they are hired out, complete with their mahouts. Some Karen men work for Thais as wage-labourers, while Yang women, who are consummate weavers, sell their handicraft.

Unusually among the hill peoples, Karen society is matrilineal, while its marriage system is matrilocal. Initially, after marriage, a man goes to live with his wife's parents, after which the new family will become nuclear. The Karens are mostly monogamous people, and are altogether rather chaste. Divorce is uncommon, and after divorce remarriage is unusual. A child born out of wedlock is a serious matter. Pre-marital sex, even overt contact between unmarried boys and girls, is frowned upon. Karen maidens, pretty with their round faces, have a studied coyness about them. This is not to say that young people have no opportunity to dally. Festivals, the harvest, work in the fields and sessions around the evening fire making jaak-leaf roofing panels provide a chance to get to know members of the opposite sex. Notably funerals are an occasion for such contact. At these, the body of the deceased, wrapped in a bamboo mat, is placed on a bier in a house, and unmarried Karen boys and girls process round and round it in groups of four, three, two and one, chanting songs to help the deceased on his or her journey to the land of the dead, but at the same time making good use of the protracted opportunity to tease, flirt and touch one another. Many a Karen youth has been heard to wish that someone would die soon, so that he would have a chance to go a-courting again.

Most Burmese Karens are Buddhist or Buddhist-animist, while Karens in Thailand are predominantly animist. The animist hill Karens believe in "the old way" - bodies of belief and spiritual practice established by their ancestors and differing (at least superficially) from village to village. They believe in a variety of spirits, which must be propitiated with offerings and animal sacrifices. Above all, harmony must be preserved between the spirit world and life down here on earth. Chief among the spirits is the "Lord of Land and Water", who has a special shrine somewhere outside the village - the only such shrine, as otherwise there are no altars either in the houses or villages of animist Karens. Also important are: the household spirits (i.e. the ancestral or matrilineal spirits who guard over the members of the household and the house itself), the spirits of the village and locality, the jungle spirits, the "Crop Grandmother" spirit, and the spirits which indwell certain singular features around the village. Offerings are made to the spirits by the village priest or, as appropiate, by the female lineage heads.

An important part of Karen mythology is the figure of the orphan. It is an objective correlative for the downtrodden state which Karens believe they languish in. They understand that - through their own negligence and oversight - they have become dispossessed. A corollary of this feeling is the idea that one day their time will come and Karens will regain their rightful inheritance. The redemption theme finds expression in a number of other myths. There is the myth that one day the time of the "Karen king" will come and all Karens will live in a magnificent palace in a great city. There is the myth of the "white brother", who will come from across the sea, bringing back the "writing" or the "Golden Book" lost by the Ur-Karens. There is the Karen legend of a single god, Y'wa, and of a "Garden of Creation". Such comforting prophecies have given rise to a number of millennial movements among the Karens during their history. A Karen sect inspired by such millennial thinking we were to stumble on later in our journey.

The notions of the foreigner saviour, the lost scripture, the single god and the garden of creation have had another far-reaching outcome for the Karens. Missionaries arriving among them for the first time could not believe their luck. Some even thought that in the Karens they had found one of the lost tribes of Israel. The Karens for their part were relatively predisposed to the teachings of the newcomers. Some saw the appearance of the "white men" from across the seas, clutching their Bibles, as the fulfilment of their old millennarian myths. But in addition, the message of the missionaries' Christianity seemed largely to confirm the substance of their own prophecies. The result was significant conversion of the Karens. Today an estimated 15-20% of Karens on both sides of the Thai-Burmese border are Christian. Most of the missionaries have been American Baptists. In the conversion of the Karens, the Baptists have scored their greatest success to date in the history of their proselytizing.

One effect of the conversion of Karens has been some improvement in their lot. Having to sacrifice fewer domestic animals to the spirits, some families have enjoyed a better standard of living. Many Karens, too, have picked up a good education from the Baptists. Baptist (later Judson) College in Rangoon used to be popularly known as "Karen College". Today virtually the entire leadership of the KNU, from Bo Mya down, is Christian. Those few who are not Baptists are Seventh-Day Adventists. But this does not mean, as is frequently assumed, that the KNU is a Christian movement, any more than the KNLA is a Christian army. As Martin Smith has pointed out, it would be unwise to try to root the causes of the Karen insurgency in the Christianity of some (upper) echelons of Karen society. At grass roots level the vast majority of the Karen population, including soldiers, field commanders and civilians, are Buddhist or animist or both. Which brings us to the matter of the Karen rebellion itself.

The Karen rebellion

The 45-year old Karen rebellion is one of the longest-running and least known-about insurgencies in the world. That would be remarkable enough, except that the Karen insurgency is just one of some dozen other continuing ethnic uprisings in Burma, which altogether form probably the world's longest civil war. Virtually since the country's independence from Britain in 1948, rebel armies have been at war with the central Rangoon-based military dictatorship of Gen. Ne Win (since 1988 Gen. Saw Maung's SLORC) in the frontier regions all round the Burman heartland. The totalitarian, "Unionist", "Socialist", essentially Burman junta cannot tolerate the secessionist, federalist, democratic aspirations of the minority peoples, with the result that for three generations a combined insurgent force of 25,000 - 30,000 guerrillas have been pitted against some 200,000 troops of the Burma Army in a vicious war of attrition, which has claimed the lives of an estimated 10,000 people a year on average, including civilians. The war would probably have been concluded years ago in the junta's favour except that Rangoon is fighting on numerous fronts in remote jungle or mountain areas against motivated guerrillas who are battling on their own patch for their very existence. Also, although the Burma Army is numerically far superior, it has never had enough soldiers to win this kind of war - military analysts calculate that to win a guerrilla war an army must outnumber the rebels by at least 10 to 1. For their part, the insurgents might easily have won earlier had they not been so disunited both among themselves and even within their own individual ethnic groupings. The Karens, along with the Kachins, now constitute the biggest faction among these groupings, and many of the most important developments in the civil war have happened on Karen territory.

The Karen uprising dates back to the late 1940s - the time of the end of WW2, the second Panglong conference (1947), and Burma's Independence from Britain (1948). The Karens' dream of the right to self-determination and of an independent state actually goes back further than this, but it was in the immediate post-war period that their aspirations became more sharply focussed, even seeming realizable. During WW2 Karen troops in the British Burma Army had remained loyal, fighting alongside the Allies or operating underground against the Japanese occupiers and collaborating Burmese. Afterwards they naturally looked to the British for reward, only to be disappointed. But in any case within three years the colonial masters were gone. The Panglong conference, which was supposed to regulate the federation of the ethnic minority territories in a Union of Burma, similarly failed the Karens. It did not create a Karen State, but instead made convoluted provision for a special Karen region to be established at some future time. Worst still, the projected territory would not enjoy the crucial right to secede after ten years such as had been granted to, for example, the Shan State. It was remarkable and cruel that at a conference so momentous provision for the most significant and pressing of Burma's minority peoples should have been so fudged. The Karens quickly understood that they would get nothing except through armed struggle. Hostilities were not long in coming. In January 1949 the Rangoon HQ of the KNU (a union of all the Karen organizations of that time) as well as Karen quarters both in the capital and elsewhere were attacked by Burmese government troops. The decades-long insurgency had begun.

Fighting flared up in many places. In the early days the Karens had a string of outstanding successes, capturing towns and even coming within an ace of taking Rangoon itself. In territory under their control they proclaimed the establishment of a Karen State. At Toungoo they instituted a provisional Kawthoolei government, with Saw Ba U Gyi, the originator of the Four Principles of the Karen revolution, as the first prime minister. Later, in 1953, at the KNU's First National Congress, held in Papun, they announced the formation of a new Kawthoolei Governing Body, informing the Thais that along the Siamese western border a Kawthoolei Free State was to be created, for which recognition would be sought from the United Nations. The initial triumphs were the result especially of a strong military. Just before the outbreak of hostilities Karen National Defence

Organizations, local defence militias still operative today, were set up throughout Yang *territory. And when fighting did start, units of the Karen Rifles in the Burma Army mutinied, defecting* en masse *to their own side. As they joined their rebel brothers, they took with them not only their weapons, but valuable military experience gained from fighting alongside the British in WW2. This was to stand the Karen people in good stead in the long years of warfare ahead, as it still does today. The modern KNLA remains modelled on the British Army of WW2, and many KNU and KNLA leaders, including Karen supremo Bo Mya, even now are veterans who saw service with the British.*

The early successes, however, were followed by reversals. As the Burma Army recovered itself, towns captured by the KNU were retaken by Rangoon, often later to be seized again by the Karens. The 1950s marked the beginning of the deadly cat-and-mouse game the Karen military and government forces have played with each other ever since. On the political front, too, there were problems. During the 1950s and 1960s the KNU, until it regained pre-eminence in the 1970s, was eclipsed as the vanguard party of the Karens by the left-orientated Karen National United Party. Maoist ideology and an out-of-character alliance with the CPB were the order of the day. A left-right split between the pro-communist KNUP and the strongly nationalist, pro-western, anti-communist KNU weakened the Karen movement, from which it did not recover until the rise of the present-day Karen leader, Bo Mya. But with that we arrive at the modern era of the insurgency.

Five factors in particular have determined the evolution of the Karen struggle from the mid-60s until today: the emergence of the modern KNU and its armed wing, the KNLA; the rise of Bo Mya; economic considerations, especially the boom in trade across the Karen-Thai border; the notorious "Four Cuts" campaign of the Burma Army; and the formation of two major alliances - the NDF and the DAB. The rise of the phenomenal Bo Mya and the emergence of the modern KNU are essentially the same story. Unlike many other KNU luminaries, Bo Mya never enjoyed a university education. His was a case of local lad made good. Born in 1926 as an animist S'gaw Karen in the Papun hills, he attended a village elementary school, breaking off his education early. Growing up in the dying days of British colonial rule in Burma, he was just a teenager of 15 or 16 when the Japanese invaded the country in 1941-42 and only 23 when the Karen rebellion erupted. For a short time during WW2 Bo Mya worked with the Japanese. Having personally witnessed some of the atrocities committed by the Burma Independence Army against his local kinsfolk, he considered this to be his best course of action. But it was not long before he transferred to the side of the Allies. His service with the British until they left at Independence made a profound impact on the future Karen leader. The outbreak of the rebellion in 1949 saw Bo Mya go underground to join the struggle. The 1950s and early 60s were the time of his meteoric rise through the ranks of the insurgent army. His military prowess and daring exploits in the eastern hills of Kawthoolei were to become the stuff of legend. While another prominent Karen commander, the wily Shwi Soe, came to control Duplaya (the 6th Brigade district of Kawthoolei's Eastern Division), Bo Mya was rewarded with Papun-Paan (7th Brigade district), adjoining to the north. The two districts, accounting for the the whole of the Kawthoolei-Thailand border, from approximately Mae Saam Laep in the north to the Three Pagodas Pass and beyond in the south, were to assume a critical importance in the struggle. Then, in 1963, with his main base at Kawmoorah, Bo Mya was promoted almost overnight to commander of the entire Eastern Division.

An event in 1964 profoundly altered the commander's cast of mind, indeed had far-reaching consequences for the political direction of the whole Karen cause. The animist S'gaw married a Seventh-Day Adventist Karen and converted to Christianity. One immediate upshot was the first of two "coups" which Bo Mya staged in the 60s and 70s. The coups stamped the KNU with the definite rightist pro-Western stance it has now. In the first days of 1966 Bo Mya ordered all KNUP troops out of his Eastern Division. At a stroke the whole Dawna region of the Karen State fell into his hands. He replaced the administration of the KNUP with a new Karen National Liberation Council, filling its posts with anti-communist hill Karens like himself. Little is remembered today of the short-lived Council, except that its military wing, the Karen National Liberation Army, gave its name to the modern Karen army.

Within a year of the coup some KNUP officials, including party chairman Maan Ba Zan, returned to join Bo Mya. The KNUP and Bo Mya's Council fused to become the Karen National United Front, the immediate precursor of the modern KNU. Initially the new body retained elements of the old KNUP ideology, but over the next ten years and in a protracted tussle between the two leaders the communist baggage was progressively dropped until everything was to Bo Mya's liking. Among other things, the name Karen National United Front was changed to Karen National Union, and the goal of a left-sounding "people's democracy" was replaced by that of a more rightist "national democracy". Finally, in 1976, at Manerplaw it was decided that the KNU should accept aid not just from any country (meaning communist ones too), but only from Western "capitalist" nations. It was at this stormy Manerplaw meeting that Bo Mya staged his second "coup". He definitively ousted Maan Ba Zan, who had been KNU president. Bo Mya already had under his khaki belt the positions of KNLA chief-of-staff, Minister of Defence and Minister of Foreign Affairs. Now he added the KNU presidency. By the mid-70s his grip on the Karen movement was complete.

Bo Mya's inexorable rise to the position of uncontested Karen leader was not without its foundations. Always a military hardman, since his early days he has enjoyed a reputation as a formidable, ruthless, even wild guerrilla commander. With a house at Manerplaw overlooking the Moei, latterly the supremo has not been afraid to exploit his reputation and power. His, it has been said, is an authoritarian, rather undemocratic style of leadership, not given to tolerating open disagreement or real debate. Announcements and policy changes, some senior figures have complained, are apt to be made without prior consultation. Since his marriage and conversion, Bo Mya's pronouncements have been increasingly interlaced with Christian sentiment and Biblical allusion. He has come to seem like a patriarch of the Karen movement, moreover guarding over the mores of his people (at least around Manerplaw) with a prudish, conservative, Old Testament eye. The Karen chief has something in common with the few other military strongmen who have ridden out Burma's civil war - one thinks of Khun Sa, Brang Seng, even Ne Win himself - and he has not escaped the criticism from friend and foe alike that he approximates to a warlord who in Kawthoolei has built up a private fiefdom. But it would be wrong to dwell on these criticisms. To the mass of hill Karens, this charismatic, anti-communist, anti-narcotics leader is a legendary father figure. Unlike other KNU leaders, university-educated and from the plains, he is "one of us". His great achievement has been to unify and galvanize the downtrodden neglected people of the eastern hills, at the same time revolutionizing the Karen movement.

Under Bo Mya's leadership the KNU burgeoned dramatically. The Karens, along with the Kachins, came to pose the biggest threat militarily to Rangoon. The KNLA swelled to a force of thousands of well-equipped soldiers, an army only ever eclipsed in strength among the Burmese insurgents by the CPB People's Army. In particular the 6th and 7th Brigade areas bordering Thailand, which had been the weakest of the KNU, were transformed, and not just transformed, but now turned into the strongest of all the Brigade areas. These had been backwaters of the Karen State scarcely touched by British or Japanese rule, let alone Burmese. But suddenly Papun-Paan and Duplaya were catapulted into the vanguard of the Karen revolution.

The rise of a powerful modern KNU together with its forceful leader was facilitated by a dramatic change in the economic fortunes of Kawthoolei. This key factor in the Karen struggle must be seen against the background of the collapse under Ne Win and SLORC of the Burmese economy. Ne Win's oddball programme "The Burmese Way to Socialism", introduced in 1963-64, led to a quarter century of ruinous economic and political mismanagement. Companies were nationalized across the board, half a million Chinese and Indian businessmen (middlemen vital to the wellbeing of the economy) fled the country, whole trade sectors folded, there were shortages of everything everywhere, and in a series of bizarre demonetizations of the Burmese currency thousands of people lost their precious savings overnight. Burma rapidly became the "Albania of Asia" and in 1987, as one of the world's ten most impoverished nations, was admitted to UN Least Developed Country status, alongside Ethiopia and Chad.

149

The economic ruin gave rise to a massive black market, which in turn engendered a vigorous cross-border trade. What was lacking at home was obtained from neighbouring countries, notably Thailand. And what could not be properly traded domestically was diverted over the frontier. But the frontier areas were almost exclusively controlled by the various ethnic rebel armies. So all the new trade, having to pass through their territory, fell into the hands of the insurgents, who taxed it. It is ironic that Ne Win's misguided strategy ended up so handsomely benefiting people he sought to crush. Nowhere was this more true than in Kawthoolei. In peak years in the 1980s the value of Burma's black economy nationwide was estimated at a staggering $3000 million p.a. or 40% of the country's GNP, while taxes arising from two-way traffic passing through KNU Eastern Division were estimated at an annual £50m - a fairytale sum for such an impecunious backwater.

Local Karen commanders cashed in on the unexpected bonanza. From the 1960s on, customs gates were opened at Mae Saam Laep, Kawmoorah, Palu, Wa Lae, the Three Pagodas Pass.... everywhere along the lengthy Karen State-Thai border. A 5% levy was imposed on the flood of livestock, hardwood, jade, antimony, dried prawns and so on flowing out of Kawthoolei, and on the medicines, foodstuffs and consumer items (such as fabrics, transistor radios and watches - anything unobtainable in Burma), flowing in. Some of these border trading posts, for example Kawmoorah or the Three Pagodas Pass, grew into bizarre jungle emporia, and the odd commander amassed a personal fortune, again raising the suspicion of Karen warlordism. It was not just the Eastern Division which was transformed. Sleepy backwoods towns on the Thai side of the border, such as Mae Sariang, Mae Sot and Sangklaburi, boomed on the back of the Burmese black economy. Mae Sot, in particular, became a pivot of the bustling new cross-border trade.

Obscure Papun and Duplaya, then, were awakened from their age-old slumber, suddenly to become of leading geographic an economic significance in the Karen struggle. But the Eastern Division's change in fortune had a further consequence. Bo Mya's old stamping ground was transformed militarily. The ever-increasing revenue from the taxes on trade flowed largely to the KNLA war coffers. The border strongholds of 6th and 7th Brigade areas became not just jungle emporia, but flourishing arms-trading centres. First American Vietnam "surplus" and then Chinese-made Khmer Rouge "surplus" found its way to these centres, where it was either bought with the new wealth or passed on to other rebel armies in Burma. The outcome has been that the KNLA has often been better equipped, especially in the field of communications, than the Burma Army itself.

The response of the junta to a robust KNU (and other rebel movements) was to initiate its infamous "Four Cuts" campaign. Originally, this was a renewed effort on Rangoon's part to silence the Karens (and other insurgents) through a series of decisive offensives. Subsequently it was an attempt to wrest control of the border from them, so that the Burmese military itself - and not its enemies - could profit from the lucrative cross-border trade. Latterly, the new SLORC has wanted to reap the benefits of the various concessions it has made to Thai logging and other companies. It should not be forgotten that until recently the only access Rangoon had to Thailand the length of the Karen and Shan State borders was puny Myawaddy (Mae Sot) and Takilek (Mae Sai). The Four Cuts campaign as a whole dates back to the late 1960s. The idea was to neutralize the rebels by systematically clearing territory controlled by them. The insurgents' supply lines were to be interdicted, their access to funds and food from their rear areas interrupted, their lines of communication severed, and their means of recruitment disrupted. Ne Win set up special new task forces to effect these "four cuts" - the feared Light Infantry Divisions. In a series of brutal offensives the LID's singled out large squares of land and then went through them, burning and destroying, confiscating, terrorizing and killing, resettling and pressganging. Today some dozen of these anti-rebel strike forces exist - they have bizarre designations such as 77th, 88th and 99th Division.

Nowhere was the campaign more vicious than in South-East Burma. In the early 80s Rangoon moved with full vigour against the Karens, and also against the Karennis and Mons. For a decade the Burma Army operated like some foreign marauding army, attacking its own people in their own country. For the onlooker it was hard not to conclude that the motivation for the Four Cuts was racial, even genocidal. All the KNU strongholds along the Dawna Range came under attack. Mae Ta Wo (Ban Ta Song Yang), just south of Manerplaw and in the heart of Karen country, fell, cutting north-south links between KNLA 7th and 6th Brigade areas. Later the Three Pagodas Pass fell, along with Wa Lae, Kloe Dae, Mo Po Kae and Palu. Other bases, such as Kawmoorah, were overrun by Rangoon, but quickly recaptured by the Karens. Manerplaw was attacked and bombarded, but never taken. The success of the campaign spelt a serious setback for the Karens, if not disaster. Up and down Kawthoolei the scene was one of devastation, with villages torched and fields ravaged. Tens of thousands of Karen refugees poured across the border into Thailand, while scores of thousands more sat poised (as they still are) to follow. The fighting badly affected cross-border trade, causing KNU revenue from taxes, vital for financing the struggle, to dip by some 60%. In the grim Burma Army offensive of 1992 an estimated 10% of the KNLA was wiped out. By the early 90s the Karens were reeling from a series of blows from which, many commentators feared, they might never fully recover.

The insurgents' response to such systematic destruction was to close ranks and form first the National Democratic Front and then the Democratic Alliance of Burma. The NDF was formed in the KNU's new Manerplaw GHQ in May 1976, at the time when Bo Mya's grip on the Karen movement was becoming complete. An alliance of a dozen ethnic insurgent organizations, the Front for the first time united minority armies from all around Burma. NDF members demanded a Union of Burma with states federated on the basis of Western models, although separatist calls were later toned down. Cohesion and effectiveness grew during the 80s, especially when the formidable KIO with its 8000-strong army returned to the NDF fold. A high-water mark was the link-up in 1986 of the NDF and CPB, meaning that for a while an unprecedented 30,000 guerrillas were allied against Rangoon. However, the alliance with the CPB rankled with anti-communist Bo Mya, and so the pact was short-lived. This was not the supremo's only irritation. Despite being its president, he grew impatient with the NDF itself. Perhaps the Karen strongman had grown too used to having his own way, or perhaps he had genuine reason for disillusion with the Front, but disagreements arose between his KNU and the other members, and Bo Mya threatened to take the Karens out of the NDF. But it never came to that, for these bickerings were suddenly overtaken by the great Burmese democracy uprising of 1988 and by the foundation of the DAB.

The popular uprising of 1988 was the result of a number of long-standing economic and political resentments. In particular it was triggered by two recent demonetizations, which made large banknotes worthless and overnight cancelled people's savings. Pro-democracy demonstrations began in towns and cities all over the country. Fuelled by long pent-up frustration, they escalated in an explosion of anger beyond the wildest expectations. The darling of the rallies was the charismatic and beautiful Aung San Suu Kyi. She soon became, almost by default, the focus of the people's aspirations and the leader of the whole democracy movement. The junta's response was characteristic - a brutal crackdown. Attacks and massacres followed, and there were waves of round-ups and disappearances. Suu Kyi was put under house arrest and held incommunicado. In the midst of the turmoil Ne Win announced his "retirement" after 25 years of misrule. In September 1988, in a bloody coup, Gen. Saw Maung seized power and replaced the veteran strongman. Claiming to have saved Burma from chaos and a communist takeover, Saw Maung announced that the country, now renamed Myanmar, would be ruled by a State Law and Order Restoration Council. The new SLORC continued with more of the old military repression and intensified its Four Cuts against the ethnic rebels.

In spite of all this, democratic elections had been promised, and in 1990 Saw Maung surprised everybody by allowing them to go ahead. SLORC was perhaps convinced that by fair means or foul it would win. It vowed it would honour the election outcome and permitted numerous political parties to be formed. They came to be dominated by Suu Kyi's National League for Democracy. The result of the election was a victory for Suu Kyi and the forces of democracy as overwhelming as the uprising of two years previously. But SLORC notoriously reneged on its promise and failed to hand over power. Suu Kyi, who by rights was Burma's new leader, remained in custody. New waves of arrests were made, all opposition was silenced, and a climate of fear as chilling as any since Independence overtook the country again.

The events of 1988 and 1990 played into the hands of the insurgents. Activists from the cities, having experienced at first hand the brutal clampdown of their own military, and exasperated by SLORC political treachery, went over to the rebels. These were not disgruntled minority people, but Burmese citizens. Many were educated professionals, but the bulk were students. It is estimated that about 10,000 went underground in the jungles and mountains controlled by the ethnic armies, about half making their way to Kawthoolei. Here they immediately started guerrilla training with their hosts, impressing with their alacrity. Aided by the KNU and the NDF, the students founded late 1988 in Kawmoorah the All Burma Students Democratic Front. This renowned organization resolved to work with the NDF. A score of special ABSDF battalions were formed (half of them in Kawthoolei), and they went into battle alongside their insurgent colleagues. Some students were killed in action - witness the ABSDF crosses in Manerplaw cemetery. Others did not go out on patrol, but became medical orderlies or village teachers.

It was in the wake of the 1988 democracy uprising that the important Democratic Alliance of Burma was formed. Established in November of that year in Manerplaw, its chairman was, once again, Bo Mya. The DAB was founded to accommodate along with its military core of NDF members another dozen new dissident Burmese organizations, like the ABSDF. At the inaugural session, the biggest meeting of insurgent leaders ever held in Burma, groups such as the General Strike Committee, the All Burma Young Monks' Union, the Committee for the Restoration of Democracy in Burma (a group of prominent Burmese exiles) and many more, were admitted to the umbrella alliance. The DAB repudiated Saw Maung's SLORC, called on all democratic opposition to come over to the Alliance's side, and in effect set itself up as a provisional alternative government. Indeed, in 1990, anticipating that the democracy elections would be rigged, it instituted a provisional Government of Burma, led by Bo Mya, and began drafting a federal constitution. Burma-watcher Martin Smith reports that at the end of 1990 a group of prominent Burmese MPs arrived at the DAB HQ to announce their own "national coalition government". Declaring a ceasefire with the Alliance, they then allied themselves with the DAB. They claimed to have the backing of scores of other MPs in the land and argued that it was they, as MPs, who along with the DAB truly spoke for the country's populace. The final turn of events, then, in the civil war was that the insurgent forces of the DAB, the NDF and the KNU had come together not just with Burmans, but also with Burmese "elected" popular representatives.

With this the story of the Karen insurgency comes up to date. At the time of our journey down the border the Four Cuts offensives were still in full swing. But shortly afterwards there was a lull in the fighting, a kind of precarious informal truce between Rangoon and the KNU. A breathing space suits both sides. With the new problems nearer to home on the streets of the cities, Rangoon welcomes an opportunity to withdraw some troops, particularly as many are in dangerously exposed forward positions with tenuous supply lines. The KNU, on the other hand, like other ethnic insurgent groupings, is growing increasingly war-weary after more than four decades of fighting. Does the struggle have to last another whole generation, Karen leaders ask? In a letter to Saw Maung which broke a silence of a quarter of a century Bo Mya spoke of the fundamental goodwill of the KNU. The war could not be solved by military means, he correctly indicated, but had to be resolved politically. Whatever their intentions (time to regroup, divide and rule?), at the moment the SLORC seems keen to enter some kind of dialogue with the rebel groups. But it will only negotiate separately, group by group. Some insurgents are unilaterally coming to an understanding with the Burmese authorities. Others, like the Karens, are only really willing to negotiate with Rangoon multilaterally, within the framework of the DAB or NDF.

CHAPTER 10

SINGING GIRLS

Manerplaw - Ban Ta Song Yang - Mae Salid - Mae Sot

It took us a long time to catch a longtail boat going south from Manerplaw. There were few settlements immediately upstream along the Moei, and the distances between them were relatively great. Also, the river was not easily navigable in places. But the main reason why few Karen boatmen would go beyond rebel HQ was that there was a danger of attack by the Burma Army, which held some of the commanding heights down that way. We stood folornly in the morning sun, waiting with our Honda on the sand and rocks of the riverbed. Finally a *hang yao*, its engine making a searing whine, came into view. We waved to it. At first it looked as if the boat was going to pass us by, but at the last moment, after some conference between the passengers and the boatman, it veered round to pick us up. The passengers were two solitary men, and we began to wonder if they had chartered the longtail. This impression was reinforced when we noticed that the boat simply ignored groups of Karens (much to their consternation) waving frantically for a ride with their bundles on the riverbank. The two men and their expressionless boatman helped us stow and lash our motorbike aboard, and we set off.

The Moei was by turns wide and languid, and narrow and fast-flowing. We passed a Karen village on the Thai side and then came to a ferry. This was at a point immediately below the third checkpoint we had walked out to earlier. We wondered if the squint-eyed girl soldier and the cheroot-smoking KNLA boy were still at their posts. The boat moved into a patch of choppy water, small waves smacking under the bow. Suddenly the driver, his face all grim concentration and his arms braced against the steering arm of the engine, headed his slender craft into some rapids. A true aim was critical. A slight error to either side, and the boat would swing round across the current and be washed backwards. The boatman misjudged. The prow veered to the Burmese side, hit the bank and got covered with earth and plants. We drifted back down the rapids until the driver recovered the boat to have another go, this time successfully, just. On these flights up rapids, the engine at full throttle, we seriously feared for our hire-bike. Everything seemed so precarious.

Over the din of the engine we shouted as much to our two fellow passengers. We should not worry, one of them replied, these boatmen made such trips everyday, and in the dry season, when the water was lower, navigation was even trickier. The man who was doing the talking seemed to be a Karen. He wore a brilliant red *Yang* smock over normal civilian clothing and spoke by turns broken English and imperfect Thai. A large and rotund man, he had a bull neck and pug face with heavy jowls and

MAP 9

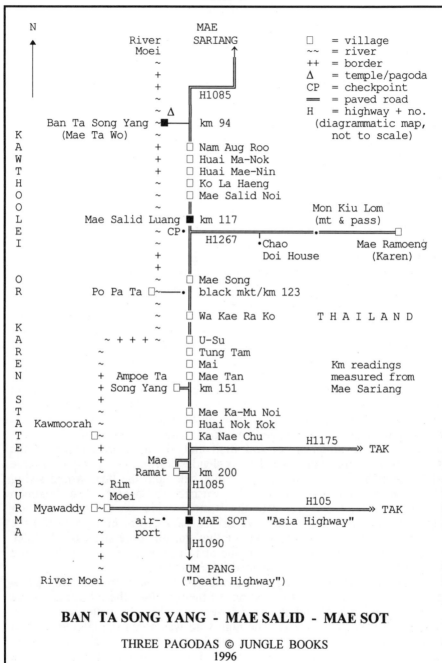

BAN TA SONG YANG - MAE SALID - MAE SOT

THREE PAGODAS © JUNGLE BOOKS
1996

short silvery hair. His skin was unusually dark, like that of southern Thais. Evidently he was a man of some consequence, for he had with him a leather attaché case crammed with documents, and his companion always deferred to him. We could not help noticing the heavy Rolex watch set off on his swarthy right arm. He had a house in Chumpon, the man explained, and was here on business. First he was going to a refugee village upstream, after which he would return "in my boat" to Manerplaw for a meeting. But what were we doing? We explained that we had just spent a few days in Manerplaw and were now trying to get to Ban Ta Song Yang.

The longtail moved into open glassy water. To our right the Dawna peaks reared up, covered in green vegetation, giving the Moei an emerald colour. It was a tranquil scene, stunningly beautiful, very remote, and with a slight but insistent note of danger. An isolated sawmill on the Karen bank glided by, and dirt tracks on either side came down to the water in the middle of nowhere. For long stretches there was no one and nothing, just a solitary man in this jungle wilderness making a dugout canoe, and another fishing from a tiny raft. Ahead lay a pointed triangular mountain, and for a long time we motored towards it. Two villages appeared, the first on the Burmese bank apparently a refugee camp, the second on the Thai side a regular *Yang* settlement. It was here that our two fellow passengers got out. We made to do likewise. But the swarthy Karen businessman motioned to us to stay in the boat. The driver would take us to Ta Song Yang and come back to pick him up later. We did not even have time to express our thanks because immediately the *hang yao* set off again. Presently the driver said to us that we were very lucky. He had been instructed to take us to Mae Ta Wo (as the Karens called our destination). Normally we would have been charged 100 baht each for the trip, even if any boat had been going there. Did we know who "the big man" was? It was Bo Mya, and we were travelling in the leader's boat. Only one thing rankled with us more than the fact we had not recognized or thanked the big man, and this was that our slide film of him and of this remarkably beautiful section of the journey was later stolen in Chiang Dao post office.

The twin villages were followed by a long lonely stretch. Now the Moei was hemmed in by mountains on both sides. Trees and greenery grew from the steep banks right down to the water. The river roiled again, with whirlpools. Swallows, fishing up insects, winged and dipped all round the boat like dive-bombers. A tributary flowed in left between two headlands, while on the right a waterfall cascaded down dark slimy cliffs. In the shade of the Dawna peaks it was distinctly cool even at midday. Rounding a bend, we saw in the distance the double village of Mae Ta Wo/Ban Ta Song Yang. Our longtail cruised past the first Karen section and finally, after a 1½-hour trip at speed from Manerplaw, drew up at the second Thai half. There we had to disembark. Karen boats would go no further - ahead lay pockets of SLORC-controlled territory.

Ban Ta Song Yang

We would have lingered at the disembarkation point, a little bay with a sandy beach where colourful *hang yao* were moored. But the drivers, who were tinkering with the engines, shouted to us to get off the beach, immediately. The Burmese claimed the river and even the beach, and they would shoot at us if they saw us. That seemed ridiculous to us. Only a week ago a *farang* had been shot just where we were standing, the men hollered sharply, gesticulating with greasy hands. And indeed, as we rode up the escarpment that separated the village from the Moei, we spotted a sign at the top which read in Thai and Burmese "Thai Border". Thus it was that we re-entered Thailand.

Ban Ta Song Yang, not to be confused with the district town of Ampoe Ta Song Yang 60 kms further south, was altogether a strange place. We scooted around the network of dreamy dusty alleyways, but found the village drained of life. No one was around and no shops were open. There was not even any stand where a noodle soup could be had - a rare thing in Thailand. We approached some children to ask why the village was so quiet, but they all ran away. Old people peered at us suspiciously from the dark interiors of houses. Finally a woman explained to us that today was the day of some special religious celebration. Everybody was at the temple. We found the temple - Wat Mong Kon Kiri Kaet, a brand-new Thai affair with high sloping roofs - and, sure enough, most of the villagers were inside.

Continuing our search for food and also for someone to quiz, we figured that the police station must be manned, so we rode in there. But the large central BPP compound overlooking the river was as deserted as everywhere else. Unchallenged, we roamed through its buildings, perused the duty book, and studied the official local maps. Our only witness was King Bhumipol, whose serious bespectacled face stared out of a large wall calendar. The station was heavily fortified, confirming that the area was a hot spot. The yard was full of sandbagged bunkers, observation points and, as all along the riverfront "promenade" and indeed all around the village, machine-gun posts. Looking out over the pale green Moei, it was difficult to believe that these defences were necessary. Over the river, completely uninhabited, thickly forested mountains rose straight out of the water. But the threat was real enough. Hanging up in the compound, just as at Wat Fah Wiang In on the Shan border, was a large piece of shell casing, a grim souvenir of recent SLORC bombardments.

If the shell had not landed in 1984, it must have fallen in 1988. In 1984, at the beginning of the Four Cuts offensives against the Karens, the Burma Army overran this area. In a carefully planned strike, 2000 44th LID assault troops captured the nearby KNLA Mae Ta Wo base. So successful were they, setting up a garrison there, that they held on to it for nearly five years. But then in the autumn of 1988 the Karens managed to regain the position. In the major month-long battle, which towards the end involved ABSDF student soldiers, there were heavy casualties. The silence of the mountains opposite and the peacefulness of Ta Song Yang were illusory. It was but a short time since all had reverberated with the sounds of exploding shells and gunfire.

Back near the "Thailand Border" sign we found a small makeshift restaurant. Located on a knoll and called *Rim Moei*, it overlooked the border river, as well at the steep track down to the longtails. The owner cooked up a mediocre fried rice for us. At the restaurant we found the policemen. Although it was only two in the afternoon, here they were on Mekhong whisky duty. They were drunk. They obviously thought that we could not understand Thai, for in the midst of their discussions one of them bragged loudly that he got 10,000-baht kickbacks for turning a blind eye when the teak logs came over. We had little desire to fraternize with these BPP men, and so soon left the village. The way out was a one-km long access road, at the end of which, where it joined the "main" road, stood a particularly splendid wooden portal, surrounded by a welter of signs. In Thai, Burmese and Karen these indicated the way to Ta Song Yang school, the BPP camp, the health centre, the police station and the jetty. We particularly liked two notices which provided an ironic comment on this sinister smuggling nest. "Welcome, visitor, to the golden honest village", one read, "where the inhabitants' votes are not to be bought." Another announced: "Welcome to Ban Ta Song Yang with its famous handcuff-making workshop."

Putting the golden honest village and also our two river trips behind us, we made ready to continue south by road. We had joined Highway 1085. To the north, 94 kms away, lay Mae Sariang, while south, 139 kms over the horizon, was Mae Sot. Route 1085, on the map a tenuous wiggly 233-km long line running clean down the border, was a road built primarily for military "border security" purposes. Few people used it (because of its great length and also because of robberies in the night), and in the early 90s there was no through public transport. In fact the road had only recently (mid-'91) been completely sealed. Without doubt it was one of the most spectacular rides in Thailand, perhaps second only to the extraordinary Mae Sot - Um Pang "Death Highway".

Much of the excitement came in the initial Mae Sariang - Ban Ta Song Yang stretch, which now lay behind us. For 60 miles the little road climbed through a marvellous alternation of airy open bushland, cool oppressive jungle, banana palm country, forests of pink, orange and white flowering trees, sun-scorched scrubby upland and eerie bald mountaintops, finally making a long descent to Ban Ta Song Yang. But the second central section was hardly less impressive. For 60 kms, to approximately U-Su, the road ran precisely along the border, shadowing the Moei and the Dawna Range. Even on the final section, from U-Su down to Mae Sot, the 1085 was never far from the border river and mountains. The motorbike dipped and swung through thrilling scenery. To the east, sunny singing mountainsides, reafforested with teak saplings, rose out of the narrow Moei valley, and to the west, in the shade with the afternoon sun behind them, a succession of dark tree-clad outcroppings soared almost perpendicularly straight out of the river. Karen villages crouched on each bank where space permitted. Those on the Thai side had intriguing names like Nam Aug Roo (= water coming out of a hole), Huai Ma-Nok, Huai Mae-Nin, Ko La Haeng and Wa Kae Ra Ko. At intervals, in the middle of nowhere, telltale unmarked tracks left the side of the road to go down to the river. We could see hardwood logs piled up on the Burmese bank, waiting to come across at night - when Ta Song Yang's police chief was looking the other way.

Mae Salid

It was not long before we passed through Mae Salid Noi (parva) to arrive at Mae Salid Luang (magna). At a distance of 117 kms by road from Mae Sariang, this Karen refugee village - also spelt Mae Sarit Luang - was the first place of any consequence going south down the 1085 and exactly halfway to Mae Sot. We were surprised to find a thriving roadside market. In front of it a number of Mae Sot *songtaews* were parked, gleaming in the teatime sun. After the poor fare at Ta Song Yang, we stopped for a snack. A Karen lady was serving up one of the most unconventional but delicious noodle soups we ate anywhere - a fiery spicy brown liquid with noodles, vegetables, a boiled egg and dried shrimps in it. She told us of a new guesthouse in Mae Salid. It was just across the road, slightly up the hill. As it was too late to get on to Mae Sot that day, we walked across to see if we could spend the night there. They had a room, a gloomy *Yang* boy said laconically.

Mae Salid GH was not one of the greatest places we stayed in. The Karens had always impressed us with their hospitality, helpfulness and integrity, and so we were all the more disappointed with our stopover in this lodging. The guesthouse seemed to be in the charge of half a dozen smoking boys, friendly enough, but lackadaisical. Of course, in a remote refugee village one does not expect overmuch. Nevertheless, a place which pretended to be a guesthouse, charging tourists 100 baht for a room for two, could have provided better amenities. The position and outward appearance of the house was fine enough. Set in a commanding position on the side of a hill, the wooden building had a spacious balcony, from which the visitor could look out over the village and the Moei to the Burmese mountains beyond. There was also a roomy vestibule, in which guests could eat supper sitting cross-legged on the polished teak floor. But we found nowhere safe to leave the Honda. The best we could do was, with the aid of a couple of the boys, to manhandle it up into the garden and park it overnight below the guesthouse balcony. But no one was really happy with this. One of boys confessed next morning that he had not slept a wink for fear of the bike being stolen in the night. Every time a dog had sniffed around in the garden, he had crept out into the moonlight to check that the machine was still there.

It was a pity that the boys' solicitude in respect of the motorbike did not extend to the accommodation and food. Our room was a stifling windowless box. With no electricity, there was no hot water, no lighting and no fan. The sole object in the wooden room was a mattress on the bare floorboards. Presumably the cracks between all the boards were for spitting through, hilltribe-fashion. In the adjacent "bathroom" a shower had been rigged up, but it did not work. With no water running either evening or morning, it was not even possible to fill up the lavatory bucket and wash out of that. Not that the idea was appealing - the plastic dipper was lined with green slime. The bathroom facilities were little improvement on the river, and actually it would have been better to take our soap and towel and wash in the Moei along with the refugees. All night long a sickly sweet smell of urine emanated from the bathroom.

For 35 baht per person the boys cooked up an all-in evening meal. From the comments in the guestbook we learnt that this was always the same - stewed chicken with rice, stewed vegetables, and fresh fruit. That would not have been so bad, except the stew was horribly greasy and the chicken all inedible bone bits with at most one nugget of tough old hen flesh adhering to it. All in all it was food reminiscent of what we had been glad to leave behind in Manerplaw. But no matter, we were able to supplement the fare with some after-dinner titbits bought from the stores down by the road and nibble them with glasses of *lao kao* on the balcony as darkness fell. And that was the redeeming feature of this guesthouse. Communication with the Karen boys was restricted (although a couple of them had a smattering of Thai and even of English) and they retired early to their own small boxes to smoke. But with the other odd traveller passing through it was a pleasure to sit there trading stories while the sun lowered behind the Dawna peaks.

During breakfast on the balcony one of the Karen lads pointed out to us a hill in the middle distance on the Burmese side. There were orange gashes near the summit, much more clearly visible through binoculars. It was a SLORC outpost of some 70-80 soldiers. From time to time, in their boredom or lust for meat and drink, they apparently came down in this direction to ambush the Karens and steal livestock and whisky. Not so long ago they had shelled the Karen settlement on the far bank of the Moei. Tired of the harassment, the Karens had moved all their families over to Mae Salid, although there were still about 200 KNLA troops left on the far side. Seeing the move, the Burma Army had then bombed Mae Salid itself, since which time the Thais had maintained a military presence in the village. The refugees were housed in an area between the market and the river. When we visited them, we found particularly wretched and impoverished people.

One km south of Mae Salid we came across the first and only real turning off the 1085 for 200 kms (counting from Mae Sariang). A BPP checkpoint and military encampment stood near the junction. It was an unusually serious affair, with sandbagging around it and obstacles across the road. The soldiers were friendly enough, if watchful. The side road (H1267) was a small metalled way which zigzagged 16 kms up to *Chao Doi House*. Exploring up there one year, we found a homely ranch-style lodging nestling in a tiny secluded valley and smothered in pink *fuang fah* blooms, run by one Mr Narong, a Thai ex-policeman and former tin-miner. Beyond his house the side road rounded Mon Krating mountain, climbed over Mon Kiu Lom (= windy col) mountain and pass, skirted Mr Narong's disused tin mine, and descended to Mae Ramoeng, an especially old Karen village (200 years). Some maps and guidebooks show a road continuing from the village to Om Koi, a mistake supported by a misleading sign on the 1267 itself announcing "Om Koi 84 kms". But at the time of our visit there was no way through here (yet) - except on foot - and the sign actually indicated Om Koi district, not town. The isolated mountainous hinterland beyond Mae Ramoeng is the source of most of Thailand's annual 25 tons of raw opium - not an area to stray into.

Po Pa Ta

From the boys at *Mae Salid GH* we learnt of the "black market" of Po Pa Ta. It lay five kms south of the 1267 junction, beyond the village of Mae Song. We would have gone clean past the market had we not been alerted by a couple of pick-ups parked for no apparent reason at the roadside. From the 1085 nothing could be seen of Po Pa Ta. Behind the trucks a path dropped down into a motley conglomeration of leaf-roofed buildings. Crammed between the highway and the Moei, this was the black market. A dark corridor ran through the shacks, lined on each side by general stores. At first sight it was an Aladdin's cave down here. Everything was on sale - from dried fish to catapults, from Karen costumes to the "best Thukhita cheroots", from milk bread to Burmese cloth. But after a while we noticed a uniformity in the merchandise and also that much of it had come not from Burma, but from Mae Sot. The goods were more to provision people in Kawthoolei than to supply passers-by with contraband.

More interesting than the goods were the marketeers and general atmosphere. Outside in the sun naked children played in the dirt, while inside men and women peered furtively out of gloomy rooms behind their stores. Did they live here, we wondered, or did they cross every day from Burma? Were they legitimately in Thailand, or were they, like the market itself, merely tolerated by the authorities in this one spot? Nearly all the men had black beards and skullcaps, suggesting that they were Muslim Indo-Burmese or Arakanese Rohingyas. But they could also have been recent Bangladeshi refugees, such as we later found in Mae Ramat. A tall gaunt old man told us that his grandfather had lived in India, and when we unthinkingly referred to the market as a "black market", he gravely corrected us with "refugee market". While prices were cheap by western standards, none of the stallholders was prepared to do any real bargaining.

At the back of the market a log bridge led to a steep path. Scrambling up it, we came to a track which led down to the Moei. Here a marvellous arena greeted us, but with a strange atmosphere. There was the limpid river itself, a backdrop of sheer mountains, a long rickety bamboo bridge crossing the water (wide at this point), and on the far bank, perched atop an escarpment, the village of Po Pa Ta. At the foot of the escarpment, in a bucolic idyll, children were playing at the water's edge, cattle were wandering along the sandy beach, and men and women were making ready to set off in a longtail. And yet the mood of this arena seemed to us even more unfathomable, shiftier, than in the market. Numerous characters were waiting around, but for what? As soon as we arrived, a crackle of small-arms fire reverberated for several seconds around the walls of the lush bowl. The shooting continued sporadically throughout our stay. What was it? As no one seemed concerned, we ignored it too (actually it was hunters on the mountainsides). The bamboo bridge and the market indicated that Po Pa Ta was a regular frontier crossing-point. But no one seemed to be in charge, unless it was the KNLA. No Thai police or military were in evidence, suggesting that things were left to look after themselves - another extraterritorial corner like Mae Saam Laep. Closer inspection, however, revealed individuals discreetly positioned, watching through binoculars. But were they plain-clothes *dorchodor*, or the KNLA watching out for Burmese soldiers, or smugglers checking that the coast was clear?

The gaunt old trader in the market had said that we could cross to Po Pa Ta village. So we went down to the bamboo bridge. This was in two sections, which met in the middle of the river on a sandbank. There seemed to be some kind of control post on the central islet. Stepping onto the first section of bridge, which creaked and swayed above the water, we arrived at the checkpoint. In a hut half a dozen KNLA men were sitting around, armed with M16s. An older man, apparently in charge, was chewing betel, spitting out red saliva onto the blinding sand. We asked him if we could look at Po Pa Ta. That would be alright, he said, but we would have to pay a toll. We asked how much, expecting this to be a nominal 10 or 20 baht. One baht each, he replied. But we had to leave our cameras with them, another man ordered. We had already hidden our cameras in our bags and said we had none with us. Then, paying our princely one baht each, we made to continue. But it seemed a good idea, before reaching the point of no return, to find out how much it would cost to cross back and whether there would be any trouble with the Thai police. We had heard horror stories of travellers being forced by rebel armies to pay extortionate sums to return or having trouble with the Thai authorities for having illegally left and then re-entered the Kingdom. The older man with the red-stained mouth shrugged his shoulders, saying that there would be no problem with the police. And to cross back over, he would ask us to pay another one baht each. It was for using the bridge.

Not entirely convinced, we clambered over the second span of bamboo bridge and stepped off, back already after only one day in Burma - or rather the Karen State. Looking back across the water to Thailand, we were struck by the strange thought that while we were in one country, our motorbike

163

and luggage was in another. We also enjoyed the irony that, while people up at Mae Sai were being milked hundreds of baht by SLORC for the dubious pleasure of looking round Takilek and saying that they had been in Burma, down here you could cross for precisely two baht or even for free. Although only a year or two old, Po Pa Ta was already relatively large. Of course, it was a refugee village, full of Karen and other victims of the Four Cuts. It was depressingly squalid, unexpectedly so for a *Yang* place. We tried to take photographs in the main street, but were immediately prevented by a number of people. They said it was for security reasons, but it may also have been because conditions made a poor advertisement for the insurgent cause. If there was a black market anywhere in the area, it was in the half-hearted shops along Po Pa Ta's "thoroughfare". Besides Thai products, there were also Chinese goods and cartons of American cigarettes at 90 baht (£2) for 200, brands unobtainable in Thailand because of the government tobacco monopoly.

Two teachers took us in hand and showed us round. They spoke reasonable English and were not Karens, but dissident ABSDF students. The nicest thing to do at Po Pa Ta, they said, was to walk in the early morning or late afternoon along the Moei where it flowed round in a great sweep before one particularly massive monolith. They showed us their school, inside which little groups of sweetie-pie infants where distractedly wrestling with the Burmese, Karen and English alphabets. But they wanted us in particular to see what was called "the Library". Of the school and the library we could take as many photographs as we liked. The library was really more a propaganda centre for the KNU and especially the Students' Front. Here were stacks of back copies of the magazine *Dawn*, stamped on the front cover "Ye Kyam Camp, ABSDF 207 Regiment". The magazine was the official news bulletin of the students. It followed developments in the popular uprising, sought to boost morale, and kept tabs on SLORC, detailing Burma Army atrocities and defections. On the walls of the library were portraits of democracy heroine Daw Aung San Suu Kyi, as well as photo displays of KNU and ABSDF activities. Posters proclaimed OUR HEADS ARE BLOODY BUT UNBOWED and KACHIN STATE - OPIUM FREE STATE 1991. There was also artwork depicting a fighting peacock. This emblem, taken from the old student journal "Khut Daung" (= fighting peacock) and much touted during the 1988 uprising, had become the logo of the ABSDF.

The guerrilla student teachers were likeable fresh-faced individuals, but there was also a certain hectoring cockiness about them, which endeared them to us less. One surveyed us the whole time from behind designer sunglasses. Whether it was to protect his identity or for preening purposes was not clear, but it was not something the Karens normally did. On our border journey we came into contact with several ABSDF groups. A similarly ambiguous message came to us from them too. Some students, in a depressed state, had taken to "smoking", while others tried to sponge off us, one individual once stealing from us a bottle of Mandalay Rum. But it is difficult to be harsh with these boys. In the last analysis theirs is a hard pitiful lot. Many are educated and from professional Rangoon or Moulmein families. They have witnessed such terrible things that they have been compelled to flee to people and places they have never seen before. After the first flush of anger and the elation at having linked up with sympathetic ethnic rebels, they have come to find themselves in impoverished jungle backwaters with no future prospect except the hopeless one of endlessly more of the same. For if they return to their home towns, they face years in prison or worse. When they arrived, they expected to find plenty of arms and western support to further the struggle, but hardly any was forthcoming. It is estimated that the majority of Front students in Kawthoolei have contracted the malaria endemic there, some dying of it. Caught between a rock and a hard place, and accepting that they are not cut out for the rigours of jungle guerrilla life, hundreds if not thousands have fled into Thailand, going underground. But there they have found no solution either. Many have been rounded up by the Thai authorities, who find them an embarrassment, put into camps and repatriated to Burma, where they have gone to their deaths or an unknown fate. Recently, those who have remained with the NDF insurgents have become a source of friction. The students, with no funds or local livelihood, are an extra burden on already overstretched insurgent resources. Some rebel leaders have found them arrogant, mere guerrilla upstarts. One ABSDF deputation which went to Manerplaw to complain was unceremonially incarcerated. The dissidents were rocking the boat. A few students have been suspected of spying for SLORC and, "just to be sure", have been executed. Guerrilla leaders are coming to appreciate that the reinforcements which were at first so welcome are increasingly a liability. They draw down on the ethnic armies especial Burma Army venom. When we once made an excusion from Mae Or to Pang Yon, we found that the ABSDF 601 battalion camp there had just been "vacated". Asking the local Karenni Army commander why the students had gone, we were told simply that "they were no good."

Between Po Pa Ta and Mae Sot there was still the little matter of some 110 kms, seventy of them mountainous - an exhilirating if towards the end rather relentless ride. For some distance the 1085 pursued its course beside the Moei, while the Dawna outcroppings on its western bank continued to rear up one after the other like an endless serpent's back. The villages of Wa Kae Ra Ko, Mae U-Su (with its nearby cave), Tung Tam, Mai and Mae Tan flew past. More sandbagged paramilitary BPP posts fished us up, some checking us, others not. One group of *dorchodor* were able to solve a little mystery for us. The strange succession of stagnant ponds we had seen on the east side of the road were places where experiments were being conducted with different strains of malarial mosquitoes. We encountered elephants. In groups of three or four and supervised by their mahouts, they were on their way to or from work. The lumbering beasts, chains jangling and a youth aloft each with red-stained mouth, were a reminder that we were still in the heart of Karen country. One oncoming tusker caravan provided a comic touch. As we rode slowly past, all seven, as if consumed with curiosity, turned round on the spot, ending up facing the wrong way, much to the annoyance of their scolding cajoling minders.

Ampoe Ta Song Yang (151 kms south of Mae Sariang) was a relatively large place. In this administrative centre lying just west of the road we found a market, foodstalls and, at long last, petrol. More villages with magical names followed - Mae Ka-mu Noi, Huai Nok Kok and Ka Nae Chu. Near the latter we finally emerged from the mountains, descending into a hot plain. The air was fragrant with oregano and oranges. Slowly the traffic began to increase. It was an uninteresting plain, and as far as the eye could see the trees had been devastated. A left turn, the first side road going anywhere since Mae Sariang, was the 1175 northern mountain road to Tak, while two turnings on the right went into the small town of Mae Ramat (km 200). After that a wide speed road thundered through numerous outlying villages until (km 233) at a T-junction we hit Route 105. This was the massive Pan-Asian Highway, which at some time in the future is supposed to link Singapore with Istanbul, if the many intervening countries can get their act together. East went to the provincial capital of Tak, and west proceeded a few kms to Rim Moei, where the road stopped short. Beyond the T-junction lay Mae Sot, which, discounting Mae Hong Son, was the only major town on the whole of our journey between Chiang Mai and the Three Pagodas.

Mae Sot

We had always imagined Mae Sot to be a small cool place by a river at the foot of some hills. Instead we found a hot noisy dusty place in a featureless plain. Joe Cummings (of Lonely Planet guidebook fame) once described Mae Sot to us as the wildest, most lawless town in Thailand, the place in the Kingdom least under central Bangkok control. It had the highest degree of corruption among its authorities and was in the grip of powerful local mafias. Many people still carried guns. And indeed, as we soon discovered, the town had an unmistakable wild-west atmosphere, a certain raw stimulating "anything goes" edge. The reason was its function as the isolated pivot of the region's arms, gems and drugs business. No other town down the western frontier had profited more from the prolific cross-border trade of the 1960s, 70s and 80s. Channelled through Mae Sot on its way to Kawthoolei's Eastern Division and deeper into Burma, went M16s and AK47s, consumer goods, medicines and fabrics, while in the other direction came jade, rubies, heroin, opium, hardwood, cattle, antiques and foodstuffs. In town the KNLA bought up dextrose-saline drips by the gross, while the numerous precious stones shops around the central *Siam Hotel* formed a gems centre in Thailand second only to Chantaburi. Mae Sot's two big cattle markets, one at the H1085/Asia Highway junction and the other near Mae Ramat, dealt expressly in livestock that had made the long trek over the Dawna.

On our Honda we scouted round our new port of call - no easy matter in the chaotic traffic-choked grid of one-way streets. The town seemed like a beefier glitzed-up version of Mae Sariang or the rich twin of swanky Loei over in eastern Thailand. The streets clotted around two main roads, running parallel through the centre on an east-west axis. The more northerly of these, the Intra Kiri Road (the one with the post office and police station), took vehicles from west to east, while the more southerly one, the Prasart Viti Road, drew traffic from east to west - at least that was the theory. The latter road was perhaps the real main drag of Mae Sot, identifiable by its midpoint *Siam Hotel* and bombastic *Thai Farmers Bank*. As we went round and round trying to get some orientation, interconnecting streets fleetingly revealed miraculous gold-covered pagodas, glowing in the late afternoon sun.

Mae Sot centre was brash, modern, westernized and tangibly artificial. Here was the vulgarity, ambiguity and sleaze of a boom town. The streets were lined with spanking rows of shophouses all gleaming white, as if cast in icing sugar. They were paradigms of that Thai speciality "wedding-cake" architecture - pastiches of modernist, vernacular and neoclassical design. Every shophouse flashed chunky gold trading signs in four languages - Thai, Chinese, Burmese and English. And indeed Mae Sot was a cosmopolitan place. *Farangs* aroused little interest here. Amid Thais from near and far, Chinese merchants, Muslim Indo-Burmese traders, Bangladeshi refugees, Karen jobbers, illegal Burmese workers, Hmong migrants and many others, Caucasians were just another group. Closer inspection revealed that the wealth-creating core was Chinese-dominated. Mae Sot oozed money. Parked in front of the gem dealers, wholesalers', bakeries, supermarkets and department stores were flashy top-of-the-range Volvos and Mercedes. The liquor stores were piled high with Scotch whisky and French brandy, and in one shop we could find English toffees but no mosquito coils.

Curiously for such a metropolis, it was not easy to find anywhere suitable to stay. There was plenty of luxury accommodation for the wealthy trader, and a number of unspeakable doss-houses, but not much in between that was pleasant, modest and clean. We thought we would give the renowned *N° 4 Guest House* a try, situated out at the western end of town (why are so many guesthouses in Thailand called "N° 4" - an allusion to the white pure N° 4 heroin?). Here, in a wooden building set in mediocre surroundings, the personnel were friendly and helpful, but the atmosphere did not appeal to us. It seemed too self-consciously laid-back, threatening to turn into a slummy semi-hippie commune. Leaving "N° 4", we almost went to the other extreme. We decided to try the *Siam Hotel*. They had some fair-priced rooms, but unfortunately, owing to some conference or fair, these were all taken. We were deliberating in the lobby about splashing out for once on an expensive room when our minds were made up for us. Suddenly a boy ran past and out of the front door with his hands, shirt and trousers covered in blood. He rampaged around the car park half demented - screaming, trying to staunch the flow of blood with his shirt, and vowing to kill someone inside the hotel. We learned that in the kitchen the cooks had been fighting with meat cleavers.

Back in the Intra Kiri Road we pulled up to have another look at the guidebooks. Stopping near the post office, we noticed by chance a place called *Old House*. It looked like a guesthouse, but we could not be sure. At that moment a *farang* walked out of the entrance. He confirmed that it was indeed possible to stay there. And so it was that we stumbled on the nicest accommodation we ever found in Mae Sot. Set well back, *Old House* was separated from the traffic-congested road by a deep front garden, full of flowers, bushes and creepers. Immediately in front of the house was an idyllic little beer area, covered over with a pergola. True to its name, the guesthouse was a sizeable old wooden building, and like all these old teak places, had that characteristic hot dusty smell that comes from dried out teak planking, but also from the town dust that has seeped in through the cracks. The rooms and bathroom inside were basic, but the restaurant was quiet and dignified, and its atmosphere magical.

The date of that first visit to *Old House* was the evening of 8th February 1990 - in the event a fateful night both for the region as a whole and for the local Karen insurgents in particular. Having cleaned up after the ride down from Mae Salid, we sat in the restaurant. After the fare of Mae Salid and Manerplaw, the food and drink was most welcome. The tables were low, and guests sat at them cross-legged on cushions on a polished teak floor. A demure Burmese girl brought the dishes, kneeling at the side of each table to serve them. Somewhere someone was gently strumming an acoustic guitar. At the next table a single *farang*, in his late thirties, sat alone. We thought no more about him, and in fact, with our spirits restored from the supper, went out to stretch our legs after the ride on the Wing.

A short way beyond the guesthouse there was a Chinese brothel. The entrance to this small ramshackle wooden building was lit by two dull red Chinese lanterns. Outside, from a trestle table, an old woman was serving an assortment of fortifying spirits and elixirs. In the glass jars were murky concoctions such as snake whisky and centipede wine. These were to give customers courage to cross the threshold and, once across, to get up their virility. A tremendous noise was coming from somewhere nearby, and it turned out that a fund-raising festival was in full swing in the grounds of a temple. The temple, Wat Manee Prai Son, housed one of the glowing pagodas we had glimpsed earlier. It was a large bell-shaped *chedi*, set on a square gold-tiled base and covered in mini pagodas. Near it squatted an ample smiling "Happy Buddha". In the monastery compound an open-air cinema was projecting some gruesome film, while on the sidelines, incongruously, a troupe of Burmese dancers was performing to traditional music. From all around came the sound of competing rock bands. In the middle of the hurly-burly, monks, installed high up on the golden pagoda, were hauling a gilt rooster up a wire by means of pulleys. People put offerings in the rooster, which the saffron-robed bonzes then received at the top. A large number of surly drunken people were hanging around, people were brawling, and dogs were snapping and snarling. It was a sinister aggressive atmosphere, which seemed to prefigure the events of later that night.

Back at *Old House*, we found the lone *farang* still sitting at his low table. He was Thorben, a Danish guy. He had a military background, had once been a captain in the Danish army, and had worked as a military advisor to the Iraquis in their war with Iran. He seemed to us a sort of educated Rambo character, who preferred semi-military clothing, talked a lot, and had a thirst for adventure. He was interested in crossing illegally into Burma "for the hell of it", and had a plan to boat on his own down the River Mae Khong. Thorben had a headful of ideas, but lacked specific direction. We, on the other hand, had a specific plan (to continue on south down "Death Highway" to Um Pang), but, not having met anyone who had done this or who could tell us anything sensible about it, were lacking in courage. So it was as if we were all made for each other. He would get his concrete goal, and we would find the moral support we were looking for, in the form of a man with substantial military experience.

While we were talking deep into the night, laying plans and questioning the owner of *Old House* about hiring a second motorbike for our new Danish friend, we suddenly became aware of the heavy crump of mortarfire and the crackle of machine guns a few kms away. We looked at each other in alarm, but the owner said that this just happened from time to time. It was the Burmese fighting again with the Karens on the border. However, this was no ordinary skirmish. The fighting continued for hours. Thorben, assaying the timbre and magnitude of the explosions like a connoisseur, kept muttering things like "82 mm mortar" and "heavy artillery". All night long the ground shook under *Old House*. What with a fullscale battle raging not far away, too much whisky coursing through our veins, the headiness of the plan to go down Death Highway, the fatigue from a long day, and the oppressive heat of the teak bedrooms, sleep was impossible.

During that night Burmese government forces, as part of their most massive Four Cuts offensive against the Karens to date, attacked and overran Kawmoorah (Ko Mu Ra), the Karen stronghold not far north of Mae Sot. Set just inside Burma, it lay opposite the Thai village of Wang Kaew, with the River Moei flowing in between. Rangoon had good reason to want to seize Kawmoorah. For years this had been Karen supremo Gen. Bo Mya's 7th Brigade base, and for years, since as far back as 1965, it had been one of Kawthoolei's most significant trading and customs posts. In its heyday up to 1000 head of cattle and 1000 porters a day had passed through on their way over the border, generating by local standards a stupendous income in taxes. Bo Mya had even set up a special KNLA 101 battalion to guard the customs gate. It was in Kawmoorah also, two years before this assault, that the ABSDF, so hated by Rangoon, had been founded. The outpost had been attacked before, but on each occasion the Karens had been able to repulse the Burma Army. Now the situation looked much less favourable.

While some Burma Army troops pounded Kawmoorah with mortars and heavy artillery, others, in an attempt to encircle the KNU stronghold, used Thailand (with the tacit support of the Thai Army, led by the now discredited Gen. "logger" Chaovalit) to attack the camp by the backdoor. In what was euphemistically described as a "fighting spillover", hundreds of SLORC soldiers twice crossed the Moei into Thai territory, precipitating the flight not just of thousands of Karen refugees, but of hundreds of local Thais. The Karens, temporarily driven out, mounted a counter-attack, fighting the Burmese on both sides of the border. They managed to cut off the retreat of numerous Burmese, inflicting heavy casualties and leaving many dead. In Wang Kaew alone, the BPP found next day nineteen Burmese and six Karen dead. The newspapers reported that altogether more than sixty people had lost their lives that night. Three captured Burma Army officers and five "porters" were later taken down to Rim Moei (opposite Myawaddy), to be returned to the Burmese side, while the inhabitants of Wang Kaew began filing demands for 20 million baht as compensation for their destroyed village.

The following day Karen rebels returned to Kawmoorah with captured weapons and munitions. Unfortunately, the Burmese, in their retreat, had left a booby-trap bomb. It exploded, killing 33 KNLA guerrillas - one of the worst death tolls of the whole Karen insurgency. Ultimately, Rangoon did not take Kawmoorah in that offensive, nor did it capture it in the following fighting (dry) seasons. On a less momentous but hardly less sinister note, there was another sequel to the events of that night in Mae Sot, which concerned *Old House*. Returning another time to town, we were disconcerted to discover that we could not find the guesthouse anymore. Were we dreaming, or had we imagined it to be somewhere along the road where it was not? Enquiries revealed that the fine old teak building had burnt down in mysterious circumstances. Someone thought that the owner and his wife had gone to Laos. With a new "wedding-cake" shophouse going up on the garden where the magical old lodging had once stood, we could not banish the depressing thought that the teak building had been deliberately torched to move the owners on - an arrangement of affairs Mae Sot-style.

Rim Moei

For the traveller Mae Sot was essentially a place either to be enjoyed for its atmosphere or to be used as a springboard for explorations north and south. But we spent a pleasant afternoon down at Rim Moei (= Moei riverbank), the settlement a few kms west of town where the Asia Highway stopped short at the Moei and the frontier. On the far bank lay Myawaddy, one of the very few places along the whole of the Thai-Burmese border firmly in Burmese hands (like Takilek opposite Mae Sai). That might not always be the case if the Karens ever manage to retake it, as they once tried in 1974. Then, in a pincer movement which turned into the biggest battle in the Dawna region since WW2, the KNU and its allies attacked the outpost from Kawmoorah to the north and Palu to the south. But after five days of savage fighting the 1500-strong insurgent force was unsuccessful and withdrew. Sometimes there was a footbridge across the river at Rim Moei, but we found none. We heard reports that occasionally it was possible for *farangs* to cross to inspect Myawaddy, depending on the whim of the Burmese authorities. Another rumour was that Rangoon was contemplating opening up Myawaddy to tourist trade, in the manner of northerly Takilek. But from the Thai bank there did not seem to be a lot to see across the water, and in the early 90s Myawaddy's significance was in serious decline. Between 1991 and 1992 the value of Thai products entering Burma along the Mae Sot/Myawaddy corridor slumped from 712 million baht to 463 million. From newspaper reports we learned of Thai-Burmese plans to construct a bridge at Rim Moei (a counterpart of the Thai-Laotian Friendship Bridge at Nong Khai), and at the time of writing work has probably started on it.

At Rim Moei we found a scaled-down calmer version of the frenetic Mae Sai-Takilek crossing. No frontier control posts were apparent, and yet official-looking people were hanging around on both sides, keeping an eye on things. Despite the absence of a bridge, a steady trickle of locals was passing to and fro. Nearly all were humping great packages of goods. A dozen longtail boats were moored at the riverbank, and people were either using these to have themselves ferried to Myawaddy, or were simply wading across the twenty metres of thigh-deep water. On the far bank, we could see, besides the jetty, a *wat*, a school, a market, some grass-roofed houses and a lot of bamboo fencing. Much of the fencing was covered with blankets and clothing, drying in the sun. On the Thai side a permanent market, consisting of a street of stalls, sold Burmese goods, but also Thai products required by the Karens and Burmese across the river. Imports from Burma included bags of dried prawns (not cheap), dried fish, cashews, quails eggs, bone chopsticks, jade and other gemstones, cottons, carved wood, lacquerware and kitschy souvenirs. From Rim Moei people were taking over to Burma wholesale parcels of T-shirts, plastic bags, fabrics, coffeemate, sugar, condensed milk and other household items.

Enjoyable down at this sleepy crossing-point was just to sit and watch the leisurely goings-on. A makeshift money-changing stall was dealing in outsize Myanmar notes of all colours. Women and children, in *longyis* and with gold discs of *tanaka* on their cheeks, were portering bales, sacks and boxes on their heads this way and that. An old Burmese monk (eyebrows not shaved off, unlike Thai monks), carrying a broad fanlike object to shade himself from the scorching sun, was being ferried in style across the Moei like some Chinese emperor. A wizened old lady, with a complete mini-restaurant on a tray on her head, went to join him in the boat. Naked boys were cavorting in the river. Dogs stood barking at the little waves. White cows were strolling around. A black-faced man, with a pagoda tattooed on his chest and some Buddhist emblem emblazoned on his back, took to the waters, swimming past the longtails. And the youths of the gaudy *hang yao* idly tweaked the throttles of the boats' outsize engines, making a gratuitous roar of noise.

A hearty meal before "Death Highway" seemed a good idea. But if Mae Sot was not bursting with good places to stay, surprisingly it was not overloaded with great restaurants either. The night market along the main Prasart Viti Road had numerous eating stalls, but the food was inevitably snacky and none of them sold alcohol, so people did not linger after eating. An exceptional stall was the noodle place outside the *Thai Farmers Bank*. This mini-triumph of pavement food was a feast both for the eyes and palate. An outstanding display of prepared vegetables in a glass cabinet spoke of the tasty noodle dishes to come. And behind the mobile stand, at a wobbly folding table, we once enjoyed the best *pat thai* we found anywhere in Thailand. A mixture of fried ribbon noodles, dried shrimps, chopped scallions, egg, crumbled peanuts, soy sauce and pepper was served with a side salad of fresh beansprouts, spring onions, cabbage, sprouting banana pods and a sprig of basil.

But the best meal - and also finest evening's entertainment - we ever found in Mae Sot was at a place called *Nueng Nut* (= N° 1 Girl). Located near Wat Manee Prai Son, this ranch-style restaurant, complete with waggon-wheel decoration, was a typical Thai "singing place". People came here to eat and celebrate, but they also came to be entertained by the *nakrong ying* and *nakrong chai* - "singing girls" and "crooning men". Here we found the good if rather pricey food we had been looking forward to ever since *Intira* in Mae Sariang. Relays of teenage Mae Sot waitresses, earning pocket money after school, brought plates and dishes while a three-piece band warmed up on stage. Savoury beef (from the Burmese heartland), stir fried in oyster sauce, was accompanied by a wonderfully fragrant *tom ka gai* - a soupy chicken curry served up in a "steamboat". In the steamboat glowing charcoal, placed in a central "funnel", continued to simmer the curry at table in a "boat" surrounding the steaming funnel. The lemony coconut sauce yielded up nuggets of chicken breast, shallots, mushrooms, lemon grass, sliced red chillies, galangal, kaffir lime leaves and other intriguing titbits. And our glasses were continually topped up with Mekhong whisky, soda and ice by the assiduous schoolgirls.

The songs in these singing restaurants were mostly lugubrious Thai ditties, not at all appealing to the western ear. But not at *Nueng Nut*. As the evening wore on, the singing and dancing grew ever more spirited. Neither were the singing girls (and boys) the usual wilting Siamese flowers. They were the raunchiest, most vivacious *nakrong* we saw anywhere in the Kingdom. It was all another sign of Mae Sot's grittiness. Considering the fact that within earshot Rangoon's war of attrition against the Karens was entering a crucial phase, it also seemed like part of some gay apocalypse. At *Nueng Nut* there were nine singing girls and two crooning men. They were accompanied on stage by the little band, consisting of drums, synthesizer and guitar. Each singer came on in turn to sing a couple of his or her own songs or old favourites suggested by the guests. Halfway through the evening the girls came on to sing together, and the culmination of the night's entertainment was a suggestive song and dance routine with all nine *nakrong ying* in a line like chorus girls. There was the languid sulky miss (much beloved of Thai men), her glossy black hair all dolled up like a film star. There was the impish little goer, perfect in all her parts, with a round face, huge mischievous mouth, tiny pussycat nose and char-coaled eyebrows. There was the leggy Karen teenager, slightly aloof, with her slender immaculate body ridiculously revealed in a red tutu. And there was the thirty-year old mum, busty, fetching, squeezed into a white dress with a flared skirt, good-natured and entering into the spirit of things.

The mum's dress had red hearts sewn all over it, another girl's blouse was see-through, and the teenager's panties were clear to see. Obviously, the function of the singing girls (and men) was more than just to sing. They paraded themselves on stage in their frilly, slinky or downright erotic outfits partly to create a floor show, but also with a view to catching the eye of the diners. And, indeed, most *nakrong* were also prostitutes. However, the prostitution at a singing restaurant was not the blatant seedy kind found in massage parlours or girlie bars. Things were discreetly arranged, and outwardly everything was innocuous enough. This was why such places were frequented also by female customers, indeed whole families. The men at this table were perhaps having a night on the town, but the lady teachers at that one were celebrating a promotion. The couple over here were eating out, while the family over there was making merry because it was someone's birthday. Singing places were an integral and authentic part of Thai life.

The relationship between *nakrong* and diner was such that if a singer sang well or tickled the fancy of someone at table, the diner bought a jasmine garland and placed it over the singer's head. A popular *nakrong* often had a number of such perfumed garlands around his or her neck. The singer noticed where the admirer was sitting and, prompted by an invitation passed up from the floor, came down to join the diner at table. Often matters went no further than this, but if *nakrong* and music-lover wanted to take the singing a step further, they went off together at the end of the evening, perhaps to a motel on the outskirts of town.

Revisiting Mae Sot a year or two after that first visit, we looked in again at "N° 1 Girl". The place was still flourishing, although prices had risen uncomfortably. Alas, every one of the nine singing girls who had pleased us so much was gone. We produced some photographs, which caused a stir among the staff. It transpired that this girl had gone to Bangkok, while that one was now singing in Korat, and a third was in Kampaeng Pet. The only *nakrong* who was still in Mae Sot was the impish little goer, who was pregnant! The new singing girls at *Nueng Nut* were somehow not as inspiring as their predecessors, and temporarily the star of "Girl N° 1" was on the wane. However, another singing restaurant had opened in a side street nearby. With equally fine food, better prices and good girls, it was the new hotspot. For the time being the real singing continued there....

MAP 10

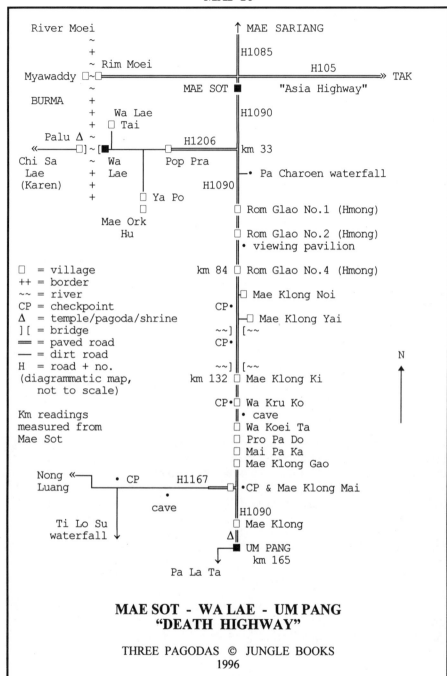

MAE SOT - WA LAE - UM PANG
"DEATH HIGHWAY"

THREE PAGODAS © JUNGLE BOOKS
1996

CHAPTER 11

DEATH HIGHWAY

Mae Sot - Wa Lae - Um Pang

The next leg of our journey was to take us further south down the Thai-Burmese border on Highway 1090 to Um Pang. Of all the trips we made on the Honda Wing, this 165-km run was the most varied and exciting - without doubt the finest ride in Thailand. A real roller-coaster of a road plunged through stunning mountain and jungle scenery. Completed only as recently as 1987, the road surface was already badly deteriorated in places, adding to the excitement. Route 1090 had the alarming designation "Death Highway". This was because during its construction a number of workers had been killed in two infamous massacres. Communist Party of Thailand guerrillas hiding out in the jungle had wanted to prevent the intrusion of the road. By the early 90s the area was quieter, and these days, as Joe Cummings puts it, the route earns its nickname more from its treacherous steep twists and turns, which give rise to numerous accidents. A notorious recent example was when in early 1995 a bus from Bangkok's Santa Cruz school crashed, killing thirty teachers. However, there were other reasons why the route deserved its name. In the border areas west of the road Rangoon continued to wage its ruthless long-standing war of the Four Cuts against the Karen people, depressing signs of which we encountered as we passed. The lonely road was preyed upon by robbers, leaving the few who ventured down the 100 miles of obscurity with a nagging feeling of unease. Specifically for us, "Death Highway" also earned its reputation because of a fatal accident we witnessed near the beginning, and because of a certain incident offroad at Wa Lae....

Our Danish friend Thorben rustled up a Kawasaki 100, which looked so puny and beaten-up that we feared it would never make the journey to Um Pang, let alone back. We stocked up with provisions and also money. The shops in Um Pang, people told us, were very limited, and the next bank after Mae Sot was apparently (incredibly) in Tong Pa Pum, beyond the Three Pagodas and on the way to Kanchanaburi town. At the Shell petrol station at the eastern end of Mae Sot's Intra Kiri Road we tanked up, at the same time setting our Wing's tripmeter to nought. A right turn at the T-junction within sight of the forecourt brought us onto the 1090. For some distance we sped southbound on a flat uninteresting road through the plain of Mae Sot until after 33 kms we arrived at a fork. Left continued another 130 kms or so to Um Pang, while right (H1206) branched off to the small district town of Pop Pra and the border village of Wa Lae. We decided to interrupt our journey to take in Wa Lae.

Pop Pra, really just an extended village, was suspiciously rich-looking, with many splendid new teak houses. It was easy to see why. Just outside was the biggest log depot we saw anywhere down the border. Precious teak trunks from Burma were piled up as far as the eye could see. There were possibly millions of them. Immediately we understood the truth of what Martin Smith has said about the indescribable destruction of the virgin forests in these parts. He reported that in one forest reserve alone (near Wa Lae), which he visited in 1989, over 100,000 trees had been cut down - all as a result of the million-dollar concessions SLORC had sold to Thai logging companies. It was a depressing sight. But that was not all. The land all around Pop Pra itself was devastated, no doubt first logged and then subjected to extensive slash-and-burn. In a scene reminiscent of a WW1 battlefield, charred tree stumps smouldered in acres of ash. This kind of burning often meant that Hmongs were nearby. And, indeed, the whole of Pop Pra District was full of Hmongs. Many had been resettled from villages around Um Pang - a relocation policy still in operation today. It seemed a pity that, in order to preserve the national parks further south, whole landscapes had to be spoiled in the north.

For a few kms the 1206, by now a poor metalled road, proceeded through this forlorn countryside, before giving over to a dust track. On each side of the track were strange compounds. The buildings inside them were barricaded behind wire fencing and wooden palings, or screened from view by bushes. Nameplates at the entrances, discreetly indicating "Muang Pon Co." or "Zilar International Trading Co. (Zitco)", gave away the occupants' business - logging. West of the road, in the distance, our old friends the Dawna mountains began to loom up. Over there, in Kawthoolei, KNU 7th Brigade District was yielding to Duplaya, 6th Brigade District. We passed a turning left to the villages of Ya Po and Mae Ork Hoo. Finally, 41 kms out from Mae Sot, we came up against a barrier. Beside it was a checkpoint, and behind that lay a fortified BPP camp. We had reached the entrance to Wa Lae.

Wa Lae

The BPP soldiers wanted to know our business. We said we wished quickly to visit Wa Lae (second part pronounced "lay"). Unaccountably, they laughed out loud, adding that a visit was out of the question. Often these soldiers tried more to discourage *farangs* from going to sensitive border villages, rather than actually prevent them, so we persisted in our attempt to get past them. However, this time they were adamant. That was a pity, not just because we had wasted time and effort coming along the dusty bumpy track, but because we had heard that Wa Lae was an interesting and important smuggling village. In fact, it faced across the border the Karen village of Palu, another major gateway (like Mae Saam Laep, Kawmoorah and the Three Pagodas Pass) to the Karen State. Traditionally the way through Wa Lae/Palu had been the main route for Karens and Thais alike to Um Pang. Passing through a corner of Burma, it had been a short cut which had obviated the long roundabout way through Thailand on the (at that time unmade) 1090 road.

Such a short cut was now impossible, the *dorchodor* explained, because the Burma Army in its latest and most massive sweep up the Thai-Burmese border had just captured Palu, in fact only the night before. We reflected: first Kawmoorah overrun; now Palu gone, and, as we subsequently discovered, the Three Pagodas Pass also lost, all of them at the same time - the writing really was on the wall for the Karens. Just as Rangoon had been greedy for Kawmoorah, so also it had wanted Palu. This stronghold had been the very first of all the new Karen customs gates that had been opened to profit from the burgeoning cross-border trade of the 60s, 70s and 80s. Established in 1964 by Duplaya KNU commander Shwi Soe, it had grown, like the other gates, into a thriving centre with an extensive "black" market. There had been shops, streets, houses and timber mills, all overlooked by a wooden temple and a large white pagoda on the hill just behind the KNU base. In 1985 the Burmese had executed forty "smugglers" near here, hoping that the example would stifle Palu's trade and also stop revenue flowing to the KNLA. In 1986 they had surrounded the outpost, burning down the timber mills a year later. In 1989 dissident student soldiers had been deployed at Palu, and now in a swingeing nighttime assault the village had fallen. The problem was, the BPP continued, that the Burmese had not just captured Palu, but were claiming Wa Lae itself, even though the village clearly lay on the Thai side of the border river. These disputes over villages or pieces of land along the frontier occurred regularly. They arose because, with the exception of some 58 kms, the 2400-km long Thai-Burmese border had never been clearly defined. Four treaties applied to the long frontier, including a British-Thai one of 1868. Of course, when the Burmese seized a piece of Thai territory, they backed up their claim with some old colonial map showing things in their favour. This was the basis of their pretence not just to Wa Lae, but also to the famous Three Pagodas.

Owing to the events of a few hours earlier, therefore, the situation in Wa Lae was extremely tense. All the Karens of both Palu and Wa Lae had fled, in fact everybody had fled except a few local Thai people in Wa Lae (the Palu Karens were later housed in Mor Goe refugee village). Presumably the Thai inhabitants wanted to look after their property and felt that the SLORC troops had no quarrel with them. Even the police and military had evacuated, withdrawing to this safer position two kms behind the village. Their instructions were not to tangle with the Burma Army, to keep a low profile, and to fire only if fired upon.

The gravity of the situation was borne in on us by the presence at the checkpoint of three utterly dejected Burmese men. They were pressganged porters, who had somehow managed to desert from the Burma Army and had been captured by the BPP on Thai territory. They were in fear of their lives, for if the *dorchodor* returned them, they would be shot on sight and dumped in the river. None of the ten young BPP boys seemed to know what to do with the unshaven men. Obviously the porters could not be returned to Burma, and yet they could not stay in Thailand either. They had no money and could speak no Thai. The soldiers for their part could not speak any Burmese, and so communication was all but impossible. It seemed that the three porters wanted to go to Mae Sot, and the BPP were prepared to let them go, except that the men would never get past the other checkpoints on the way. For the moment at least, the *dorchodor* chain of command seemed to have broken down. But in the end the porters would be taken to Mae Sot and returned to the other side at some safe point further up the border.

The thrill of a genuinely extraterritorial Wa Lae made us (foolishly) all the more keen to go down there. We fraternized with the BPP boys for half an hour and then badgered them again to let us go down to the village. It was too dangerous, they said. Much as the Burma Army hated the Karens, it hated *farangs* even more, whom it took for spies or agents helping the insurgents. Two *farangs*, a girl and a boy, who knew the locality well, on both sides of the border, had gone down to the village a couple of days earlier, but had not returned and were now presumed dead. And recently a western TV unit which had come to film the Karens' plight had been shot at, with ten people injured. We asked the soldiers if they would come down to the village with us, forming an armed guard. They would not, they answered, and when we asked why not, they confessed that they were simply too scared to go.

Finally, the checkpoint guards relented. They said that we two men, Thorben and I, could go down on our own and at our own risk, but that, if anything happened to us, they would know nothing about it. We should not stay any longer than five minutes, we had to leave all our valuables at the checkpoint, and we must sign the duty book. So we divested ourselves of passports, money, cameras, backpacks and jackets, and entered into the logbook our names, nationalities and the exact time of our departure. Then, saying goodbye to everyone at the checkpoint, we set off on the two bikes. It was exhilirating riding unemcumbered down the dirt track to Wa Lae, but, while for the Danish army captain it might have been just another routine sortie, for me it was also terrifying, and I trembled like a leaf.

We rode into a street lined with low wooden houses. They were deserted, and the place seemed like a ghost village. At the bottom end, a narrow river was visible immediately behind the houses. All along its rim and in the gaps between the houses were rolls of gleaming new butterfly barbed wire. The rolls had been put there after the *farang* couple had disappeared. An old man came out of a house and said that we could get a better view round at the market place. We rode warily through the empty alleyways until we found it. It was a dusty square which sloped down to the river. A number of local Thais were standing around there, chatting but watchful. Their faces showed great surprise when they saw us. There was something eerie and chilling about this small market place, so we turned the bikes around, parked them facing uphill, towards the village exit, and left the engines running. In the middle of the square was a military post, surrounded by sandbags, but there were no faces at the observation slits. All round the square, where it bordered the river, ran the same coils of barbed wire. Behind the wire a small footbridge, consisting of a wooden gangplank, crossed the meagre river. It was blocked in the middle by a boarded-up gate. Some wag had attached to this obstacle a nude pinup of a Thai beauty queen. It was a strange conjunction of mortal danger and beauty - Death and the Maiden.

On the other side, just a few feet away, Burma Army soldiers were roaming around. Three were loitering on the bridge itself, relaxing after the fury of the night assault. They were tall thin men, wearing ragged uniforms, belts laden with pouches, grenades, water bottles, knives and the other paraphernalia of war. One had a beaten-up straw sun-hat, and another a red bandanna, which was pulled tight behind his head in a knot. They looked a duplicitous semi-hippie outfit. Of course, they all spotted us immediately, and on seeing the *farangs* stirred into activity. Inexplicably, many seemed to walk away, perhaps to go and get guns. Thorben chose this moment, of all moments, to go down to the water's edge. It seemed to me that we had already stayed too long and that we should get back to the idling motorbikes. Concerned, I asked him what he was doing - did he want to look into the faces of the SLORC fighters eyeball to eyeball? Back came the unconcerned reply that he only wanted to see what the fishing was like. Just then there was a terrific explosion, and Thorben, myself and all the villagers were showered with water and mud. Someone on the other side had lobbed a grenade, but it had hit the barbed wire, falling back into the river. The villagers shouted "Get down, get down", and themselves lay flat in the dust. But it was not my idea to wait for a second attack, so I ran to the bike, jumped on it and retreated to a safe distance, there to wait for the Dane. I saw him go to his bike, get on it - and then stall the engine! In that burning sun-bleached square he kicked at the baby Kawasaki for a good half minute. Finally he came up the hill, and we rode straight out of the village. "What was the hurry?" he said above the din of the engines. "They were trying to kill us", I shouted. "They were fishing with grenades", he replied. "A strange way of fishing", I retorted, "more like they were fishing for you!"

The BPP boys and the others back at the camp had heard the explosion. They all thought we were done for. In spite of what they had said, they sent out a rescue party. Two soldiers immediately came down to the village on motorbikes. But because we rode a different way out of Wa Lae from the way we had come in, they did not meet us. Soon we reached the camp again, much to everybody's relief. The two soldiers soon got the story that we had not been captured or killed and also returned to base. We thanked them for their efforts and sheepishly gathered up our possessions. Then we rode back to Pop Pra and the fork in the road. It was the end of the little ill-advised side-trip to Wa Lae and our encounter with the Burma Army.

"Death Highway"

Death Highway proper began back at the 1090/1206 junction (km 33). The road headed south over a plateau, past numerous villages, houses, experimental farms and agricultural research projects. Through the heat haze mountains began to appear in front of us. Not far down the road we found a sign pointing left down a track to Pa Charoen waterfall. As the fall was near the road, we decided to have a quick look. We were not disappointed. It was a multi-cascaded waterfall with dozens of tiers and basins. But the best thing about Pa Charoen was a little mobile foodstall at its foot. The owner prepared for us an excellent *somtam*, a refreshing salad of grated green papaya, tomato, raw green beans, lemon juice, dried shrimps, shrimp paste, peanuts, garlic, fish sauce, fresh palm sugar and a prise of deadly "mouse shit" chilli peppers.

Following Nam Tok Pa Charoen the 1090 continued straight and long through a blisteringly hot plain of burnt fields and tree stumps. It was another environmental catastrophe up here. In every direction the denuded shimmering beige landscape receded as far as the eye could see. The occasional charred tree trunk made the plateau look as if it had been the scene of a nuclear attack. It was the worst ecological devastation we had seen anywhere in Thailand. This depressing setting was the home of the Rom Glao villages. These were three Hmong settlements, all with the same name, but distinguished by a different number. Rom Glao N° 1 greeted us first (km 45), soon followed by N° 2, but Rom Glao N° 3 we never found - perhaps it lay offroad or in the mountains. As at Pop Pra, the land had been devastated partly through logging, partly through the clearing away of trees to make room for crop-growing, and then through slash-and-burn agriculture. We hoped only that the numerous agricultural projects and research farms strung along the road would somehow manage to reverse the despoliation.

It was in the midst of this desolate landscape that we came upon a tragic accident. From a distance we saw a couple of pick-ups parked oddly at the side of the road. Some figures stood huddled near one of them, and as we approached, the story of what had happened began to emerge. There were the telltale long black skidmarks veering off the road, a mangled bicycle on the asphalt just beyond them, and a woman lying across the centre of the road, with a pool of blood coming from her head. She was dead. She lay face down, her hair flopping onto the tarmac, an arm up around her head as if to shield herself from a blow. What made the situation all the more unbearable was the fact that it was obvious she had died only a minute or two earlier. Her body was no doubt still warm. The bystanders seemed instinctively to know this, because they kept their distance, as if recoiling from some ambiguous object. No one had the courage to go and cover the woman up. Even passing vehicles gave her a wide berth, creeping round by her feet on the scrub verge. Her loneliness out there on the road in the sun was absolute and terrible.

DEATH HIGHWAY

Our horror began to turn to anger - anger that one of these pick-up drivers, either through speeding or drunken driving, had so casually obliterated a life. But then it occurred to us that the woman herself might have caused the accident, perhaps wobbling out of a side track into the road, not so much as giving a glance to see if the way was clear - as people so often did in Thailand. And then our anger gave way to a sense of waste, of futile loss. This woman, no doubt a wife and mother, had got up this morning as usual, but by lunchtime was dead, while her husband and children, still unknowing, were probably working in the fields.

Thailand was famously a country full of *sanuk* or fun, but there was also no shortage of death. Like two sides of the same coin, they often seemed locked together in a kind of gay Siamese apocalypse. In the Kingdom the visitor saw a delight in eating, drinking Mekhong, conviviality, going places, doing business, developing tourism and patronizing singing girls. But the pleasures had a darker side - hedonism, alcoholism, exploitation, pollution, logging, environmental destruction, graft and corruption, and AIDS. Sometimes it was difficult to escape the impression that a charming, affable, almost childlike people was cheerfully bent on self-destruction - careering down a larger "death highway", lacking in commonsense and self-control, self-indulgent and avaricious. It was a situation reflected in miniature on the roads. Carefree self-centred drivers, like children with a new toy, hurtled down an asphalt death highway, grinning behind the wheel. In 1991 some 25,000 people died in the country in traffic accidents, making death on the roads the number two killer in the land of smiles (second only to death from heart disease). One person died in a car accident every 21 minutes, like this young woman near Rom Glao. Life was cheap (8000 baht one person told us), so why worry too much? And, anyway, did not Buddhism teach of reincarnation and many more lives to come?

The Rom Glao area was also the site of the two massacres that had taken place during the long construction of Highway 1090. According to contemporary newspaper reports, some thirty roadworkers were attacked and killed at km 43, apparently by Thai, Hmong and Karen CPT terrorists wanting to stop the road from penetrating Um Pang district (one of the principal communist strongholds in Thailand in the 60s and 70s). The attacks were one of the factors which had delayed completion of the road for so long. Following them, the Thai authorities deployed anti-communist KMT forces from places like Kae Noi to guard the project and its construction workers. The security situation was alleviated in 1982-83 with the mass surrenders in the province of hundreds of heavily-armed communist rebels and thousands of sympathizers. Nevertheless, until the late 80s, when "Death Highway" was finally finished (a decade late), the CPT remained active in the region south of Mae Sot.

Our minds full of all these unsettling thoughts, we headed into the mountains. The road swung left and then right, ascending rapidly. Most of the traffic stopped on the plateau. Anything still continuing was probably going right through to Um Pang. It was a creepy little road in poor condition. It skirted steep mountainsides, which dropped away to streams in valley clefts, hundreds of feet below. Mysterious footpaths branched off to each side, disappearing in the vegetation, only to reappear much higher up or much lower down. Soon we emerged in grassy upland country. Magnificent views opened up on all sides, with wooded hills and valleys receding like the waves of the sea towards bluish cordilleras on the horizon. The road snaked along ridges, dipping up and down between scrubby bald mountaintops. In the end it was not the plateau of the Rom Glao villages which we found the most sinister section of Death Highway, but this first mountain stretch. Back at Pa Charoen waterfall, the *somtam* lady had spoken of a robbery which had occurred the previous evening at a viewing pavilion on a hilltop up here. Now we came to the sala, involuntarily shivering as we rode past. Far and wide there were no signs of human habitation. The only people for long distances were parties of careworn Hmongs, beating brushgrasses at the roadside and laying them out to dry on the hot asphalt. They did not even look up as we passed.

Around km 80 on a steep climb we rounded a corner to find a brand-new pick-up upside down in the water drainage channel on the inside of the road. The driver, coming too fast down the other way, had evidently lost control on the corner and crashed. He was lucky that he had not gone over the edge. Strangely, his shiny pride-and-joy was being guarded by a wandering monk, who was perhaps unhappy about seeing the truck abandoned. The highway at this point had been gouged out of the rocks of the high mountainside. Soon it rounded a spur and presented us with a completely new view over a broad secluded valley. Down a series of hairpin bends we rapidly lost height, to roll into Rom Glao N° 4 (km 84). This shabby Hmong village, exactly halfway between Mae Sot and Um Pang, was where everybody, *songtaews* included, stopped for a rest or a snack. Most of the village lay to the east of the road. An enterprising Hmong family had set up a makeshift canteen there, and passers-by could get a noodle soup or a drink. When Thorben and we arrived, it was well past lunchtime, and the noodle soup was all gone. However, the friendly stallholders soon cooked up three packets of instant noodles, adding any scraps of leftover vegetable and meat they could find. There was always a camaraderie among the people stopping at this canteen, as if to say "we are all adventurers down Death Highway together".

A road sign just beyond Rom Glao N° 4 said "Ampoe Um Pang 80 Kms" - not so far, apparently, and yet there was another cool fifty miles of steep mountain and jungle road to go, virtually uninhabited until the run in to Um Pang. Two or three hours of hard riding still lay ahead. Fortunately, the road surface was better after the halfway village, and for a while we swung speedily down the valley. Somewhere along here a 6-ft brown snake slithered across our path, just before the front wheel. It was not the first time that this had happened. The snakes always seemed to wait until we were upon them, before darting across. It was an unnerving experience, which again sent cold shivers up our backs. Obviously, at speed no sudden evasive action was possible. The vision flickered through our minds of what would happen if we ran the serpent over. In its agony it would writhe up and bite us in the ankles.

Snakes were not the only problem. In one isolated stretch of jungle we rode into a swarm of bees. Stopping precipitately to flick them off our clothes and out of our hair, we had the uncanny feeling that we were being watched from out of the green-gold wall on either side. Were not those two spots of dappled sunlight the eyes of a tiger staring out unblinking, and was not that trembling leaf the faintest switch of a tail at the end of its motionless body? The air of the impenetrable undergrowth seemed to bring us an acrid smell, redolent of the fell of wild boar or big cats - the sour smell which assails one in certain corners of zoos or circus compounds. We hurried on our way. The road wound on through more jungle and new mountains. Progress·was slow, the bikes began to heat up and we to tire. The strategy of the highway seemed an odd one. It did not follow the valleys, but preferred to skim from mountaintop to mountaintop. There must have been a logic in it. A rare track east (km 94) was signed Mae Klong Noi, at km 100 we came to a checkpoint, and shortly after it another way went east to Mae Klong Yai.

Somewhere along this central section we passed a pick-up with a dozen Hmong men aboard. The vehicle struck us as odd because it was just sitting at the roadside. The men were neither relieving themselves, nor collecting anything, but just waiting. The ones in the open back of the truck were wearing those black balaclavas which leave nothing of the face showing except the eyes, which watch out through a slit. Their sinister appearance did nothing to alleviate our fears. After we had passed, we noticed in the rear-view mirror how they pulled out and began to follow us. They shadowed us for a long way. Mostly they kept a short distance behind, but sometimes, on the steep climbs, we could pull away and get clear of them. However, on the next level piece of road they caught us up, or even overtook us. When that happened, we dawdled to let them get well ahead. But then, just when we thought we had shaken them off, we would round a corner to find them parked, as if waiting for us. Thoughts of an ambush began to nag us. Once we stopped for a longer time to definitively lose them. But when we started off again, there they were the same short distance ahead.

After a bridge over over the River Mae Klong (km 106) the big climb began. Up and up the road went like a corkscrew, necessitating frequent changes down into first gear. Wafts of heat rose up from the engine. We were crossing the biggest and last ridge before the descent to Um Pang. Another checkpoint greeted us (km 116), after which the road entered elevated rainforest. If the first section of Death Highway, up to Rom Glao N° 4, was the most sinister, this stretch was the most beautiful. As we passed from open sunny patches to dark corners, the roadside vegetation alternated between rank brilliant green foliage and cool damp recesses of dark evergreen. Massive trees rose up, standing silent, dripping, covered in lianas, moss and other epiphytic plants. Peering anew into this dense jungle, we could once again almost see the glint of amber eyes and smell the fetid exhalations of forest beasts. Our increasing tiredness from the ride, our fear of the Hmongs, and the coldness both from the altitude and the rainforest made us tremble on the bikes, almost uncontrollably.

The breaks between the trees revealed marvellous views northwest of forested mountains, rolling uninterrupted and uninhabited, like a green carpet, right across into Burma. Suddenly, coming round from the cold shady side of the ridge, we emerged into the sun and onto a short stretch of high-level road (km 126). It was the pass, the highest part of the journey, and the most spectacular piece of Thai roadbuilding we had yet encountered. A ledge had been carved out of the rock just below the ridge crest. Cautiously it bore the narrow road around the curves of the mountainside above a 1000-metre precipice. In places the roadside was unprotected, and a wrong manoeuvre here would have spelt certain death. With a queasy feeling, not looking left over the abyss, we edged forwards, hugging the inside (wrong side) of the road, hoping that no vehicle was coming the other way. In an little lay-by right under the rockface we parked the bikes and walked on unsteady legs to enjoy the view. To the southeast, also, mountains rolled away into the far distance, blanketed with virgin forest. Looking south, we could see the last forty kms of Death Highway heading off into flatter land. It glittered silver in the sun like a river, before vanishing in the heat haze.

After the big climb: the great descent. With a series of sharp twists and turns the highway ran down and down a spur of the ridge. The heat of the afternoon came up to meet us. Finally, the road bottomed out in the valley of the River Mae Klong. Crossing the river, we arrived at Mae Klong Ki, a Karen village on the eastern side (km 132). While we were coming down the last hill, our Danish companion suddenly called out to us. He was out of petrol. He pulled in the clutch, coasted over the bridge and came to a stop right outside the entrance to the village. The little Kawasaki 100 was out of fuel, and in the middle of nowhere! Certainly there was no fuel station at Mae Klong Ki. We looked at each other with consternation. Time was getting on - it was already late afternoon - and there was still thirty kms to go. On the other side of the road, we saw a lot of building going on. Then we noticed that, facing this, on the far side of the river, there was an army camp. We recrossed the bridge, went to the guardhouse, and explained the position. The guard said that they had no petrol for us at the camp, but we could probably beg or buy some in the village. We asked about the housebuilding opposite. It was a brand-new Karen refugee camp, still in the process of being set up. The guard offered to show us round.

Everywhere men, women and children were busy fetching and cutting up bamboo poles, plaiting wall panels, thatching roofs, and hammering and sawing. In the centre of the compound stood a communal shelter. Besides being a kind of meeting place, this housed all the community's sacks of rice. Several battered pick-ups were parked around it. With the help of the

Thai soldier and the leader of the group, we pieced together the refugees' story. A month earlier, when the Karens feared another Four Cuts offensive, they had sent a "spy" to Mae Klong Ki to sound out the possibility of using the village as a fall-back position. When things had become dangerous, the women and children, together with the food supplies, had come on ahead. The men had arrived just a day or two before our visit, fighting a rearguard action as they went. This accounted for the fact that every one of these handsome friendly men looked utterly exhausted and dejected. The SLORC troops had chased them across the border to here, even though it was several kms inside Thailand. To prove the point, the men showed us bullets in the coconut trees. It was the same sad story as at Kawmoorah and Wa Lae. When things were quiet again on the other side, the Karen leader said, the refugees would return home.

We thanked the Thai soldier for his trouble and went across to the real village, on the east side of the road. In Mae Klong Ki we found people willing to sell us petrol. Thorben bought five litres, measured out in five old Mekhong whisky bottles. With the aid of a plastic funnel, we poured the red liquid into his completely dry tank. Coming down off the mountain into the Mae Klong valley was like dropping into a different world. And in fact we were entering a national park - the Um Pang Wildlife Sanctuary. At the village of Wa Kru Ko (km 140) there was another checkpoint, which constituted the formal entrance to the park. Here we made as if to pass, head ducked, under the half-raised barrier, but the soldiers manning the box insisted that we sign our names and nationalities into a duty book. A sensational karstic landscape unfolded before us. To the left and the right of the road, the hilly wooded countryside was punctuated with needle monoliths, hundreds of feet high. These jagged grey Rachaburi (also called Kanchanaburi) limestone outcroppings were partially covered with trees, bushes and creepers, giving them a hirsute appearance. Many were bizarrely eroded. The effects of water and weather during their 350 million-year history had left them with clefts and pock marks, fissures and caves. One monolith with a cave stood directly at the roadside.

Near the Karen village of Wa Koei Ta (km 145) we found a *songtaew* parked by an isolated roadside dwelling. Stopping to check the distance to our destination, we noticed cartons of dextrose-saline drips being unloaded from the vehicle. Opposite, an unmarked track disappeared into the scrub, heading west towards the border. The boxes would find their way up there to KNLA troops, wounded in the latest fighting. A string of small villages ran down the valley - Pro Pa Do, Mai Pa Ka, Mae Klong Gao and Mae Klong Mai. A turn-off west by the checkpoint at this last place was the beginning of the old way up from Um Pang to Mae Sot passing through Burma. There remained just one more village, Mae Klong, after which the 1090 passed a well-known local shrine on the right. It was the resting-place of the spirit of a dead man, called Pra Wo. The custom here was for vehicles to toot their horns when passing - to say hello to the man's spirit. We did so too - out of relief that we had safely reached the end of Death Highway. For almost immediately the road reached the brow of a steep hill and after 165 kms plunged down into Um Pang.

Um Pang

Discounting Karen settlements deeper in the jungle, Um Pang had to be Thailand's ultimate remote village. To go shopping in Mae Sot meant a two-day round trip, and anything not produced locally had to be hauled over the mountains and around Death Highway's 100 bends by truck or *songtaew*. For vehicles there was no exit from Um Pang, so the way out was the way back. *Changwat* Tak, the administrative centre responsible for the village and the area, was a cool 250 kms away, while Bangkok, although not so distant as the crow flies, could only be reached by a circuitous route indeed.

Until recently Um Pang had been even more cut off. Tong Lor Toed Yotin, the old man who ran the telephone booth at the "Five Ways" (that nodal point in the village centre where five streets met), told us why. Until 1987, when Highway 1090 was completed, it had been difficult to get there at all. He had moved down to Um Pang from Mae Sot in 1968. In those days there had been no road, not even a track. The journey had taken the "short" cut via Wa Lae through Burma - a four-day walk on foot or by elephant, camping three nights in the jungle on the way. In 1971 people had begun building a cart track south from Mae Sot, so that rice could be transported from Um Pang up to town in four or five days. In 1975 the first motorized vehicles had started using the new cart track. Work on turning the cart track into a proper road had been unusually slow because of local CPT guerrilla activity and because of the two massacres in the Rom Glao area. As late as 1984 the route through Burma had still been in regular use, some people continuing to use it until, of course, it had been interdicted by the Burma Army. In the rainy season the new dirt road had often become impassable, leaving Um Pang cut off from the outside world for months on end. Finally, in 1987, "Death Highway" had been metalled right through.

With the completion of the new road Um Pang's first tourist visitors arrived. They were mostly just a few Thais wanting to view the nearby Ti Lo Su (Tee Lor Soo) waterfall. Local people also vividly remembered the first *farang* visitor, who came the same year. The number of visitors, both Thai and *farang*, had remained to this day a trickle. We estimated that during the clement season an average of one *farang* a day made it to Um Pang. Almost none came off their own bat. Nearly all arrived in small organized (and costly) parties, passing straight through the village to go trekking in the surrounding jungle or rafting down the River Mae Klong.

Um Pang village itself, with a population of 2000, was a sleepy little nest. It was one of those places, like Mae Sariang, which could grow on the visitor. A first stay perhaps disappointed. The thrill of the adventure down Death Highway raised false expectations as to the excitement of the goal. But, of course, Um Pang was just another rural settlement at the end of the road. Even on a second visit the village hardly overwhelmed. But to the patient visitor it eventually began to yield up its charms. As the romantic illusions fell away, its real self could start to speak. This magical corner, that droll character, or this unexpected detail delighted, and one wondered

MAP 11

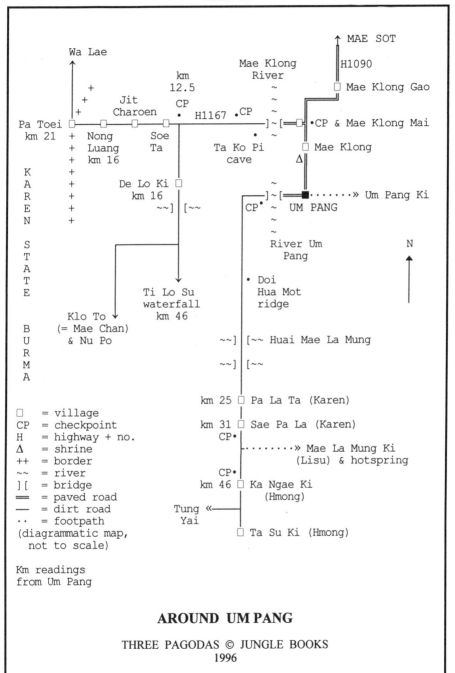

AROUND UM PANG

THREE PAGODAS © JUNGLE BOOKS
1996

how one could have missed so much in the first place. The end of all our exploring would, indeed, be to arrive where we first started and to know the place for the first time, or, to put it another way, the secret of travelling was never to be in too much of a hurry. Given the chance, Um Pang could easily seduce for a week or two. Far from the madding crowd, it offered a tranquil little world all of its own. This isolated but intact Thai-Karen outpost, with its own feel and rhythm, offered nothing, but also everything. A nexus of quiet dusty alleyways formed around the village's two main parallel streets. The houses, often with shops at the front, were mostly single-storey wooden buildings. It was a community laid out in a coconut grove, and over the homesteads towered immense palms, stirring lazily. Of a morning the odd truckload of Chinese-looking Hmongs breezed in from outlying Ka Ngae Ki. Traditional Karens, colourful with their costumes, shoulderbags and pipes, wandered around, making purchases. A group of serious enigmatic *loe-si* people, in green and pink, proceeded in single file past the market. Later, in the sizzling afternoon heat, while Um Pang's inhabitants napped, extravagant butterflies with four-inch wingspans fluttered in the silence, which was broken only by the whooping noises of monkeys in the trees beyond the village.

The hill down into Um Pang was lined on the left by a BPP base, a meteorological station and an agricultural office. On the right, set back, stood a primary school. In front of it the road forked, dividing into the village's two main streets. In our usual fashion we rode round and round, getting our bearings. The righthand way dropped down past the post office, a fuel station, the police station, *Gift Shop*, and a daytime restaurant *Khun No* with green tablecloths. A side road running left by *Gift Shop* headed up to the central Five Ways, while the next turning right ran off past the abode of the *kamnaan* (mayor) towards the bridge over the River Um Pang. Continuing straight on, we arrived at the bottom end of town. Here the road swung left, skirted the *ampoe* or district office (right), and then bore left again, bringing us to the bottom end of the other main street. Riding up this, we passed several shops, a motorcycle repair place, a *wat*, Five Ways, a small market, more shops, and the generating station which supplied Um Pang's power. With that, we were back at the fork at the top end of town. In the side streets east of Five Ways, up on the hill, stood a small hospital and a second monastery. Many of the shops in the two main drags were general-purpose, selling the same ubiquitous fish sauce, tinned sardines, soap, washing powder, doughnuts.... Some also supplied petrol out of drums. The price, as at the new fuel station, was a baht or two higher per litre than normal. And there was no bank to be seen.

Accommodation was in short supply too. Somebody told us that the *kamnaan* had rooms, but in our tiredness we could not find them. Asking again for directions at *Gift Shop*, we were told by a lady that she had a house we could rent for 60 baht per person. It was just outside Um Pang, and we followed her on our bikes as she rode on a moped up the steep hill and back towards Mae Sot. After three kms, and saluting Pra Wo again with our horns, we turned left down a track among the houses of Mae Klong. Here we were given the keys to *Gift House*, a brand-new well-appointed villa in a banana grove. We could not believe our luck. We foresaw a problem with food, but the lady said we could have whatever we liked. She would bring it out to us later. After we had cleaned up, a moustachiod young man arrived with supper in a plastic bag, slung from the handlebars of the same moped. We tucked greedily into a feast of stir-fried chicken and vegetables, fresh fruit and iced beer. The young man began to serenade us with music on a synthesizer. What with the food and drink, the gentle music, the peace of the banana grove, the relaxed review of the day's events, and the balmy air of the veranda under a starry sky, it seemed as if on the fringes of Um Pang we had found heaven on earth.

The young man went by the name of So. With his cultivated dashing good looks, So fancied himself as the local popstar (in fact he was a teacher). He subsequently presented us with a cassette of some of his music, entitled "So - So Easy" - it was accomplished stuff. Through the "popstar" and also the *Gift Shop* lady we became friendly with So's brother Sombat, who worked in the district office. This modest sincere man was to become our most valuable contact in Um Pang, but just how he fitted into the picture only emerged later.

Because *Gift House* was rather cut-off, we decided to move the next day back into Um Pang itself. A diligent search turned up more lodging possibilities. In fact, in the end it began to seem to us that almost anybody in town would offer us floorspace if asked. We tracked down the mayor's accommodation, *Um Pang House*. It lay a short way down the road leading to the bridge. A vaguely fanciable ladyboy, working as a maid for the *kamnaan*, greeted us. She (he?) showed us first some bleak noisy rooms in a block beside the road and then, in a grassy area behind, a set of bungalows. All were overpriced, even after haggling, so we showed a clean pair of heels. As we left, we heard the *kateuy* wailing that we could have one of the block rooms for 100 baht - still too much for Um Pang. In the same road we found other places to stay, but again the owners were charging inflated prices, considering the state of the rooms and the status of the village. The people of Um Pang did not seem much amenable to sensible bargaining, or perhaps they reasoned that visitors, trapped down here, had nowhere else to turn. In the end a man stopped us in the street and offered to lend us a kind of secondary garden-home he owned. He was the 2-i-c at the *ampoe*, and his house lay in an obscure back alley. Only one storey high and made of wood, it was built on piles in the middle of a small lake, on which floated a carpet of pink-flowering lilies. The lake was set in a marvellous garden, full of tropical plants. The house was reached by a gangplank from the garden. All this we could have to ourselves for a ridiculously cheap thirty baht each per day. And so for a number of idyllic days and nights we lazed in the quarters which we came to know as "The Lilypond".

THREE PAGODAS

One thing that Um Pang lacked, even the locals agreed, was a decent restaurant. From an early hour tea and coffee was served in a shed at Five Ways, and our preferred breakfast came to be hot coffee or Milo there with coconut cake bought from a store. *Khun No* and a couple of other modest eating places in the two main streets offered during the day fried rice, *pat thai*, or noodles with meat and greens in gravy (*raad na*). In the early evening many housewives, in traditional Siamese style, sold snacks and takeaway food in front their houses, but what was on offer was not to everybody's taste. Down by the *ampoe* a couple of stalls offered typical Thai sweetmeats. With these possibilities exhausted, the one remaining eating place was the questionable *Ti Lo Su* restaurant in the *kamnaan's* backyard, also known in northern Thai dialect, more appropriately, as *Karngtong* (= in the middle of the field).

This desultory ranch-style place, with its long wooden tables and benches on the bare earth floor, had no menu, either in Thai or English. On enquiring, we learned that we could only have whatever was available. That should have simplified things, but when we asked the lackadaisical cooks and waitresses what they had got, back came the answer: What did we want? Meanwhile they fiddled up at the front with a cassette player, which crackled out lugubrious Thai songs. Of course, whatever we wanted they had not got. *Mai mii, mai mii*, they replied breezily. Finally, a stir-fry of vegetables and sliced sausage was borne to our table by the same passable ladyboy we had snubbed earlier. "She" gave us a cool look through half-closed eyes. In fairness to *Ti Lo Su*, the food improved the more we ate there. Also, the better the staff got to know us (including the willowy *kateuy*), the better the service became and the more reasonable the bill at the end of the evening.

The real problem with this eating place was drunkenness. BPP soldiers from their border posts, forestry boys from the jungle and off-duty policemen all homed in on *Ti Lo Su* to drink away their boredom or frustration. The drunkenness in itself would not have been so bad, but all these characters passed through that intermediate stage, having supped on watery *tom yam* from a clay pot and emptied two or three bottles of Mekhong, when they spotted us minding our own business, latched onto us and thought it enormously funny to ask endless forward and fatuous questions. One evening this unwanted attention became so tiresome that we rebelled. The manageress, noticing that things had gone too far and failing to shift a pair of drunks from our table, called the police. The police arrived, but they were also drunk and started fraternizing with our importunate tablemates. Finally, the bosses of the two drunks, accompanied by a senior official from the *ampoe*, arrived, but, far from restoring order, these local eminences merely suggested that it was we who should leave "because it was not good for us to see such a thing". We were preparing to depart from *Ti Lo Su* in utter disgust when the *kamnaan* himself arrived, saving the day, or rather evening. He had brought a length of elephant chain with him and proceeded to chain up the two men, tying them to a post out in the darkness.

DEATH HIGHWAY

Um Pang had originally been a Karen settlement until Thais from the northern provinces began to settle there. The village was at least 100 years old because records showed that in 1889, when Um Pang district belonged to Utai Tani province, it had been an immigration point for people from Burma. This might account for its name, which is said to derive from the Karen "um pa", meaning "issue pass". In 1898 *changwat* Tak made nearby Mae Klong an *ampoe* (present day Mae Klong Gao). With two district seats so close, it was inevitable that they should merge. In 1926 Mae Klong was subsumed under Um Pang, but at the same time the newly enlarged *ampoe* Um Pang was reallocated to Tak province.

Ampoe Um Pang now had the distinction of being the largest district in Thailand, with a surface area of 4325 sq. kms. Its population, however, was a mere 13,000, distributed throughout some 37 villages. It was bordered to the north by Pop Pra district, to the south by Sangklaburi and Si Sawat, and to the east by the districts of Klong Lan, Laad Yao and Ban Rai. To the west lay the Tanon Tongchai mountains, which divided off Um Pang district from Burma. The River Um Pang ran past town on the south side, flowing into the River Mae Klong to the west. This larger river ran south to join the River Mae Chan, and both ultimately flowed into the River Kwae Yai, down in Kanchanaburi. Almost the whole of the district was mountainous. Its agricultural economy had to make do with only some 3-5% of flatland. Local produce was sold mostly to Mae Sot. The area had reserves of tin, wolfram, lignite and antinomy, but as yet these had not been exploited. For eco-political reasons they might never be so.

About 70% of Um Pang district was real jungle. With such a large area of mountainous jungle so sparsely populated, it was a largely undisturbed zoological and botanical treasure trove. Fortunately, this had not been lost on the Thai authorities. With so many other parts of the Kingdom depredated from logging, slash-and-burn and erosion, they had been commendably quick to add Um Pang to other contiguous fastnesses to form one giant nature reserve. Thus, combined with Um Pang Wildlife Sanctuary to the north, Klong Lan and Mae Wong National Parks to the east, Huai Ka Kaeng Wildlife Sanctuary to the southeast, Tan Lot and Erawan National Parks to the south, and the vast Tung Yai Naresuan Wildlife Sanctuary and Forest Protection Zone to the southwest, Um Pang district formed the greatest and the last real wilderness in Thailand (said to be one of the most significant in Asia). A look at the map confirmed this. It was one huge inaccessible area, with not a single road running into it. The reserve was home to tigers, gaurs, wild elephants, bears, deer, barking deer, gibbons, leaf monkeys, wild boar, civet-like linsangs, serows (goat-antelopes), peacocks, Chinese pheasants, forest chickens, snakes and a multitude of birds. There were forests of teak, ironwood, rubber trees, betel, *mai daeng, teng, rang, pradu, tabaek*, and *takien*.

One result of the formation of this giant nature reserve was that increasing numbers of people were being moved out. There were next to no Thais living in it, so the villages which were being resettled were hill-tribe, mostly Hmong, but also some Lisu. As we saw, they were being moved north to the Rom Glao and Pop Pra areas. They were being moved not just for the sake of creating uninhabited national parks. As Prasert Leksakhun Deelok, head of the district office explained to us, especially the Hmongs were involved not just in slash-and-burn, but in illegal logging, poaching and opium-growing. He showed us press cuttings detailing a scandal in which local Hmongs had hunted and killed a female elephant with a calf. On the subject of poppy-growing, as the authorities became increasingly successful in suppressing cultivation, the Hmongs apparently moved deeper and deeper into the jungle to evade detection, cutting down more trees to make room for new fields. Thus, villages had been moved out of Mae Wong National Park between Um Pang Ki and Klong Lan, and we heard rumours that the Lisu villages beside the River Mae La Mung (Ra Mong), near the hotspring, had gone. It seemed that even strategic Mae Chan Ta was due for resettlement.

Karen villages did not seem to figure much in the relocation program. In a sense this was right, for if anyone could claim to be the region's indigenous people, it was the Karens. By contrast, the Hmongs were migratory people who had entered the area relatively recently. In addition, however, the subsistence economy of the Karens, who were mostly lowland farmers, was much less environmentally destructive than the highland slash-and-burn economy of the entrepreneurial Hmongs. Also, the *Yang* did not grow opium and certainly never poached elephants. At most some outlying Karen hamlets would be amalgamated with more established "central" villages, such as Pa La Ta.

Finally, a second result of the creation of this huge nature reserve was that public access to it was under threat. Visitors, we were told, would increasingly be prevented from trekking either in it or through it. Some tracts had already been closed. The path through Mae Wong National Park from Klong Lan to Um Pang via Um Pang Ki (even marked on some maps as the H1117) was absolutely forbidden, the way having been closed eight or nine years previously, with all villages en route shut down. The truth of this we found out to our own cost when once we tried to take a short cut from Kampaeng Pet to Um Pang. Other parts would no doubt follow. Perhaps in the future it would not be possible to go beyond Ti Lo Su waterfall, or one would only be allowed to make specific walks care of the Wildlife and Forestry departments. But, in addition, with villages in the jungle disappearing, any trekking, whether independent or organized, would become increasingly difficult. If a logistically important village such as Mae Chan Ta went, it would be all but impossible to get down to the Three Pagodas unless one mounted a regular expedition, with porters carrying food and tents. The upshot of all this was not lost on us. Adventure south of Um Pang seemed about to be nipped in the bud, and so if we were serious about our dream of trekking through the 200 kms of jungle to the Three Pagodas, there would never be a better time to try to realize it than now.

CHAPTER 12

THE DRIVERLESS KOMATSU

Um Pang - Sa Kaang Thi - Nu Po - Kui Le To

One evening, when we were talking to Sombat, the *ampoe* man who was the brother of "popstar" So, he began speaking about the village of Lae Tong Ku and of the enigmatic *loe-si* people who lived there. The village lay south of Um Pang on the Burmese border and could only be reached on foot. The people were a small colourful Karen sect, who worshipped a *loe-si* - a kind of rishii or sage. This demigod lived in the village in a *wat*, and somehow elephant tusks figured in the group's religion. The people ate only the meat of jungle animals and wore their hair long, twisted up in top-knots. The *loe-si* sect was unique in Thailand and little was known about it. Needless to say, the subject fired our imaginations, and we immediately determined to reach the mysterious village.

We asked Sombat if he thought we could visit Lae Tong Ku. It might be possible, he said thoughtfully. Had he ever been there? He occasionally went there on district business, and once he had stayed a longer time because he had had to organize a census and prepare the ground for a helicopter visit by some member of the Thai royal family. We plagued the sober Sombat with many questions, and he patiently tried to answer them. How could we get there, and were there other villages on the way? What language did the *loe-si* people speak, and would we be able to communicate with them? What about the problem of food? And did other people ever visit the village? The *ampoe* official thought that it would take us about two to three days to get from Um Pang to Lae Tong Ku and the same amount of time to get back. So a round trip would take one week. We had first to go down to the Karen village of Nu Po and then start trekking. There were villages on the way, but we would need guides. After Nu Po there were two ways on to Lae Tong Ku - a long roundabout path remaining in Thailand and a short cut through Burma. All the local people, of course, took the short cut, but he was not at all sure about the wisdom of a *farang* trekking through Burma, all the more so with the war raging on the other side.

Lae Tong Ku, we imagined, lay broadly speaking on our route to the Three Pagodas Pass, and so it seemed a good idea to try to use the village as a first stepping-stone. We plied our informant with more questions. Did the *loe-si* community lie far from the route to the Pagodas, and what did he know of the territory beyond it? But here our friend's knowledge was exhausted. Lae Tong Ku was on the edge of Um Pang district. Beyond it was another district (Sangklaburi) and another province (Kanchanaburi). Sombat knew nothing about that outer darkness. It seemed anyway that we

MAP 12

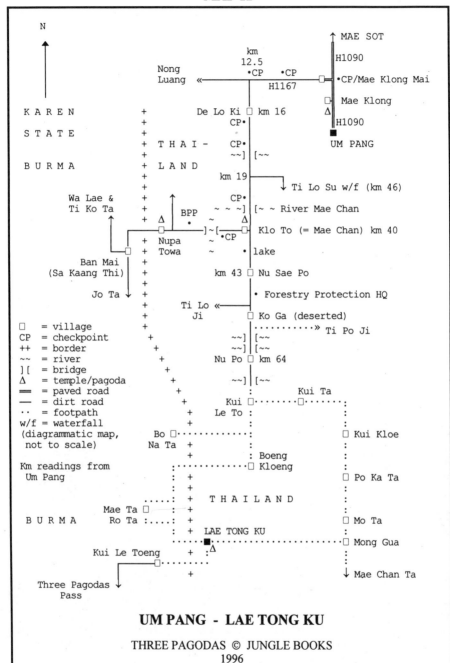

UM PANG - LAE TONG KU

THREE PAGODAS © JUNGLE BOOKS
1996

should at least be able to reach Lae Tong Ku. The problem now was to research the lie of the land on the far side. As this was the more obscure part of the journey and also, we estimated, the lion's share, we spent several more days in Um Pang trying to gather further information. The results were hardly encouraging. But one thing sustained us in our enquiries. We had once met someone who had trekked from Um Pang to Three Pagodas, so the journey had to be possible. This was Wachara Liu Pong Sawat, the young owner of *Ta Mi La Guest House* in Chiang Khong. He had taken part in a joint BPP paramilitary and Thai adventure-club expedition. The group had taken ten days to trek through the jungle, starting at Ti Lo Su waterfall. He had told us that the trip had been hair-raising, so much so that in one place on the mountains he had cried with fear. Remembering Wachara's words, we were filled with apprehension, but at the same time spurred on. What we did not know until later was that the way taken by Wachara had been a different, more easterly, route than the one which we finally took.

The obvious person to quiz next was one Boonlum, an ex-Thai Army ranger of Um Pang who sometimes organized trekking and rafting trips. At first he warmed to our idea, but then the complications began to pile up. Yes, he could come with us, but there would have to be a minimum of two guides. The trip would last about a week, and at his charge of so-and-so-much per guide per day that would work out at thousands of baht for the trip. On top of that, we would have to pay for the bus tickets to get the guides from Sangklaburi back to Um Pang. Or, rather, we would have to pay for them (and ourselves) to get to the bottom end, because now the onetime *tahaan praan* planned to start down there and trek up. The mounting expense of the trip, not to mention the enormity of our plan, began to dawn on us. We told Boonlum that we would think the matter through, but soon anyway his interest went off the boil, and he drifted away, saying that we knew where we could find him. We then studied the guide's maps. They seemed not to accord with the accurate administrative map we had wheedled out of the district office. Also, it became clear to us that the ranger's real stamping ground was restricted to Um Pang district. Details on his map further south were sketchy. Seeing his heart go so quickly out of the project, we even wondered if he had ever trekked right through.

We turned next to the *kamnaan*. He knew nothing about what happened beyond Lae Tong Ku, but thought that from a place called Boeng Kloeng to the *loe-si* village it was a 20-km hard day's hike. (In fact it turned out to be a four-hour walk.) He imposed the stricture on us that we should on no account do anything unless it was sanctioned and organized by the BPP. Beyond that the village head seemed more interested in coaxing us away from the "Lilypond" into his guestrooms. Seeing that we were not amenable, he finally suggested we try for information at the police station. At the police station on the main street deputy commander Rong Moet could add little to what we already knew, except to say that he thought it would be alright to proceed to Boeng Kloeng, the village the *kamnaan* had mentioned, where we should report to the BPP camp and ask about the local situation.

It was becoming increasingly clear that all roads led to the BPP and that nothing could be achieved without enlisting their help. Accordingly, we summoned up our courage, rode to the edge of Um Pang, past the sentries at the entrance to the BPP Base, and up to the camp offices. Here, working our way up the chain of command, we finally spoke to the base commander. This was a mistake, for, quite apart from getting nothing out of the *dorchodor*, we merely apprised them of what we were up to, with the result they they would probably radio through to the first checkpoint to turn us back. While sympathetic to our cause, the commander explained that he himself could do nothing for us, neither give us permission, nor arrange back-up. We would have to go through headquarters in Mae Sot. Not only that, but we would have to get permission from the Forestry Protection HQ in Tak. Moreover, he could not radio through for us to get permission. We would have to appear in person at the two places, make an application and wait for a written permit.

This news came like a bombshell. Had we come so far just to be sent all the way back, frustrated by bureaucracy? A round trip to Mae Sot and Tak would take a minimum of three days, not allowing for any hitches. Worse still, the whole thing squared with what Wachara of Chiang Khong had told us, for he and his friends had had to go through exactly these official channels. There really seemed now no other option. Seeing our despondent faces, the commander then began to slightly attenuate what he had said. He himself did not mind what we did, but he had strict orders from above and was obliged to stick to them. He did not want to be held responsible for us if anything happened. It seemed to us that he was trying to communicate to us an interstice through which we might slip. It was as if he was intimating: go if you want, but I have now put myself in the clear. We thanked him politely and left.

As a last resort, we went to Um Pang district office. We remembered how helpful Somsak, the chief of *ampoe* Wiang Haeng, had once been to us. Through Sombat and also through our "Lilypond" landlord (deputy *ampoe* head), we secured an interview with the chief. But in his room the door to our little jaunt seemed to slam shut forever. *Mai dai*, came his repeated response as we unfolded each new element of our plan, *mai dai*. The situation with the Karens was far too fluid at the moment. In short, he flatly forbade us to set off for Lae Tong Ku, let alone for the Three Pagodas. In a last-ditch attempt we produced Somsak's letter and tried to shame him into assisting us. Could he not produce a similarly helpful letter? But the chief would not even consider the idea.

The fluidity of the Karen situation which the *ampoe* chief had mentioned referred not only to the latest offensive of the Burma Army against the KNLA. In the days before we reached Um Pang and also during our stay there, we began to receive disturbing reports of some serious incident near Mae Chan Ta in the south of the district. The newspapers were full of lurid horror stories that *loe-si* people had attacked and killed a number of BPP soldiers and Forestry Protection officials deep in the jungle. This rather contradicted the impression we had gained from Sombat of the *loe-si* people of Lae Tong Ku, whom he had described as quiet peace-loving folk, but there was no denying the press cuttings or what was on everybody's lips in Um Pang. On top of the discouragement which we had garnered at the hands of the authorities, all this was bad news indeed. It seemed that not only were the very people we wanted to visit embroiled in some kind of bloody conflict, but that we would absolutely be prevented by the military from going anywhere near the area for our own safety.

One newspaper report spoke of the brutal murder of five BPP soldiers and one Thai villager by members of a little-known religious group, the Talarku. These cultists were followers of a godlike leader who lived in a monastery in the remote Karen village of "Letako". The Talarku wore their hair long, tied up in a knot on the tops of their heads. For religious reasons they ate the meat only of wild animals. The cultists were extreme in the devoutness of their beliefs, and if anyone criticised their faith or tried to put obstacles in its way, they could resort to violence. It was thought that while the *pu chaik* or *pu kyaik* (as the man-god was titled) was not himself directly responsible for the incident, his most fervent followers were. Two possible motivations for the attack were given. On the one hand, the Forestry Department had been trying to prevent the Talarku from entering and hunting in the wildlife preserves (i.e. frustrate their precept to eat only jungle game), and on the other, the cultists had believed that the *dorchodor* were trying to suppress their faith in favour of Buddhism. So they had moved to protect their way of life, and this had resulted in the killings. In nearly every detail the newspaper report tallied with the picture we were building up of the *loe-si* people of Lae Tong Ku.

Another account ran along the same lines, if marked by the occasional difference. Talarku cultists had ransacked and burnt a Forestry office in the jungle south of Um Pang, before going on to attack a nearby BPP base. The "Karen splinter group" of "voodoo fanatics" had hacked five BPP officers and one Thai civilian to death with machetes and had abducted three Forestry officials, who were later released. However, the incident had not taken place at Lae Tong Ku, but in and around Mae Chan Ta, a village some hours' walk away. Further, the perpetrators were not the "white thread" Talarku of Lae Tong Ku, but members of a breakaway "yellow thread" group, who lived in villages within the ambit of Mae Chan Ta. Numbering some hundreds, they had set up a "hermit centre" of their own with their own *rishii* in the outlying settlement of Chong Pae. The rival man-god and his followers, so the second newspaper report continued, were ex-CPT communists. As to the motive for the attack, the upstart "yellow" cultists had wanted to expand their sphere of influence to villages such as Lae Tong Ku and Mong Gua, where the "whitethread" *loe-si* religion was already firmly established. Ultimately their goal was to drive out the traditional Talarku from such places. The killing of the BPP soldiers had been an attempt by the "yellowthreads" to impress the orthodox Talarku with their prowess and so gain influence. In the wake of the attack large numbers of BPP had been helicoptered in to track down the culprits, resulting in the encirclement of about 300 cultists around Mae Chan Ta and the arrest of 21 of them. The "yellowthread" *pu chaik*, however, followed by dozens of his most ardent disciples, had fled deeper into the jungle, towards Kanchanaburi province, where they were still at large.

The news of this serious incident put an even bigger question mark over our already doubtful project. It was still not clear whether it was the cultists of Lae Tong Ku or of Mae Chan Ta who had been responsible for the murders. And even if we knew, we had no idea which of the two villages we might have to pass through on our way to the Pagodas - perhaps through both. But, further, assuming that Lae Tong Ku was safe and that we could also give Mae Chan Ta a wide berth, we would still have to pass through the jungles of Kanchanaburi province, where dozens of murderous fugitive "yellowthreads" were on the run. Added to this, there were all the regular problems and dangers associated with jungle trekking. The more we contemplated actually embarking on our adventure, the more they weighed down on us. Would we not get lost? Would we find people to guide us? Would we be able to communicate with them? Were there any tracks going where we wanted to go? The jungle was full of poisonous snakes, bears, big cats and other large wild animals. What was the risk with these? Especially the border areas of Tak and Kanchanaburi provinces were notorious for malaria. What was the risk of catching the disease? The same areas were a hideout for fugitive criminals and cross-border bandits. How real was that danger? And, then, it was not clear to what extent we might have to go through Burma. Sombat had hinted that to get to Lae Tong Ku we would probably have to trek some hours on the wrong side of the border, but what about beyond the *loe-si* village? Passing illegally through Burma brought a new set of problems. The Karens in Kawthoolei were every bit as hospitable as those in Thailand, and no doubt the KNLA of 6th Brigade district could be very helpful, but in Burma we were beyond the help of the Thai authorities and at the mercy of people we could not fully know. A major Four Cuts offensive was in progress. Apparently it had now mostly swept further north, but the situation was extremely volatile. What was the latest? Even more unfortunate that running into "yellowthreads" would be to fall into the hands of a Burma Army foot patrol, or be seen by an informer or a government spotter plane, or step on a landmine left in a deserted village.

Our round of the authorities in Um Pang had left us despondent enough. Now all these new concerns threatened to overwhelm us. In the Um Pang offices we began to realize that the more we enquired, the more we only generated discouragement, conflicting information, dis-information, confusion, *mai ru's* and *mai dai's*. Instead of building towards setting off, we were being pushed ever further back in the direction of Mae Sot or even Tak. However, there was one avenue, so simple and obvious that we had overlooked it, that we had not explored - just to set off and see what happened. Policeman Rong Moet had even almost suggested this. Go to Boeng Kloeng, he had said, and ask again there. Warming to this possibility one evening in *Ti Lo Su* restaurant, we figured that the worst that could happen would be that we would be sent back from Boeng Kloeng with a flea in our ear. So after relaxing for a week in Um Pang, we decided to start next morning.

The area south of Um Pang was the last great unspoilt area in Thailand, and a trek through it to the Three Pagodas Pass the last great adventure left in the Kingdom. After an assessment of the possibilities and risks, our concern now was with practicalities and preparation. Real jungle trekking, Sombat told us, was more than twice as exhausting as ordinary trekking. The heat and humidity made it difficult to go very far or carry much weight. Accordingly, on the eve of our departure, we divided our possessions into two piles - the things we would leave behind and those we would take with us. The unnecessary things we bundled up and gave to our *ampoe* friend. Traveller's cheques, airline tickets, excess money and other valuables went into the district office safe. Onto the pile of indispensable things we threw: jeans, trainers, long-sleeved shirts (against mosquitos), pullovers (cool evenings), underwear, one change of lightweight clothes (pyjamas or a sarong seemed a good idea), lightweight sleeping bags, a mosquito net, washing things, plasters, Autan insect repellent, sun cream, water purifying pills, antiseptic cream, diarrhoea pills, a wide-spectrum antibiotic, vitamin tablets, toilet paper, matches, a torch, notebooks, cameras and film.

The biggest problem, we foresaw, would be food. Of course, wherever there were people, there was cold rice to eat. Villagers may or may not offer other food. But if they did, it was another matter as to whether one could stomach it. In Mae Sot we had taken the precaution of stocking up with tins of tuna and sardines in various sauces, and now in Um Pang we loaded up with packets of Ma-ma instant noodles. The famous Ma-ma were a godsend. They weighed very little and provided a tasty snack wherever someone had a fire going to boil water.

We had long since taken leave of our Danish friend. Seeing us getting ever more deeply entangled in Um Pang, he had left to chance his arm bobbing down the River Mae Kong in a boat. Now all that remained was to seek out Sombat, tell him of our exact plans, and hand over our dispensable possessions. He wished us good luck and gave us a slip of paper, on which he had scribbled the name of the BPP commander in Boeng Kloeng and a couple of other words. This scrap of paper was to prove the most important of all our items of preparation, crucial to the success of the whole venture.

To go forward we had first to go back. We rode out of Um Pang a couple of kms in the direction of Mae Sot. Tooting our horn for the last time at the Pra Wo shrine, we passed the turn-off at Mae Klong for *Gift House* in the banana grove, where we had started out all those days ago. At the police box we bore left onto the 1167 road, immediately passing through Mae Klong Mai (mai = new). In this pleasant market village we crossed a bridge over the Mae Klong, the river which gave both this village and others in the vicinity their names. Beyond the bridge the asphalt gave out, and a gravelly dirt road dipped up and down through hilly country, wooded with teak. A sign left pointed to Ta Ko Pi cave. Rumour had it that there was a way right through this three-km long cave to Mae Klong Tai (tai = south). Two checkpoints followed, the second (12.5 kms from Um Pang) marking a junction. Straight on (west) led to the Thai village of Nong Luang and to the Karen refugee village of the Pa Toei (Ba Tui), situated on the border. It was the beginning of the old short way up to Mae Sot, not used any more now that Highway 1090 was complete. Our way went left (south) down a dirt highway. Not far along this we came across a sprawling low wooden building with a grass roof. In front of it were some of those large brown earthenware waterjars found everywhere in Thailand, as well as sacks of rice and baskets of vegetables. Bunches of bananas were hanging up, trays of soft drinks were stacked up, and many other provisions were for sale. In among them we spotted an urn with hot water on the go. We stopped and drank an *oliang*, a strong Thai coffee. It turned out that this ramshackle building, resplendent in the early morning sun, was the last roadside store for some 200 kms, until Sangklaburi.

De Lo Ki (16 kms from Um Pang) was the first village down the south-bound dirt road. Two more checkpoints followed and a couple of bridges. After the bridges, the way divided, left proceeding a further 27 kms to the famous Ti Lo Su jungle waterfall, and right continuing to Klo To. The stretch between the fork and Klo To was as lonely and scary as any we had ridden on our journey. For twenty kms it snaked up and down through uninhabited jungle and forest. Bizarre sinister limestone monoliths stuck up through the canopy like teeth. Behind them, to the west, lay the Tanon Tongchai border mountain ridge. The road was totally devoid of traffic. With relief we found ourselves descending into a broad valley, past another checkpoint, to the village of Klo To, already forty kms south of Um Pang.

Klo To, known also as Mae Chan, lay west of the dirt road. A Karen village dominated by a white pagoda atop a karstic needle, it marked a significant unofficial border-crossing point to the Karen State and Burma. Some kind of market was taking place on the playground of Klo To school, and here people told us about a big black market over the border at a place called Ban Mai (= new village). Ban Mai was seven or eight kms away, and we could visit it if we wanted. As the morning was not far advanced, we decided to have a quick look. A very bad 4WD track led past a checkpoint, over the River Mae Chan, past a military camp, to the Karen settlement of Nupa Towa. Spread out along the route in three sections, the village had its own white *chedi* and was enhanced by many red-flowering trees. As we continued through woods and jungle, outcroppings in the form of a razor blade reared up above the vegetation to the south. A post at the trackside with no sign on it led us to believe that we had reached the border. Picking our way through a maze of criss-crossing tracks and paths, we went down a hill to arrive suddenly at a KNLA checkpoint and customs gate. We were at Ban Mai or, in Burmese, Sa Kaang Thi.

Sa Kaang Thi (Ban Mai)

Although only three or four years old, the village was surprisingly large. Some 180 houses, twenty well-provisioned stores and a school bore witness to the fact that this was indeed a major border crossing-point for both people and vehicles. Sa Kaang Thi seemed to us like a cross between Po Pa Ta and Mae Saam Laep. Set in a bowl, and backgrounded by a bald ridge, it was surrounded close at hand by three small jagged tooth mountains. Parking the bike, we wandered up and down the streets of leaf-roofed houses. In front of every store were bundles of Thukita cheroots, 50 for 10 baht, and also all the paraphernalia of betel chewing - lime leaves, pastes and so on. Conspicuous too were pyramids of cartons of cigarettes, mainly imported into Burma from Singapore. The brand names pretended to luxurious internationality, or affected the swank of American limousines. The smoker could indulge himself with Long Beach, Monterey, Fortune, Lucky Strike, Eagle, Classics, Perilly's, Monte Carlo, Hunter or Modern. Those of a Chinese smoking persuasion could light up a Duya, a Xinxing or, strangely, a Horse.

What struck us most about Sa Kaang Thi was the large number of Muslim Indo-Burmese traders and their families in this Karen village. As at Po Pa Ta we were surrounded by tall dark wiry men with beautiful piercing eyes, chintuft beards and white skullcaps. Some were Arakanese *rohingyas*, others Burmese Indians, a few perhaps Bangladeshis. Mostly they were not refugees, but people who had been living in Burma a long time who had recently been displaced. Muslims had traditionally traded along the old Moulmein-Um Pang-Mae Sot route. It was just that in the recent fighting many had been pushed up here to the border from the interior. Very possibly the Muslim Liberation Organization provided at Sa Kaang Thi one of the Muslim units that still operated within the KNLA.

We were taken in hand by a soft-spoken refined young man, who was a dissident student from Moulmein. In convincing English he told us that there were no fewer than three revolutionary student camps in the village. Two, only a year or so old, were ABSDF camps, Battalions 206 and 216, while the third, his own, was called Sa Kaang Thi Students' Camp, consisting of fifty men. Perhaps on account of his English, our Moulmein friend (name suppressed) was charged with "looking after foreign matters and supplies". We expressed to him our desire to take an early lunch in Sa Kaang Thi. We had spotted numerous Muslim tea shops, but found no regular eating place. He brought us to a Karen-run "restaurant", called *Family*. Operated by a Mr Jo Thu, it turned out to be the local KNLA nerve-centre with an adjoining

KNU propaganda room. The walls were covered with information and slogans. Meant less for outside consumption and more to boost insurgent morale, the slogans announced: "The race is not to the swift, nor the battle to the strong", "A house divided against itself cannot stand" and "The darkest hour is before the dawn". One slogan, chalked on a back wall, particularly caught our eye. DON'T KISS ME, it admonished and seemed to form a counterpart across the intervening miles of the enigmatic "I KISS" which we had found incised on the lady guard's flip-flops at Manerplaw.

In the black-market village we had seen goats wandering everywhere. Now, inevitably, goat was served up for our early lunch - curried and eaten with the fingers. There was a great deal of coming and going in and around *Family*. Women and children with discs of *tanaka* on their cheeks played in dark corners. An invalid guerrilla with a wooden leg came in to read the paper over a mid-morning Hong Tong whisky. Outside three elephants plodded past. Battered trucks arrived and departed. One delivered up a squad of heavily-armed security men. Nearly all had long hair, done in pigtails or ponytails, or just loose, adding to the racy atmosphere. A minah bird in a bamboo cage chattered in Karen, while at the main table in *Family* a group of people sat huddled around a transistor radio, listening to the news in Burmese from the BBC World Service.

We were eating the goat curry when a Suzuki jeep drew up outside. The local KNLA commander, accompanied by a driver and two armed body-guards, got out. Word had reached him of our presence and he wanted to check us out. He was Sor Tae Tu, a pleasant chap of about forty with a square face, moustache, and red teeth. Sitting down at our table, he asked us our business. During the interview he made no move to make himself more comfortable. He sat there with his green beret on, complete with KNLA badge (British Army style), and a much-bepocketed safari jacket, heavy with bits and pieces. From a waist belt hung, on one side, a pistol in a holster and, on the other, a hand grenade, shiny from rubbing against his camouflage trousers. As he enquired, we noticed on one of his fingers a gold ring with green jade set in it. Satisfied with our account of ourselves, he relaxed and turned the conversation to other things. Why did we not go and visit the Karen New Year celebrations at Jo Ta across the Dawna Range, he asked? We explained our intention of going to Lae Tong Ku. In the restaurant we had noticed a mysterious set of jars up on a shelf. What were they, we asked? That was *lapat tho* or tealeaf mixture, Sor Tae Tu said. He motioned to Mr Jo Thu to bring the jars down and prepare some. It was a kind of nutty snack made of sesame seeds, peanuts, *bae yi* (split beans), *tua noi* (little peas), fried grated coconut, fried garlic, and green tealeaf paste mixed with oil and fish sauce. The idea was to dip into each jar, taking according to one's taste, and stir the ingredients together. Doubtfully we tried some of the *lapat tho*. It was surprisingly good. As the commander made to go, we asked him about the wisdom of leaving our motorcycle with the headman at Nu Po, as we planned. That would be alright, he said, "and come back and see me again sometime."

Back in Thailand again at Klo To, we rejoined the dirt road south to reach after a couple of kms a Karen village signed Nu Sae Po. Here we found the way blocked and a bridge under construction. It seemed like the end of the road. Back at Um Pang Sombat had said that the road terminated at a place called Nu Po and that we should leave our motorbike there. We asked several people if it was Nu Po, but either they could not understand Thai, or they indicated that it both was and was not Nu Po - very confusing. Tiring of riding round the dusty alleyways of the village, we went back to the entrance by the road. We had seen a school on the top of a hillock there, and wandered up. Ragamuffin children gawped in silent astonishment from every window of the school building, and finally a single all-purpose teacher with some deformity came out onto the veranda. The village was Nu Sae Po, he stated. Nu Po lay another twenty kms down the road, and to get past the bridgeworks we had to make a detour through the village.

We continued on our way, passing a Forestry Protection office and the deserted village of Ko Ga, which had been amalgamated with Nu Po (or was it Nu Sae Po?). Otherwise there was little else on this stretch of road, which penetrated ever deeper into forest country. The compacted gravel and dirt surface began visibly to deteriorate. The way was littered with fist-sized stones, some of which catapulted up from the front wheel. More than one struck me painfully on the shinbone. After that the surface degenerated into soft, churned up earth. It seemed that we must be nearing the roadhead, and as if to confirm the fact, we passed a wayside navvies camp, two half-built bridges, and a small quarry with a rock-crushing machine. Just when we were on the verge of giving up because the way was virtually impassable, we spied houses in the trees to the right. A long 64 kms south of Um Pang it was the Karen village of Nu Po - the end of the road.

We biked into this unprepossessing collection of twenty wooden dwellings, situated around a dry grassy compound, and asked for the headman. At his house we found that he was away, but relatives said that it would be alright for us to leave our bike under the house in among the stilts, pigs and chickens. Everyone seemed very vague, which made us uneasy about abandoning a hire machine so lightly. But, remembering the assurances of both Sombat and Sor Tae Tu, we did just that. (When finally we came to retrieve the Wing, it was exactly where we had left it, untouched and covered with a layer of dust.)

At Nu Po we enquired about a guide to Kui Le To (To = Tor), our next station. As luck would have it, a party had just left. A boy went round the village asking if anyone else was going to Kui, but at two in the afternoon we had arrived too late. The last people had now gone, and no one else was prepared to guide us there. This left us in a quandary. Nu Po did not look like a good place to stay, it was too far to get back to Um Pang by nightfall, and we did not know the way forward. That did not matter, everybody said in the typically blithe manner of the Karens, we would easily find the route. All we had to do was follow the course of the new road and then turn off it onto a well-marked path, which would bring us in an hour to Kui. People went this way all the time. A group with a laden elephant had set off earlier, and we would undoubtedly catch them up. Against our better judgement, but with no satisfactory alternative, we shouldered our backpacks and set off. Right at the beginning of our adventure we broke one of the cardinal rules of jungle-trekking, never to go without a guide. The imprudence nearly led to our undoing.

We trudged a few kms through the deep orange powder of the rudimentary road. Reassuringly, small groups of red-clad Karens came against us. Especially to the east there were breathtaking views through vivid green banana palms of spiky monoliths piercing the jungle canopy. We passed two giant yellow Caterpillar bulldozers slicing into the shoulder of a hill, shoving piles of rock and earth, and tipping them unceremoniously over the edge, where the debris rolled down the hillside into a tangled mass of bamboos and trees. From under their parasols the drivers, faces masked by triangles of cloth, waved to us. Clambering through their worksite, we came onto a pilot track. The track was no more than a tunnel which had been smashed through the tall dense bamboos. We walked along this for another km or two, following the profile of the mountainside. Presently, we came upon a surreal sight. A third giant bulldozer, this time a Komatsu, stood unattended in the depths of the jungle, its massive diesel engine gently idling. Beyond its shovel was virgin jungle. This was the absolute cutting edge of the new road to Kui le To and ultimately to Boeng Kloeng. We looked around, expecting to see someone in the trees having a snack or a nap, but there was nobody. We even waited for fifteen minutes, hoping that the driver would return because we wanted to ask what had become of the path to Kui. But nobody came. It was a weird situation.

The position was further disquieting in that it was clear that our path could not lead beyond the bulldozer. That way the vegetation was impenetrable. So somehow we had missed the turn-off. We backtracked for a while until we saw what looked like a little path dropping down from the pilot road. The beginning was marked with a stick. We scrambled down the steep mountainside until the ground levelled out among trees and bamboo. For some reason we had the illusion that we were near a habitation. But there was nothing. The path fragmented increasingly until it became clear that the ways were just animal tracks through the bamboos. We stopped to look and listen. Nothing. The sweat was pouring off our bodies, our shirts were sticking to our backs, and winged insects kept bothering us by settling on our forearms and faces. We looked at our watches - nearly 4 p.m. In a couple of hours it would be dark. Alarmingly and humiliatingly, only forty minutes out from the motorbike, we were already lost in the jungle. It was hopeless to go on, so laboriously we climbed back up to the pilot road. There we noticed that the stick we had seen was just one of many marker sticks, telling the bulldozer driver where to push the road. How stupid we had been! At the same time our ears picked up the low tones of the Komatsu ticking over.

In fact it was just around the corner. So for a second time we visited the bizarre spectacle of the machine left running in the middle of nowhere. But where before the sight of this juggernaut had vaguely sickened us because it seemed to be an instrument of the rape of the virgin jungle, now we greeted it with relief as a sign of civilization.

We trudged back along the pilot track. A night in Nu Po looked inevitable. Suddenly a battered Land Rover approached us. We waved it down. Inside were five boys with long-barrelled guns poking out of the windows. We thought we were done for, but it was just the Komatsu team returning to work. They offered us water from a dirty bottle, which we drank greedily, disregarding everything we knew about doubtful water. The boys said that the Kui path went off from the east side of the "road", not the west, and started about one km back, near the two other machines. We cursed the imprecision of the Nu Po Karens and set off again. Sure enough, there was the beginning of the path, although it was easy to see why we had overlooked it.

Far too late we began the two-hour mountain trek to Kui. Essentially the path crossed a mountain. Relentlessly it climbed up through the trees, before dropping steeply down an even greater distance on the far side. During this long hour of clambering we met not a single person, but the way was clear enough. At the bottom there was a river. The river at that point fragmented into a network of tree-covered islands and rivulets, and we could not see where the path went or where it emerged on the other side, even if it did. Nor was it clear whether we had to go upstream or down. So, blindly we thrashed about among the islets, watching the sun make its steady tropical descent. We picked up scraps of path, only to lose them again. In our hearts we knew what we did not dare to admit to ourselves, that with the light beginning to fade we were lost for a second time. Categorically we promised to ourselves that we would never again make the idiotic mistake of trekking either without the most precise instructions or without a guide.

We figured that if we proceeded downstream, we must eventually come to some village. Suddenly, 100 metres away we saw half a dozen buffaloes being led by an old man, who had a mighty bundle of straw on his head. We hullooed to him, shouted more urgently, and chased after him. But he ignored us totally. We skipped across the islands, splashed through the rivulets and felt sure we would soon catch him up, all the more so because we saw that he had to cross a deep pool. But when we got to the pool and waded through the waist-deep water, he and his animals had vanished. It was uncanny. Were the buffaloes and the man real, or were they just some chimera? We found no further trace of them. But we did find a path. The path led through some tall trees until suddenly we came across a wooden sign nailed to an outsize tree. In hand-painted white letters it said (in Thai) - Ban Kui Le To.

Kui Le To

Around a parched clearing we found about twenty wooden thatch-roofed Karen houses. On the platforms of some of them families were sitting cross-legged in a circle eating supper. It was clear to us that we would have to spend the night in this unpromising-looking place. Perfunctorily we asked at one dwelling how far it was to Boeng Kloeng. It was far too late to set off now, the people said. The last group had left two hours earlier. Kui Le To, although unimportant in itself, was significant in that the way divided there, one path leading to Kui Ta, Mo Ta and Mong Gua (the long roundabout way to Lae Tong Ku), and the other path going to Boeng Kloeng (the short way to Lae Tong Ku).

As was the custom in these situations, we reported to the *pu yai baan* or village headman. We clambered over the bamboo stockade marking off his front garden and addressed him as he sat with his family over rice, stewed vegetable, a dried fish and chilli dip. Fortunately he spoke some Thai. He motioned to the covered part of the balcony behind him, where we could stay the night. Beyond that neither he nor his family took much interest in us. They were not unfriendly, but not friendly either. We unpacked our bags and, as there were obviously no toilets or washing places, went down to the river to wash both ourselves and our filthy trousers. On the far bank we saw more houses, and in full view of these we began to wash. We balanced our clothes, comb and soap tray on a tree stump and, half in the water and half on the sandy riverbank, attempted to juggle soap, shampoo and towel. While we were thus engaged, Kui Karen women came down to the river to fill up fat sections of bamboo with water for the evening. This was for drinking and cooking, and we noticed that where they drew their supplies, the river was fouled not only by our soap and shampoo, but also by big buffalo droppings.

On the way back to the headman's, we made a brief tour round the dusk-bound village. In fact there was not much to see. Like Nu Po, Kui Le To was a less interesting Karen village. It did not even seem to have a shop. Of course, there was no electricity in the village and no vehicles. The only way to arrive here was on foot. All necessities had to be transported either in baskets on people's backs or by elephant. In among the houses and all over the central compound domestic animals wandered around - buffaloes, pigs, goats, cows, chickens and cocks. As night fell, their owners herded them behind the bamboo fences of their respective plots. Otherwise not much was happening. After a day out in the fields, the villagers were sitting around, smoking, chewing betel nut and spitting. They watched us with a kind of distant curiosity. It was a backward, impoverished, rural scene, as if the clock had been turned back 200 years. However, the clock was all set to leap forward. Soon the dirt road down from Um Pang would reach Kui Le To. We were told that it would cut right through this central patch. When that happened, the lives of these people would be transformed forever. They would have improved access to the outside world, but equally the outside world would have easier access to them. In one corner of the compound, behind a house, we found the elephant that the people of Nu Po had talked about. Chatting to its youthful mahouts, we learned that the beast was going to Boeng Kloeng next morning. If we wanted to join the party, the lads said, we should turn up at 8.30 a.m.

In a forlorn attempt to dry our jeans, we laid them over the headman's fence. Then we turned our attention to food and drink. We were famished and parched. We had eaten and drunk nothing all day except a doughnut for breakfast, an *oliang* at De Lo Ki, morsels of goat curry at Sa Kaang Thi, and some dirty water from the bulldozer boys. Meanwhile we had scrambled down to Nu Po, walked all round a black market, climbed over a mountain, got lost twice and sweated profusely. But we had nothing to eat or drink except our emergency provisions of tinned fish and instant noodles. Were we to start on them so soon? We scrounged some cold rice from the wife of the *pu yai* and topped it off with sardines in tomato sauce. Bed that night was embraced with gnawing hunger pains.

The situation with drink was even more problematic. But it had a humorous side. The good lady of our hut thought she was doing us a kindness when she brought us some water poured out of a bamboo section into a bronze bowl. We thought of the river water contaminated by soap, buffalo shit and, who knows, perhaps a dead goat upstream. When she saw that we did not drink the water, she removed the bowl. Presently we had to ask her to bring us some more water. When no one was looking, we slipped a couple of water-purifying tablets into the bowl. It took an hour for these tablets to work, and for a long time they sat stubbornly and visibly on the bottom of the bowl. Our problem was that for an hour we had to stop anyone from taking the drinking bowl away from us. For a long dry-mouthed sixty minutes we defended the bowl, pretending to drink from it from time to time and hiding it behind our backs, but when the time was up, we greedily gulped down long draughts of the purified river water.

While we were minding our own business on the *pu yai's* platform, virtually the whole of Kui, on the pretext of visiting the headman's family, came round to have a look at us. People were actually much more interested than we had first thought, and yet they maintained a kind of studied indifference, stealing sly glances at us from behind pillars. The majority of our onlookers were females, and old and young alike, even quite young girls, smoked. They puffed on pipes, homemade cigarettes and green cheroots, and spat incessantly through the cracks of the raised floor. Darkness had meanwhile fallen, and we were surprised by the chill of the nighttime jungle air. People began lighting fires in front of their houses. The evening's social activity seemed to consist of standing or squatting next to one of these fires, warming first one's front and then one's rear. The villagers wandered from fire to fire, exchanging the latest tittle-tattle. We decided to join the group around "our" headman's fire. But when I stood up, I made an unpleasant discovery. I could not get my left foot into my shoe. The ankle had swollen up, throbbed painfully and was difficult to stand on. We thought immediately of the large stones which had struck my shinbone on the ride down. The headman and a lot of other concerned faces peered at the reddish purple ankle in the light of an oil lamp. Of course, there was nothing to be done in Kui, and it was 75 kms back to Um Pang. But the *pu yai* muttered something about a field hospital in Boeng Kloeng and suggested we talk to the elephant boys. So, hobbling, we went over again to the house where the elephant was and began protracted negotiations with the mahouts. In the end they agreed to take me on the tusker to Boeng Kloeng (an all-day ride) for the very modest charge of 150 baht. In fact, they said, seeing that the beast was a female, we could both ride, although it might be difficult for the second person to find much space because the elephant would also be loaded up with goods. Apparently men may ride on both male and female elephants, but women may not ride on males.

Back at the headman's fire, the socializing went on for a long time. One thing that struck us was that nobody ate or drank anything, not even tea or water. This seemed strange, for in most societies conviviality is marked by nibbling or nipping. Again we thought: perhaps these people really were as economically depressed as they looked. Two Thai boys wandered in with torches. They were from the roadmakers'forward camp beyond the village and were looking to buy a chicken from the locals. They were involved in the surveying and marking of the new dirt road. We were pleased to see them because we were uneasy about the inhabitants of Kui, even wondering about the wisdom of sleeping there. But the roadmarking boys put our minds at rest. Except for the flicker of the fire and the occasional pinpricks of light from torches, the night was as black as pitch. Overhead the stars twinkled brilliantly. It was freezing cold, and the people who were not grilling their backsides at the fire squatted huddled in blankets. In the gloom some were nimbly assembling roofing panels out of *jaak* leaves. It was past midnight before everyone had drifted away.

Sleep was virtually impossible. My ankle throbbed painfully, and we were afraid that we might have to abort our whole expedition. We were hungry and cold, and the floor was uncomfortable. Bit by bit we realized that we were not alone on the platform. In dark corners shadowy shapes in crumpled blankets tossed and turned. What with these, the night owls by the fire, and people creeping backwards and forwards across the balcony, it was like trying to nap in a marketplace. There must have been up to a dozen *Yang* staying that night in the headman's house. The noise and commotion went on into the small hours. Between the last person coming to bed and the first getting up there was a quiet interval of a couple of hours, but even this was punctuated by the cries of a baby, old folk coughing and muttering, people heaving themselves up on one elbow to expectorate through the floorboards, and others clambering across the platform and down the ladder to go and warm themselves on the embers of the fire. As we hovered between sleep and wakefulness, we had nightmare visions that these stealthy figures were coming to slit our throats. At four in the morning a cock began to crow under our heads, and soon afterwards people started operating a rice pounder directly beneath the house.

CHAPTER 13

EXTRATERRITORIAL

Kui Le To - Boeng Kloeng - Lae Tong Ku

The next morning, after putting on our cold wet jeans and breakfasting on water and peanut crunch by the fire, we made it to the elephant house at the appointed hour. There, to our annoyance, we found that the elephant and its retinue had left soon after dawn. We returned to the headman and explained the situation. "Never mind", he said, "you will soon catch them up." We thought that in two or three hours they would have got a long way and asked him to find us a guide. This he did, and soon we were on our way with a boy and two youngish men. One of the men was going to branch off into Burma, and the other two were going to fetch something from Boeng Kloeng. Karens, no matter whether young or old, flew along the mountain paths in their flip-flops and with their *yaams* and machetes as if there were no tomorrow. It had often puzzled us why they raced along like this, but probably it was just that they were fit, were used to the heat and the climbing, and travelled light. The trek from Kui Le To to Boeng Kloeng was to take us a brisk three hours. Our guides told us that, after making it to Boeng Kloeng and picking up their goods, they would run-walk back to Kui in an hour. This fleetness of foot made Karens underestimate times and distances by our standards, so that when they said that a village was "fifteen minutes away" or "just around the corner", actually a haul of fifty minutes still lay ahead. "Just over this hill" meant an exhausting climb over that distant ridge.

The guides set off at a cracking pace through the trees and over some dried-up paddy fields outside the village. We trudged after them. Then for some distance we all splashed in single file through water and mud along a riverbed. It seemed hopeless to try and keep our trousers and shoes clean or dry, and from that moment on we never again attempted to do so. Quite soon we came across the road surveyors' camp beside a stream. This was an orderly affair, with three or four roomy bamboo huts, a field kitchen, a washing-up place and a long bamboo table with fixed benches on each side - big enough to seat a dozen workers. Washing was drying in the sun, theodolites and other surveying paraphernalia were lying around, and we could see communications equipment. The marking boys were all out with their red sticks in the jungle. We learned that they had got so far with their surveying and marking that it now took them two hours to walk to the forward edge and two hours back. Soon the camp would have to be moved.

Round at the back of the camp, we surprised three older men. They were tall, thin and Chinese-looking, with droopy Fu Manchu moustaches. Clearly they were the brains behind the operation. They were lolling in shirts and tracksuit bottoms on the balcony of their office, reading girlie magazines. Amid the tits and bums of Thai cuties were military maps and piles of paperwork, which they toyed with from time to time. In spite of their agreeable existence down here by the stream, they welcomed us as a pleasant distraction. They offered us Milo and Nescafé, pointed to a large thermos of hot water, and told us to help ourselves. A man got up and fetched mugs and a barrel of chocolate biscuits. The boss wanted to show us round. After our austere night in Kui we could not believe our luck. The three Karen guides fidgeted in the background.

We helped ourselves to a mugful of Milo, a cup of coffee, another mugful of Milo for good measure, and ate about a pound of chocolate biscuits each. Then we took advantage of the roadmakers' incomparable maps. These stretched well into Burma and a good way beyond Lae Tong Ku. We jotted down the names of villages which seemed to be on our route. The men were very interested in our plan to try to strike through to the Three Pagodas. They thought that from Lae Tong Ku it should take us two days on foot (drastically inaccurate, as things turned out). Also, they said, there was a 4WD track down that way, but mostly on the Burmese side. If the Burma Army had not interdicted it, we might be able to make use of that.

As the boss showed us round the small camp, we noticed that it was a veritable arsenal of weapons. We commented on all these guns, and the boss explained that some were for hunting, but others were for self-defence. Roadmakers were popular with tigers, bears and snakes, and unpopular with some of the local people. He may well have had in mind the Death Highway massacres. Interestingly, his team, now constructing this road, had previously engineered Highway 1085, the new Mae Sariang - Mae Sot road. The present project was slow stepwise work. It was going to take at least another two years just to reach Boeng Kloeng - a matter of a couple of hours on foot. There the new road would stop for the moment. There had been a plan to push the road at some time down to Three Pagodas, but this would probably never happen, partly because it would take decades to build, and partly because nobody now wanted a road through the Tung Yai - Naresuan Forestry and Wildlife Preservation Area.

Finally, we consulted the surveyors about my swollen ankle. They thought that nothing was broken, but that the bone was bruised, and that if I was careful, I could walk to the field hospital in Boeng Kloeng. They produced some deep-heat cream, which we rubbed in. Besides, they said airily, if we continued we should soon catch up with the elephant, which had passed their way earlier. Fortified with the coffee and biscuits, we set off again with almost a spring in our stride. Somehow the troublesome ankle was already feeling better.

The guides continued as we found they often liked to go, with one in front, one bringing up the rear, and us sandwiched in the middle. This was a good arrangement, because then they could not speed off, leaving us behind. Also the leading Karen could warn of dangers, such as snakes or bees nests, but also point out items of interest, which strangers to the jungle often did not see. The peril from snakes was very real, as on this very stretch of our trek we ran into one, just as we did on later sections. Our three guides said that they often encountered snakes and also bears on the Kui Le To - Boeng Kloeng path.

The path climbed up a long way through a bamboo forest. At the top was a deep narrow cutting through orange clay. It looked as if it had been worn down by generations of *Yang* walkers and elephants. In the defile we stopped for ten minutes to get our breaths back. Ahead we heard cracking noises and low insistent cajolings. Slowly a massive bull elephant, piled high with goods, and a Karen mahout perched on top of its head, came into view. The dark sinister shape crashed through the jungle gloom under the forest canopy, its chains jangling. Everybody got well out of its way, especially the little boy, who out of fear hid behind a tree. Our guides and the mahout exchanged information, and we learnt that "our" elephant was not far ahead. This was good news as my foot was throbbing more than I cared to acknowledge. After the bull elephant, we encountered next an officious off-duty BPP soldier, hiking alone back to Um Pang. He told us to turn back because the area ahead was troubled. He asked to see our BPP permits and even our passports and visas. While not exactly telling him to mind his own business, we largely ignored him and said that the *dorchodor* commander in Boeng Kloeng was expecting us.

An hour out from Kui Le To we emerged into open sunny upland, covered with sizzling 5ft-high elephant grass. To the west lay the high Burmese mountain of Doi Mo Ga Tu, which we were now to follow for some way. Appropriately enough, in the elephant grass we caught up with our elephant. The party, including the mahout, three or four Karen boys and a dog, had stopped to adjust the load. The young men were not at all embarrassed about having left without us. They merely said that the elephant had been too heavily laden to take the two of us. But it would be possible for the *farang* with the hurt foot to ride. So in the end one of us at least came to get on the elephant, and for free too.

The ride was not at all as I had expected, and afterwards I was never again in a hurry to get up on an elephant. I had envisaged swaying comfortably along in a wooden howdah, but the howdah was so full of sacks and cartons that there was nowhere else to ride except on the beast's neck. Also there was no stepping aboard from some mounting block, but an unseemly scramble up the side of the animal past its ear. Even with a leg-up from the elephant and a good pull from the mahout kneeling on its head, this was a strenuous climb up the beast's neck chains. The mahout lashed our backpacks to the netted bundle of goods, shinned down his animal and led the way. All the others followed behind. It seemed awfully high and exposed on the elephant's neck. The neck was some eight feet from the ground, and, adding another three feet of human torso length, my head looked down from a height of eleven or twelve feet. Worse than that, there was nothing to hold onto. The broad smooth top of the animal's head lay immediately in front at lap level, offering no handhold; and the tops of its

211

ear flaps were unsteady. So I gripped my legs around the animal's neck and in behind its ears, and where necessary leaned back to grab hold of the corners of the wooden basket.

Then we began to roll. As the beast lumbered slowly forward, its shoulders pummelled up and down in my bottom, making things uncomfortable after a while. Walking on the level was harmless enough, and even going up the steep narrow paths was not too bad. Each time the elephant set a front foot in one of the well-established plod marks, there was a sudden and exhilirating heave up into the air. But the slow step-by-step negotiation of the precipitous, rocky, sometimes muddy descents of the trail was alarming. As the beast set a front foot down, we seemed for a sheer second to be in free fall forwards through empty space. Going down, the animal's head did not rise to meet me, but dropped clean away. I lay back and held on tight to the lurching howdah. Another problem was that the elephant seemed to have no sense of obstacles lying across the path, which it could go past or under, but which I had to evade or duck. In fact it seemed to take a perverse delight in making a beeline for these. Thus I was lashed by overhanging bamboos and, had I not paid constant attention, would have been struck in the face by a thorn tree or simply dismounted by a low bough. It was while passing close to the branch of a tree that the first brush with a snake occurred. Suddenly one of the boys behind shouted out in Karen "Snake!". But by the time this was translated into Thai and then English, I had no time to take precautions, and the ends of a branch swished past my head. When I turned to look, I saw a bright green snake with scarlet diamonds, a metre long, lurking on the foliage of the branch. The snake was a poisonous one, and it had passed within inches of my face.

Our whole progress was accompanied by a litany of calls and clicking noises, wheedlings and cajolings, entreaties and curses on the part of the Karen boys. Sometimes, to gee the old lady up, the mahout leapt up in front of me and slapped her on the head or prompted her with legkicks under the ears. Once, to our horror, he beat her on the skull with his machete, adding fresh cut marks to numerous old ones. But the old lady was not to be hurried and just took it all uncomplaining. In fact she had a mind of her own, and her wilfulness led to the amusing side of the ride. She would go off down the wrong track and refuse to turn around. Or she would crash off into the pathside undergrowth and snack on something she fancied. Sometimes, not bothering to do this, she just took a titbit in passing, casually twirling her trunk around a young succulent 4-ft banana plant, uprooting it and chomping it on the move. Once the sly tusker farted loudly into the faces of everybody traipsing behind, and she never tired of frightening the dog. She would lash out at it with her trunk or crash her trunk down on some dry bamboos behind where the dog was sniffing, sending him scampering for dear life.

Almost my most vivid impression was of the dome of the elephant's head - perhaps because there was plenty of time to observe it. The skull seemed to have two distinct mounds or lobes, which moved independently of each other as the animal lurched along. The skin was leathery and dusty, and it sprouted hairs as bristly as a wire brush. The ride had a legacy which plagued me for days afterwards. Hundreds of itchy red spots appeared all over my upper body. This dermatitis may have come from sleeping in sweaty clothes or on dirty blankets. Or it might have been an attack of prickly heat. It could even have come from some jungle plant brushing against my skin. But I felt sure that it had come from the dirty head of that elephant.

Progress with the elephant was so slow and uncomfortable that after an hour I climbed down. It was going to take all day to get to Boeng Kloeng, and our guides were getting restless. In spite of my ankle, we decided to walk on. We thanked the elephant boys and presented them with a couple of tins of sardines in tomato sauce. While we were retrieving our backpacks and shouldering up, they lost no time in opening the tins. They took some fresh banana leaves from the jungle, spread out sticky rice on them, levered open the tins with machetes, mixed the fish and tomato with the rice, and ate balls of the mixture with their dirty fingers.

We journeyed on through a forest of immense trees rising up as straight as a die. Their two-metre thick trunks were buttressed at the base with giant moss-covered vanes. Also along here were fig trees and the dense dark salacca woods which were a favourite haunt of bears. Two hours out from Kui and with still an hour before Boeng Kloeng, we came to an unmarked fork in the path. Left was our way, and right went fifteen minutes downhill to the village of Bo Na Ta, in Burma. One of our guides was going there, and he took his leave. We began next a long descent through mixed country until we hit a cart track. The cart track intertwined with a watery muddy riverbed, and for a some distance we splashed our way through. Down in the valley the heat was oppressive, and we envied some children and their mothers bathing naked in a pool. At the sight of a grubby *farang* limping by, the children ran away and the mothers shrieked. Finally, we passed through a grove of betel nut trees and came to the first houses of Boeng Kloeng. Our other guide and the boy left us here. We thanked them for their patience and paid them 100 baht to be shared among the three of them (100 baht per day was approximately the going rate for guiding), and they looked well pleased with their morning's work.

Boeng Kloeng

Boeng Kloeng was much bigger than Kui Le To. With around 300 inhabitants, it was a mixed Karen, Burmese, Indo-Burmese and Lao place. This "Lao" puzzled us because we could not understand how people from Laos could have got so far from home. We had a theory that they were the descendants of Khmu teak workers who had perhaps been brought here from Laos in the early years of this century by British logging companies operating in Thailand and Burma. But in fact they were just Thai people - "Lao" was an old word for "northern Thai". The village was one of the most picturesque we saw anywhere on our journey. Set against a backdrop of rocky cliffs and pitted denticular mountains, it lay astride a long dusty, but shady and tranquil "street". Considering how rural and remote Boeng Kloeng was, many of the wooden houses lining this thoroughfare were surprisingly large and ornate. Some had lovingly tended front gardens with a profusion of colourful blooming plants and bushes.

We were surprised to find the main street humming with activity. In both directions there was a steady flow of people, old Chinese bicycles and bullock carts, piled high with rice and other goods. Even more astonishing, we found one or two beaten-up motorbikes and pick-ups. Where did they go? Did they no more than ply the main street? And where had they come from? Had they been helicoptered in? The mystery was solved when we learned that there was a track behind Boeng Kloeng across the border and that most of these people were Karen refugees from Burma. In fact, in the days before our arrival there had been a massive influx of people, vehicles, food and animals into Boeng Kloeng, all fleeing in the face of a swingeing SLORC offensive. They were mostly being housed in a refugee camp at the bottom of the village near the river, and, when we went down to have a look, we found everybody in the process of settling in.

The flood of refugees and the nearby fighting made everyone jumpy. We had hardly gone a few paces up the street when a BPP boy tumbled out of somebody's house and challenged us. Where were we going? What were we doing? We could see from his red eyes that he had been drinking. He was joined by four more colleagues from the same house. They were all drunk, yet it was only noon. We told them we were going to Lae Tong Ku. *Mai dai*, they said, impossible, the whole area was active and it was from the Lae Tong Ku direction that the refugees were coming. We would just have to go back to Um Pang. We told these aggressive *dorchodor* that we would think about it over lunch, and wandered off. This first encounter with the Boeng Kloeng authorities was not encouraging, and the news of fighting towards our goal made us even more despondent. Now it really seemed that we would get no further.

While we were looking around the main street, a tall thin mustachiod character called Sampan from Ko Samui came up to us. He was also BPP, but his attitude was much more conciliatory. He said he recognized us from *Ti Lo Su* restaurant in Um Pang a couple of nights earlier. We mentioned that Sombat had encouraged us to come to Boeng Kloeng and produced the magic slip of paper with the local commander's name on it. We called Sampan "Mr Fixit" because from then on his sole concern seemed to be to want to fix things for us. He radiod through to the BPP camp base and escorted us there to meet the commander. We climbed up a long steep flight of steps and found on the top of a hill a regular fortified encampment. In a kind of open mess-building the commander interviewed us. He wanted to know in particular if we were journalists. We flatly denied this, adding that we were a travel writer accompanied by his Thai guide. To demonstrate the fact, I produced my diaries and also the photographs we carried with us precisely to "oil" such occasions. The commander was much taken with the pictures, and so the shots of Darkie and the Long Neck women came to be passed from him to Sampan and then to the assembled orderlies. We explained that we had come to visit the *loe-si* people of Lae Tong Ku and, if possible, the divine guru himself.

Our cards were on the table, and the moment of truth had arrived. Either we would now be sent back to Um Pang with a flea in our ear, or we would be officially allowed to go to Lae Tong Ku. A lot of radioing went on next. Contact was made with the Karen headman of Boeng Kloeng, the BPP commander at Lae Tong Ku and the local KNLA commander across in 6th Brigade district. News from the latter was especially important not just because the next part of our trek went through Burma, but because it was feared that an attack by the Burma Army exactly in that part of Duplaya opposite Lae Tong Ku and Boeng Kloeng was imminent. The rebel commander better than anyone would know the latest position. While the transceivers crackled, our BPP commander motioned to the cooks to provide us with some lunch. They dished up catfish with green chillies, rice, two cans of sardines in tomato sauce, purified water and nips of *lao kao*. While we were tucking into this little feast, Mr Fixit drew up a protocol detailing: Mr Christian, nationality, age, passport number, profession travel writer, our goal and intentions. Finally, to our great surprise, the commander said that if we went tomorrow morning everything should be alright. Further, he offered to organize a guide for us, or, if we preferred to wait a day or two, we could accompany the next detail of BPP going to Lae Tong Ku. We said we would be happy to take the guide the next morning. He shook our hands, wished us good luck, and suggested that we fill up with water at his camp before setting off.

We could not believe our good fortune. Not only had the commander not been interested in any permit from Um Pang or Mae Sot, but he had not queried our plan. We regretted having wasted so much time enquiring in Um Pang. From the encounter we learned two things. Firstly, that the attitude of the authorities (notably the BPP) in the field could be quite different from what it was back at headquarters. And secondly, that the *dorchodor*, far from not cooperating with the insurgents (as one read in the newspapers or as was put out diplomatically for SLORC consumption), were still working hand in glove with them. Intelligence was shared, communications were good, both the KNLA and refugees freely came and went across the border, and the Thai Army crossed with impunity through rebel-held Burma. But above all, from our point of view, the BPP, far from stopping us from going on, were trying in conjunction with the KNLA to help us, even apparently encouraging us (illegally) to leave Thailand and then step back in. The same helpfulness and tolerance we found all down this frayed section of border. It was a different world down here. From Boeng Kloeng on, the way was extraterritorial in both senses of the word.

As yet we had found nowhere either to stay or take supper. We walked up and down the long main street in the hope that somehow a solution to the problem would present itself. There were four little shops, two of them well-stocked, but no eating-place or noodle stall. On our reconnaissance we found the village school, the field hospital, plenty of elephants (Boeng Kloeng was a big elephant place), a *wat* and numerous houses with betel nuts drying in their front gardens. In the street a Karen woman buttonholed us and asked us to examine the eyes of her son, who she was dragging along behind her. The poor boy was blinded in one eye, apparently by cataracts, and had half lost the sight of his other eye. He squinted at us hopefully and folornly, and his mother implored us for some medicine to cure him. We tried to reason with her that we were tourists, not doctors, but the naive woman thought that as westerners we surely had all the answers. We told her that she should seek help at a hospital in Mae Sot or Kanchanaburi. She had already been to Mae Sot, she said, but they could not help her. The hospital had told her to go to Chiang Mai, but that was too far away and she could not afford the journey. Our visits to remote areas often led to such painful situations.

Down by the refugee camp, where there was a constant hammering and sawing, coming and going, unloading and stowing, we met two Karen boys. They were from Jaddhur in Burma and had walked to Lae Tong Ku and on to Boeng Kloeng. Their village had been overrun by Rangoon and they were not so much fleeing, as migrating. They intended to push on to Klo To (Mae Chan), where they thought they could get some kind of legitimation papers. After that, they proposed to move up to Um Pang and Pop Pra, where one of them had a sister. They hoped to find some kind of work there or in Mae Sot. With scarcely a bean between them, the plight of these naive happy-go-lucky boys was typical of many people in the area.

Although they had never been to Boeng Kloeng before, the boys had that easy familiarity with everybody and everything which we had noticed before among Karens. We explained that we were looking for a place to stay, but had not been able to find anywhere. "No problem", they exclaimed, "you can stay anywhere!" And within minutes they had fixed up lodging space for us on the platform of a large house near the refugee camp. Not only that, they rustled up blankets for us and even *longyis* (Burmese sarongs), so that we could wash and change. They themselves preferred to stay in another house nearby, where there were certain girls.... At dusk we used the *longyis* to wash in the river. We washed surrounded by some hundred doleful but inquisitive Burmese Karen refugees - a humbling experience. The night spent in that large strange house was, if anything, even more public and uncomfortable that the night at Kui, but in the morning the boys brought round a tray of rice cakes coated with sticky toffee.

With my ankle still painfully swollen, it seemed a good idea to visit the field hospital. We were unlucky in this because when we stepped into the small wooden building, we learned that a Thai doctor and nurse, who had come to attend the refugees, had just left, going north. A couple of local paramedics were kicking a football around behind the hospital, and after a while they came in. They poked and twisted my ankle to see if it was broken or infected or what, causing excruciating pain, and pronounced that the bone was bruised. Then they rummaged around for medicines, but found that they had only two large sweetie jars full of paracetamol and antibiotics. They gave me a fistful of each free and said that on no account should I walk to Lae Tong Ku the next day.

That evening, outside Boeng Kloeng's best-stocked shop, we found a rough table and benches. It did not look like an eating table, but we sat down anyway. We had seen that the store sold instant noodles, so we bought two packets and asked the lady serving if she could prepare them for us. While we were waiting, we inspected her provisions. Amongst the more conventional items, such as the inevitable tinned sardines, we spotted Anchor beer from Malaysia, Burmese gin, and fruit liqueurs from China. There was also Nescafé, Milo, Pepsi and other soft drinks, as well as stacks of cheroots and homemade *lao kao* at only 10 baht a large bottle. The evening looked more promising than the one before. Presently, the Karen owner called us into her house, where the Ma-ma noodles were steaming in bowls. To our pleasant surprise, we found in addition a mini-banquet laid out for us on the floor - stewed aubergine, okra with dried shrimps, rice, and huge glass mugs of coffee. In the lamplight we sat and gorged ourselves, watched by a sea of placid faces of all ages. The lady said that if we returned in the morning, she could make us coffee or hot chocolate for breakfast at 5 baht each.

It transpired that the shop was also the home of the elephant we had ridden earlier. It had arrived meanwhile with its retinue and was penned round the back. After supper, its *Yang* owner, the mahout, joined us at the rough table. We asked him to bring *lao kao*, cheroots and glasses. The man spoke broken Thai, and mixing the hooch with Green Spot, we spent a convivial and informative evening with him and his family under the stars. The *lao kao*, he said, was made of rice and sugar cane, and was 20% alcohol. Everyone was cracking and chewing betel as usual, so we asked the man about this habit. They just chewed betel nut as we did chewing gum, for fun, the man said. The bitter taste made the saliva flow, hence the frequent spitting. But the mahout was much more interested in our story, and soon we noticed that not only his family, but half of Boeng Kloeng, Burmese refugees and all, were squatting in the gloom around our table listening. They would all have heard of the "long-neck" women, but our tales of Manerplaw, Wa prince Maha San, the great Shan pagoda of Piang Luang, and legendary Chiang Mai had them all transfixed.

The BPP commander had arranged that the man escorting us to Lae Tong Ku should come for us next morning at 9 a.m., but the Karen guide was already waiting outside our hut at 7.30, while we were still in our mosquito net. But we need not have worried, for after delaying him while we washed, ate sticky cakes, went to the shop for Milo, and got water from the BPP camp, he then kept us waiting while he stopped off to chat at a friend's house. Not many people went to Lae Tong Ku because it was out on a limb. For the locals, the paths beyond the *loe-si* village went nowhere.

So it was correspondingly hard to find anbody willing to go there, and often the best hope was to tag along with some passing *loe-si* people. The first guide who was sent to us upped his price from 100 to 200 baht, after which he lost interest altogether. But we were well pleased with the second candidate, who was now waiting for us.

This was Sooksi, a fine fellow. This tall, slim, gentle man, with short hair, a handsome square face and broad flared nostrils, was a father of five and came from Boeng Kloeng. He trekked in flip-flops, a calf-length wrap-around skirt and a KNLA camouflage jacket. Of course, there was also the obligatory machete and Karen *yaam* or shoulderbag. We struck out with him along a muddy riverbed, and almost immediately crossed into Burma. The riverbed was the border, Sooksi said. We considered what we had so often thought before - that it was this easy to wander out of the Kingdom and into xenophobic "Myanmar". There was no fuss, no barriers and no controls. With typical *Yang* understatement, everybody had said that the journey passed through only a small bit of Burma - we understood perhaps half an hour. But in fact almost the whole of the four-hour trek to Lae Tong Ku was on the wrong side of the border. Had we known, we might have gone via Mong Gua because we were not interested in passing through a war zone "just for the hell of it". But there was no going back now.

After a short distance we deviated from the Lae Tong Ku path and headed off deeper into Burma. We grew increasingly anxious about this and asked Sooksi what was going on. But our guide merely said that we had to meet his local commander. The land was flatter here, and although it was only ten in the morning, the temperature was rising uncomfortably. Presently we picked up a 4WD drive track, which brought us into a village with the delightful name of Mae Ta Ro Ta. It was a diffuse Karen place, scattered among trees and bush. An hour out from Boeng Kloeng Sooksi presented us to the area KNLA 6th Brigade commander.

The commander received us high up on the balcony of his spacious wooden house. We could see that he was a man of some consequence not just from the size of his house and the way everyone deferred to him, but from an entourage of beautiful women and girls, who looked on in the background. Sor Kyi Shwi was an affable urbane middle-aged man with a round face, balding head and gold teeth. He was dressed like our guide in flip-flops, sarong and a khaki army shirt, and even spoke some English. He bade us sit down, called for water, and frankly asked us what we wanted in this area. We told him that we were tourists, that I was collecting material for a book, that we were on our way to Lae Tong Ku, and that we hoped to press on to the Three Pagodas Pass. At first, for security reasons, Sor Kyi was unwilling to divulge his name, let alone pose for a photo. But when he got used to the idea that we were neither spies nor gun-runners, he loosened up. In particular this vain man was not proof to the blandishments of his many comely females, so that in the end he had to relent and pose with the *farang* before the camera.

We picked up some useful information from the leader about our onward journey. For Three Pagodas we would have to proceed after Lae Tong Ku to a place called Sa Kae. Sa Kae could be reached either by continuing on down through Burma, or by striking east across to Mong Gua and then south via Mae Chan Ta through Thailand. But this latter route involved a difficult mountain path which everybody feared and avoided. As far as Sor Kyi knew, there was no direct way from Lae Tong Ku to Sa Kae. The commander's information, though substantially correct, turned out to be inaccurate in some respects. It went to show just how difficult it could be to obtain reliable data when on the move, even from well-informed sources. But what interested us particularly was how safe the next part of our journey would be, especially in view of the SLORC advance. The KNLA had scouts out, the commander said. Normally the scouts went out every second day, but at the moment they were out every day. The path should be safe. We could have stayed for an early lunch, but we did not want to detain our guide, and something told us that we should press on while the situation remained favourable.

After Mae Ta Ro Ta the three of us followed the 4WD track for some distance. We passed through a countryside of mixed bamboo, scrub and trees. The sun was reaching its zenith, making the trudge along the dusty trail devastatingly hot. Sooksi tore a branch off a bush and used it as a parasol. We did likewise. I remarked to him that we looked like a band of *pi tong luang* (Spirits of the Yellow Leaves) on the move, which amused him greatly. Presently we left the track and rejoined the direct Boeng Kloeng to Lae Tong Ku path. Mercifully, it was shaded by overarching bamboos and trees, making the going cooler, if more humid. Most of the way to Lae Tong Ku was fairly flat, and for some distance the path followed the steep eastern bank of a stunningly beautiful river. The Suriya, which like the River Moei flowed unusually from south to north, was beautiful both because it meandered lazily through pure jungle, with rank green foliage pitching straight into the water on both sides, and on account of its remarkable turquoise colour. Upstream, into the sun, the water shimmered a glaucous colour, and downriver, it was a fuller aquamarine. Where the waters reached in under the gloom of the overhanging vegetation, they shaded off into a dark emerald.

Sometimes the path ran low, virtually along the river bank, and sometimes it skirted the precipitous hillsides high up. But always there were glimpses of the blue-green Suriya through the tree trunks and knotted twisted lianas. Where the narrow path climbed or dropped steeply, we found again the deep plod marks of elephants, and it was not long before another such beast came against us. We scrambled out of the way as best we could. This elephant, although heavily laden, was moving at a fair speed. It was accompanied by only one mahout, perched high up on the animal's head, feet tucked in under its ears. He was a *loe-si* boy, with a topknot of hair just above his brow. Boy and animal had established a steady rhythm, and we saw now how we should have travelled the day before. As man and mount trundled past, Sooksi exchanged words with the mahout. The man had come with his elephant from Lae Tong Ku.

In a small clearing we stopped for a rest. Our guide pointed out termite mounds in amongst the stands of giant *mai huak* bamboo. He also told us something of his life. One thing that surprised us was that his five children were relatively grown-up, and yet to us he looked no more than thirty. He had four girls and one boy. Two of his children were still with him, but three were in Kanchanaburi province. One daughter was working as a labourer on a building site. While we were talking in low voices, we heard a sudden crack of bamboo from the way ahead. Purposeful footfalls drew closer. We filled with alarm. It was certainly an advancing Burmese column. Four youths, in single file, swung into view. They were wearing combat jackets and military backpacks. Even Sooksi looked concerned because he could not recognize them as KNLA guerrillas or *dorchodor*. In fact they were four more Burmese Karen boys fleeing from the oncoming Burma Army. Evidently they had never seen a *farang* before because they were mightily taken with us. One produced a primitive pocket camera and insisted on being photographed by my side in front of the River Suriya.

After the refugees had got on their way to Boeng Kloeng, two *loe-si* boys in their early teens caught us up. In their green skirts and azure and pink shirts they looked striking. Scarves were wound around their heads in such a way that their topknots were revealed in an opening. Augmented to five, we set off again - a strange international band. One *loe-si* boy took up the lead, an English *farang* and a Thai were sandwiched in the middle, and the Karen Sooksi and the other *loe-si* boy brought up the rear. For some reason the two *loe-si* boys seemed disgruntled and switched restlessly at passing twigs and bamboos with their machetes. Suddenly, as we were labouring up a path through deep jungle, the leading *loe-si* boy in front of me leapt high in the air, landing with his legs wide astride the path. I could not work out what had turned him so and stood rooted to the spot in amazement. Sooksi had seen everything. The *loe-si* boy, just as he had been about to tread on a snake, had spotted it, sunning itself on the path. He had leapt into the air, startling the creature. The snake had slithered off down the path, but had encountered my ankles. Wriggling around the obstacle, it had then darted off into the undergrowth. The escape was perhaps even luckier than the earlier encounter with the tree snake.

All along the Suriya we saw signs of refugee movement. People were ferrying family possessions and rice supplies across the river on bamboo rafts. Some were washing themselves or clothes in the water. Men were hastily constructing temporary shelters in the trees on the side of the river away from the enemy. And in an open, burning hot field we found a new refugee *loe-si* village - Kui Kloe. Wherever we saw people, or people passed us, our guide and they would briefly chat. Seen from the air, this must have looked like a tenuous column of ants encountering each other, exchanging information, and passing on. At the deserted *loe-si* village of Le Ka Nae Ta (the people had mostly moved to Lae Tong Ku) we found a betel grove intergrown with wild starfruit, papaya and grapefruit trees. The white flowers of the grapefruit trees were heavy with sweet perfume. Sooksi got down some starfruits and cut off slivers with his machete, and we enjoyed a tart refreshing snack on the fly.

The last hour of the trek was the most gruelling. It was here that we learned the true meaning of Karen understatement about time and distance. Perhaps to encourage us when the path was most strenuous and we were most weary, Sooksi kept saying that Lae Tong Ku was just over that hill and that there was only another fifteen minutes to go. There were two ways into the village from Boeng Kloeng - a longer flatter route in through the backdoor via a waterfall, and this steeper, more direct path, which aimed straight for the BPP camp. We battled up an endless mountainside in the blazing sun towards a col. After four hours with the backpacks in the torrid heat, this was the killer. The sweat was streaming off our faces and bodies, and we had to stop every ten minutes, every five minutes, to drink water and get our breaths back. We each had a two-litre bottle of water with us. Nearly all of it was drunk on this last ascent. Sooksi and the *loe-si* boys drank too, but they did not carry water bottles, rather drank from the Suriya and any passing spring they found.

Finally, in the distance we saw the BPP camp - on the top of a hill. Behind its fortifications a flag was flying. We crossed some baking open ground and with our last reserves of strength toiled up the hill. There we threw ourselves on a bench, all in. Red-faced, dry-throated and with sweat running freely, we tried to cool off in the faintest hilltop breeze. Sooksi looked cool and fresh and amused, ready to do the same again, which in fact he presently did. Suddenly it dawned on us to our great joy that we had made it. Three days out from Um Pang we had reached the first principal objective of our jungle adventure - Lae Tong Ku.

CHAPTER 14

A JUNGLE MAN-GOD

Lae Tong Ku

Contrary to our expectations, the Border Patrol Police were excited to see us. The commander must have known that we were coming, but it appeared that the ordinary soldiers did not. They began rushing around to make us comfortable. The royal reception we had from these *dorchodor* at Lae Tong Ku was such as we experienced nowhere else down the border. Pineapples appeared, water, some round yellow peanut cakes and, marvel of marvels, cans of iced Coca Cola. Looking back on this, it is clear that the Cokes were not iced, as there was no electricity in the village. In our euphoria they had seemed chilled, when in fact they had probably just been cooled in the river. The soldiers made us eat salt with the juicy pineapples to counteract our dehydration. They took down our details in a duty book, invited us to supper that evening, and escorted us to a canteen at the foot of their eyrie.

Here more fruit and water appeared, also a dish of sardines, while a cook knocked up a large omelette in a wok. Unfortunately, when he served this on the mess table, we all saw that it was full of ants. Unperturbed, the chef cooked up another one. When we expressed our concern about the wasted omelette, he said that out here nothing was wasted. The boys up above would eat it. And in fact somebody straightway carried up the ant omelette, where it was shared out. Surrounded by M16 weapons hanging from nails, we tucked into the new offering. At the back of the kitchen we spied a barking deer (muntjac), tied up by one leg. The soldiers had trapped it in the night. The future did not look too bright for this poor little animal.

Sooksi left us at that point. He wanted to hurry back to Boeng Kloeng. We paid him his 100 baht and thanked him sincerely. We were sorry to see the Karen go. We could not have hoped for a more charming, informative guide. When he had gone, one of the BPP soldiers escorted us to the school, where we could stay. It was lucky that he did, for we would never have found the way ourselves. The first thing we noticed about Lae Tong Ku was just what a spread out village it was. Actually, it was more like a village within a village, with a strict *loe-si* hub and *wat* located amid a wider outer band of mixed Karen and *loe-si* dwellings. We thought that our walking was over for the day, but it was a good km to the school, and another one beyond that to the village proper.

The school consisted of a wooden tin-roofed building with about four classrooms, as well as a corrugated iron latrine block. Further, there were a couple of teachers' huts, a guest hut, storeroom and mess area. Two teachers greeted us - a third was away. Our hut was a bamboo affair, raised on poles, with a leaf roof, split bamboo floor, and no door. We hung a

222

towel in the doorframe to provide some privacy. The teachers brought blankets, mats, an oil lamp and a torch. Later they rigged up a short strip light, powered via wires in the trees by an old car battery on their balcony. There was a dribbling tap in the ovenlike latrine block, otherwise washing was done in public from a standpipe and pail outside our hut, or in the river. Four young *loe-si* boys worked for the teachers, and two of them were assigned to us. In particular they had to look after our breakfast.

We would dearly have loved to unpack our rucksacks, wash and rest, but the teachers insisted on taking us straightaway across the playing field to the so-called Karen hospitality house. We got the impression that the teachers, now that the *dorchodor* had flirted with us, wanted to have their share of our company. And indeed there was a certain element of jealousy and ill-feeling between the teachers and the soldiers. The Karen hospitality house was a gloomy wooden building, situated on the perimeter of the inner *loe-si* village and run by an old woman. There we were regaled in the afternoon heat with a spread of very hot food, laid out on the floor. There was grilled wild boar, barking deer curry, other unidentifiable curries, *somtam* with dried fish in it, and sticky rice. The wild boar had been salted first and was surprisingly lean and tasty. It was reminiscent of smoky bacon, but was chewy and salty too. Politely, we ate as much of this as we could stomach. When we asked the teachers how much we had to pay, they said the food was free. At the time we did not know how much we would come to rely on this house, nor did we fully appreciate the quality and generosity of the hospitality. It transpired that the *Yang* grandmama was famed far and wide for her welcome.

We finally got our wash and nap. When we were making ready to go up to the *dorchodor* camp for the supper to which we had been invited, the teachers came round and said it was time for us all to go over to the hospitality house again. We remonstrated, saying that we had been invited by the BPP. But they insisted, saying it would be bad form not to accept the Karen hospitality. So they trooped us across the playing field once more, and for the second time we picked at the grilled salted boar and barking deer curry. We were getting near to breaking into another of our precious reserve tins of tuna salad, nursed all the way from Mae Sot, but we thought first we should see what the soldiers served up. We ate several more times at the hospitality house, but, no matter whether it was breakfast, lunch or supper, the food was always exactly the same as on that first day.

Honour satisfied, we were free to go to the camp. We dared not ask the teachers to guide us, so we got one of the *loe-si* boys to lead the way. It was already dark, and he headed off with his torch down a path we had not taken earlier. We followed the lad downhill and up, through bits of jungle and across slimy single-log bridges over black rivers and muddy ravines. Lae Tong Ku by night was a perilous maze, punctuated by the feeble pinpoints of torchlight of Karens hurrying hither and thither. The soldiers again greeted us extravagantly. It seemed from their high spirits that they had already been at the bottle. They ushered us up the steep hill with its controlling daytime view over the whole area and sat us down at a table in a kind of open-sided command post. They were celebrating a colleague's birthday. The colleague was not actually present - he had gone to Um Pang - but, well, never mind. Also, they wanted to celebrate our arrival. In fact, in our honour they had decided to take the rest of the day and the night off. The fact that the commander had also gone away had nothing to do with the matter, of course. So the camp and, indeed, the whole area was under the control of his deputy. This unshaven rogue, in his early twenties and sporting a red baseball cap, was drinking away like the best of them. If the Burma Army had swept across the border at that moment, as it could easily have done, heaven only knows what would have happened.

In the corner of the command post the soldiers had stood up a cardboard cut-out of their absent friend, and at intervals we toasted the symbolic figure with gulps of Mekhong and Coke. Then the cooks proudly brought in the party meal - rice with a tureen of wonderful barking deer curry. In the space of six hours we had already had enough muntjac curry to last us a lifetime. What made it even more difficult to force down another plateful was the thought of the little hobbled deer we had seen earlier, who would now bark no more. We asked the *dorchodor* about the eating habits of the *loe-si* people. It was true, they said, that the cultists ate only the meat of game, not of domestic animals. They ate deer, boar, monkeys (four kinds), snakes, jungle fowl, fish - whatever they could hunt in the wild. Within the confines of the village we would find no chickens, ducks or pigs. There were elephants, buffaloes and cows, but the people did not eat these, only used them for work. Neither did the *loe-si* drink alcohol, although they did smoke. This was why the school and the army camp, even the hospitality house, were outside the real village. Anybody who liked chicken or pork, or who liked a drink, lived, literally, beyond the pale. We asked the boys why the *loe-si* Karens did not eat domestic animals. Their answer was an explanation as apocryphal as any we heard. When domestic animals came into *loe-si* houses, the inhabitants cursed them. The cult followers then avoided eating the animals because they did not want to eat their own curses.

It interested us to find out from the soldiers if *farangs* ever came to Lae Tong Ku. None had come recently, although they thought that a few years previously two had somehow orienteered their way here. (A year later, when we revisited the village, the teachers said that no *farangs* had been in the meantime.) Occasionally foreign missionaries came to Lae Tong Ku in a futile attempt to convert the devout *loe-si* people. They mostly came up from Kanchanaburi and stayed only a short time. We had heard that a Karen Christian missionary woman, who spoke some English, was living near the mini-waterfall, but we never encountered her. In the early 1990s the principal trouble in the village was religious conflict between the *loe-si* and a Californian missionary, Mr Christopher. Cultural imperialists like him generated considerable ill-feeling, which was then indiscriminately directed against any visitor, as we were later to discover.

A JUNGLE MAN-GOD

When the cool evening air began to bite, the *dorchodor* rolled down tarpaulins over the open sides of our post. The atmosphere became cosier, more convivial, but also steadily more inebriated. The boys ran down to the storeroom to fetch more bottles of Mekhong, Coke and whatever titbits they could rustle up. Then the sound of distant fighting started, thundering in the Dawna Range. We hearkened to it for a while, but nobody paid much attention. Someone had the idea of trying to teach us a few words of Karen. Thus we learned: *omi* = rice, *oti* = water, *lor omi* = I'm hungry, *goh poh gah yor* = full, *tabloe dumah* = thank you very much, *soe koh* = hello, *jor lai le loh* = where are you going?, *or chua* = how are you?, but also, as the evening became progressively sillier and more drunken, things like *chi cha* = wee wee. A helicopter dropped supplies to the BPP jungle camps every ten days. On that evening the boys, with our help, drank up the whole of their ration of Mekhong and ate nearly all the food. Afterwards we were not invited to any more meals and drinkies at the camp. Worse still, only a few hours after our arrival, we were shamefully stotious in this ultimate teetotal village of stoics.

The next morning, when we appeared in the teachers' open-air canteen area, our two *loe-si* boys brewed up coffee for us. From an early hour the teachers had been blasting the immediate area through a tannoy with the Thai national anthem and Isaan pop music. This they did every morning. Seeing us arrive, they made to take us to the hospitality house, but we bridled and instead ate up the stale remains of some coconut cake we had brought from Um Pang. Over breakfast we enjoyed the marvellous surrounding scenery. To the east a long sheer cliff formation began to emerge from the morning mist. One of the teachers went off to school. The school was visible from where we sat, but we were surprised to see him together with only seven pupils, lined up before the Thai flag. We commented on the small number of children, and the other teacher explained that mostly the pupils did not come during the day. They went out cutting *jaak* and teak leaves to make roofing, and came to class in the evening. Altogether there were 57 schoolchildren, aged between seven and fifteen years.

The second teacher took us on a guided morning tour of the village. Again we were struck by the distances we had to walk and by how fragmented the place was. Often houses stood quite isolated among the trees and fields. We saw also how relatively prosperous and established Lae Tong Ku was, compared to, say, Kui Le To. It was a study in self-sufficiency. There were rice and cereal fields (altogether some 100 and 50 *rai* respectively), and cotton, sugarcane and tobacco plantations. Fruit was a significant part of the local economy, people cultivating durian, grapefruit and betel trees. Of course, growing wild, were coconut and banana palms. Another important crop was chillies and sesame. In many places we saw chillies and betel nuts drying in the sun, and in one spot we found a rotary mill, driven by an ox, grinding the oil out of sesame seeds.

In many parts of Thailand cereals were harvested more than once a year. Here there was just one annual crop. Some of the rice and other products were sold to Karens in Burma or exchanged with them for salt, dried fish, shrimp paste and tobacco. Most families were engaged in weaving, both of cotton and bamboo. The finished cloth, mats and baskets were mainly for personal use. In one house we watched black gunpowder being prepared. Considering that the *loe-si* people did not eat domestic quadrupeds, we were surprised to see so many cows and buffaloes wandering around. A recent census in Lae Tong Ku (by our Um Pang friend Sombat) counted 81 cows, 39 buffaloes and also 7 elephants. But nowhere did we find a single chicken, duck, pig or goat.

The headman, Tra Nai, was out of the village at the time of our visit, but we did see his deputy, Mong Aemi. The deputy *pu yai* spoke good Thai, and we quizzed him at length. We were also introduced to a key character called O-Sae-Tae. This 65-year old man had been born in the village and had seen four *loe-si* leaders come and go. It was under his direction that the fine new second monastery building had been constructed in 1991. Evidence of his skill as a craftsman could also be seen in the design of his own house. A sign of O-Sae-Tae's influence was that he was a confidant of the present *rishii* and owned two elephants. During our stay at Lae Tong Ku we spoke at length both with Tra Nai and O-Sae-Tae, but also with the teachers, the BPP, and the *loe-si* himself. The information we gleaned from them is included here not in the form of a series of interviews, but as a digest.

History and culture of Lae Tong Ku & the loe-si sect

Lae Tong Ku, everyone agreed, was about 140 years old. The original inhabitants had come from Burma. Between 1852 and 1860 they were chased two or three times out the country by the Burmese, finally settling in this spot during the 1850s beside Kao Saam Rom mountain, just inside Thailand. The River Suriya, one mile west, formed the border. Between the village and the Suriya was a small waterfall. "Lae Tong Ku" meant "the village above the waterfall". The villagers were Talarku loe-si people, one of the many Karen subgroups. In 1992 the population numbered 610 or 109 families (excluding a Karen refugee camp nearby), consisting of 365 males and 245 females. The major discrepancy in numbers between the sexes was explained by the fact that the male contingent was swelled by the disciples of the loe-si, many of whom came from outside the village. Lae Tong Ku was situated at 210 m. above sea level and consisted of approximately 15 sq. kms of houses and fields, with an additional 12 sq. kms of jungle and mountain.

Most of the 109 houses were of wood and bamboo. All were roofed with teak leaves, except five, which had tin roofs. Only two of these dwellings had "proper" toilets (i.e. with pot and dipper), 65 had just a hole dug in the ground, and 42 had no toilet at all. Three small rivers ran through the village - the Ti Mo Ko, the Lae Pra Ko (= bat cliff river) and the Ba No

Krae Ko (= lemon river). The rivers were used for washing, irrigating and drawing water. Drinking water was derived from two shallow manmade wells and from sand wells along the rivers. The water in the taps near the school was stream water piped down from the mountain. There was no hospital in Lae Tong Ku, although the BPP could sometimes provide emergency aid. Villagers walked mostly to the health clinic in Boeng Kloeng for treatment, or they waited for the mobile (airborne?) hospital which came three times a year. The most common complaints of both adults and children were thyroid problems, respiratory and intestinal ailments, and malaria. Lae Tong Ku was one of the deadliest places for malaria in Thailand.

What made Lae Tong Ku interesting, of course, was that it was a centre for the loe-si *cult. What made the village unique was that it was the home of the only* loe-si *in Thailand. The* loe-si *cultists were of the Lagu (Talarku, Telakhon) denomination. They were peculiar to this area and lived on both sides of the border, but mainly in Burma. Altogether there were 31* loe-si *villages with an estimated total of 16,000 followers. Six of these villages were in Thailand, all of them in the remote southwestern reaches of Um Pang district. Lae Tong Ku was the principal village of the six. The other five were: Mae Chan Ta, Mo Ta Lua, Chong Pae, Ti Wa Kae and Kai Wo Ta. Apparently there were a couple more* loe-si *leaders in Burma, but not in every cultist village. Where a village did not have its own* loe-si, *the faithful went from time to time to worship the man-god of a central village.*

The loe-si *cultists were devout people with austere practices. They could always be recognized by their characteristic topknots. As a subgroup of the Karen peoples, they wore Karen costumes, but with some flamboyant modifications. However, whereas most Karens were animists or even Christians, the* loe-si *Karens were essentially Buddhists. Theirs was a Buddhism interwoven with animism and shamanism, and overlaid with the cult of the* loe-si. *More recently the Lae Tong Ku* loe-si *people had overlaid their version of the religion with another cult - the cult of elephant tusks. The word "loe-si" was actually a Thai word (roe-sii, rishii) and signified a holy man, an ascetic hermit, a jungle sage with magical powers. The* loe-si *cultists believed in their* loe-si *(or pu chaik, as he was also known), as Thais believed in the Lord Buddha.*

Loe-si cultism and Buddhism shared the same five central precepts. They differed, however, in their interpretation of the first. Where Thai Buddhism said that you should not kill animals, the loe-si *followers believed that you could - for eating. Why it was that the cultists did not eat domestic animals such as cows and buffaloes, and yet did eat wild animals, we never established, but it might be because of Hindu influences. In many ways the Lae Tong Ku* loe-si *people, with their elephant cult, their ascetic sadhu or guru, their long hair and their made-up faces, were reminiscent of some exotic Indian sects. Each year, at Lae Tong Ku, there were four main religious ceremonies - at* songkraan, *prior to the rainy season, after the rainy season and after the harvest. Also, every month there were the three ceremonies of the full moon, half moon and no moon.*

When loe-si *villagers transgressed, they were first admonished and then, if they repeated the transgression, shorn of their hair and paraded round the village. On a third occasion, they were expelled from the village and the sect. The wrongdoer could be re-admitted by apologizing, by being purified with holy water, and by bringing five kgs of pure beeswax and also flowers, incense and a candle. A villager with shorn hair was not necessarily a wrongdoer. A* loe-si *villager might cut off his hair to get rid of lice or fleas. When villagers died, they were not cremated as in Buddhist practice, but buried. The burial took place on the day of the death without a* wat *service. When cows and buffaloes died, the people did not eat them, but likewise buried them.*

In 1993 the loe-si *of Lae Tong Ku had 82 disciples. These were different from the rank-and-file followers in the village in that they lived at the monastery and learned from the holy man. At the time of our visit their ages ranged from 11-28. The young disciples had to serve a minimum of three years and three months and during that time could not, like the* loe-si *himself, enter people's houses or marry. After three years of the ascetic life, they were free to leave or marry. However, if they did so, they could not then re-enter the discipleship. The newest and youngest acolytes had the hardest work to do and lived with the master himself in the original* wat *building. They fetched water, gathered wood, cooked rice and served the* loe-si. *The older ones lived in a separate building and made baskets and other things for use in the monastery or to give to villagers. Local people sometimes brought food offerings to the* wat. *In order to become a disciple, a young man had to be bathed in the leader's holy water and had to offer one coconut, three bunches of bananas, one kg of pure beeswax, and food. He brought, further, his personal requisites, including three knives, one axe, a sleeping mat and a pillow.*

Unique in Thailand, the Lae Tong Ku loe-si *was a kind of Dalai Lama or spiritual head, but was also a demigod in that people actually believed in him and worshipped him. The present one was titled Monnae and named Ujae (English: Ujay, "U.J."). In 1995 Ujae was aged 44 and was the tenth* loe-si *since the founding of Lae Tong Ku. He was a relatively new incumbent as the last man-god, hailing from Burma, had died in August 1989. Technically, Ujae was the eleventh* loe-si, *as there had been another one, Jae Hor Wae, before the lineage of ten. But that very first one had been caught and killed by the Burmese, and the Lae Tong Ku cultists had begun counting anew with their second leader. For the record, the ten official cult leaders have been: Jae Bae (died 1852), Jor Yor, Jae Moe, Jae Lia, Gaeng Kor, Soe Tia Boei (died 1942), Jae Chouai (1942-1955), Toh (1955-1965), Du Yoh (1965-1989) and Ujae (1989-).*

Before he died, a loe-si *normally nominated his successor. Du Yoh and Ujae had inherited the mantle in this way. But if an outgoing* pu chaik *died without having chosen, a meeting was called of all the* loe-si *villages in*

Thailand and Burma to nominate the successor. The loe-si *could not marry or visit villagers' houses, and stayed mostly in the* wat. *His daily life was to instruct the disciples and the cult followers in general. He ate twice a day, morning and evening, preferring fish, fruit and jungle bipeds (monkeys and wildfowl). In the rainy season, he ate once a day, after sunset. The leader was endowed with certain shamanistic powers. Illness in a villager was regarded as possession of that person by an evil spirit. The* loe-si *could exorcize such spirits. It was said that he did not actually arbitrate in disputes, but could act rather as if the disputants had taken a "truth drug". The Karens came to the man-god and told their conflicting stories. They believed that whoever told lies would die. If the Talarku sect's numbers were holding steady or were even on the increase, belief in the magical powers of the* loe-si *himself was on the decline.*

Our morning round of the village with the teacher ended with a visit to the *wat*. The teacher thought he might be able to secure us an interview with the holy man, but he held out no great hope. We for our part knew that this Thai teacher was a particularly religious (Buddhist) man and hoped that he might have some leverage with the *loe-si*. We came down to the monastery complex. It lay sheltered in a coconut grove at the foot of "Bat Cliff" escarpment. The atmosphere was peaceful and friendly. *Loe-si* boys and men sat or strolled around, and cows and buffaloes wandered at will. We found five buildings - the original *wat*, the new quarters constructed by O-Sae-Tae for the older disciples, a meeting place, a shed housing elephant tusks, and a storehouse for rice and food. Besides the compound itself, a further thirty *rai* of land belonged to the monastery.

At a certain point on the approach to the compound there was an invisible line beyond which no one could go without taking his or her shoes off. We were just about to overstep this line when the teacher and some of the disciples firmly reminded us that now we should proceed barefoot in the dust. Beyond this line, at the level of the *wat*, there was a second invisible line, marking off territory which no woman could enter, not even the Thai Queen, Sirikit. A third line, behind the *wat*, demarcated a sacred area running back to the cliff, accessible only to the *loe-si* and his disciples. Apparently there were elephants in there, and rumour had it that in the cliff face there was a cave for the personal use of the jungle hermit.

We particularly enjoyed the colourful extravagance of the *loe-si* followers. These were handsome wide-jawed men in bottle-green or blue sarongs, and wearing shirts which were typically green, azure, or pink. Their long black hair, rubbed with coconut oil to make it shine, was twisted up behind the head and brought over the crown to be knotted above the forehead. Mostly the knot was worn centrally, but sometimes it was sported above the right eye. Almost every follower had a white or pink scarf, often fringed with magenta, which was wound around the head in such a way that the topknot appeared in a front opening. It was the habit of the *loe-si* people to beautify themselves with gold facial painting, red lipstick, earrings, necklaces and flowers in their hair. Altogether they looked very pretty, and sometimes it was hard to remember that the young ones were not girls. The *loe-si* women were no less striking. Married ladies wore wine-red sarongs and red or blue or black blouses, while the unmarried girls dressed in long, off-white, pink-edged shifts. All the *loe-si* people, like all good Karens, never went anywhere without their cerise shoulderbags. The Pwo Karens, who along with the S'gaw Karens make up the two principal Karennic groups in Thailand, have a theory, drawn from their mythology, that they represent the female lineage of the tribe, while their S'gaw counterparts form the male. The *loe-si* people, inclining to the feminine, seemed to have something in common with the beautiful Pwo.

The original *wat* building, which, judging by its state, must have been a good century old, was smaller and more ramshackle than we had imagined. It was made of old brown wood and rusty beaten-up corrugated sheeting, and was raised high enough on stilts for buffaloes to be able to wander underneath. The jungle hermitage was in the Burmese style and appeared in essence to be a deep rectangular box, although, of course, we could not look round the back. At the front was a porch, and low wings with sloping roofs abutted on each side. The whole building was surmounted by a curious stunted square wooden tower and was shaded by the trees. I was not permitted to enter this building and tried instead to look through the open door, which was about 6 feet off the ground. But it was so gloomy inside that it was impossible to make out anything except a photograph of the previous *loe-si* and numerous baskets. I had the impression of peering into a dusty run-down junk shop.

As an offering for the jungle man-god, the teacher had brought some peas roasted in batter. He called into the *wat* and asked for the holy man to come out. After a while the *loe-si* appeared from the interior gloom and sat cross-legged in the doorway. The teacher handed the "sweeties" to him via one of the acolytes. Monnae Ujae was simply dressed in an off-white robe wrapped around his body and over his left shoulder, leaving bare a muscular right arm and shoulder. Of course, he had a topknot, but no headscarf, and we noticed cotton strings (spirit cords) tied around his wrists. His face was severe, angular, unsmiling, crosspatch. Wisps of hair grew out of his chin, his eyes were rather too close together, and the pronounced furrows which slanted upwards and outwards from the bridge of his nose made him look more diabolical than godlike. Our teacher guide could not speak Karen, and the *loe-si* no Thai, so communication was difficult. However, through one of the acolytes, who spoke some broken Thai, the teacher tried to convey that we had come all the way from Um Pang to visit the leader. But the *loe-si* was a model of calculated indifference. He said almost nothing the whole time, avoided our gaze, and, when I tried to photograph him (with his permission), looked steadfastly at the floor beyond his knee. Finally, he cleared his throat and spat demonstratively onto the ground, whereupon he disappeared back into the gloom of his ramshackle jungle *wat*.

A JUNGLE MAN-GOD

We were disappointed with this audience with the *loe-si*. After having come so far, we were peeved that he had had so little time for us and had shown so little interest. It must have been a rare event for a *farang* to come and see him. But beyond that, he did not even show the common courtesy and welcome one might have expected of any holy man, whatever his persuasion, and so we formed a poor opinion of this man-god. On top of everything, I knew that the half dozen photographs I had sneaked were failures. Thoughts were running through our minds that the divine could not be interviewed or photographed, and, less charitably, that at the end of the quest was nothing. Later we found out that the *loe-si* had mistaken us for missionaries, and we roundly cursed all missionaries and even the pious teacher for not making things clearer.

While we were thinking evil thoughts outside the *wat*, one of the disciples shinned up the long trunk of a coconut tree and began hacking football-size nuts down. Although there were only three of us, he had to get four because one of them, after plummeting to the ground, burst open with a spectacular spray of milk. The boy then deftly lopped off the tops with a machete and presented each of us with a fresh coconut. After we had drunk the milk, he then split the green nuts in two, allowing us to scoop out the thin slimy flesh. Apparently all visitors were at least accorded this courtesy.

Later that evening, after we had supped once more on wild boar and barking deer, we returned to the school area to find two monks, an old one and a young one, who had wandered in from Supanburi. We also found a couple of BPP boys who, far from inviting us for food and drink, were trying to heavy it up with us to leave Lae Tong Ku. Evidently, visitors were not allowed to spend more than a night or two in government property except by prior arrangement with the authorities. In Lae Tong Ku, seeing that it was impossible to stay in a *loe-si* house, anyone passing through was more or less obliged to stay in the school guest hut. Insofar as Buddhist monks could express such feelings, the two whacked bonzes, shorn of their hair and eyebrows, looked reproachfully at us because we had taken the only free accommodation and they were going to have to double up with one of the teachers in his hut.

The *loe-si* boys had made a fire, and we all sat round it in the betel trees under the moon and stars. The fire was a criss-cross of dried bamboo sections, and at regular intervals everybody pushed the end nearest to them further into the centre of the fire. We were a strange gathering - a brace of wandering monks, the religious Thai teacher, the two *loe-si* boys, an Anglo-Thai and an English *farang*. The other teacher was busy in the school, and from nearby came the drone of multiplication tables or the Thai alphabet being chanted by the pupils. We asked the two monks which route they had taken. They had wanted to go from Mong Gua to Boeng Kloeng, but had got lost after half an hour and had followed by mistake the dreaded path from Mong Gua to Lae Tong Ku. They had set off at 9 a.m. and had arrived here at 4 p.m. The path had not been so difficult, especially coming this way round.

But if one started from Lae Tong Ku, there would be a long steep climb over "Bat Cliff" ridge.

Reviewing with the teacher our unsatisfactory visit to the *loe-si* earlier that day, we came to speak of the confusion surrounding the two groups of Talarku cultists, the "yellowthreads" and the "whitethreads". At the same time we were able to make more sense of the confusion surrounding the attack by *loe-si* tribesmen on BPP soldiers. There were indeed two rival Lagu subgroups - the old "whitethread" sect based here on Lae Tong Ku, and another breakaway "yellowthread" cult, which was trying to establish itself near Mae Chan Ta. The murders had had nothing to do with either Lae Tong Ku or the "whitethread" *loe-si* followers living there, but had taken place in a different place, fomented by a different group of people - the troublesome "yellowthreads". It was said that the splinter "yellow" sect, numbering some hundreds, were partly ex-communists local to the area. They and their rival *loe-si*, one Ti Liang Eng or Dhi Liew Eng, had set up an alternative hermitage, Sitti Ariya, in the far-flung settlement of Chong Pae. From here they wanted to establish a fiefdom in the heart of the giant Tung Yai/Huai Ka Kaeng wildlife sanctuary. Actually, there was a rumour that the new self-proclaimed "yellow" leader was already dead. In a juicy detail (or piece of nonsense) that could only have emanated from the depths of the jungle, we learned that the upstart cultists believed that, if they carried a piece of their *loe-si*'s yellow robe, they were invincible, incapable of being hurt even by bullets. To prove the point, Ti Liang and three of his most devout followers had allowed themselves to be ceremonially shot at, with the unfortunate result that they had been killed.

Unlike the Lae Tong Ku cultists, who cooperated to a degree with the authorities, the rival sect sought total autonomy in its area, subject to the control of neither the "whitethread" *loe-si*, the paramilitary *dorchodor*, nor the forestry *anuraak*. But the BPP and the forestry authorities had bases in the sect's "territory" and, even more provocatively, had forbidden the group to hunt the wildlife of Tung Yai or to cut down sanctuary trees to make space for agriculture. For a while relations with the authorities had been distinctly strained. But what had brought matters to a head was not so much the belief of the "yellowthreads" that the authorities were trying to suppress their Ariya cult, or the ban on hunting, as a particularly galling and all-too-human detail. In revealing this telling detail to us, our pious teacher friend provided an insight into the resentment he and his colleagues felt towards the BPP soldiers and also the *anuraak*. The *dorchodor* and forestry boys, not content with forbidding the cultists to hunt, had then themselves proceeded to hunt, openly flouting their own interdict. One might perhaps have expected that the BPP would engage in a bit of surreptitious poaching, but not the very guardians of the wildlife sanctuary. Yet the *anuraak* too had openly hunted under the very noses of the "yellowthread" *loe-si* people.

So it had been the hypocrisy of the military and the forestry authorities that had so incensed the cultists, triggering the violence. The mechanics of the raid we gleaned from BPP soldiers themselves. One night, 30-40 "yellowthreads" had come to the Mae Chan Ta forestry office, ordered two young men staying there to leave, and burnt the place down, including all the paperwork and communications equipment. Later the same night, between 4 and 5 a.m., the same band of cultists had gone to the local BPP camp, about one km away. The soldiers had all been sleeping except for a sentry and one cook, who had got up to prepare the camp breakfast. The cook had seen the cultists coming and raised the alarm. But it had been too late, and the *loe-si* followers had killed six soldiers with machetes. One soldier had managed to get out a machine gun and shot half a dozen of the assailants. The rest had run away, to Supanburi and Kanchanaburi. Those who had not been rounded up in the subsequent Army action were still at large down that way.

The next morning, sick of grilled boar and muntjac curry, we went in search of food which we could buy and prepare ourselves with the aid of the teachers' utensils. In a house near O-Sae-Tae's residence we found the beginnings of Lae Tong Ku's very first shop. We purchased there some yellow Burmese noodles, shallots and greens, and later cooked these up into a wonderful pottage, flavoured with fish sauce, oyster sauce, garlic and black pepper. It was the best meal since Um Pang. O-Sae-Tae was doing some detailed woodwork on the balcony of his house. Meeting him again, we had a piece of luck. The village elder introduced us to one Toom Yai, who was sitting with him. We joined the two men on the balcony. The fetching 35-year old Toom Yai, who sported a stylish bushy bobtail topknot, spoke good Thai as well as his native Karen. Amongst other things, Toom Yai offered to guide us on the next leg of our journey, wherever that might take us.

The role of the elephant tusks in *loe-si* religion puzzled us, and O-Sae-Tae, through Toom Yai, seemed to be the very person to ask about it. The story, as told to us by the elephant owner, was as follows. In the old days a large wild elephant had frequented the village area. It was a smart animal because it used to come to the *wat* each time there was a full or half moon - the days when people brought food offerings for the *loe-si* and his disciples. The people saw this as a sign of good luck, a sign from the Buddha, and began to incorporate the elephant in their cult. When the elephant died, the *loe-si* of the day cut off its outsize tusks and had them carved by a Burmese craftsman. The tusks were the enormous pair in the ivories house near the *wat*. If we liked, Toom Yai and O-Sae-Tae could take us down to see them. We took up the offer at once. We also told them about our disappointing visit to the *loe-si* the day before. The two were quite upset about this and resolved to put things right. And so it happened that we secured our second and successful audience with *loe-si* Ujae, this time equipped with one of his confidants and an interpreter.

We waited on the benches facing the porch of the old hermitage while O-Sae-Tae explained behind the scenes to the *loe-si* that we were not missionaries, but had journeyed with no other intention than to see him. Could not the holy man come out again and answer our questions? After a long time Monnae Ujae appeared for a second time. This time he did not skulk in the doorway, but came right out to sit cross-legged on a kind of dais between the doorway and the benches. Behind him was an array of eighteen disciples in their colourful finery. We quickly realized that our second audience was an official reception, making it a somewhat daunting occasion. In other respects, however, it was the same seedy spectacle as before. The *loe-si* sat patiently on his makeshift platform in his dirty cotton robe. Because he was sitting in a shaft of light burning down through the tree canopy, beads of perspiration formed on his forehead. As he emerged from his *wat*, he picked up a handful of betel nut and crammed it into his mouth. For a long time he chomped on this, spitting out streams of saliva in a way that was not at all godlike. Behind him his entourage of young girl-boys lolled around, likewise chewing betel and expectorating, but also smoking pipes and fat homemade joints. The spectacle would have been absurd or even suspect if it had not been so riveting.

Through Toom Yai we asked the *loe-si* as many questions as we could think of. We asked him if he could leave the village or if the sect could uproot and move to somewhere else. No, they had to stay here in the appointed place. We wanted to know if his sect was proselytizing. No, their cult was non-expansionist. How tolerant and forbearing these people seemed in comparison to the missionaries who intruded into their jungle retreat. The subject led on to "yellowthread" cultists, who had attacked the BPP. Here, Monnae Ujae, who had been a picture of composure, quietly picking at his toenails under our noses, became agitated. His face darkened and the lines fanning out from between his eyes deepened into that infernal frown. This was a splinter group, and they were false *loe-si* people, the "whitethread" leader hissed. They wore trousers and other degenerate things. They had nothing to do with the Lae Tong Ku group and were bad people.

The rival sect troubled Ujae in another way that was not easy for us to understand. He said that in his cult if the *loe-si* dreamed three times of yellow thread, he had to change the colour of his robes from white to yellow. He had recently had a second dream of yellow thread, and he was afraid that he might soon have the third and final dream. The photo we had seen of the previous leader, taken shortly before his death, showed the predecessor wearing a yellow robe. It was possible that the colour yellow was associated for Ujae with something bad, the need to nominate a successor, or some great change in the sect. The rise of the breakaway "yellowthread" group may have seemed for him like the harbinger of some apocalyptic change.

Toom Yai explained to the holy man that I was sure that the photos I had taken the previous day were no good, and he asked if it was possible for the *farang* to take some fresh ones for his book. Ujae nodded approval. Where earlier the *loe-si* had resolutely avoided looking at the camera, now he scowled into the lens with such a vengeful thunderous stare that I thought the lens, film and my eyeball would be burnt out. After the photographs, the *loe-si* expressed an interest in the camera and began asking questions about it. It seemed he was taken with the idea of becoming a snapper himself. We suggested that he buy a pocket Kodak from Mae Sot, a notion which brought to his face the only smile we ever saw him make.

Our last question concerned the religious ceremonies. It was answered in an unexpected way. By good fortune there was to be a half-moon ceremony the next morning, and if we liked we could come and watch. The jungle man-god rose to return to his hermitage. As he disappeared, O-Sae-Tae asked if we might look at the ivories. It was arranged that some of the disciples would show them to us.

The sacred tusks were housed to the left of the old *wat* building in a special shed raised high off the ground on stilts. As the ivories lay behind the second invisible line, women were not permitted to see them. My eyes peered at floor level into the gloomy repository. Inside were two pairs of tusks, one large and one small, and many Buddha figures, mostly rather small. The two large tusks from the local elephant were massive indeed. Standing at 155 cms high and weighing 35 kgs each, they were mounted on their stump ends and arched up and inwards, framing the smaller ivories and some of the figurines. Both giant tusks were elaborately carved with scores of standing and seated Buddha images, which diminished in size as they approached the tip. We were told that the carving had been done by a Burmese mastercraftsman. The two smaller tusks, two kgs in weight and one foot high each, had come from Kanchanaburi and were remarkable, although damaged, for their exquisite intaglio work. It looked as if a lacework of ivory had been wrought around the core of each, itself carved with Buddhas, and yet the tusks were all of a piece. There had once been a third pair of tusks at Lae Tong Ku, but these had been given away to another monastery.

The two largest Buddha images were a twelve-inch golden standing figure in the Ayuttaya style and a similar black figure in the Burmese style. There were a pair of white jade Burmese Buddhas five inches wide by seven inches tall. In addition there was a small Burmese clay figure two inches wide by three inches tall, covered in gold. Seven Burmese images with similar dimensions were covered with silver and had heads of gold. Further, some thirty or so other small figures resided in the shed. At one time there had been a Buddhist *wat* in Lae Tong Ku, manned by one monk. When he had died, all the temple's Buddhas had been moved to the *loe-si wat*. Considering how valuable the big tusks and some of the Buddha figures were, in terms both of their material and spiritual value, it was remarkable to see them on display outside unguarded. After we had inspected the ivories house, we were again treated to a fresh coconut each.

On the fourth day of our stay in Lae Tong Ku we got up very early and went down unaccompanied to the *wat* to witness the half-moon ceremony. People were arriving from far and wide. Some had got up in the small hours to trek from far-flung *loe-si* hamlets. About 200 people had congregated in the temple compound. The disciples were brushing up dead leaves to make the bare earth spick-and-span. In several places fires were burning, and the dust and smoke drifted up through the shafts of early morning light filtering through the trees. People were busy changing into special ceremonial clothes. The men were donning ankle-length white shifts, edged with pink and bearing four vertical red stripes, an attire which made them resemble unmarried girls.

People were bringing food offerings for the *loe-si*, and these were transmitted to him by the *ukoh*, a special male intermediary. Presently, everybody sat down, sorted in receding bands. At the front were the disciples, behind them ordinary *loe-si* men, and at the back women and children. The ceremony seemed to be conducted by the *ukoh*, for the *loe-si* himself was nowhere to be seen - perhaps he was at the back of the *wat*. A short religious service followed. It was difficult for us non-initiates, relegated to the side lines, to see. The *ukoh* said prayers and chanted, and intermittently the assembled *loe-si* followers chanted with him. At the end of each chanted section, they exclaimed a loud "Hey!" and as they did so, turned their upper bodies to face another direction. Occasionally, the man conducting the prayers went to the rear of the *wat*, where some bamboo posts were erected with candles on them. Their function was unclear to us. The end of the ceremony was marked by the beating of gongs and bells.

Back at the school a visitation of BPP soldiers made it abundantly clear to us that we should quit Lae Tong Ku as soon as possible, and, as we did not want to completely outstay our welcome, we decided to go the next morning, our fifth day. The only problem was how to continue. Nobody did go on, not the *loe-si* people, nor the *dorchodor*. We tried to glean any further information we could in the village and review our options. It seemed that whichever way we went we had to get to a place called Sa Kae, the village the KNLA commander had mentioned back at Mae Ta Ro Ta. Going the shortest way, down through Burma, this was apparently two days' hard walk away. Beyond that, as we subsequently found out, it was a further 60 kms or three days of hard trekking to the Three Pagodas Pass. We had estimated that it would be two days on foot from Lae Tong Ku to the Pass, and the roadmakers near Kui Le To had confirmed this. How wrong everybody turned out to be! Lae Tong Ku was not even half way - a good 100 kms of jungle lay between the *loe-si* village and the famous Pagodas. Already, one week out from Um Pang, we were beginning to get tired and dirty and demoralized, and yet a second tougher week lay ahead. Our problems seemed only now to be starting, and we seriously wondered if we would ever reach our goal.

Once Um Pang had seemed like the end of the world. Then it was Nu Po or Kui Le To. Now it was Lae Tong Ku. Each new remoteness relativized its predecessor, and from this distance Um Pang, with its choice of shops and eating places, looked like home indeed. But would not Lae Tong Ku also become, relative to later stops, a new home? The *loe-si* people and their guru demigod certainly did not see the village as the end of the world, but rather as the beginning of a world. And in fact, after we had got used to the village and then travelled on, Lae Tong Ku did come to seem like a civilized friendly restful place. However, the comparison with Um Pang was not exhausted there. Like that distant idyll, this new one, which at first had seemed like the end of the trail, now proved that it too was just the beginning of a new set of routes.

There was, of course, the way we had come in, the path back to Boeng Kloeng. There was the mountain way east to Mong Gua, which the monks had negotiated. There was a way west, so we had discovered while reconnoitring, to Kui Le Toeng, which then swung south down through Burma, possibly to Sa Kae. And there was a fourth possibility, which went due south. We learned of this only on the very eve of our departure. We were sitting after supper as usual in the darkness, pushing the bamboos into the flames, when a small old man with a wispy beard stopped by chance to warm his bottom on our fire. He revealed that there was a direct route from Lae Tong Ku to Sa Kae which stayed in Thailand, thus avoiding the hazard of Burma. This was good news. But then came the bad news. It took this wiry old Karen a full nine hours to make the journey, and he was renowned as the fastest walker in the village. Carrying no baggage, he started at 5 a.m. and reached Sa Kae at 2 p.m. The journey had to be made in one day because the path ran through the jungle without passing a single village or house the whole way.

Examining the various possibilities from every angle, we ruled out this last one first. What the fastest Karen could run-walk in nine hours might take us with backpacks 18 or 24 hours. Obviously, we did not want to return to Boeng Kloeng. That left the path east to Mong Gua or the route southwest via Kui Le Toeng through Burma. The easterly route via Mong Gua and Mae Chan Ta we next excluded partly because it was a roundabout way of getting to Sa Kae, but also because it passed straight through "yellowthread" territory. In the wake of the killings even Karens had given up walking the long jungle path (feared and rarely used at the best of times) from Mae Chan Ta to Sa Kae. Which left only the southwesterly route via Kui Le Toeng - possibly the best and shortest way, but also potentially the most hazardous, as it ran mostly through Burma.

MAP 13

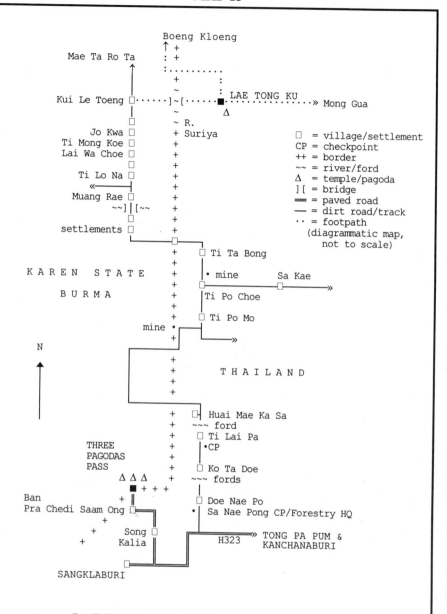

LAE TONG KU - THREE PAGODAS PASS

THREE PAGODAS © JUNGLE BOOKS
1996

CHAPTER 15

ELEVEN TIGERS

Lae Tong Ku - Kui Le Toeng - Ti Po Mo

On the morning of our fifth day in Lae Tong Ku the teachers made enquiries about a guide who might take us to Kui Le Toeng. Over breakfast they radiod with a walkie-talkie to the BPP camp. The base commander had meanwhile returned, and it transpired that he had just had a meeting with the local KNLA commander of Kui Le Toeng as well as with the headman of that village. If we hurried, we might be able to catch them up as they walked back home.

We scampered off with one of the teachers to the beginning of the path. The path seemed to cross somebody's garden, which was surrounded by a stockade. Sliding aside a couple of bamboo poles which acted as a gate, we entered the patch. Here, at a house, we caught up with the headman. He had stopped for a natter with some Karen friends while the KNLA commander and an interpreter (just someone who knew Karen and Thai) had gone on ahead. The headman was a Burmese *loe-si* man in his twenties, and although he could speak no Thai, he soon understood what we wanted. We said goodbye to the teacher, thanking him and his friends for all their trouble. And so it was that we set off on the next stage of our journey not with Toom Yai, as we had imagined we would, but with this young Burmese cultist headman.

Strikingly handsome, like many Karens, he was dressed in an azure shirt and emerald wrap-around skirt, knotted at the stomach. A cerise *yaam*, slung over his right shoulder, hung at his left side. Around his head was wrapped a piece of cloth, something like a Terry nappy, which revealed a glossy black topknot. The Karen was also wearing, we noticed, cotton wristbands and a gents watch. For some reason the headman was carrying a 5-ft crowbar. He sauntered off with us in tow through a pineapple field and through a maze of crisscrossing paths. The stretch from Lae Tong Ku to Kui Le Toeng took only an hour, but it was one of the most varied and appealing treks that we made anywhere. Our spirits rose because finally we were on the move again.

The headman led us down a steep muddy V-shaped defile, through close steamy dripping jungle, through sunny airy bamboo groves, and into wooded country. In the bamboos we met an extraordinary old *loe-si* hunting man. He was naked except for a skirt girded up around his loins and some old plastic shoes. But he was heavily laden. He carried a green game-bag, two long dibbling implements, a homemade stovepipe rifle as long as himself, and, on a tumpline suspended from his forehead, a basket full of jungle produce. Although sweating from his exertions and bothered by insects, the old man was very pleased and also surprised to meet us.

His lined face and Chinese-style moustache wrinkled up into a broad grin. Extending his free hand, he amazed us by saying "Good morning, Sir". One or two other old people had done this to us in Burma. Probably they were remembering English learned in colonial times fifty years earlier or during service with the British Army in WW2.

In the wooded country we met a party of three *loe-si* women coming the other way. In their magenta outfits against the sappy green background, they were the picture of beauty. The ladies were glad to see us, for it gave them an excuse to have a rest. Like the old man, they were heavily laden. Jokingly, we tried to hump their baskets of rice and betel ourselves, but found the loads almost too heavy to lift, and yet these women were only a shade over 4-ft tall. The woods gave over to a bright spacious betel forest. Betel trees had always seemed to us to have a simple primordial appearance. Their slender silver trunks rose up unadorned and straight-as-a-die to a considerable height, to be topped off by a couple of fronds. They were absurd plants. In their competition with one another for sunlight, they all shot up to a uniform height, producing nothing on the way, when they could just as easily have had the same competition six feet off the ground, wasting much less energy in growing.

In the middle of this betel forest I had something of a mystical experience - not Buddha under the bodhi tree, but a Brit under a betel. We had stopped for a little rest. Each of us sat on the scrubby woodland floor, our backs propped against a betel trunk. While I was vacantly staring at the ground between my feet, my eyes suddenly caught sight of a strange crescent-shaped object in the dry leaves. Picking it up, I found that it was a small carved piece of antique ivory. It was four or five inches long, in the shape of a miniature tusk, and had a hole drilled through the stump end to accommodate a piece of string or a silver chain. Evidently, it was a pendant which somebody had lost. Later, in Kui Le Toeng, we showed it to several *loe-si* people, and they all confirmed that it was old ivory. It was too heavy to be bone, they said, and finding such a thing was a great piece of luck.

What was remarkable about the find was that of all people I should happen to find it just in this spot. The chances of anybody at all finding it were remote, for why should anybody stop just by that tree? But the chances that a *farang*, me, should find it were billions to one, or so improbable that it seemed that somehow, miraculously, the ivory had been specially put there for me to find. But who could have put it there? The only possible explanation was that it was the *loe-si* himself. It was as if the man-god had wanted to make a sign to us. It seemed as if through the sign of the elephant's tusk he had wished to communicate his regret that he had received us so discourteously during our first visit to him and also perhaps wanted to bless our onward trip. A supernatural pattern was building up - the ride on the elephant between Kui Le To and Boeng Kloeng, the *loe-si* cult of the elephant tusks at Lae Tong Ku, and now the antique ivory. In Kui Le Toeng we got a length of string, and I wore the pendant as a lucky charm around my neck for the rest of the journey.

The remainder of the short trek was characterized by many stream and river crossings. The bridges over these were of three kinds. There was the greasy pole type of bridge, where we did not know whether it was better to risk the single slimy log or splash through the mud and water underneath. There was the bamboo suspension bridge, swaying high above the river. And across the wide Suriya, which we learnt was called Juai Ya Kru in Karen, there was the rickety bamboo pontoon bridge. Near the pontoon bridge a *loe-si* man was building rafts out of bamboo. Several examples of his handicraft were moored by the bank. We stopped to admire again the turquoise Suriya and also to pluck up courage to broach the pontoon. Before crossing, I turned to look at the path by which we had come down to the river. A short piece of planking was nailed to a tree with the word THAILAND crudely painted on it, together with a picture of the Thai flag and some words of Burmese or Karen. We were beginning the long Burmese section of our onward journey.

Kui Le Toeng

On the far bank the path proceeded for some way through woods, passing deserted and burnt houses - the result of a recent Burma Army attack. People were in the process of building them anew. Finally, we emerged into the dry dusty compound of Kui Le Toeng. This small *loe-si* village, consisting of about forty houses, was a poor scruffy affair compared to Lae Tong Ku. Chickens scratched around, a bullock cart stood idle under a tree, and in a couple of huts women were weaving. We found two basic shops and, near them, a lot of people hanging around, we knew not why. They looked at us with a degree of suspicion. Nobody spoke a word of Thai. The late morning heat was building up. It was an uncomfortable situation.

Our guide, the young headman, conveyed to us that we should wait by the bigger of the two shops. A small veranda provided some shade, in which we sat. The shop was stocked primarily with pulses, but there were also sweeties, biscuits, torches, batteries and Coya Pearl make-up. In addition, as at Sa Kaang Thi, there was every kind of smoke for sale, both cheroots and cigarettes - Monterey, Monte Carlo and Seven Diamonds. Glancing by chance up into the roof of the little store, we noticed laid out across the rafters a sizeable cache of automatic weapons. We were back in the war zone. While we were waiting, a number of children came to watch us. The girls, in their white full-length shifts, were wearing cosmetics, perhaps the Coya Pearl from the store. Once again we were struck by the heart-rending beauty of Karen lasses. It was a beauty all the more poignant for blooming in the midst of so much death and destruction.

The headman returned with the local KNLA commander as well as the man who had mediated between him and the Thai commander of Lae Tong Ku. The "interpreter", with his bare top, terrycloth turban, hairy underlip, wispy beard and moustache, not to mention a fearsome stomach scar, looked rugged enough, but the commander, one Mor Thaing Chor, was one of the wildest characters we met anywhere on our journey. Very different from the urbane Sor Kyi Shwi of Mae Ta Ro Ta, the ageing commander of Kui Le Toeng district, perhaps sixty years old, had permanently half-closed eyes, making him look as if he was sleepy or drugged out. A set of six deep lines stretched across his brow, he had dark straggly flyaway hair with wispy white sideboards, and long isolated hairs sprouted out of his chin. In a dark blue and red sarong and with a black sweatshirt, Mor Thaing Chor did not appear to be cultist. We could scarcely believe this man capable of a spirited defence or a counterattack against a SLORC assault force, but perhaps he was the wiliest guerrilla leader of them all. A commander he certainly was because he had a transceiver with him. We spotted this by his side in a kind of green military-style *yaam*. He had wrapped it up in a plastic bag, but the telltale stump of a telescoped aerial stuck out of the top.

A 4WD track could be seen passing through the central compound of Kui Le Toeng, and from the bizarre trio of the commander, the headman and the "interpreter" we learned that a solitary truck plied it some days. Coming from Mae Ta Ro Ta, the vehicle mostly terminated here, in Kui, but occasionally it went further to Sa Kae. Hearing the magical words "Sa Kae", our ears pricked up. A whole new perspective began to unfold - the possibility of riding to Sa Kae. Apparently, it was a three-hour drive to the staging post or a full two days' walk. Naturally, hearing these times from Karens, we took them with a pinch of salt (in fact they proved substantially correct). On the way there were other villages. Through the "interpreter" we asked the commander if the truck might come that day or if perhaps it had already come, but he did not know. Finally, the villagers said that no vehicle had been that day yet. We asked him if he could radio to Mae Ta Ro Ta to establish whether any vehicle would set off or indeed had set off, adding that Sor Kyi Shwi had suggested we approach Mor Thaing Chor for help. Patiently, the old man radiod through, not only querying the truck, but verifying our story. Hearing from his opposite number that we had indeed passed through Mae Ta Ro Ta and were "OK", the commander relaxed a bit. However, the message he received did nothing to dissipate the general vagueness. No one knew if the truck had departed or would depart. And with that the little band of the wild guerrilla leader, the crowbar-bearing headman and the scarred interpreter left us.

We considered our position. We had planned to trek from Kui Le Toeng. However, seeing that a jeep track ran through the village and that, moreover, from time to time transport ran down it, this began to seem increasingly senseless. Also, because of the vehicle, no one was prepared to guide us. It was easy to walk, the villagers of Kui said, just follow the track. But we already knew that tracks had a horrible way of dividing or petering out. Further, we were unhappy about spending more time in Burma than we had to, particularly on foot, and it seemed a fair distance down to Sa Kae. But, above all, we really wanted to get on. The length of the journey still to go - an estimated 100 kms - was weighing ever more heavily on us. We feared we might never get to the end of it. So the truck looked like a good option for speeding on our way. The trouble was: where was it? Even if it came, would it by chance be going beyond Kui Le Toeng? For a lift to Sa Kae we might have to wait three or four days, while trekking would take only two, or so they said. A prolonged wait in such an impoverished place was out of the question, but equally we could not go back to Lae Tong Ku. The only realistic option, therefore, seemed to be to start walking for Sa Kae and hope that the truck might catch us up.

Transplanting ourselves to the back of the compound, where the 4WD track passed through, we looked folornly up and down the dusty way - nothing, just silent withered countryside sizzling in the midday heat. It was like waiting for a train on a disused railway line in a heatwave. We settled on a compromise. We would wait for an hour, have some lunch and then start walking. By the side of the track, at the southern edge of the village, we found a house with a shop rather better stocked than the two others. We stationed ourselves there, ready to leap out and intercept any vehicle that might pass. From the lady owner of the shop we bought two packets of Mama, and asked her to cook the noodles for us. Then we sat down to wait. Our concern was infectious because soon everybody was straining their ears for the sound of a distant motor. A false alarm had us all unnecessarily excited when someone in the village started up the engine of a rice-dehusking machine. But otherwise there was nothing.

When it was clear that no truck was going to come, we started walking. No one seemed concerned, but no one seemed much interested either. We were very concerned. We had no guide. Communication with the locals was problematic. We were illegally out of Thailand and illegally in someone else's country - and not just in any other country, but in a country whose authorities were murderously xenophobic. Further, we had entered an area where a Four Cuts offensive was in progress, yet we did not know where the nearest Burma Army LID might be. But the worst thing was that, where before we had trekked towards some BPP camp, which had been forewarned of our arrival, now there was no *dorchodor* base ahead, and no liaison had been made - either with a BPP chief or with some KNLA commander. Wild-looking Mor Thaing Chor had radioed back to Mae Ta Ro Ta, but not further down the line. Nevertheless the mystical lure of the Three Pagodas drew us on, and we figured that somehow the find of the ivory was auspicious and that the pendant would protect us.

The two of us walked alone down the track, wondering what lay around every corner. It was flattish country with mixed cover. The powdery laterite track was scarcely wider than a vehicle and lined with dense headheight bamboos. Any spot would have been perfect for an ambush. We were trudging down this way, searching ahead and glancing nervously over our shoulders, when suddenly we heard something remarkable - the sound of an engine. Behind us a white Toyota Hilux Hero pick-up swung into view. Not caring if it belonged to the Burma Army, bandits or the KNLA, we flagged it down. It drew up, enveloping us and its occupants in a cloud of russet dust. It was a high-ride 4WD job, and looked fairly new. As it had no numberplates, only a sign like a red hand, we could not tell who it belonged to. Probably it was a KNLA general-purpose truck. In the cab was an older man, a youth and a boy. All had jet-black hair and Burmese-style *longyis*. In the back were three dubious-looking youths in tattered T-shirts, slashed jeans, sunglasses and military caps. One fancied himself and sported earrings. Each carried a small backpack. In Thai we asked the driver where he was going, and the answer back came - Sa Kae. We could not believe our ears. We asked if we could travel with them, and the swarthy unsmiling driver motioned us to climb aboard at the rear.

After the discouraging wait in Kui Le Toeng and the trudge along the track, our spirits soared again. We could be in Sa Kae by nightfall. The truck set off hell-for-leather, making the ride dreadfully bumpy. Karens evidently drove at the same lick as they walked. On the floor of the open-backed Hilux was some knobbly cargo, covered with a blanket. The boys, not wanting to sit on this, perched with amazing ease on the tailgate. We took up position behind the rollbar, just behind the cab. Standing there, with legs slightly flexed to absorb the shattering blows as the truck rattled along, we had a commanding view, although repeatedly it was necessary to duck overhanging bamboos to avoid being slashed across the face. The bumping of the truck caused some of the cargo to slither out from under the blanket. It was a cache of semi-automatic weapons and older rifles.

Presently the truck stopped for no apparent reason in the middle of nowhere. The driver got out and went off into the jungle. The boys fidgeted at the back. They looked at us all the time, seeming to allude alternately in a language we could not understand to our backpacks and to us. Nobody smiled. We began to regret the alacrity with which we had accepted a lift with this dubious outfit on their questionable errand. But after a while the driver returned with some other men, bearing roofing panels of *jaak* leaves. It transpired that in the bushes there was a settlement. We all got down from the truck and the men piled the panels high in the back. The new load made the ride even more uncomfortable. The *jaak* leaves had long spiny ends and, as we bounced around on top of the panels, their treacherous points speared our legs and bottoms. It was one more complaint to add to the bruised shinbone, the elephant rash, bedbug bites, sunburn, prickly heat, deficient diet, diarrhoea, inexplicable fevers and whatever else had assailed us since Um Pang.

The Hilux ploughed on a good way, the countryside changing from more open, wooded land to denser jungle. We passed the small Karen villages of Jo Kwa, Ti Mong Koe, Lai Wa Choe, a nameless settlement and Ti Lo Na. At one point our vehicle took a turn east, alarming us because we seemed to be heading ever deeper into Burma. But there was little we could do. Delivered into the hands of inscrutable people, we could only trust them blindly. At Ti Lo Na our lift stopped for a while. We had been told that the village was three hours' walk from Kui Le Toeng, and, if we had been on foot, we would probably have spent the night there. It was strange to view the place hypothetically as a point we might have stopped in. A relatively large Karen settlement with fine houses and a school, Ti Lo Na was set against a backdrop of craggy mountains to the west - the continuation of the Dawna Range. We got down to stretch our legs in the dusty central compound. Some urchins kicked a football around us and over our heads.

Following the halt, the truck continued a fair distance through mixed countryside. Isolated dwellings punctuated the route, and at one of them we were held up by a gate built across the "road". At a fork, the main track veered off east, but fortunately we went west down a narrower, less promising way, indicating that we were at least heading back towards the border. Before too long, at a place called Muang Rae (= mine), we came upon a river. The water was knee deep, and people were bathing and washing clothes in it. The place was a ford, because we could see the track continuing on the far bank. Our driver plunged the Hilux straight into the middle of the river, stopped and switched the engine off. He motioned everybody to get out. We all jumped down into the water and tried to find out what was happening. We thought that perhaps the truck was stuck. One of the three boys who had sat with us in the back spoke a few words of Thai, and he conveyed to us that the driver was going no further. We tried to remonstrate that the man had said that he was going to Sa Kae. We tried to cajole and even to bribe him to complete the trip, but it was hopeless. He ignored us and with his two mates began washing the Hilux. So this was the new pretty pass. After a 2½ hour ride from Kui Le Toeng we were abandoned in Burma in the middle of nowhere. What was more, the afternoon was well advanced.

We had no idea where we were, how much further it was to Sa Kae, or what lay ahead. Our greatest fear was that the three boys might now also separate from us. But it turned out that, like us, they were heading for Sa Kae and were as disconcerted as we were at being let down by the lift. So, far from eyeing the boys warily, we now sought to make common cause with them. They enquired of the washerwomen in the river which way went to Sa Kae, and we all set off together. We soon discovered why the truck-driver had been unwilling to go further. In places the track was so rugged that even a high-ride 4WD vehicle would have had difficulty clambering over it. The three boys continued to behave oddly, making us feel uneasy. They did not walk with us, as one might have expected, but lagged far behind, or disappeared altogether, or suddenly reappeared ahead of us, apparently having taken some secret short cut. Evidently, they knew the lie of the land better than we thought or were having little conversations with locals as they went along. Often it seemed to us that we were guiding them, and we could not understand why they did not take up the lead. The thought was never far from our minds that the shifty threesome might try to ambush us. They had looked once too often at our cameras.

We pressed on as fast as we could, trying to put some distance between the boys and us. The sweat began to pour from our faces, and the shoulder straps of our backpacks cut into our shoulders. We had hardly eaten all day, and hunger pangs were starting to gnaw in our stomachs. The track followed a spectacular series of limestone needles, to the sides and tops of which clung small trees, like hair. The outcroppings glowed in the teatime sun. Presently, we passed a small village, followed by two even smaller villages under construction. The people and their mode of house-building were unfamiliar to us, and yet they looked Karen. We waited for our laggard companions and asked the boy with earrings, the one who had a smattering of Thai, who these people were. They were "just a kind of Karen", came back the unsatisfactory answer. Then, in the company of the three ne'er-do-wells, we trekked into Titabong (Htitaban).

This large ramshackle poverty-stricken village was inhabited by the same strange people as we had seen earlier. They looked in some ways like Karens, and yet there was no trace of pink or red. In fact, mostly they wore no costume at all, except for a few, who were dressed in a kind of brown costume. We knew that we were approaching Mon territory, and at first we took the villagers for Mons. But discreet enquiries brought back the firm answer that they were not Mons. Which led us to suppose that the people of Titabong and of the nearby settlements were refugee Burmese Karens in ordinary "civilian" clothes - plains *Yang* rather than the traditional hill Karens. That they were refugees was borne out by the newness, meanness and incompleteness of their dwellings. And indeed, near Titabong we found a whole village newly wrecked and deserted. We were told that the villagers had abandoned the old place "to be nearer the road" at Titabong, but it seemed to us that once again the Burma Army had just swept through here, causing the inhabitants to flee and then return to rebuild their village on a new site. Evidently, Titabong lay on the border, and it looked as if the people had simply moved their village from inside Burma to the relative safety of the frontier.

We were so hungry and tired that we held up our little party in Titabong to brew up more instant noodles. The boys proved their worth here, for with that easy familiarity which all Karens seem to have in each other's villages they commandeered someone's house and set the inhabitants to work. Water was boiled over a wood fire, and bowls and spoons appeared. We decided to break once more into our emergency rations, nursed all the way from Mae Sot, and levered open a tin of tuna in masman curry sauce. The consumption of this rare luxury was watched by a circle of awe-struck Titabongers, who had probably never seen a *farang* before, let alone a *farang* scoffing tinned tuna.

Like ourselves, the boys were getting concerned about whether we would ever reach Sa Kae by nightfall. Everyone seemed vague about how far it was. We set off again at a cracking pace, with the three Karen youths in front for a change. As we left Titabong, we struck out once more into Burma. It quickly became clear why the boys had taken up the lead. They had been instructed about another short cut. Leaving the 4WD track, they guided us down a jungle path. After a while we filed in silence through the spooky village so recently deserted. Rejoining the track, we entered more open country. There were no villages here, but isolated dwellings - some deserted - lined the way. As the sun lowered and our shadows lengthened, we consoled ourselves that in an emergency we could pass the night in one of these rural shacks. We at least had our mosquito net with us. People passed us coming home from working in the fields. They were astonished to see us, but very friendly, and all confirmed that we were heading for Sa Kae.

A long hour later we chanced upon something strange. At a fork in the route, we saw imprinted on one of the two ways the unmistakable marks of a tracked vehicle. Either a tank had passed down here or a bulldozer. We had visions of another driverless Komatsu in the middle of nowhere. We all followed the caterpillar tracks, thinking that, even if they did not lead to Sa Kae, then they must at least go somewhere, to some form of civilization. How wrong we were. Soon we caught the sound of distant engines and, climbing over the brow of a hill, came upon a mine in the middle of the jungle. It was only a small affair, with some rock-crushing and processing machinery. The plant was stepped in sheds down a hillside. Below it were three or four tipper trucks, noisily making their final manoeuvres for the day. The scene was surprising enough, but the weird thing was that the tippers were being conducted like an orchestra by a fine Indian-looking gentleman in a suit and yellow hard hat. The trucks bore on their sides the words BHOL & SONS CO. LTD - LEAD CONCENTRATES. We picked our way through them and approached the Indian man. He was taken aback to see a *farang* and four others wandering in from Burma, and even looked perturbed, as if I might be a snooping journalist who could discover here some dark secret. Above the deafening roar of the trucks I shouted: "Are we still in Burma here?" "No, Sir", he replied in supercorrect English, "you are back in Thailand now. The men are just finishing work for the day. If you go over there and wait by the office, I will be with you in a minute." As we turned to go, we noticed a nameplate pinned to the breast of this black-faced upright Indian. It announced: MR JOHN SAVARIES, MANAGER - more and more bizarre!

In front of the office, we threw ourselves down on a bench, exhausted. It was gone five o'clock, and the light was beginning to fade. But at least we had arrived somewhere. We contemplated the prospect of staying the night at the mine. It was not appealing. Around the office there was a small shanty settlement, consisting of squalid workers' huts and oily repair bays for the vehicles and machines. Like us, the three boys were disconsolate. Now that we had a good source of intelligence of our own, they knew that they were marginalized, and they shifted uneasily in the background. For once, we thought, the boot was on the other foot.

Mr Savaries strode over to us. On the one hand he seemed like some colonial ex-army officer, transposed in place and time, and given a new name; and on the other he was reminiscent of some Mr Kurtz at the heart of a new heart of darkness. "You come from England?" he enquired, extending a hand and fixing me with glittering eyes. "Yes." That seemed to reassure him slightly, as if "German" or "American" would have been unsatisfactory. "Where have you come from?" "From Lae Tong Ku." He did not know where that was, so we explained that we had stayed there after trekking south from Um Pang. Our story surprised him, and now that we came to think of it, it surprised us too. How faraway Um Pang seemed, while Mae Sot was some mecca over the horizon. We mentioned that we, for our part, were surprised to find him, Mr Savaries, here. He explained that he had been born in Burma of Indian parents and now managed the mine here. Here, it transpired, was the Karen village of Ti Po Choe. We told the manager that our ultimate goal was the Three Pagodas Pass, but that we thought that initially we had to get to Sa Kae. However, as it was getting dark, could we not stay the night here at the mine?

That was not possible, Mr Savaries replied, without elaborating. What we should do was walk to the next village, Ti Po Mo, and stay with a man called Mr Joi-ae. He was a Karen Baptist and would look after us. Then, the next day, we could return and move on to Sa Kae. Or, if we really wanted to get on to Sa Kae today, we could wait and get a lift with a mine lorry later. The only trouble was, the Indian manager continued, he did not know when one might be going - perhaps at ten o'clock. We asked how far it was to Sa Kae. About ten kms - too far to walk now. And to Mr Joi-ae's village? About twenty minutes on foot. And how was the way to Ti Po Mo? That was easy - "all we had to do was follow the track"! The whole situation was confusing, made more impenetrable by the fact that we had to try to fathom it and make a decision with tired minds and with the pressure of night falling fast. One thing was clear, however. We could not stay at the mine, but had to go on to either Sa Kae or Mr Joi-ae's village of Ti Po Mo.

As Sa Kae was our immediate goal and lay on our route, we decided to go there. We did not know about accommodation there, but at least a truck would carry us there. We told Mr Savaries of our decision. That was good, he said, because next day, or even the same night, a lorry could take us much further along the same route, bringing us nearer our destination. The lorries hauled their lead concentrate from Ti Po Choe to Sa Kae, and then 110 kms through the jungle to a place called Kwitti (Kriti?). After that they continued for some unspecified distance, before emerging onto the highway to Kanchanaburi near Tong Pa Pum.

Hearing this last detail, we immediately changed our minds. Tong Pa Pum was going in quite the wrong direction, leading us away from the Three Pagodas. Also we were not taken with riding on a lead concentrate lorry, whether off or on the highway. So our last question to the Indian manager was which direction Ti Po Mo lay in and what he thought was beyond the village. Ti Po Mo was south of Ti Po Choe, but he did not know what lay beyond. No one went that way. Mr Savaries thought that there was a path for about sixty kms through some Karen villages towards the Pass. That clinched the matter. We stood up, thanked the mine manager and wearily set off again. And so it was that, after all the brouhaha about Sa Kae, the village did not lie on our route, nor did we ever go there. We heard reports, though, that it had a BPP camp, but was in other respects a small place like Ti Po Choe or Ti Po Mo. As the shifty trio of Karen boys were going to Sa Kae, we now abandoned them at the mine. Judging by their faces, it looked as if they feared that they were going to be eaten by Mr John Savaries for supper.

The way to Ti Po Mo was a track which had been pounded to six inches of ultrafine orange bulldust by vehicles. We found out why. Near Ti Po Mo there was another mine. The track immediately plunged into the most spectacular virgin jungle we had seen anywhere. The primary canopy was still intact, and gigantic trees soared hundreds of feet into the air. In the twilight, monkeys whooped and birds called. We were filled with consternation at embarking on another trek at nightfall, and only prayed that the Indian man was right. After twenty minutes there was still no village. After thirty minutes, just when we were getting ready to turn back, we emerged from the forest. The last thing we saw before darkness came promptly at 6 p.m. was a massive monolith immediately to the west. Chao Tao (= rocky hill) dominated the small Karen village of Ti Po Mo and was peculiar in that a chunk of its southern edge had fallen away, leaving a cavity beneath an overhanging section - like a mouth and nose. This gave the outcrop an anthropomorphic quality. Silhouetted against the brown of the dying western sky, the face of this monolith looked sinister. We stumbled into Ti Po Mo in darkness, there to be greeted at the office of the second mine by the fabled Mr Joi-ae. Evidently he had been tipped off by Mr Savaries by radio that we were coming.

Ti Po Mo

Joi-ae, a Karen man in his late forties with a round face, receding hair and scrubby greying chintuft beard and moustache, led us to his house. His good nature, ready smile and unshakable composure made him instantly and lastingly likeable. His dwelling was not the usual simple Karen affair of wood, bamboo and leaf, but a well-constructed wooden house with an upstairs. There was the customary open but covered platform, where anyone could linger or sleep, and in front an open-air dining area. Joi-ae said we could use the platform and also sleep there. We had hardly unpacked when a thermos of boiling water appeared, together with pint-sized mugs, Ovaltine, tea, condensed milk and biscuits. After an arduous day and in the middle of the jungle, this was luxury indeed. We each drank off about three pints of Ovaltine and tea.

Our clothes and bodies were filthy from fording rivers and kicking through laterite powder. We asked Joi-ae to take us to the washroom. At that moment his son-in-law "Edu" appeared. This brusquer, less mellow man in his twenties was detailed to show us the way. He led us across the village with a torch. On the far side of the dusty village street, behind a vegetable garden, he pointed the torch at the black waters of a small river. There he left us. It was pitch dark, the bank of the river was 4 ft high, there was a slimy gangplank descending to the water, and the riverbed was squelchy mud. In our dispirited state, the difficulties of trying to wash almost made us want to cry. The shampoo got lost in the grass of the riverbank, the soap dropped into the water, and we, far from getting cleaner, got steadily dirtier. But the worst thing was that, standing naked in the river in the blackness, we were savaged by mosquitoes. How it was that we did not get malaria we never were able to explain.

Picking our way back to Joi-ae's, we were surprised to see electric lights burning. It turned out that there was a generator in the village, which provided wobbly power every day from 6-9 p.m. But what astonished us more was the spread of supper which had been put out for us on the long table. When Mr Savaries had said we could stay with the Baptist Mr Joi-ae, we had pictured a frugal repast with austere religious people. But here was stir-fried cabbage, potato curry, omelette, fried salted dried fish, barking deer curry, chilli dip, fresh pineapple, papaya, and *lao kao*. In our experience Karens were unsurpassed among the "hill-tribe" peoples for their hospitality, but the food and attention we enjoyed with Joi-ae's family over the next three days was outstanding even by these standards.

While we ate, most of Joi-ae's extended household came to join us. There was the master and his wife, his daughter and son-in-law Edu, their baby, a brother of Joi-ae's, a grandmother-in-law, and others we never identified. Granny was a phenomenon. She claimed to be eighty and had apparently taught English in Burma when she was young. This sprightly and remarkably well-preserved lady said she owed her longevity to alcohol. She had a few nips every night and periodically let go with more expansive drinking sessions. It seemed that today was the occasion of one of these bouts, for according to Joi-ae she had been at the bottle since early morning. Our arrival merely confirmed to her that she had chosen the right day to have her "little medicine" and "look after her health". She drank more and more, grew steadily louder, put her arm around me, cooed in my ear, and began telling tall stories in a mixture of Karen, Thai and incomprehensible English. She also introduced us to some of the arcane practices of her tippling. Besides the rice spirit, she had a bottle of runny wild honey and also a tin of "Eleven Tigers Ruby Blood Tonic". This latter red medicinal powder was supposed to "clean ladies' blood". Granny mixed the Eleven Tigers and *lao kao* together, adding a dose of honey. The resulting dark red, savoury, sweet, biting concoction was not at all unpleasant, and it was easy to see how, if one lived in a mining outpost in the jungle, one could become quite attached to it.

In the pauses between the old lady's expatiations, we quizzed Joi-ae about Ti Po Mo and our onward route. Apparently, the village was only about ten years old, although Joi-ae himself had been living in the area for twice as long (he had grown up in Moulmein). There had once been a BPP camp in Ti Po Mo, but it had moved to Sa Kae. Chao Tao was the border with Burma, and it was possible to climb to the top of this enormous precipitous rock. We asked Joi-ae how he liked living in such a remote place. He said he had been to Sangklaburi, the nearest town, only four times in eighteen years and preferred hunting in the jungle to town life. While we were talking and eating under the single naked lightbulb, a succession of people either looked by or reported to the house. They came from the village, the mines, from Kwitti, from Sangklaburi, from as far away as Boeng Kloeng, and from Burma. This happened all the time we were there, and we soon realized that the Baptist Karen's house was the nerve centre of Ti Po Mo, indeed of the whole area, while Joi-ae himself was the kingpin.

On the subject of our onward journey, Joi-ae said our best bet was to ride in the cab of a lorry from Ti Po Choe down to the main road and Tong Pa Pum, and then take public transport up to Sangklaburi. When we said that we were unhappy to do this because it was out of our direction and was not in the spirit of our adventure, he replied that the alternative was not good. There was a way through from Ti Po Mo to the area of the Three Pagodas Pass, but it was rarely used. The 60-km way was a poor track and passed through three Karen villages - Ti Lai Pa, Ko Ta Doe and Doe Nae Po. The problem was that the first stretch to Ti Lai Pa was 24 kms long, went down the Burmese side through pure jungle, and passed absolutely nothing on the way. It was too far to walk in one day, and nobody would go with us. Beyond Ti Lai Pa it was a further eight hours on foot to Ko Ta Doe and then another three hours to Doe Nae Po. On the other hand, 4WD trucks passed from time to time down that way in about four hours, on average one every three or four days. But, unfortunately, one had gone today. Not only that, a mini-convoy had gone with it, meaning that the potential supply of lifts would have been exhausted not just for three days, but possible for a week. It was always the same two or three vehicles which plied the route, and before they could set out again, they would all have to come back.

It was bad news. However, Joi-ae promised to ask in the mine office the next morning and suggested we walk down to the mine itself - about ten minutes away - to check the latest vehicle situation. Beyond that we could only trust to luck. Promptly at 9 p.m. the lightbulb gave two warning flickers, and the power was finished for the night. Granny was quite far gone and wanted to continue the conviviality, but the others got up to retire and dragged her away remonstrating. She grumbled for a long time in a back room, knocking bottles over and repeatedly lighting a pipe. We strung up our net on the public platform and arranged ourselves for sleep. By 9.30 Ti Po Mo was extinct. But these *Yang* villages were never really quiet in the night. Soon we realized that others had come to sleep on the veranda, and there was the usual shuffling and spitting. Occasionally, a lorryload of lead concentrate rumbled through the outpost, and upstairs Edu's baby cried. We reviewed our day's progress. It seemed remarkable, even epic, knocking something like another forty kms off our journey. We had breakfasted in Lae Tong Ku, met commander Mor Thaing Chor, despaired in Kui Le Toeng, ridden wild with gun-runners through Burma to Muang Rae and the river, trekked with the shifty trio past Titabong to Ti Po Choe, interviewed Mr John Savaries, and blundered into Ti Po Mo to the unexpected welcome of Joi-ae's family....

The following morning, while we were breakfasting on Ovaltine and biscuits, we saw the old lady leave the house on some mission. She greeted us as if the previous evening had been as nothing. It transpired that granny was going fishing, and by all accounts she was a champion fisherwoman. Joi-ae returned from the mine office in the village with the news that no truck would be going to Ti Lai Pa either that day or the next. We voiced our concern about outstaying our welcome at his house. "Never mind", he said in Thai, "you can stay as long as you like." However, he did mention that there was a man in Ti Po Mo who might be persuaded to take us in his pick-up down the way we wanted to go. We would have to negotiate a price with him.

Presently, this selfsame wily truck owner arrived at our table. We haggled with him until he would lower his price no further. He was prepared to take us down to Sangklaburi for 900 baht. Although by western standards this was not so much for two people down a jungle track (£25), it still seemed too much for a four-hour 60-km ride. We had hardly spent much more since leaving Mae Sot. So we rejected the man's offer. We figured that he would return later with a more reasonable price. Actually, after we had been holed up in Ti Po Mo for two long days, it was we who returned to the man. But the man simply upped his price to 1500 baht, causing us to reject his offer once and for all. Our not accepting the man's original proposition was possibly the biggest mistake we made on this last leg of our adventure. For, as things turned out, his offer proved to be a very favourable one. In the end the track was so atrocious that he would surely have done at least 900 bahts' worth of damage to his vehicle. Moreover, if we had gone with him, we would have had our "own" transport and driver, enabling us to stop where we wanted and proceed at our own pace. In the event we were hustled down that nightmare stretch at breakneck speed, half the way in darkness.

Our morning's occupation was to visit the Ti Po Mo mine. We followed an orange bulldust track south of the village for about one km until it divided. The principal way continued to - we never found out. A turn west went to the "Moniko & Korea Mining Company". Near the entrance was the site office. The wooden buildings were deserted, almost abandoned. However, the door to the bookkeeping office was unlocked, and we looked inside. The wages and employment records for each worker lay in dusty pigeonholes. The information was an eye-opener. For an eight-hour shift the most junior worker received forty baht a day (£1), while the most senior took home a princely 50-60 baht. Opposite the site office there was a kind of vehicle repair station. The grease and disorder here was considerable. Various ancient lorries lay around in different stages of cannibalization. It looked as if the two mechanics were trying to make one viable vehicle out of the others. We asked the men if any truck would be going down to Ti Lai Pa that day, but they could not say. We further asked a more senior-looking supervisor at the mine itself, but he did not know either. All that anybody could say was that if a vehicle was going, someone would come up to Joi-ae's to tell us.

Between the site office and the mine lay a squalid shanty settlement. The huts were of split bamboo and grass or *jaak*. There were a couple of primitive shops, and people eyed us doubtfully. These impoverished Karens enjoyed one thing - an impressive view from their backdoors of the monumental Chao Tao. Behind the huts we came across an interesting scene. Some men were making sugar. Harvested sugarcanes lay piled up, and armfuls of them were being introduced into a press. The press was driven by a poor buffalo, which walked endlessly in a circle with a black blindfold over its eyes. When it stopped to rest in the heat, a boy beat it with a stick. The sap dribbling out of the press was gathered and put into four steel pans, like giant woks. These were boiled over a fire until the sticky juice was reduced to a thick brown liquor. From time to time the men skimmed off a white froth. The fire was ingenious in its simplicity. It consisted of an underground tunnel beneath the four pans. Long sections of bamboo flamed in the tunnel, and as they burnt down towards the entrance, they were simply kicked further in. The heat, added to the blazing morning sun, was withering. Finally, the molasses was decanted into trays, where it set into slabs of toffee-like cane sugar. We were given a shard to try. It tasted very good.

At the back of the shanty camp was the mine, stepped down a hillside and surrounded by jungle. To be accurate, the Korean mine at Ti Po Mo, like the Bhol mine at Ti Po Choe, was really a processing plant. The raw rock was quarried somewhere nearby and brought by tipper truck to these plants. The rock was dumped at the top of the hill and then descended down the hillside through various machines as it was processed. The end-product was a grey metallic sludge containing antimony. It was dried out and taken away in bags, presumably for refinement.

An inspection of the plant was a depressing experience. At the bottom end the Sb sludge dribbled out like slurry from a pig farm. Above it machines were activating the pulverized ore, spraying it with what looked like oil or solvent. In this reeking treatment shed a man sat by the hour, tending the machines and breathing in air laden with suspended particles of antimony and spray. In two minutes my spectacles were covered with fine droplets. Above the shed was a series of crushing drums. They reduced the ore to a powder with a deafening roar. Above the crushing machine, a chute funnelled the rock into the mouth of the first and largest drum. Underneath the end of the chute two Karen girls squatted on the hillside. In an endless cloud of toxic dust, and amid the frightening thunder of the crushers, they were employed to encourage the chunks of ore down the hopper and into the machine. Their only tools were a wooden spoon and their fingers. We infinitely pitied these poor children, exchanging their health and young lives for thirty or forty baht a day. In the middle of this jungle wilderness, this was the real heart of darkness.

Ti Po Mo itself was understandably not the most beautiful of Karen villages. There were too many oil and diesel drums lying around, as well as broken vehicles and bits of vehicle. But there was an interesting makeshift *wat* on a knoll just outside the village. It was run by two monks, one an older Mon man, and the other a younger fellow of the enigmatic Tuwai group, from southern Burma. The tall striking Mon spoke some English, while the Tuwai knew Thai. They invited us in for refreshments, and we were treated to pint mugs of Ovaltine or tea or coffee, which seemed to be standard in this region. School began presently, and the one multi-purpose class was held in the *wat*. But before the class could begin, the *Yang* infants had to endure a prayer session. In unison they chanted an interminable Pali rigmarole, doing their best not to laugh at our smiles. Finally, the lesson began, with the shorn Mon bonze trying to teach some Burmese to the children, many with gold *tanaka* discs on their cheeks.

Back at Joi-ae's, we got excited because a KNLA driver arrived in a battered Toyota pick-up. We asked Joi-ae to find out from this rugged man in a peaked military cap if he was going further. But it was a false alarm. The dust-covered driver was going only as far as Ti Po Mo. He was a jovial fellow and helped himself to the *lao kao*.

The evening of that second day was enlivened by a special prayer ceremony. After another feast, which featured granny's catch of fish with extra helpings of potato curry, we were invited upstairs onto a central landing. Some twenty people were sitting on the wooden floor with their backs to the walls. We learned that Joi-ae's eldest son was setting off into Burma the next day, and they wanted to pray for his safety. Some hymns were sung, and passages were read from a Karen Baptist version of the Bible. Then a young man made a kind of sermon. As this was in Karen, we could not understand what it was about, but it became intriguing and memorable because the text was frequently interspersed with the words "Stonewall Jackson" and "Ti Lo Su" (= waterfall). The sermon went on for some time, and we were able to study the posters on the walls. They were a strange collection of icons - a picture of the Thai King and Queen, a KNU calendar, a photo of some eminent Baptist, and a few pinups. After the little ceremony everyone partook of tankards of ultrasweet tea with cream biscuits.

On our third day in Ti Po Mo we were largely left to our own devices. The novelty of our arrival had worn off, and people just got on with their business. As usual, after breakfast, Joi-ae reported back that no trucks were going to Ti Lai Pa that day. A trip to the Korean mine drew a similar blank. We were beginning to fear that we might be holed up in this unprepossessing village for a long time, caught up in a disheartening waiting game. But we could not walk on and did not want to go backwards to Ti Po Choe and Sa Kae. We moped around the houses for a while, hoping against hope that something might happen. But nothing did.

ELEVEN TIGERS

Two tracks skirted Ti Po Mo, enclosing the village like an envelope. At each end they met. It seemed a good idea to station ourselves at the place where they met on the southern edge of the village. We figured that if any vehicle did happen to pass, we could not miss it there. So we took up position in the shade of a stand of bamboos, prepared a mat of banana palm leaves, and settled down to wait. The heat was stifling and the waiting boring. To pass the time, we smoked some of the Best Thukhita cheroots we had acquired in Sa Kaang Thi black market. We reflected on how since Um Pang our journey had proceeded in fits and starts. A day of intensive progress was followed by several of time-biding. Apart from smoking and reminiscing, the only other thing to do was study the monolithic Chao Tao. Depending on one's viewing position and also on the time of day, it changed its aspect. On the evening of our arrival it had seemed like a sinister human head. But now, from our forsaken mid-morning post by the bamboo clump, it looked more like the mocking head of a parrot or the uplifted snarling head of a tiger. As long as we waited, nothing came, and after two or three hours we gave up the waiting game as ridiculous.

CHAPTER 16

THREE PAGODAS

Ti Po Mo - Ti Lai Pa - Pra Chedi Saam Ong

Deliverance came on the fourth day. A truck was going from Ti Po Mo to Ti Lai Pa, but no further. We figured that we should take the lift because, even if the vehicle was going only to this first village, it would take us across the long untrekkable section, and after that we might be able to walk the rest of the way. Very likely the pick-up was Joi-ae's own, or at least on loan from the Korean mine. The master was no doubt getting tired of seeing our long faces and wanted to send us packing before we either became too morose or ate him out of house and home. But we did not feel too guilty about the arrangement because, as we stowed our backpacks and ourselves in the back of the truck, many other people materialized, climbing in too. In the end there were ten of us aft and three, including Joi-ae and Edu, in the cab. The vehicle was another white Toyota Hilux Hero (4WD, 2.4 litre diesel engine, kicked-out suspension), which seemed to be the standard means of transportation in these parts.

It was a great relief to be on the move again. After three days of enforced confinement in hot dusty Ti Po Mo, it was exhilirating to have the morning air blowing into our faces. Um Pang and our forgotten Honda seemed like ancient history, and we were more than ever anxious to complete our journey and embrace the Pagodas. A sign of our battlewornness was that I was now sporting nearly a fortnight's beard growth. Almost immediately we had a little surprise. One km out from Ti Po Mo, instead of following the main track, the pick-up forked right into the Korean mine. It stopped there while some consultations were made. To our delight we spotted Mr John Savaries, sitting in front of one of the "shops". It looked as if it was his day off and he had decided to spend his free time by making an outing from one mine to the other, for he was wearing not the corporate clothing we had once seen him in, but holiday dress. A Burmese *longyi* was complemented by a Thai T-shirt, a Karen shoulderbag, and flipflops. But best of all, his coal-black face was surmounted by a dapper azure pith helmet. This colourful character, part Indian, part Burmese, part Karen, part British colonial military man, was cleaving forcefully into a coconut with a machete.

We left the mine area by a track we had not previously noticed. It was the way down to Ti Lai Pa. Crossing over the border once again, we straightway plunged into primary jungle. Joi-ae drove steadily but carefully. Nevertheless it was a bumpy laboured ride, with the 4WD truck grinding over rocks and tree roots. Skirting mountainsides, we climbed over a ridge. The whole of the 24-km journey ran through Burma, and all of it cut through dense jungle. We saw at once the difficulty of walking through here. There was not a single dwelling on the way, and we passed not a single person on foot.

256

The only event of the ride was an encounter halfway with another truck. This almost led to an accident. The vehicles met coming round a corner, and as there was nowhere for Joi-ae to go, the other truck ploughed up into the foliage. It was an antiquated affair, with battered, riveted, dark green bodywork, an upright cab and wooden sides at the back. It looked like one of those Dinky toys children used to play with years ago and may have been Burmese or Chinese. Otherwise the vehicle was equipped with an array of searchlights and a winch. There were ten men aboard, but quite what they were doing was unclear. They had some drums of diesel in the back and had possibly been to collect fuel. The two vehicles drew up alongside, and the drivers conferred loudly through their cab windows. Some critical situation had arisen which necessitated Edu transferring from our truck to theirs and returning immediately to Ti Po Mo. The lonely meeting of the vehicles with their small bands of occupants was one of those Stanley-meets-Livingstone situations. But we were struck by another thought which we had often had as we crept through the jungle, that the jungle was a place which could inspire fear, but also a certain profound contentment. The reasons for the fear were obvious, but the reasons for the contentment might be that in the jungle human beings had an obscure feeling of returning "home". After all, the theory was that we all originated there, a bountiful environment which even today supplied all the needs of, say, the prehistoric "yellow leaf" (Mrabri) people. Maybe when modern humans visited the jungle, some deep-seated sympathy for that long-lost primordial habitat resonated within them.

After a long hour of jolting and shaking, Joi-ae pulled up in the middle of nowhere by a small wooden sign. It pointed one way to the Huai Mae Ka Sa Karen refugee camp and the other to Ti Lai Pa. He explained to us that if we continued down the track for a while on foot, we would come to the village of Ti Lai Pa. It was the parting of the ways. We thanked Joi-ae for his incomparable hospitality and helpfulness, and watched him disappear towards the camp. One km on, we came to the River Mae Ka Sa. A fair-sized flow, it formed the Thai-Burmese border at that point, and for the umpteenth time we crossed back into the Kingdom. The track led straight through the thigh-deep waters, up a precipitous riverbank on the far side, up a rise, and to a checkpoint of the Forestry and Wildlife Protection authorities. Near it was a makeshift notice nailed to a tree, saying in Thai, English, Burmese, Karen and another language we could not identify, possibly Mon, "WELCOME TO TEA LYE BAA - our world heritage".

Ti Lai Pa

Such a portentous notice led us to have high hopes of the checkpoint and the village in terms of facilities and the possibility of getting on. We were quickly disillusioned. The barrier was manned by a short Karen youth, Tirapon, who lived in a shack to one side. A couple of other Karen youths also loafed around at the little outpost. It was a beautiful peaceful spot. Trees grew all around, and the boys had laid out well-kept flowerbeds.

Outsize butterflies drifted by on the warm air. We asked the youths about the chances of onward transport. They were not at all hopeful. They produced a record book of all the traffic movements in both directions. Most of the days were blank. Just as Joi-ae had said, there was on average one vehicle every three days. Entered for three days ago, for our first morning in Ti Po Mo, was the convoy of four trucks we had heard about. As the minutes ticked by, the peacefulness of that isolated spot began to grow rather too quiet for our liking. We contemplated the distinct possibility that we had escaped one place, only to become holed up in a worse one, for there were not even the facilities of Ti Po Mo here.

Opposite the guard box by the barrier, was an outdoor canteen area, backed by a row of dilapidated huts. We retired to the mess table to have a mid-morning snack and review our position. Here we broached our last-but-one tin of food, consumed with cold rice begged from the Karens. We could either walk on, or wait in the hope that a truck might come that day, or stay the night and start again the next morning. With the last option in mind, we inspected the huts, where the boys had said we could sleep - although there were no blankets. Two of the rooms were locked up, evidently in use, one was a store, and the remaining free one was so filthy that we straightway ruled it out. Someone had evidently been using the cubicle for stripping down a motorcycle. While we were making our inspection, our ears suddenly discerned the miraculous sound of an engine. As it drew closer, we realized, however, that it was coming from the wrong direction. And soon a white Hilux drew up at the barrier, signed into the book, crumped down the embankment and breasted the river.

We consulted with Tirapon, the short Karen boy. The white Hilux was a KNLA truck, was stopping at the Huai Mae Ka Sa camp, but might go on even as far as Mae Ta Ro Ta. No one knew when it would return. As for walking to Ko Ta Doe, that was an eight-hour trek along a route exactly the same at the one we had just come down, and at 11 a.m. it was too late to start out now. It would be better to wait until next morning and set off early in the cool. The one straw of hope that Tirapon could offer us was that when vehicles came, heading south, they usually came around midday. We clutched at that straw and decided to wait until midday. But by midday nothing had come, and by one o'clock still nothing had come. The boys went off to snooze, and we decided to take a look at Ti Lai Pa village. We left our backpacks with the Karen, saying that if any vehicle came, he should let us know at once. Vaguely, he promised to send word.

Ti Lai Pa was a relatively large *Yang* place. We found the headman and some of his friends shredding tobacco. Judging by bundles of freshly picked, white fleece lying around, they also grew cotton nearby. The village was laid out among a lush mixture of betel, coconut and vivid red-flowering trees. In an open area there was a fine old Burmese *wat*. Raised high off the ground on wooden piles, it consisted of a perfectly square wooden box with a two-tier corrugated iron roof. Another feature of the village were some remarkable swaying bamboo bridges over the Mae Ka Sa river. But the most spectacular thing about Ti Lai Pa was its setting. It lay in a valley sided by steep mountains. In particular, it was dominated by two conjoined outcroppings, the Song Pinong. On the summits of these, two flags were flying. But the flags were not the same. One monolith was in Thailand, while its twin was in Burma. The Thai peak, of course, had a Thai flag, but its Burmese counterpart, ironically, was flying KNU colours.

The flags were a reminder of the continuing hostilities between the Karens and Rangoon. But the area had been the scene of other earlier conflicts. An engraved border stone near the barrier told that from 1538-1854, during the Sri Ayuttaya and Rattanakosin periods, the Mae Ka Sa river had been used by both the Siamese and Burmese armies for ferrying supplies in their long-running wars with one another. The headman told us that more recently the Song Pinong had been a CPT hideout. Then, in 1973, the Thai military had set up a camp in Ti Lai Pa. The result had been a battle, which the Thai Army had lost. The area had remained under the control of the Communists until 1981, when government forces returned, this time defeating the local CPT for good. In a for us tantalizing detail the headman mentioned that from the top of the Song Pinong it was possible to see the Three Pagodas Pass.

Our problem exploring down among the village houses was that we were away from the track and could not keep an eye out for passing traffic. So, rather than wait in the village, we decided to return to the barrier. Up there we found an older Thai man, also waiting. He had a little knapsack, and his identity and purpose were inscrutable. Quizzing him, we realized that our plight was as nothing compared to his. He had been waiting for a lift for a whole week. When we mentioned the mini-convoy, he said that he had missed that because he had been out walking all day over the border. We asked him what he was doing in Burma, but he replied evasively: "just looking around". The border areas were full of such oddball characters on unaccountable missions.

The waiting game at the deserted checkpoint area continued through the baking early afternoon heat. Again it was borne in on us just how awkward it was journeying down this way. We reflected on how crazy we were spending our holidays holed up, wasting our time. Sometimes we wondered if we were not demented, our minds turned by the heat. In fact, everyone here seemed demented. When we shifted our waiting station down to the ford in order to be cooler, a man came to the river to wash his dog, yet he did not just toss the dog into the water, but carefully washed it with washing powder. When the dog was perfectly clean, it bounded out of the river and rolled twenty times in the dust of the track. A ten-year old refugee girl repeatedly appeared sirenlike on a little promontory of riverbank just out of reach from where we were sitting. Each time she did a little dance, erotically aware of her body, flirted outrageously with me, and teasingly scampered away. Was this reality or a figment of the imagination conjured up by jungle fever? She seemed to be an embodiment of the spirit of the quest, luring us on, only to frustrate us, taunting us with the promise of a lift, only to leave us waiting.

At teatime the villagers came down to the river to bathe. We went up to the barrier to speak again with Tirapon. The friendly Karen had cooked up some food and invited us and the Thai adventurer in. We all sat with long faces, dipping rice balls into a curry made with the tender core of a banana palm stem. We told Tirapon that we had decided to wait until 5.30 p.m. and then go to stay overnight with the *pu yai baan*. It transpired that the short Karen was himself waiting for a lift, in fact had been waiting for two days. He wanted to get down to Sangklaburi for some time off. So now we were a band of four. We were just clearing away the dishes, when we heard the sound of a truck. What was more, it was coming south through the river towards us. We all leapt up in great excitement, scattering the dishes. Fortunately, the barrier was down, so the vehicle was obliged to stop. Clutching our backpacks and knapsacks, the four of us ran out to the truck. It was the same white KNLA Hilux we had seen that morning. It had been up to the Huai Mae Ka Sa refugee camp and was returning with some sacks of rice, bought in from Burma. As if by magic, half a dozen other people also materialized out of the trees and descended on the trapped truck. Without even asking, all ten of us scrambled aboard and sat in the back, utterly grateful that the waiting was over.

The barrier went up and the Hilux moved forward. But on the other side of the checkpoint it stopped, and the Karen driver, one Sawoei (= eat), and a burly Thai BPP officer in civilian clothes got out of the cab. They said we could all get down because the truck was going no further than Ti Lai Pa, where the two of them were going to spend the night. They seemed to dispense this news with some relish. Cruelly disillusioned, everyone got down. We asked the Karen Sawoei if he was driving on the next morning, but he did not know - it depended on the BPP man, who was conducting a census in the vicinity. And sure enough, the truck disappeared down a side track into the village.

The stranded crestfallen hopefuls held a council of war at the barrier. Some people dropped out at once and went off. We decided to try our luck with the headman. The rest, a party of five which included Tirapon and the Thai adventurer, made the singular decision to start walking to Ko Ta Doe, trekking the eight-hour journey through the night. This left us on the horns of a dilemma. On the one hand we knew that it was senseless and even dangerous to trek through the jungle at night. It would be pitch black, with - as things turned out - not even a moon to light the way. But, on the other, we knew that the party would be guided by Tirapon, who was familiar with the route and had a torch. Further, the little band would be walking when it was pleasantly cool. But the most aggravating thing for us was that the party of five would be getting out of Ti Lai Pa and would be in Ko Ta Doe before dawn, whereas we would be left behind, separated from them, and faced with the prospect of trekking the long distance alone the next morning. However, for us, commonsense in such a predicament was paramount - the idea of stumbling blindly over rocks and roots in the blackness of mosquito-infested jungle was foolhardy - and so we let the band, led by the diminutive *Yang* youth, set off, and folornly waved them goodbye. They departed down a short-cut path, which branched off from the 4WD track.

With heavy hearts we made our way down to the headman's house. There we found the truck, Sawoei and the *dorchodor* officer. The two men were tippling *lao kao* with the headman. They looked sheepish when they saw us arrive and invited us to drink with them. We asked the headman if we could stay with him overnight so that we could trek the following morning. That was not necessary, he replied. The truck was leaving for Sangklaburi that night and we could ride with it. We could scarcely believe our ears. We verified the news with the BPP man, who said: yes, it was true, although he himself was not going, but we were free to ride with Sawoei. We asked them why they had made everybody get out at the checkpoint and had come into the village. Oh that, they confessed, was a trick. Too many people had climbed into the truck and they had wanted to get rid of some. Besides, they had found it bad manners of everybody simply to jump aboard. We could not help feeling that for once discretion really had proved the better part of valour. By setting off too precipitately down the short cut, the others were going to miss the lift, whereas we, who had played prudently, were going to get the ride. Just as much as our luck had been down, now suddenly it was up.

Sawoei, "Mr Eat", helped us rearrange the sacks of rice, and we installed ourselves behind the roll bar, seated on a sack each. Finally, when it was absolutely dark, we left Ti Lai Pa and set off into the jungle. It was a pity to complete the last leg of the journey at night, but we were too tired and emotionally drained to care. Besides there was a certain attraction about making at least one jungle trip in the night. We soon changed our minds about that. Sawoei drove the next thirty kms like a bat out of hell. It was more nightmarish and dangerous that the two rides together with Joi-ae and the grumpy gunrunner who had dumped us in the river at Muang Rae. Quite why these drivers attacked the route so ferociously was a mystery. They perhaps gained twenty minutes, but destroyed their vehicles in the process. Nor was it clear why Mr Eat should want to travel by night, unless it was because there was something dubious about his errand. We later found out that these KNLA trucks liked to flit down the border during the hours of darkness - perhaps to outmanoeuvre the Burma Army.

After a while the headlights of the Hilux picked out the trudging figures of the little band. The driver did not have the heart to pass them by, and gratefully they clambered in. We were surprised that they had got so far. They were surprised to see us and were not a little peeved that we had outwitted them and got the best seats. Meeting again with the five, everything came together. With the shady Thai adventurer and our new friend Tirapon, we were all now in the same truck that we had seen earlier, and we were all finally heading in the direction we wanted to go.

The rest of the journey was not so much a question of when we would get to our goal, but whether we would reach it alive. The Hilux Hero sped through endless jungle tunnels, with bamboos lashing our faces, and thorny branches lacerating our sides. It groaned up steep gradients, scraping its underside on protruding rocks, and lurched alarmingly to left and right, threatening to spill us all out. It tipped over precipitous riverbanks with a sickening slithering thud, and forded rivers, the water lapping around the bottoms of the cab doors. Then, with the engine screaming, Sawoei smashed the truck up the far riverbanks, sometimes, from a standing start in the water, having to take a second shot at them.

On several occasions, for no apparent reason, the pick-up stopped in the middle of nowhere and the driver got out to check something. He seemed bothered by one of the wheels or the suspension. Naturally, this did nothing to allay our fears. The truckload of people seemed like a fragile island of humanity in the black threatening immensity of the jungle, and we kept willing Sawoei to get back in and drive on. On one such occasion, we all had a real turn. The Hilux drew up and we searched the track to see what the matter was. At first nobody could see anything, but then someone noticed in the headlights the body of a man lying right across the path. How it was that the truck had not run him over was amazing. Nagging thoughts of the murderous "yellowthread" *loe-si* cultists ran through our heads. Also we knew that ex-communist bandits and fugitive criminals hid out in these jungles of Kanchanaburi province. Even the Karens Tirapon and Sawoei, who were better able to interpret local irregularities, were visibly uneasy. They glanced nervously around into the blackness.

On either side of the man, large bamboo sections had been placed across the track to stop vehicles. Everyone feared an ambush, and the two Karens flashed their torches into the surrounding bamboos. The Thai adventurer produced a gun. The remnants of a smouldering fire were burning near the man. It seemed that he had made a little camp for the night there and had put the bamboos across the path to stop vehicles running over him, but no one was sure and the man could not be roused. Either he was drunk, or half bitten to death by malarial mosquitoes, or dead. The thought occurred to us that, if we had tried to trek to Ko Ta Doe in the night, this could be us lying here. The two Karens moved the body to one side, removed the bamboo obstacles, and cautiously drove around the man. Then we hurried on in silence.

It was a long way to Ko Ta Doe, but finally the truck headlights illuminated a checkpoint. Sawoei got out to report to the guard hut, and then we were off again. Between Ko Ta Doe and Doe Nae Po came the famous score of river crossings - we counted nineteen. It seemed that on this section the track intertwined with and continually reforded the same river. Some of the crossings were up to 100 m. long and 1 m. deep. Often the boulders on the riverbed were round and slimy, making progress difficult and slow, even with 4WD. As if to annoy us, Sawoei began stopping the truck in the water to shine his torch along the riverbanks in search of jungle frogs. From everywhere came a chorus of croaking calls in the night. In the end, the driver's desire got the better of him, and on the approach to one ford he drew up the Hilux definitively, switching off the engine and lights. It was so dark that it was impossible to see anything, not even the nearest person in the back of the truck.

Sawoei came round to the back and explained to Tirapon that he wanted to get some frogs "for a garden pond he had built", but that he needed the other's help to find and catch the frogs while he himself held the torch. Tirapon, as an employee of the Wildlife Protection authority was understandably unhappy about this, but the driver leaned on him, reminding him that he was after all getting a free lift. Perhaps an element of Karen brotherliness came into the equation. And so the two of them went off along the pitch-black riverbank, abandoning the rest of us to our fate. Like Tirapon, we also wanted to remonstrate. It was no fun being ditched in the dark in the jungle. But our position was even weaker than the Karen's.

The men were gone a long time. The cool night air was alive with the croaking of the big jungle bullfrogs. In the back of the truck we were constantly pestered by insects. As the moon had not yet risen, it was still incredibly dark. Nothing could be seen of our companions except the tiny glowing cones of their cigarettes. Over and again the absolute impossibility of trekking down here at night bore in on us. Someone spoke of bears and tigers in the trees. Our own thoughts circled around the idea that the unscrupulous Sawoei was making a rendezvous with some accomplices to double back and ambush us. Everybody was distinctly unhappy. Then the Thai swashbuckler suggested making a fire. It would keep us warm, illuminate the immediate area, drive away insects and animals, and just pass the time. Soon a fire of dry bamboo was crackling merrily. The situation was so hopeless and absurd that it began to seem amusing.

After a good hour, the pinpoint of the torchlight came dancing erratically back towards us. The two Karens arrived clutching by the legs a dozen foot-long frogs. They put them in a sack and then went to get a spear of bamboo. We were afraid they were going to spit the animals and roast them over the fire. But they merely used the bamboo to fasten the sack. At around 10 p.m. we set off again. The driver seemed in an even greater hurry now, trying to make up for lost time. We trawled through the remaining fords and then passed through what looked more like open country, even elevated ground. Certainly that latter section was back onto bulldust tracks. In our minds we tried to translate the ghostly scenery outlined by the headlights into the stunning countryside it must have been in daylight.

Sleeping Doe Nae Po passed by, and then, not far short of the main road, we drew up in front of yet another barrier. This was no lackadaisical post manned by Karen boys, but a serious checkpoint. In fact it was the Sa Nae Pong Wildlife and Forestry Protection HQ and, at the same time, a southern entrance to Tung Yai - Naresuan National Park and Wildlife Sanctuary. Something funny happened here. After the paramilitary *anuraak* guards had logged the arrival of our truck and quizzed everybody, especially us, as to their business, they began to search the vehicle. They inspected the sacks of rice and then, inevitably, found the bag of frogs. Sawoei, of course, could come up with no plausible explanation whatsoever for the freight of frogs, and Tirapon kept remarkably quiet. The bullfrogs were confiscated. Sawoei was visibly sore about it. Tirapon whispered in our ears that the frogs would certainly not be returned to the wild, but would be eaten by the *anuraak*. Poor Mr Eat could only watch as the treat that he had envisaged for himself passed into the hands of other eaters. The rest of us were just exasperated that the long hour which we had been forced to wait had all been for nothing.

At the checkpoint we enquired of the guards about the route ahead. The main road was only eight kms away and the turning for Three Pagodas not much beyond it. But the truck was bound for Sangklaburi, which was in a different direction. Also, midnight was not a good time to arrive at a strange town. So we asked the Forestry officials if we could spend the night at their Sa Nae Pong camp. Without enthusiasm they agreed. They seemed doubtful about a shattered-looking *farang* dropping out of the jungle in the night with a red face and a jawful of stubble. In fact, after the frog episode, they viewed us all with deep suspicion.- and rightly so. We thanked the questionable Sawoei for the bone-shaking ride, and bade farewell to both the shady Thai adventurer and our friend for the day, Tirapon, as well as the others. The red taillights of the Hilux vanished in the dust and gloom.

The reserved *anuraak* led us to an A-frame bungalow nearby and, as it was late, let us get on with things. We strung up our mosquito net and rolled out our sleeping bags on a pallet bed. A late snack consisted of our very last tin of food, lugged from Mae Sot, and the rest of a bottle of lukewarm water, which had a snow of fragments of purifying tablets rolling around in the bottom. Reviewing the confused events of the day, we tried to get some details down in the diary. Could it really be that we had breakfasted with Joi-ae in Ti Po Mo? And were we actually sleeping within striking distance of our final goal? As we drifted off to sleep, it seemed to us that we heard the contented murmurings of the *anuraak*, turning jungle frogs on a grill over their fire....

The next morning, over a breakfast of eggs, rice and coffee, we learned that a Land Rover was going to Sangklaburi. If we wanted, we could travel with it as far as the turn-off for Ban Pra Chedi Saam Ong (= Three Pagodas village). We accepted the lift and bumped along for eight kms. The terrain in these upper reaches of Kanchanaburi province was every bit as rugged as what we had been seeing. The same Dawna Range lay over to the west, separated from us by scrubland. Suddenly we came to a T-junction and the 323 Kanchanaburi-Sangklaburi highway. It was a shock. It was the first tarmac we had seen since Um Pang, two weeks earlier. And the odd cars and trucks swishing by were the first real traffic since Mae Sot, in quite another part of the country. Even though it was still early morning, we noticed that it was significantly hotter and more humid down here. We were almost on the same latitude as Bangkok.

A roadsign pointed southeast some eighty kms to Tong Pa Pum and more than 200 kms to Kanchanaburi town. Northwest went to out-on-a-limb Sangklaburi and the border. Our Land Rover turned right and drove the few kms up to the turn-off for the Pass. We alighted there and were made to sign our names and nationalities into a book at a police box on the junction. Then we waited for the first passing *songtaew* to take us the last eighteen kms to the Three Pagodas. Finally an empty one arrived, charging us 25 baht each. It was strange to be handling money again. Except for paying guides and buying the odd packet of Ma-ma noodles, we had been given everything free since Um Pang. The Thais were reconstructing the road up to the Pass, engineering a highway out of all proportion both to the traffic on it and the meagre village at its end. The first section had already been paved, while the remainder was still dirt. In keeping with so much of our journey, we completed the last stretch with a generous coating of yellow powder.

Halfway up the dust highway lay the mixed Mon and Burmese village of Huai Song Kalia (also Chong Karia and variations), named after a nearby river. The countryside to the left was desolate scrub, while to the right loomed the same craggy Dawna mountains we had followed down the border, sometimes on the Thai side, sometimes on the Burmese side, all the way from Ban Ta Song Yang. They were the outermost foothills, the dying ripple, of the Himalayas. The *songtaew* ascended to a shallow pass (altitude 1000 ft.), crossed over, and dropped down the other side into the large squat village of Pra Chedi Saam Ong. Here our transport parked, and it was but a short walk further to the Three Pagodas. We could see why the Burmese claimed the pagodas. Both they and the village clearly lay west both of the pass and the border mountains. On the other hand, it was understandable why the Thais should also claim (want to keep) the pagodas. They formed one of the most celebrated shrines in South East Asia.

The Three Pagodas Pass

And so, alighting from a humble *songtaew* in the early morning, this was how we came to behold the goal that we had so long journeyed towards. After the anticipation, the reality of the pagodas was inevitably a trifle disappointing. They were not pieces of monumental architecture, but three piles of whitewashed stones. Encircled by a little garden fence, and with flowering bushes growing in among them, the *chedis* were swathed Buddhist-style in lengths of red, green and yellow gauze. People had placed offerings before them. Nearby were a couple of feeble stalls. The big dirt road led up to the pagodas and ended by swinging around them. To put it irreverantly, the Three Pagodas looked like nothing so much as pert little oriental breasts sticking up out of a roundabout.

THREE PAGODAS

The shrine was marred not just by the road, but by the paraphernalia of an adjacent Burmese border crossing and military checkpoint. For 130 baht (Thais, of course, only 5 baht) visitors could put a smile on the faces of the Rangoon authorities and cross over to see the village of Payatonzu (also Pia Tong Su = "three pagodas" in Burmese). Beyond the village the road continued for 100 miles to Moulmein and the Andaman Sea. The crossing point was quiet. Flags were flying, and authoritarian notices abounded, such as: WELCOME TO MYANMAR - LOVE YOUR MOTHERLAND, RESPECT THE LAW and WELCOME TO PHAYATONZU - THIS CITY WAS ESTABLISHED BY THE ARMY AND PEOPLE IN 8-2-90. The joint presence at the pass of SLORC troops and the Thai Army reflected the current disposition of ownership and control of the pagodas. Judging by the way a Thai highway ran up to the shrine, it looked as if the cairns were firmly part of the Kingdom, but actually they sat more in a piece of no-man's-land or "extraterritory", ruled by neither power or both.

The Burmese notices reflected just the latest chapter in the long chequered history of the Three Pagodas. When not in itself a flashpoint, the Pass had often been the vehicle of invasions going in both directions. More than a few times the Burmese and the Siamese, traditional enemies who even today remained mutually suspicious, had crossed the pass to conquer each other's kingdoms, sack each other's towns, and steal each other's most important Buddha figures. The Burmese, for example, had come this way when in 1765 they infamously destroyed Ayuttaya, the wondrous former capital of Siam. In calmer times the Three Pagodas had been the age-old and principal link between Burma and the fertile plain of the Chao Praya River, channelling traders, pilgrims, diplomats and migrants. These individuals, when leaving their own land and before entering the territory of the "enemy", used to pause at the pass to make an offering. They found the frontier marked by three little cairns, and in fact the Three Pagodas Pass was originally known as "the three cairns". By adding a stone to the cairns, the wayfarers sought to draw down blessing on their journey, and this was how the *chedis* started life. In 1929 Pra Sri Suan Kiri, the governor of Sangklaburi, brought the local people up to Pra Chedi Saam Ong to transform the cairns into the pagodas as we now know them.

In more recent times the Three Pagodas Pass was the conduit of a much larger invasion. During WW2 the Japanese used the route to help launch their attack on Burma from occupied Thailand. They invaded also from other points further north, for example Mae Hong Son and Wiang Haeng, but the pass was of especial significance because it was the only route for hundreds of miles by which they could forward large quantities of heavy supplies. To enable them to sustain their offensive, the Japanese had the idea of building a 415-km long railway over the pass, linking the Thai and Burmese railway systems. It was projected that a 304-km Thai stretch and a 111-km section in Burma would meet at Pra Chedi Saam Ong. The idea gave birth to the infamous "Death Railway", associated with the Three Pagodas.

THREE PAGODAS

Work began on the railway in June 1942 at the existing terminals of Nong Pladuk in Thailand and Thanbyuzayat in Burma. It had been estimated that the line would take five years to build, but work was completed in September 1943, in little more than a year. The two railheads met just south of Three Pagodas. Such an extraordinary feat of engineering through mountainous jungle terrain was only possible due to the forced labour of an army of prisoners of war and pressganged coolies. Of the workforce, estimated to number approximately 200,000 men, some 13,000 POWs (principally Australian, British and Dutch) and perhaps as many as 90,000 coolies (from Thailand, Burma, Malaysia, Indonesia, India and China) perished. They died from malnutrition, disease (notably malaria), exhaustion and accidents, but quite especially from the bestial treatment meted out to them by their Japanese captors. Two celebrated war cemeteries at Kanchanaburi honour the Allied dead.

The story of the building of Death Railway up to the Pass is well-known on account of one of the line's bridges, the one which spans the River Kwae Yai near Kanchanaburi. The construction of this bridge was famously documented in Boulle's book *The Bridge over the River Kwai* (should be "Kwae") and subsequently celebrated in the film of the same name. The bridge was in use for almost two years before it was bombed by the Allies in 1945. After the war the bridge was rebuilt and is still in use today. Of Death Railway itself, the first 77 kms on the Thai side still exist, running as far as Nam Tok, near the Sai Yok Falls. The rest has been dismantled or reclaimed by the jungle.

Until a short time before our visit, the Three Pagodas Pass had always stood in territory historically Mon, but latterly controlled jointly by the Mons and the Karens. We had come across our first Mon man, the monk, back at Joi-ae's village. Song Kalia, just before the Three Pagodas, was full of Mons, and other villages in the vicinity were also Mon. The nearby district seat of Sangklaburi was in essence a Mon town. With our route ending by brushing the Mon homeland, it is appropriate to say a few words about this last minority people of our border journey.

The Mon people
The Mons are classified as belonging to the Austro-Asiatic Mon-Khmer group of peoples, also thought to include the Wa and Lawa. They are the oldest inhabitants of Burma still surviving today, predating the Burmans by hundreds of years. In Thailand, disregarding the even older Wa, the Mons were probably the first people with an advanced civilization to settle in the plains of the Chao Praya river. The marginalized and suppressed Mon ethnic minority of the present day are the descendants of a race of people who once had a mighty South-East Asian empire. More than 1000 years ago their Dvaravati imperium extended from the Indian Ocean in the west, to the Malay peninsula in the south, and to the high plateauland of northeast Thailand. The Mons used to be called the Talaings, after a region

on the Madras coast of India, and their culture appears to have Indian roots. As early as the 5th century AD they had taken over Hinayana-Buddhist doctrine from the Indian subcontinent. The ancient Mons had their own language, writing and masterly sculptural style. Their empire was a loose association of principalities, the chief one, the "capital", being Lopburi. In the modern Thai town of Lopburi stones have been found dating back to the 8th century bearing old Mon script, while in Lamphun, near Chiang Mai, artifacts have been dug up with Mon inscriptions.

From the 9th century AD onwards the Mon empire was squeezed from the east by the Khmers and from the west by the Burmans. Later the Tai, coming south, pushed the Mons out of central Thailand. The Burmans, themselves displaced by the Chinese and migrating south from the Tibetan area, established their own empire, subjecting the Mons. The animist Burmese conquerors took over from their subjects Buddhism and Mon culture. The Mons were left to inhabit the area where they now live - mainly in the Tenasserim mountains of southeastern Burma, but also to a small extent in western Thailand.

In the mid-20th century, the Mons got the same raw deal as the Karens at Panglong (1947). Occupying land that was either shared with the Karens or contiguous with their territory, it made sense for the Mons to make common cause with the Yang. Accordingly, in 1948, the year of Burma's independence from Britain, the Mons allied with the KNU. The two peoples agreed to work for a joint Mon-Karen independent state, particularly in territory inhabited by both groups. The Mon uprising began in 1949, the same year as the outbreak of the Karen insurgency. The alliance held in one form or another until the 1980s, when simmering discontents over land and taxation in the region of the Three Pagodas began to boil over. Back in the mid-60s KNU 6th Brigade district had opened a new trading post/customs gate at the pass. Controlled jointly by the Karens and the Mons, it rapidly grew (like Palu and Kawmoorah further north) into one of the most important of all Kawthoolei's frontier outposts, boasting a population of some 5000 Karens, Mons, Indo-Burmese and others. Travellers to the Three Pagodas "blackmarket" reported seeing temples, churches, a mosque, and even a cinema hall. With the revenue from taxation booming, each side must have secretly considered how much it would have liked to have all the income for its own purposes.

At the beginning of the 80s the Mon insurgent movement fissured into two rival factions. The split, which lasted six years, seriously compromised the Mon cause. It also weakened the Mons vis-à-vis their allies - in spite of the fact that one faction, the 1000-strong New Mon State Party (Army), stayed with the KNU. In the matter of control of the Three Pagodas, the Karens, who at that time were anyway gaining in absolute strength, were in the ascendant. In 1987, however, the two rival Mon factions reunited, restoring Mon military clout. Overnight the Mons felt confident enough again to challenge the Karens for overall control of the pass. There was a new twist in the spiral of tension between the two ethnic armies. The *resulting skirmishing between old allies was senseless enough, but it was utterly absurd in view of the offensives against both of them by a common foe, Rangoon. In 1977, 1980 and 1986/87 the Burma Army, pursuing its Four Cuts campaign, repeatedly attacked Karen/Mon bases at and around the Three Pagodas. Finally, the allies themselves achieved - incredibly - what the Burmese had for so long failed to do. In a major battle in July 1988 between the KNLA and the NMSA, the Three Pagodas village and base was virtually razed to the ground.*

But that fatal and tragic mistake, which cost the lives of more than one hundred Karens and Mons, was as nothing compared to what was about to happen. In early 1990 the Three Pagodas became the scene of the last in the long line of invasions through the pass. This time it was a cross-border incursion by SLORC troops into Thailand. But the Burmese were not, as so often in history, after the Siamese, but the insurgents. On Friday 9 February Rangoon forces captured and destroyed what was left of the black-market immediately behind the pagodas, paving the way for a larger offensive. Then, at midnight Saturday 10 February, they launched a major attack on the NMSA HQ at Nam Koek, a few kms north of the pass. However, the Myanmar troops did not make a frontal assault on the rebel stronghold, but used Thailand as a springboard to attack it unexpectedly from the rear. It was the same tactic as they had used almost contemporaneously up at Kawmoorah. The Mons were furious that the Thais had "allowed" the Burmese to use their territory. But for the moment they, like the Karens, were a casualty of thawing relations between Bangkok and Rangoon. Burma Army troops manoeuvred on Thai soil with the tacit support of the Thai military, as directed by Army supremo Gen. "logger" Chaovalit.

1000 SLORC soldiers, led by Col. Chit Maung, poured through a corner of the Kingdom to capture Nam Koek village and base on the morning of Sunday 11 February. There were heavy casualties on both sides. All Sunday 11 and Monday 12 the junta forces made helicopter drops of supplies, transporting these and marching across Siamese soil southeast of the Three Pagodas. They even passed a tellingly empty Thai Army Ninth Division outpost. The upshot of the fighting was that between 4000 and 7000 Mon civilians fled to Song Kalia, while 200 or more Thais sought refuge in Sangklaburi. Numerous Burmese people also fled to the Thai side to escape the fighting and avoid being pressganged. The Mon insurgents retreated from Nam Koek to regroup. With a view to "stretching" their assailants and counter-attacking, they buried their differences with the Karens and linked up with KNLA troops operating nearby. However, the Burma Army, far from crumbling, held on to the pass area. It did not even completely withdraw from "Thai" territory, but held onto the Three Pagodas, claiming that they belonged to Myanmar. To back up their claim, the Burmese produced an old British colonial map showing the pagodas inside their country. While they were there, they gave the ancient venerated chedis a coat of white paint, ironically using Thai paint to do the job. The following day an incensed Thai nation awoke to see pictures of marauding gun-toting bandanna-clad Burmese infantrymen roaming around the freshly whitewashed pagodas. Needless to say, the Burmese were soon dispatched from regular Thai soil, but they were not entirely removed from the pass - witness their presence now immediately beside the Three Pagodas.

The Three Pagodas made a fitting end to our journey. Purely on their own account, these ancient, famous, revered and remote *chedis* would have been an appropriate enough destination. But, marking a frontier pass, they formed an especially apt conclusion to a journey which had passed down the border, zigzagging across it. The three cairns which had guided generations of wayfarers going east and west now greeted new travellers coming from the north. Travelling is in some respects a quasi-religious quest, and what better goal could there have been for such a pilgrimage than this shrine? In the early morning sun, untroubled by anyone except for a man making a votive offering, we sat in a crude shelter, savouring undisturbed both the magic of arrival and the mystical presence of the pagodas. The three wild piles of stones stood silent and gleaming in a desolate forbidding arena. Behind them squatted the shacks of Pra Chedi Saam Ong village, in the middle distance lay what looked like some abandoned *wat* construction, and in the background towered the precipitous tree-covered Dawna mountains of the border ridge. We were tired, dirty and very hungry. Our clothes were grimy and our faces burnt red by the sun. My ankle was as painful and swollen as ever, and the red spots of the elephant rash had still not gone. A fortnight out from Um Pang, a good cm of traveller's stubble had grown. But all these discomforts were as nothing now that we were finally able to joyfully embrace the Three Pagodas.

The latest Burmese incursion at Pra Chedi Saam Ong was still a fresh event. The praying man, when he had finished his offering, came over to us and pointed out holes in the tin roof of our shelter. They were bullet holes from that assault. This reminded us of the other darker side of the Three Pagodas. Their chequered history and the conflicting claims to them reflected the continuing sporadic warfare all up and down the disputed territory of this western border, not least at the pass itself. Even if for the moment the traditional enemies, Thai and Burman, were sharing the spot in an uneasy standoff, it was a place where Mon had fought Karen, and Burmans had fought both - just as further up the border other ethnic minorities continued to fight each other, with the Burmans fighting everyone.

Finally, the pagodas symbolized in a more abstract way. Their ambivalence reflected not just the deadly freedom-fighting up and down the border, but dubious developments in the countries on either side. In the name of "Burmanization" Burma had been economically, politically and militarily wrecked by the longstanding Ne Win military dictatorship and latterly its SLORC replacement. Now too the country was a source to be plundered of hardwood, opium and young girls. We only trusted that Thailand would not suffer a similar fate, but from more insidious causes. We hoped that the Kingdom, as it changed from being a traditional Buddhist third-world country to a developed nation, would not destroy itself in a riot of headlong modernization, mechanization, road-building, exploitation, tourism, greed and hedonism - that Mr Donut would delay his coming for a while longer, that Shangri-la would persist in spite of the *tuk-tuks*, and that the driverless Komatsu would thrust only so far into the virgin jungle. In his book *Golden Earth* Norman Lewis wrote that during crucial moments in the history of Burma a prophecy had often become current. It had been heard again during the pagoda-building mania which had preceded the Mongol invasion. People had said: "The great pagoda is finished, and the country is ruined." As we rested at our journey's end, contemplating· the celebrated Three Pagodas, we hoped that Burma's Siamese neighbour would not be ruined by a modern-day invasion.

Above: Shan pagoda at Wat Fah Wiang In, Piang Luang
Below: Shan Buddha figures at Wat Wiang Haeng

Above: Opium poppy field on border near Kae Noi
Below: KMT house front, Kae Noi

Above left: Wa lady in costume
Above right: Pipe-smoking Lawa woman
Below: Lahu Sheh Leh people near "Spirit Well"

Above: Wat Jong Kham, Mae Hong Son
Below: Jong Kham lake, Mae Hong Son

Above: Longtail boats on River Salween at Mae Saam Laep
Below: Provisions in market stall, Mae Saam Laep

Above: Karen National Liberation Army GHQ, Manerplaw
Below: Democratic Alliance of Burma HQ, Manerplaw

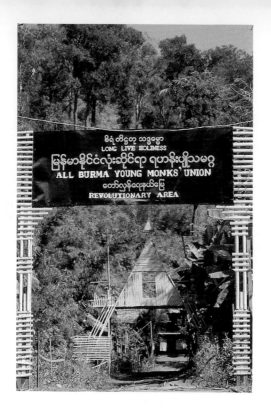

Above: All Burma Young Monks' Union compound, Manerplaw
Below: Insignia of National Democratic Front members, Manerplaw

Above: "Death Highway"
Below: Karen elephant going to Boeng Kloeng

Above: Main street, Boeng Kloeng
Below: Karen house, Boeng Kloeng

Above left: Two wandering monks, Lae Tong Ku
Above right: Border sign in jungle near Kui Le Toeng
Below: Two *loe-si* disciples, Lae Tong Ku

Above: Author's wife trekking through jungle to the Three Pagodas
Below: Three Karen women between Lae Tong Ku and Kui Le Toeng

Above:In Joi-ae's truck in the Burmese jungle between Ti Po Mo and
Ti Lai Pa
Below: KNLA commander flanked by two *loe-si* cultists, Kui Le Toeng

Above: Wa National Army officers Jerng & Kong Mong
Below: Wa mud house

Prince Maha San,
Wa leader and chairman of the Wa National Organization

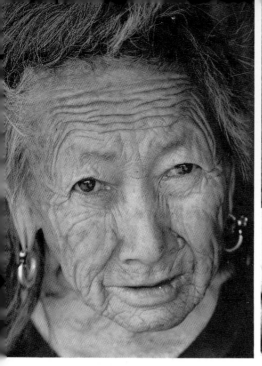

Above left: Hmong grandma at Ka Ngae Ki, south of Um Pang
Above right: Padaung grandma, Mai Nai Soi
Below: Two shots of Wa girl "Darkie"

Ma Ja, Padaung "long-neck" girl, Mai Nai Soi

Ma Nang, Padaung "long-neck" mother of Ma Ja, Mai Nai Soi

Above: Northern entrance to rebel HQ, Manerplaw
Below: KNU finance office, Manerplaw

Above: By longtail boat down the River Salween
(Burma & Dawna Range left, Thailand right)
Below: Karen boys posing with KNLA truck at Jo Ta, near Sa Kaang Thi

Above: Mae Sot "singing girls"
Below: Karen Baptist Joi-ae with Karen driver at Ti Po Mo

Above: KNLA commander Sor Kyi Shwi with author, Mae Ta Ro Ta
Below left: Sooksi, one of our KNLA guides
Below right: Toom Yai, our *loe-si* interpreter at Lae Tong Ku

Above: *Loe-si wat* at Lae Tong Ku
Below left: *Loe-si* jungle hunter, near Lae Tong Ku
Below right: *Loe-si* disciple at half-moon ceremony, Lae Tong Ku

The *loe-si* man-god of Lae Tong Ku

KNLA commander Mor Thaing Chor, Kui Le Toeng

POSTSCRIPT

By 1995 Mr Donut had arrived in Chiang Mai - in the company of Col. "finger-lickin' good" Sanders and the Burger King. In the winter of 1993/94 we found Wiang Haeng closed off (as it sometimes is) because of the Burmese offensive against Khun Sa across the border in the Shan State. Piang Luang was more inaccessible than ever. Nor could the help of the local district chief be called upon - Somsak had meanwhile been posted elsewhere. The SLORC offensive against Khun Sa failed, and it is thought that the junta will try again to move against the opium king in 1995, after first dealing with the Karens (see below).

Journeying again down Highway 1095 (Mae Ma Lai - Mae Hong Son), we found that the road had at last been sealed right through. Soppong had mushroomed considerably along the main road outside town. In Mae Hong Son we discovered that the *Sanguan Sin Hotel* was defunct. It was also disappointing to find that that useful alternative, the *Siam Hotel*, had jumped on the tourist bandwaggon, virtually doubling its prices. In the "town of the three mists" our missionary friends had moved to a larger house and had started a mission with a nursery. Outside of town the "long-neck" people had been relocated to a new site more accessible to tourists. The human zoo was now complete. Miss Silver had left the Padaungs, preferring to work at the desk of a travel agency in town. Down at Mae Sariang, the 1194 road to Mae Saam Laep was undergoing drastic improvement. It should soon be possible to scoot down to the Salween with ease. Even further south, the mini-market at Mae Salid had been moved away from the road west towards the river because of a number of accidents in front of it. The bamboo bridge across the Moei at Po Pa Ta had been severed on the Thai side, making it necessary to use a boat to cross. The Karens were anticipating a Burma Army attack - correctly, as things turned out. The night market of brash Mae Sot had been moved off the Prasart Viti road into accommodation of its own in a precinct off this central drag.

In Mae Sot the lure of sinister Wa Lae again proved irresistible. By a strange coincidence, just as the Burma Army had taken Palu only hours before our first visit, so now, immediately before our return in 1994, it had withdrawn from the former KNU base (just after New Year in fact). The bridge by the market square was open, although nothing was using it. The square itself was empty, and many of the buildings around it looked disused. There was still some barbed wire around, but mostly it had gone. Curiously, a checkpoint by the bridge was unmanned, and anybody was free to wander across. Just the usual wooden sign announced "Thailand", under which another amateurish board exhorted "No Arm, No Uniform". An old couple in a nearby shop told us we could go across. We could go to Chi Sa Lae, a Karen village 6 kms distant or, indeed, all the way to Nong Luang and Um Pang - the old way was open again.... On the far bank Palu was deserted. In fact there was nothing left of Palu, it was completely destroyed. Every building had been smashed or burnt at some time during the four years of SLORC occupation. Jungle had already reclaimed some of the old streets and households. Among the ruins were a couple of small timber workshops, and further up the road a checkpoint. It seemed to be a BPP guardbox (inside Burma!) controlling logging traffic. The guards were fast asleep. Picking our way through the overgrown ruins of Palu, and with the thought of left-over landmines nagging, we tried to get up to the big white pagoda on the hill. But it was impossible. Over in that direction the countryside was ablaze everywhere. But we did get to the wooden *wat*. Just as we arrived, however, the burning bushes around it set fire to the temple, and before our eyes the monastery conflagrated. Through a door we could see a wardrobe with mirrors in flames, and some votive banners hanging from the ceiling dripped fire. Hurrying away, we saw that the bush fire was just beginning to engulf the pagoda. With the Burmese gone, Wa Lae/Palu was no less disquieting than on the first visit.

South of Um Pang at Boeng Kloeng we were pleased to find during a revisit a year after our first stop there that the place had reverted to its usual idyllic self. We wandered up an almost deserted main street, with a few children playing in the dust and the sun filtering through the trees. It was as if the refugees had never been there. In the village we learned from an aid worker that Joi-ae's house down at Ti Po Mo had burnt down soon after our departure. Hopefully he made no connection!

But all these changes were as nothing compared to the calamity which overtook virtually the entire western border during the winter of 1994/95. Most affected were the long-suffering Karens. At the end of November 1994 the SLORC junta broke its two-year unilaterally declared ceasefire with Burma's rebel groups and began attacking the Karens, Mons and ABSDF dissidents. That in itself would not have mattered so much - after all, it was nothing new. Much more worrying was that simultaneously conflict broke out in early December within the Karen movement itself. Some Buddhist soldiers of the Karen National Union grew increasingly discontented with regard to their Christian counterparts. They felt that they were being passed over for promotion and that the Christian-dominated leadership of the KNU was practising religious favouritism. Rumours circulated that the Christians were persecuting Buddhist Karen civilians and soldiers, and there were reports of each side attacking the other. The Buddhists began focussing themselves on the so-called River Junction Pagoda, a pagoda and *wat* on a strategic hill at the confluence of the Salween and Moei rivers. Run by a prominent abbott, Myiang Gyi Ngu Sayadaw, the confluence monastery in turn became a source of discontent for the Christian KNU leadership. Not only was the abbott gathering hundreds of disgruntled Buddhist Karens around him at a sensitive point, but he was also building temples and pagodas in other parts of Kawthoolei, some in militarily restricted zones. The leadership, which suspected the hand of SLORC in all this, objected that the *wats* compromised KNU security, allowing the enemy to infiltrate Karen territory. For a few days the crack was papered over with an agreement between the two factions.

But then in the dying days of 1994 a sizeable number of Buddhists definitively split off from the KNU. Five hundred armed guerrillas and hundreds of followers took over River Junction Pagoda as their base and proclaimed an organization of their own, the Democratic Kayin (Karen) Buddhist Organization/Association (DKBO/DKBA). The mutiny was a serious, possibly fatal, blow to the Karen movement. Not only was it now riven and weakened by internal dissension, but the defectors seemed to have gone over to the side of their "Buddhist brothers", the Burmese enemy. As if that was not enough, an organization apparently in the pocket of SLORC also controlled the KNU's vital Salween-Moei supply line from Mae Saam Laep to Manerplaw. Confirmation of the treacherous alliance was not long in coming.

In the last week of January 1995 the Burma army launched a three-pronged attack on KNU positions up and down the border. The aim was no less than finally to capture rebel HQ. After a week of fighting, the unthinkable happened. Manerplaw fell, an event that not only stunned the Karens and their NDF/DAB allies, but triggered a chorus of protest and condemnation around the world. Six other bases north and south of the insurgent nerve centre were also captured, precipitating the flight of thousands of refugees and many KNU leaders into Thailand. Few documents could be saved, and there were reports of the "capital" being torched as the defenders withdrew. During this latest SLORC campaign, about 10,000 - 15,000 new Karen refugees crossed the border (an estimated 5000 from the Manerplaw area alone), pushing the total of displaced Karens in Thailand to some 70,000. There was no mistaking the hand of the Burma Army LIDs in the seizure. Possible smarting from outraged world reaction, SLORC sought to play down its involvement, claiming it had merely provided logistical support for the Buddhist Karen mutineers, who had actually made the attack. Judging by the suddenness of the fall, suggesting that there had been an unexpected assault through a side door from Karen kinsfolk to the north, the DKBO would indeed seem to have been implicated.

Following the fall of Manerplaw, KNLA troops withdrew to Kawmoorah (Ko Mu Ra), reinforcing the defenders there. The Burma Army had already laid siege to the base in December. Now, on 30 January 1995, they began attacking this last Karen outpost in the northern sector. Although of little strategic value, Kawmoorah had great symbolic importance not just for the defending Karens, but also for SLORC, which desired to take it at all costs. Over the years Rangoon had lost hundreds of troops trying to rush this virtually impregnable old stamping ground of Bo Mya. Situated not far north of Mae Sot, it lay on a piece of land backed on three sides by a horseshoe of river (the Moei) and connected to Burma by a thin neck of land. This strip, mined and booby-trapped, with three rows of trenches and a dozen layers of barbed wire entanglements, and overlooked by ten two-storey reinforced concrete bunkers, was called by the Karens "the killing zone". With some 1000 KNLA and ABSDF soldiers on one side of the zone and 1500 SLORC troops on the other, the scene was set for a vicious and protracted battle.

After a week of preparations, the Burmese began round-the-clock shelling of the camp with up to 100 artillery pieces in an attempt to grind the resisters down. Thai Army observers reported hearing 120 mm mortars, 130 and 155 mm howitzers, rockets and heavy Chinese-made siege guns. Possibly as many as 50,000 shells were fired during the two-month siege. Then on 9 February the Burma Army launched an unsuccessful frontal "suicide" assault on the defences. The Karens believed that many of the 200 attackers had been drugged, so impervious did they seem to the danger, and reported that civilian porters had been used as "minesweepers". After the attack some 40 dead and 60 wounded littered the 600 x 500 m. area of "no-man's-land" between the two forces, among them apparently Buddhist KNU renegades. It was at this time that further up the border Daungguin (Dagwin), the ABSDF headquarters, situated 30 kms north of Manerplaw (near Mae Saam Laep), fell to the Burmese. Before evacuating their HQ, the student fighters torched their buildings. For the KNLA defenders at Kawmoorah the last straw was when, as they alleged, chemical shells (possibly teargas) landed around their bunkers. On 21 February the thousand rebels withdrew, leaving the Burmese to cut through the fortifications and take the last major Karen stronghold on the Thai-Burmese frontier. The KNU survivors regrouped further down the border, vowing now to resort to guerrilla warfare in the southern sector. They would conduct operations in Tavoy and Mergui, and target key installations such as the proposed Burma-Thailand Unocal/Total gas pipeline.

Following the fiasco and with the wisdom of hindsight, analysts pointed out that the KNU should have seen trouble coming. The leadership had indeed been too Christian-dominated, whereas the bulk of the KNU rank-and-file was animist or Buddhist. Bo Mya was out of touch with his people, he had grown too autocratic, and his KNU seriously lacked democracy. Suddenly many realized that no real party conference had been held since as far back as 1974. Bo Mya countered by saying that the disaster had happened not because of any weakness in the KNU, but because of the treacherous machinations of Rangoon. The trouble at River Junction Pagoda had been fomented by SLORC agents, who had financed the DKBO's operations, setting Karen against Karen. Manerplaw and the other bases in eastern Kawthoolei had fallen not because of a lack of democracy, but because Rangoon, aided by the Buddhist Karens, wanted to clear the border area of opposition prior to developing it. The Burmese wished finally to reap the full benefits of their logging concessions to the Thais and above all intended to cash in on the lucrative business of selling power to their energy-hungry Siamese neighbours. But they could not build dams across the Salween or lay the Unocal/Total gas pipeline from the Gulf of

Martaban to the Bong Ti pass (Sai Yok district, Kanchanaburi) if the KNU controlled the area. Critics of Bangkok noted that it was this - the routing of ethnic minorities and not any political reform of the junta - that was the real fruit of Thailand's hollow policy of "constructive engagement" with SLORC. Even as Manerplaw fell, the Thai government was signing a 30-year agreement to buy annually $400m of natural gas from an illegal dictatorship. And while Kawmoorah succumbed to its pounding, senior Thai Army officials, no doubt mindful of their private business interests, were inviting SLORC top brass to visit the Kingdom "to strengthen ties between the two countries".

For the traveller in the region the repercussions of the calamity have been that boating on the Salween and Moei rivers north and south of Mae Saam Laep has been stopped as too dangerous. In February 1995, on the sandy riverbank opposite Mae Saam Laep, from where most of the longtails start, some 120 trigger-happy SLORC troops were roaming around, while on the Dawna mountaintops Burma Army artillery positions had been set up. A visit to rebel HQ is out of the question, and even if one managed to get there, KNLA GHQ as well as the headquarters of organizations such as the NDF and DAB may well have been razed to the ground. Similarly, the KNU/ABSDF camp at Po Pa Ta is almost certainly unvisitable - no more crossings of the bamboo bridge there. Palu (Wa Lae) could well have been reoccupied, the old Wa Lae - Nong Luang route to Um Pang interdicted yet again, and Boeng Kloeng swamped once more with Karen refugees. Following the SLORC/DKBO seizure of large parts of the Burmese side of the border, there have been numerous newspaper reports of cross-border banditry, raiding and pillaging, intimidation and kidnapping (even a senior Buddhist KNU official, Pa Do Ma, was apparently abducted by the DKBO from Thailand into Burma, causing the Karens in Thai refugee camps near the border to move further "inland". Because of this fighting and its ugly aftermath, during the winter of 1994/95 tourism down much of the Thai-Burmese border dropped by 80%, with visits to Um Pang decimated.

GLOSSARY

This is a glossary of Thai and other non-English words (Karen, Burmese etc.) as well as acronyms and abbreviations frequently used in this book.

4WD: four-wheel drive
ABSDF: All Burma Students Democratic Front
ampoe (amphoer, ampher, amphur): district, district office
anuraak: forestry protection officials
ban (= muban) (pronounced "barn"): village
BPP (= Border Patrol Police), dorchodor: paramilitary force operating in the border
  areas
changwat: province
chedi: pagoda or pratat or stupa, a monument with a thin pointed spire, containing
  a relic of the Buddha (allegedly) or the ashes of some prominent person
CPB: Communist Party of Burma (also BCP)
CPT: Communist Party of Thailand
DEA: (United States) Drug Enforcement Administration, American anti-narcotics
  agency
DKBO/DKBA: Democratic Kayin (Karen) Buddhist Organization/Association
doi: mountain, Mount
dorchodor: Border Patrol Police (BPP)
farang: Caucasian foreigner, typically from Europe, Australia or the USA (derived
  from 'farangset', a Thai attempt at 'français')
hongnam: typical Thai ablution cubicle combining washing and toilet facilities, the
  water coming from a big earthenware pot or cement tank to be scooped up
  with a plastic dipper
huai: mountain stream
Isaan (Esarn, Isan): large area in NE Thailand, marked by Lao influence
jiin/Jiin: chin/Chin (Chinese)
kamnaan: village mayor or headman
kateuy: ladyboy
kao soi: tasty dish of yellow noodles served in curry soup, accompanied by a side
  salad of pickled cabbage and shallots
kap klaem: appetizers, food to accompany drinking
kru (yai): (head)teacher
KKY (= ka kwe yae): local militias set up by the Burmese authorities around 1963-
  73 with a view to bringing rebel/private militias over to government side
KMT (= Kuomintang): Chinese Nationalist refugees loyal to Chiang Kai-shek,
  ousted by Mao Tse-tung's Communist revolutionaries in 1949 and forced
  to flee to Taiwan (Formosa) and also south to Burma, Laos and Thailand
KNLA: Karen National Liberation Army
KNU: Karen National Union
ko: island
lak muang: town pillar or phallus
lao kao: white spirit, schnaps, made from rice and palm sugar
LID: Light Infantry Division
li kae: traditional Thai costumed burlesque theatrical performance, folk dance-
  drama

loe-si (lur-si, lercy) = roe-si or rü-si: Thai vernacular word derived from Sanskrit 'rishi', the Indian hermit-ascetic sage of early vedic times; refers now to the spiritual leader or 'pu chaik', meanwhile endowed with magical knowledge and supernatural powers, of the Talarku (Lagu/Telakhon) Karen sect
longyi: Burmese wrap-around skirt worn by men and women
mae (short for maenam): river
mai dai: can't, not possible
mai mi: don't have
mai ru: don't know
MTA: Mong Tai Army, private army of warlord Khun Sa
naga ("naak" in modern Thai): snakelike river dragon
nakrong ying: singing girl (nakrong chai: male singer)
NDF: National Democratic Front, major alliance of a dozen ethnic insurgent groups in Burma, based in KNLA GHQ, Manerplaw
ngaan ledou nauw ("now"): Winter Fair
oliang: strong Thai coffee
pat thai: meal/snack of rice noodle fried with beansprouts, egg, diced tofu, preserved shredded turnip, dried shrimps, crumbled peanuts etc., and served with raw green side salad
pi tong luang: Spirits of the Yellow Leaves - prehistoric Mrabri people from Nan province, north-northeast Thailand
po luang: dialect word for pu yai, headman
pratat (phrathat): grand pagoda or chedi
pu chaik = loe-si
pu yai (baan): (village) headman
rai: area of land comprising approx. 1600 sq. metres (40 x 40 m.)
samlor: (= three wheels) a three wheeler or tricycle, either pedal-powered (pedicab or trishaw) or motorized (tuk-tuk)
sanuk: fun
sawbwa: traditional feudal lord or princeling in former Shan States
silor: (= four-wheels) four-wheeler, open-sided public-transport pick-up
SLORC: State Law and Order Restoration Council
soi: side road, lane, alleyway
songkraan: religious festival to mark the Thai new year, held in the hot season and now associated with a lot of water-throwing
songtaew: (= two benches) a small public means of transport with two rows of seats in the back
stupa: chedi
SUA: Shan United Army, former name of Khun Sa's MTA
SURA: Shan United Revolutionary Army, name of warlord Mo Heng's force before it became TRC, later MTA
tahaan praan: crack Thai military force, the rangers who wear the black uniform
tai/Tai: pertaining to/someone belonging to one of the many subgroups of the ethnic Tai family of peoples
Tai Noi: (= little Tai in contrast to the Shan Tai Yai) the Siamese Thais of modern Thailand
Tai Yai: (= big Tai) Shan
tambon: subdivision below ampoe, precinct
Thai: citizen of modern Thailand

tanaka: a kind of complexion-enhancing cosmetic made from powdered bark and
worn mostly as a white or gold disc on the cheeks
tanon: road, street
TRA: Tailand Revolutionary Army, formerly SURA and later MTA, Mo Heng's
force, which amalgamated with Khun Sa's SUA
TRC: Tailand Revolutionary Council, political wing of TRA
tuk-tuk: motorized samlor or tricycle, half-car half-motorcycle, so called because
of the sound of its engine
tung: long thin banner of woven material presented to a wat for votive purposes
UWSA: Wa Daeng ("Red" Wa) United Wa State Army
viharn: the building in a temple complex where the Buddha figures are housed
wai: traditional Buddhist greeting, palms of hands pressed together below the chin
wat: temple-monastery
wiang/wieng: moated fortified town
WNA: Wa National Army, Maha San's force
WNC: Wa National Council, Ai Hsiao-hsu's (and also Li Ching's) force
WNO: Wa National Organization, political wing of WNA, affiliated to NDF
yaam: smallish thin square bag, made of handwoven cloth and slung from the
shoulder, used by the hill-tribes, especially the Karens
Yang: Thai name for the Karens, also Kaliang/Kariang
Yellow Leaves = "pi tong luang" or Mrabri people
ying tong: water pipe

BIBLIOGRAPHY

Belanger, Francis W.: *Drugs, the US and Khun Sa*, DK Books, Bangkok, 1989

Boucaud, André & Louis: *Burma's Golden Triangle. On the Trail of the Opium Warlords*, Asia Books, Bangkok, 1992.

Boyes, Jon & Piraban, S.: *Hmong Voices*, Hilltribes of Northern Thailand Series, 1988.

Cummings, Joe: *Thailand. A Travel Survival Kit*, Lonely Planet Publications, Hawthorn, 4th edition, 1990.

Davies, John R.: *A Trekker's Guide to the Hill Tribes of Northern Thailand*, Footloose Books, Salisbury, 2nd edition, 1990.

Touring Northern Thailand, Footloose Books, Salisbury, 1991.

Evers, Cornelis B.: *Death Railway*, Craftsman Press, Bangkok, 1993.

Falla, Jonathan: *True Love and Bartholomew. Rebels on the Burmese Border*, Cambridge University Press, 1991.

Forsyth, Tim: "Refugees and Freaks: Plight of the Long Neck People" in *Bangkok Post*, 9-11-1991 (Vol. XLVI, No. 313), Section 3, pp. 21 & 23.

Greenwood, Nicholas: *Bound Tightly with Banana Leaves. A South-East Asian Journal*, Right Now Books, London, 1992.

Khun Sa, *His own Story and His Thoughts* (undated MTA propaganda)

Kunstadter, Peter: *The Lua (Lawa) of Northern Thailand. Aspects of Social Structure, Agriculture and Religion*, Center of International Studies Research Monograph No. 21, Princeton University, 1965.

Lebar, F. M. et al.: *Ethnic Groups of Mainland S-E. Asia*, Human Relations Files Inc., New Haven, 1964.

Lewis, Paul & Elaine: *Peoples of the Golden Triangle*, Thames & Hudson, London, 1984.

Lintner, Bertil: *Land of Jade. A Journey through Insurgent Burma*, Kiscadale & White Lotus, Edinburgh & Bangkok, 1990.

Loose, Stefan: *Thailand-Burma Traveller Handbuch* (Vol. 2), Stefan Loose Verlag, Berlin, 2nd edition, 1988.

McCoy, Alfred: *The Politics of Heroin in South-East Asia*, Harper & Row, New York, 1972.

McKinnon, John & Bhruksasri, W. (eds.): *Highlanders of Thailand*, Oxford University Press, Kuala Lumpur, 1986.

McKinnon, J. & Vienne, B.: *Hill Tribes Today*, White Lotus Co. Ltd., Bangkok, 1989.

Pragadwootisan, Kanchana: *The History of Doi Mae Salong - Ban Santikiri*, Siamrat (SR) Ltd., Chiang Mai, 1992 [in Thai].

> *The 93rd Regiment and Nationalist Army in Doi Pa Taang*, Siamrat (SR) Ltd., Chiang Mai, 1994 [in Thai].

Smith, Martin: *Burma. Insurgency and the Politics of Ethnicity*, Zed Books, London & New Jersey, 2nd impression, 1993.

Stern, Theodore: "Ariya and the Golden Book: A Millenarian Buddhist Sect among the Karen" in *Journal of Asian Studies*, 27 (2), 1968, pp. 297-328.

Tettoni, Luca I.: *Introduction to Chiang Mai and Northern Thailand*, The Guidebook Company Limited, Hong Kong, 1992.

Tribal Research Institute: *The Hill Tribes of Thailand*, Technical Service Club, Tribal Research Institute, Chiang Mai University, 3rd edition, 1989.

Unkovich, David: *The Mae Hong Son Loop. Northern Thailand*, Compustyle Publications, Grafton, 1991.

> *A Pocket Guide for Motorcycle Touring in Northern Thailand*, Jareuk Publications, Chiang Mai, 1988.

Young, O. Gordon: *The Hilltribes of Northern Thailand*, Journal of the Siam Society Monograph No. 1, Bangkok, May 1961.

> *Tracks of an Intruder*, Souvenir Press, London, 1967

JUNGLE TOURS

Experience the
peoples and villages
culture and nature
mountains and jungle
of northern Thailand
in small groups
guided by experts

Touring and trekking on foot & by motorcycle

For further information
write to:
Jungle Books (Halesworth)
P.O. Box 15
Halesworth
Suffolk IP19 0DY
England